TRUE HOLLYWOOD STORY®

TRUE HOLLYWOOD STORY®

The Real Stories

Behind the Glitter

Edited by

Lanford Beard

CHAMBERLAIN BROS.
A MEMBER OF PENGUIN
GROUP (USA) INC.
NEW YORK
2005

CHAMBERLAIN BROS.
Published by the Penguin Group
Penguin Group (USA) Inc., 375 Hudson Street, New York, New York 10014, USA • Penguin Group (Canada), 10 Alcorn Avenue, Toronto, Ontario M4V 3B2, Canada (a division of Pearson Penguin Canada Inc.) • Penguin Books Ltd, 80 Strand, London WC2R 0RL, England • Penguin Ireland, 25 St Stephen's Green, Dublin 2, Ireland (a division of Penguin Books Ltd) • Penguin Group (Australia), 250 Camberwell Road, Camberwell, Victoria 3124, Australia (a division of Pearson Australia Group Pty Ltd) • Penguin Books India Pvt Ltd, 11 Community Centre, Panchsheel Park, New Delhi–110 017, India • Penguin Group (NZ), Cnr Airborne and Rosedale Roads, Albany, Auckland 1310, New Zealand (a division of Pearson New Zealand Ltd) • Penguin Books (South Africa) (Pty) Ltd, 24 Sturdee Avenue, Rosebank, Johannesburg 2196, South Africa

Penguin Books Ltd, Registered Offices: 80 Strand, London WC2R 0RL, England

Published simultaneously in Canada

Library of Congress Cataloging-in-Publication Data

E! true hollywood story : the real stories behind the glitter / edited by Lanford Beard.
    p. cm.
    Contents: My name is—Slim Shady, the Eminem, story—Stop! in the name of love, the Diana Ross story—The doctor is in, the Phil McGraw story—America's funniest woman, the Ellen DeGeneres story—Her mother's daughter, the Liza Minnelli story—Lone star stunner, the Anna Nicole Smith story—I did it, I liked it, so what? the Ginger Lynn story—Sister act, the Paris and Nicky Hilton story—America's sweetheart, the Katie Couric story—Eight days a week, the Heather Mills McCartney story—The girl next door, the Doris Day story—Key to Camelot, the John F. Kennedy Jr. story—Triple threat, the Naomi, Wynonna, and Ashley Judd story—Blond ambition, the Goldie Hawn and Kate Hudson story—Unlikely romance, the Arnold Schwarzenegger and Maria Shriver story.
    ISBN 1-59609-091-X
1. Celebrities—United States—Biography.   2. Celebrities—Biography.   3. United States—Biography.   I. Beard, Landord.

CT220.E13   2005   2005041330
    920.073'09'04—dc22

Printed in the United States of America
10 9 8 7 6 5 4 3 2 1

Book design by Jaime Putorti

Photo credits: Eminem on page 1 by Kevin Mazur/WireImage.com • Diana Ross on page 19 by Jeffrey Mayer/WireImage.com • Phil McGraw on page 53 by Steve Granitz/WireImage.com • Ellen DeGeneres on page 71 by Michael Caulfield/WireImage.com • Liza Minnelli on page 101 by Jeff Vespa/WireImage.com • Anna Nicole Smith on page 129 by Ron Galella/WireImage.com • Ginger Lynn on page 163 by Jean-Paul Aussenard/WireImage.com • Nicky and Paris Hilton on page 195 by RJ Capak/WireImage.com • Katie Couric on page 213 by Scott Suchman/WireImage.com • Paul McCartney and Heather Mills McCartney on page 229 by Jeffrey Mayer/WireImage.com • Doris Day on page 245 by Jim Smeal/WireImage.com • John F. Kennedy Jr. on page 273 by Barry King/WireImage.com • Wynonna, Ashley, and Naomi Judd on page 307 by Barry King/WireImage.com • Goldie Hawn and Kate Hudson on page 339 by Kevin Mazur/WireImage.com • Maria Shriver and Arnold Schwarzenegger on page 371 by Jim Spellman/WireImage.com

Special thanks to Betsy Rott, Natasha Selver, Laticia Headings, Edward Zarcoff, and Mya Alexander for all their help.

DVD credits: Footage of Liza Minnelli at the Academy Awards® courtesy hollywoodnewsreel.com • Photo of Liza Minnelli and Vincente Minnelli courtesy Nancy Barr-Brandon • Photo of Liza Minnelli in Cabaret © Alan Pappe 1971

CONTENTS

CHAPTER 1

MY NAME IS . . . SLIM SHADY

The Eminem Story

"The most satanically possessed class clown that's ever lived."

—*Anthony Bozza, Eminem biographer*

When [he] first came up there was no history of white rappers having success and being critically respected," summed up music journalist Toure, "so it was sort of like 'A white boy who's going to get respect? Yeah, Columbus, you go sail to America. Yeah right. Fall off the end of the world. We'll see ya later.'"

It was 1999. America faced an invisible foe labeled the Doomsday Virus Y2K. Meanwhile, another powerful force loomed on the horizon: M23, better known by his original name, Marshall Mathers III, and later known as Renegade, Trouble, Lady-Killer, Mr. Controversy, Slim Shady, and Eminem. This is his story.

Ironically, the world of rap music didn't even exist when Marshall Mathers was born near Kansas City, Missouri, on October 17, 1972. Marshall's father left the family before his son's first birthday. Manager and lawyer Paul Rosenberg described Eminem's childhood as being a challenge from the start, saying, "He was forced to grow up with a handicap. He didn't have a father and certainly didn't have a father figure." Em's longtime friend Proof of D12 saw in Em's fatherless childhood the beginning of his me-against-the-world attitude. "I don't think his father's abandonment hurt him or scarred him, 'cause he's like 'Everybody don't got no father, f**k it,'" he offered, adding, "but I think he envied people with both mother and father."

In 1980, eight-year-old Marshall and his mother, Debbie Mathers, moved to the Motor City. According to *Detroit Free Press* columnist Brian McCollum, "Eminem was shuffled back and forth by his mom. He lived with his grandmother at times and moved around house to house, trailer to trailer. He had a childhood that was probably not that stable." Marshall's surroundings didn't help. He lived on the wrong side of an unmarked border between safety and danger. Racial tension festered, and warring gangs ruled. Rosenberg explained that 8 Mile, the road where Em grew up in Detroit, is like one of those two-lane streets with opposite-end traffic divided by an island. It represents the other side of the tracks.

For most kids, life on the streets of this broken-down neighborhood was rough. For Marshall, things only got worse when he went home. His mother had no idea how to support herself, much less a young son. Throughout the 1980s, Debbie Mathers was kicked out of one shabby trailer park after another. In school, Marshall became the target of bullies. In the fourth grade, he was beaten to a pulp by an older kid, and suffered a near-fatal cerebral hemorrhage. He recovered but felt even more isolated than before, retreating into his own world of comic books and TV until his uncle Ronnie Polkinghorn came to the rescue, becoming Marshall's one true confidant and friend. "He idolized Uncle Ronnie. The reason he's rapping was probably because of Uncle Ronnie," said Proof.

Through his early teens, Marshall also worshipped emerging rap artists like LL Cool J, the Beastie Boys, the Fat Boys, and Run-DMC. In the mid-1980s, Marshall began channeling his sound and fury into rap. The young "Mike Controller," as he was then called, battled other MCs in local Detroit clubs. Proof offered, "An MC battle is saying, 'I think I'm better than you,' gladiator-style, to see who's the top dog at that particular moment." Young Marshall soon snagged the attention of Detroit's local DJ Bushman, who said, "You could never deny his skills and his battling technique, because he would slaughter guys, just literally slaughter them."

As his battles were heating up, Marshall found a different kind of love with high school girlfriend Kim Scott. "Kim and Em met in high school, when Em was, I think, fifteen years old," said Rosenberg, quipping, "and they have gone out ever since. High school sweethearts—Joanie and Chachi." Proof saw firsthand the beginnings of the tumultuous relationship for which the couple is now infamous. "They broke up like three times a day, but it was still good. It was true love, I guess," he said. Marshall had a new girlfriend and was enjoying some success in local rap battles, but at home the situation became desperate.

To help pay the bills, he took a job as a short-order cook at a lodge in nearby St. Clair Shores. According to the restaurant's manager, Linda "Flip" Ulrich, Marshall's mother called regularly for seemingly no reason. "She depended on him, instead of him depending on her," Ulrich said. In 1986, Debbie had a second son, Nathan, and Marshall had another mouth to feed. With barely any support, something had to give, and it did. The kid from the wrong side of 8 Mile failed ninth grade three times. Teacher Robert Blair recalled asking the struggling teen what he wanted to do with his life, to which Marshall responded without missing a beat, "I want to rap." Dumbfounded, Blair said, "Well, go for it," not realizing that he "was going to be talking to the number one rapper in the world."

Taking Blair's advice, Marshall formed a rap group called Bassmint Productions, thus named because, according to Paul Rosenberg, the group made their demos and performed in local basements. Proof joined the Bassmint ranks as the group made the rounds at local radio stations that would give fledgling artists a chance. They even took the high school talent show by storm. Blair, who witnessed the beginnings of Eminem's greatness, says he now looks back and thinks, "Had I only known!" However, Marshall's burning desire to pursue his rapping career came at a price. He saw no need to waste his time on education and even encouraged his friends to quit school. "He felt like, 'I don't need high school to be a rapper,'" remembered Proof. Added Proof, Em would argue, "Proof, why are you going to school? We're rappers. Drop out. Don't go to school. We're going to be rappers." In 1989, Marshall Mathers III dropped out of school to chase his dream.

"Hip-hop is birthed out of pain—out of the harsh realities of the streets, and crack sales, and drugs, and in that pain that we suffer, we come out on top," affirmed Reverend Run of Run-DMC. Em's personal pain was strong. Ignored by his father and his mother, and harassed by his peers, the kid who would rattle the music world as Eminem grew up an outcast. In the late 1980s, Marshall's movement into the Detroit hip-hop community became, in some ways, his saving grace. It was a club that nobody messed with. By 1987, fifteen-year-old Marshall began fanatically honing his rapping skills. "We all heard him rapping," recalled Linda Ulrich. "In the kitchen, he used to sing songs. We used to hear demo tapes long before he had a record deal." Described Proof, "Em's home life was basically him in his room writing raps, listening to rappers like CO Smooth, Grand Puma, and Treach from Naughty by Nature, or drawing rappers or females naked—female rappers naked."

As he was drawing and dreaming about other worlds, Marshall realized that every up-and-coming rapper needs a catchy name, and Marshall's was a stroke of pure genius. "Eminem is simply his initials—Marshall Mathers," explained Rosenberg, "and he was smart enough at the time to figure out that he wouldn't want to get sued by a certain candy company, so he spelled it out phonetically."

Marshall had a new name, but in early 1993, he lost an old friend when Uncle Ronnie committed suicide. Eminem was too distraught to attend the funeral, but he vented through his sound and his new identity, said Proof. "I remember the impact of Uncle Ronnie dying, Em going to the studio and recording a song called 'Troublemaker.' The song explained to his family how nobody listened to him when he was crying for help all the time."

Things began to look up for Em when he met the production team of Marky and Jeff Bass, who gave him studio time to rap, develop, and essentially invent himself. As Proof put it, the free time from Marky and Jeff Bass "honestly made Em a perfectionist to hone his skills." Paul Rosenberg shed light on how crucial it is "for an aspiring artist, particularly a rapper, to have someone interested in you and give you studio time." During these sessions, Eminem dreamed up his rapper alter ego—a diabolical fiend named Slim Shady—appropriately, when he was "on the toilet." In 1995, Em and Slim joined forces with an all-star posse of local Detroit rappers called D12. Said Rosenberg, "They formed the pact, 'Well, if I blow up first, then I'm going to come back and I'm going to get all you guys signed.' There are six guys, and each one has an alter ego. So D12 technically stands for Dirty Dozen."

As his career started to show some promise, Em had something more than music to think about. He was feuding with his girlfriend, Kim, who announced she was having Em's baby. Biographer Anthony Bozza, who has written extensively on Eminem for *Rolling Stone* and in his biography, hung out with the couple. He attributed their roller-coaster relationship to the fact that they "love each other clearly, or else they wouldn't have such a tumultuous relationship if there wasn't passion." By December 1995, Em was in no mood for Christmas carols. Instead, he composed three brutal songs about his girlfriend, titled "Ho, Ho, Ho." It wasn't the gift Kim expected, and she said to Em, "You're sick. You're twisted. You've got problems." The couple stayed together, and on December 25, 1995, Hailie Jade Scott was born.

Eminem was an extremely proud papa, but he was terrified of becoming an absent dad like his own father. "I've never seen anything but a good father out of him. Just the way he talks about her and speaks of her, you could tell in his eyes," commented Linda Ulrich. Em himself admitted in an interview, "Having my little girl was definitely a wake-up call for me to get my ass in gear, to do something and make something of my life. It made me try ten kadrillion times harder." Nevertheless, cash was tight.

Still, Em stayed focused on cutting his first album. In the fall of 1996, *Infinite* was released. The first album, said McCollum, was a learning experience when "he was still finding his voice. In a lot of ways he was imitating what he heard on records and on the radio. They only pressed up five hundred copies." The album didn't exactly fly off the shelves. Eminem was being robbed blind by a crack head at home, but he couldn't give away copies of his record.

Eminem desperately wanted to prove himself, and on October 24, 1997, he got the chance. Wendy Day, founder of the Rap Coalition, organized the Rap Olympics in Los Angeles. Em almost didn't make it, because his living situation was so unstable, said Paul Rosenberg. "He was really down and out. He was staying in a house with a group of friends, and they got evicted," he explained. "So Em breaks into the house and sleeps on the floor in the room that he used to sleep in before, because he didn't know what else to do. He still tells me that he's amazed that he woke up in time to get on the flight to L.A." Despite the preflight turbulence, Em arrived pumped to win and gave it his best shot, but he came in second. Em lost to a rapper named Otherwise. Snarked Rosenberg, "He's Otherwise nowhere to be found at this time," adding, "the prize was $500, and Eminem needed the money. But more than that, he really wanted to win just for the sake of getting that validation." Em was back where he started—broke in Detroit.

Eminem's first album was a flop. He had a baby girl and no job. His relationship was on the rocks. The former Marshall Mathers was going nowhere fast. "After the *Infinite* album, he was like, 'I'll quit if they don't accept me.' He always was trying to quit. He always gave up, but it's in his heart. You can't quit rapping when you're an artist. It's impossible to give up," said Proof. Eminem cut a new album, *The Slim Shady LP*, and returned to L.A. for a radio guest spot that won him the title of "Freestyle Rapper of the Year." That caught the attention of Dr. Dre, a renowned rapper who was starting his own record label, Aftermath, a division of Interscope Records. According to Rosenberg, "Dre was launching Aftermath and said, 'I want to go in a new direction,' and that's when he started signing guys like Eminem. Everyone was afraid to touch a white rapper." Eminem went totally against the grain—just what the Dr. ordered—so he invited Eminem to a meeting of the minds. "For a kid coming from Detroit who basically has nothing, to be sitting in a room with Dr. Dre with the potential that he might get a record deal, it's just mind-blowing."

In 1998, Em signed with Aftermath Records. With Dr. Dre on board, the stigma of "White Rapper" melted away. Paul Rosenberg remembered Dre at the time saying, "I don't care if he's purple as long as he can rap." Said Touré, "The moment that Dr. Dre gets involved and brings those hot beats to the table, it gives him credibility, because Dr. Dre is NWA and Snoop Dogg and Tupac. The moment that happens, suddenly his whiteness becomes a huge marketing tool, a huge positive. So now the white kids in the suburbs of Dallas and Kansas can say, 'Hey, he looks like me.'"

But the poor white kid from Detroit was cracking under the stress. Em popped Ecstasy and vented through his alter ego, Slim Shady, spewing foul-mouthed lyrics about murder and mutilation. Slim's pure rage became a hit machine. "He went in the studio with Dre, the first day they recorded like four songs, I think," said Rosenberg, "and the first song that they recorded was 'My Name Is.' He hit a home run on the first ball."

Advance word on *The Slim Shady LP* spread fast. Writer Kris Ex recalled the rap star Busta Rhymes's reaction, saying, "When Busta Rhymes heard 'Guilty Conscience,' there was a commotion at the front of the bus. I came out to see a crack in the windshield that was maybe a foot long and very thick, about an inch wide. Busta Rhymes broke the windshield with his forehead from listening to 'Guilty Conscience.' Something about the music, or as he says, 'You don't know how I feel about this music—something about this kid. Oh my God, this is crazy,' and that was it for the windshield." On February 23, 1999, *The Slim Shady LP* was released. Within two weeks, it shot to number two on the *Billboard* charts.

Not everyone was a fan. Gay rights advocates and feminists protested Em's homophobic and sexist lyrics. Detroit radio DJ Coco said, "Every other hip-hop or rap artist uses 'ho' or 'bitch' or whatever. There's no sense in acting like it's brand-new. You've heard 'ho' and 'bitch' unless you grew up in a bubble, so it's not like you're not familiar with the verbiage. I think it's the fact that we expect a white boy not to talk this way." Defying the odds, the LP went platinum four times.

In the summer of 1999, twenty-six-year-old Eminem embarked on a sold-out national Slim Shady Tour. "After they got a chance to really sit and listen to the album, people started telling other people about it, and it went back up the charts. I believe that's the reason," said Dr. Dre. The money flowed.

So did the drugs, as witnessed by Anthony Bozza. "Eminem was very open about the fact that he liked Ecstasy," he mentioned. "I was actually in the limo, and someone came to the window and had a bunch of pills. I was sitting by the window, so basically they got handed to me. He held his hand out, and I figured that they were for him. He was popping those a lot during his performances and stuff." Proof put it more bluntly: "We were high all the time on the first tour, so I don't remember it." Bozza continued, "When he wasn't onstage, he was still kind of onstage. This was a guy who was living every second as if it might be his last. I think that he thought it wasn't really happening to him."

It was happening. So were lawsuits from family members who were livid about how they were portrayed on Eminem's album. *The Slim Shady LP* skyrocketed Eminem near the top of the hip-hop world, but the higher the climb, the more perilous the fall. "There was a time not long after Eminem broke out nationally that I started getting calls in the newsroom from various family members—Grandma, Mom, assorted uncles—who wanted to air the family's dirty laundry," recalled Brian McCollum. Gary Graff, a columnist for the *Oakland Press*, also watched the accusations fly. "He's like a lightning rod—'Look, I'm big and successful. I have millions and millions of dollars, so, hey, see if you can get a piece of me. See if I'll pay you just to go away,'" he explained. By the summer of 1999, the Eminem backlash divided his family and much of the country. He was loved, he was hated. There was no in-between.

For most of the 1999 Slim Shady Tour, Eminem was fueled by a high-octane mixture of women, cash, and drugs. "There was a point when Eminem's hedonistic lifestyle caught up to him," observed Kris Ex. Em's trash-talking demeanor on his album began to frighten people. In particular, the song "97 Bonnie & Clyde" riled up critics, who thought the lyrics were downright sick. According to Proof, "Kim said that she's going to take Hailie away or something like that or you won't be able to see her. Or she was using Hailie against him in some kind of way. And that song was his way of saying, 'Guess what, I'll kill you, and I can be with my daughter.' So it's really like a twisted love song." While Paul Rosenberg mentioned that Em was using his lyrics to "vent his frustration with his relationship with Kim," McCollum added, "not only has his music been kind of a therapeutic exercise, but it's also been a chance to get back at people who he feels have crossed him."

Revenge was sweet for Slim and Em. "Slim Shady got to be the sinister guy, the mischievous guy. For a lot of people it's been this refreshing blast of political incorrectness," said McCollum. Kris Ex noticed that Em's rogue behavior was "when he talks about acts of crime and more bizarre acts of sex, it's kind of the 'Na na na na na na,' brattish, childish side—it's definitely the Slim Shady side." DJ Bushman also noted, "Slim Shady is the real funny character side of Marshall and Eminem. Eminem is the person that you get when he's on stage and he's just giving it to you, you know. And Marshall Mathers is the guy who cares for and loves his daughter." In fact, Em cared so much for Hailie that he asked her mother, Kim Scott, to marry him despite their rocky relationship. The couple made it legal on June 14, 1999.

Later that year, Debbie Mathers-Briggs jumped onboard the

lawsuit express. On September 10, 1999, she sued her son for $10 million, claiming defamation and emotional distress.

The jury was out on Eminem's personal life but, professionally, the verdict was clear. In September, Em was honored by MTV with three major awards. Five months later, the GRAMMY Awards were held. Em was nominated for Best Rap Album and Outstanding Solo Performance. In his typical style, Em "didn't really understand what the GRAMMYs were. To him, it was like, 'Some award that a bunch of sixty-year-old men are going to give me? I don't know if I should go. I'm going to be in the studio.'" Em snubbed the ceremony but still won the Best Rap Solo Performance for "My Name Is." More success followed. *The Marshall Mathers LP* was released on May 23, 2000, and became the fastest-selling rap album of all time. "There's a speed with which he rhymes. There's a speed with which his mind works. There's a speed with which his mouth works and flowing through the lyrics and getting the rhythms right. I mean, it's sort of an athletic genius," summed up Touré.

Of *The Marshall Mathers LP,* the rap ballad "Stan" was a standout. "When they got that beat," explained Proof, "we had just got back from Milan, and it was a crazy fan in Milan named Stan." For Em, "'Stan' was a way of also dealing with his own success and fame where he tried to understand the fans," said Paul Rosenberg. The album had a lighter side, too, including goofy skits with Rosenberg and marketing executive Steve Berman. "Dr. Dre put me in one of his videos, Dr. Dre and Snoop Dogg's 'Dre Day,' and I played a scumbag record executive. The first time I met Eminem, he thought it was real and so it grew out of that," laughed Berman. *The Marshall Mathers LP* jumped from comedy to tragedy with the song titled "Kim": once again Eminem verbally attacked the woman who was now his wife. Said McCollum, "It was very hard not to have a very visceral, negative reaction to a song like 'Kim' that starts with a baby daughter cooing on the record and ends with mom getting thrown into a lake, dead."

The *Marshall Mathers LP* was dark. "It's an album that's definitely influenced by altered states of mind," said Kris Ex, who continued, "He rapes his mother, kills his girlfriend, has a whole song dedicated to the use of drugs, and kills Dr. Dre twice on the album, I believe." Rosenberg described the tumult, saying, "I heard from somebody who worked over at the studio that he was bringing his gun to the studio, and he didn't have a concealed weapons permit. Somebody also informed me that he may have fired it out behind the studio just testing it out." He quickly called Em and sternly told him to leave his guns at home.

But Em's violent tendencies continued to catch up with him. According to police reports, on June 3, 2000, Em faced off with Douglas Dail, the manager for Insane Clown Posse, or ICP, a rival rap group. Said Brian McCollum, "Eminem and ICP began feuding where they were trading jibes on record. It ultimately manifested itself in an incident where Eminem pulled an empty gun on an ICP associate." At the end of what Gary Graff called a "heated exchange," police broke up the fight in the parking lot of a car stereo store, but Em was just warming up. "The following morning, Eminem apparently heard that Kim was at a club in Warren with another man. He went down to assess the situation, saw them kissing in the parking lot, and assaulted this John Guerra with the pistol, which Eminem has always contended was unloaded," reported Graff. Police charged Em with possession of a concealed weapon and assault with a dangerous weapon. Commented Rosenberg, "He was struggling between trying to be a normal person and this superstar that he'd become. At the same time, he was having personal problems with Kim and with his family, and it all just sort of collided at the same time. He screwed up."

By the spring of 2000, twenty-seven-year-old Eminem was one of the biggest recording stars in the world, but the volatile rapper seemed intent on destroying his career and his life. Em was right on when he fessed up in his song "A Drug Ballad," saying, "These drugs really got a hold of me." The drugs and the exhausting concert tour schedule seemed hard on Em and his wife. "Any time one of the partners in a relationship isn't around, it puts a strain on a relationship. And if a relationship doesn't have a solid foundation to begin with, it's going to make it worse," said Rosenberg. Going to court only added to the strain. On Valentine's Day 2001, Em pleaded guilty to possession of a concealed weapon; the assault charges were dropped.

Still, Eminem was facing up to five years jail time in the Guerra case and more penalties for the ICP incident. On June 28, 2001, the sentencing took place with the court requiring Eminem to go through drug and alcohol testing. Em was slapped with an additional year probation for the ICP brawl. This time, Eminem seemed to hear the message. Proof thought that Em learned "not to take life for granted and slow down because I'm a successful person now, and my stupidity almost took it all away."

Em's run-in with the law was soon overshadowed by a crisis at home. Em's wife became so depressed she attempted suicide by slashing her wrists. Kim's near-lifeless body was discovered by her mother. Kim survived, but the marriage didn't. In February 2001, she filed for divorce. The couple later reached an undisclosed settlement and agreed to share custody of Hailie Jade.

Professionally, Em could do no wrong. On February 21, *The Marshall Mathers LP* was nominated for four GRAMMY Awards. For the first time in history, a rap album was up for Album of the Year. Eminem's fans were thrilled, but human rights activists were outraged. "This is someone who's just spewing poison and venom to make money, and this has touched, I think, all of us as he comes up for a nomination for a GRAMMY for Album of the Year, which is the top award in the industry," said one protester. The uproar was a hassle for Em's publicist, Dennis Dennehy, who called his client "Public Enemy Number One" in other people's estimation.

Since his splash entrance on the national stage, Eminem has pushed just about everybody's buttons. His decision to perform at the GRAMMYs ignited an international frenzy. Said Dennehy, "There were talk shows devoted to how he was corrupting the youth of America." There was one way to stop the outcry from the gay community. It was the unthinkable, and as Rosenberg remembered, initially just a joke. "Either Marshall or myself said, 'Well, we should do something really crazy and shut people up. Like go out there and perform with Elton John.' And we were half joking when we said it. We said, 'Well, we better ask what Dre thinks.' So we go to Dre, and he said, 'Hell yeah, do that.' Because, you know, Dre is all about shocking people, too." Eminem's "Stan" duet with Elton John went off without a hitch, but close to 30 million viewers—along with nervous GRAMMY and network executives—braced themselves when *The Marshall Mathers LP* was named Rap Album of the Year. Em walked onstage and shocked everyone by not shocking everyone. In his acceptance speech, he started, "I guess first of all I want to thank everybody who could look past the controversy or whatever to see the album for what it was." Eminem sat by as *The Marshall Mathers LP* was passed over for Album of the Year.

His mother Debbie appeared on the *Sally Jessy Raphael* show to talk about the defamation suit filed against her son, saying, "I'm in the midst of trying to resolve things because I have to forgive him." She didn't stop there. She took part in a song called "Set the Record Straight," to counter what she considered Em's lyrical slander. "I mean, I think all that you can really do is let the facts speak for themselves," said Anthony Bozza. "She's suing her son for malice, she's kind of exploiting what he's put on record about her in a song by recording a song of her own and selling that for profit." On June 27, the judge ruled. He awarded Debbie $25,000. After legal fees, however, Em's mom wound up with just $1,600.

After winning major awards and wrapping up one chapter of his controversial relationship with his wife and his mother, Em was still unsatisfied with his place in the spotlight. "He got a lot more focused. Then his work became a lot heavier," said Kris Ex. In May 2001, twenty-eight-year-old Eminem signed on to star in *8 Mile*, a semiautobiographical film about a young white rapper from Detroit who struggles to prove himself. Some of the cast had doubts that Em could carry a movie. Mekhi Phifer, who eventually went on to costar in the film, admitted, "At first, I wasn't even going to read the script. I wasn't interested in doing a quote-unquote Eminem nostalgic movie." To prove the skeptics wrong, Eminem rehearsed long hours with director Curtis Hanson. Brian Grazer, producer of *8 Mile* said the rehearsal "gave me enormous amounts of confidence as a producer to have Curtis do the six weeks, and then just to see Marshall Mathers perform persuaded me to believe how perfectionistic, how talented he is."

When Em came on set, the cast grew increasingly confident in his ability to carry a major movie. "Once we started reading the words and the lines and stuff, I saw he was serious. He wasn't just trying to come in there and capitalize on his popularity. He wanted to really, really make a good movie, and really wanted to be good in it. And he was insecure and unsure, and I thought that was cool," Mekhi Phifer said. Brittany Murphy, who played Em's character's love interest, noted, "He's actually the most professional person I have ever shot any sort of kissing, making out, love scene with in my life." In fact, during the shoot, tabloids linked Eminem with two of his female costars, Murphy and Kim Basinger, who was nineteen years his senior. All three stars denied the reports. Em, it seemed, had no time for affairs. In addition to his film work, he was also completing a new album, *The Eminem Show*.

In July 2002, *The Eminem Show* was released. Once again, Em scored with the public and the critics. And, according to Kris Ex, he silenced at least a few of his inner demons. "Eminem has proven that he does not need the drugs to make good music. His third album was his best work to date. He started attacking Bob Dole and Tipper Gore and dealing with issues of race in America," Kris Ex remarked. In *The Eminem Show*, the rapper shared his most personal secrets. "He came out talking about his childhood on 'Cleaning Out My Closet,' which was just a phenomenal song that's very autobiographical." Another emotional song came in the form of "Hailie," Em's ballad for his daughter. Said Proof, "The 'Hailie' song meant a lot to him, because it's like Em's whole motivation to his success today is because of the love for his daughter. And that was his time to freeze it in time to talk to his daughter. She got a lullaby for the rest of her life." *The Eminem Show* eventually sold more than 5 million copies.

Meanwhile, the premiere of *8 Mile* was looming, and Em knew the success of the film was riding on his shoulders; he appeared in nearly every scene. "It's one of those things where it can make or break you in several aspects. I mean, look at Vanilla Ice's movies," said Mekhi Phifer, "but Eminem just wanted to be credible and have a good film on his hands. It could be detrimental, or it could make him incredible." On November 8, 2002, *8 Mile* hit movie theaters across the country. Critics raved about Eminem's magnetic performance. The film shot to number one at the box office, raking in more than $50 million in its opening weekend. "There was a period where Eminem really could have lost his head and lost everything," said Anthony Bozza, "but he didn't. He stopped himself. He calmed down, and he's diversifying."

As the film soared, so did Eminem's single from the movie, "Lose Yourself," which topped the *Billboard* charts. Most of Eminem's harshest critics changed their tune. "You suddenly had op-ed columns in the *New York Times* waxing philosophical about what Eminem meant in the broader cultural sense. To be at this point where you've got baby boomers sneaking into record stores to buy an Eminem CD to listen to in the SUV on the way to work, I think it's a big signal," said Brian McCollum. So was the announcement out of Hollywood in February 2003: Eminem was nominated for an Academy Award for Best Original Song. For now thirty-one-year-old Eminem, this coup signaled his power position—few could deny his talent. Eminem had captured countless music awards, but the approval of mainstream Hollywood was more surprising. On March 23, 2003, he won the Academy Award for Best Original Song for "Lose Yourself." True to form, Em was a no-show at the ceremony. McCollum noted that

Eminem "recognizes that's not really his audience and that there's a danger in showing up in Hollywood wearing a tuxedo."

Eminem, a born underdog, continues to remain true. He supports his city. Said McCollum, "He didn't leave Detroit. He could have easily moved somewhere else at this point. He's got plenty of cash. I think it's been pretty important to him to stay around things he knows, because I sense that if he leaves Detroit, then Detroit might leave him." He remains loyal to his friends, promoting D12's career (and his own) with songs like "My Band," which appeared on the group's 2004 album, *D12 World*. Em also insists that he remains loyal to his ex-wife, Kim Scott, despite their rocky relationship.

But above all, Em's heart and soul will always belong to his music. By the end of 2004, Em had once again shown his staying power in a big way. He released *Encore*, the much-anticipated follow-up to *The Eminem Show*, and shot to number one on the *Billboard* charts with singles like the GRAMMY-nominated "Just Lose It," the politically charged "Mosh," and the controversial "Like Toy Soldiers." He also made a cameo in the spoof movie *Pauly Shore Is Dead;* launched a clothing line, Shady Ltd.; and found his way onto satellite radio with an uncensored hip-hop station called "Shade 45." And now that the name Eminem has become imprinted in American minds, what remains of Em's maniacal alter ego, Slim Shady? Laughed Kris Ex, "Well, according to Slim Shady, ten years from now he's going to be in a nursing home, j**king off with Jergens, or doing something with Mariah Carey and in some sort of psychiatric ward." Summed up Proof, "I think Slim Shady is all our therapy, because it's everything that everyone thinks but never says."

At the end of the day, what is the difference between Marshall Mathers, Eminem, and Slim Shady? Marshall Mathers, says Reverend Run, is merely "what his mother named him." DJ Coco calls Slim Shady "the comedian" and Eminem "the business person, the sensible person." Anthony Bozza adds that Slim is "the most satanically possessed class clown that's ever lived" and Em "the mastermind. You put them all together, and you have the sense of this guy who's really just a kid from Detroit." Marshall Mathers rose from no worth to a net worth of millions. The dream is alive—and rapping. "He embodies all of America, all of these trends that are bubbling up in our society," said Bozza, "and he communicates the reality of it in a way that crosses every border, from fifty-year-olds to fifteen-year-olds, black, white, men, women—people whose value systems say that they should not like Eminem probably have one of his CDs."

CHAPTER 2

STOP! IN THE NAME OF LOVE

The Diana Ross Story

"I am a diva. I think I've earned it."

—*Diana Ross*

She is the supreme Supreme, an Oscar-nominated actress, and, of course, a diva. "I am a diva," she once said. "I think I've earned it." The voice, the look, and that killer attitude—through decades of life in the spotlight, Diana Ross has become one of the most beloved and talked-about pop icons of our time. Her story travels from the Brewster Projects to supreme stardom, through two failed marriages and numerous passionate affairs, to the triumphs and exploits that have made her larger than life—and the heartaches and scandals that have brought her back down to earth. This is the story of an ambitious and talented woman who settled for nothing less than superstardom . . . then found it very lonely at the top. Miss Diana Ross is driven, dramatic, and all diva, and this is her story.

Even at birth, Diana made a unique entrance in Detroit, Michigan, on March 26, 1944. Though her intended name was Diane, a mix-up on her birth certificate named her Diana. Diana was the second daughter born to Fred Ross, a worker at the American Brass Company, and his wife, Ernestine, a teacher. Both parents worked hard to give their children a good home. "Diana Ross came from a very stable family, a very sort of upswinging kind of family, a family that stressed education and those kind of values and really had a lot going for it," described Randy Taraborrelli, author of *Call Her Miss Ross*. But the arrival of three more children forced the family to move to bigger quarters on Belmont Avenue.

One of their neighbors was a slick teenager named William "Smokey" Robinson. Diana admired Smokey, but she was really competing for the attention of another older man—her father. "Many people in the family felt that [Diana's] sister Barbara was sort of the favorite of Fred's," noted Randy Taraborrelli, and there was a little bit of a rivalry going on between Diana and Barbara, who was pretty and smart. Diana's decision to become a singer infuriated her hardworking dad because "[h]e had bigger aspirations in mind for her. He wanted her to go to college. In fact, when I interviewed him and asked him how he felt about her huge success after Diana was a major star, he told me that he still thinks that she should go to college."

By 1958, Fred and Ernestine Ross had six children to support. Money was getting tighter and tighter. They decided to move their family once again, this time to a brand-new housing development near downtown. On Diana's fourteenth birthday, the Rosses settled in on Saint Antoine Street in the Brewster Projects. Though the "projects" developed a shady reputation, Taraborrelli countered, "The Brewster Projects at that time was not a terrible place to be. No matter what's been written historically about it, those were rather nice dwellings for these kids." At the Brewster Projects, fifteen-year-old Florence Ballard was turning heads with her curvaceous figure and booming voice. In 1958, Flo and neighbor Mary Wilson made a fateful connection. Along with neighbor Betty McGlown, Ballard and Wilson set out to find a fourth girl to complete their group. They turned to the new arrival, Diana Ross, and took the name the Primettes.

From the get-go, the Primettes looked beyond the projects. "Florence, [Diana,] myself, and Betty all decided that we were going to pursue getting a record deal, and that's when we had the audition with Berry Gordy," Wilson recalled. Berry Gordy Jr. was a Detroit-based songwriter who had some success writing songs for R&B crooner Jackie Wilson, but by 1959, Gordy and his buddy Smokey Robinson were fed up with substandard royalties. Gordy took Robinson's advice. He borrowed $800 from his family and formed his own label, Tamla. They then formed a second label, Motown Records.

Gordy set up shop in a small house at 2648 West Grand Boulevard in Central Detroit, then used his considerable charm to lure talent to his new label. "He recruited the best musicians in Detroit. He went to the Detroit neighborhoods and handpicked the very singers, the Miracles, Martha and the Vandellas, Mary Wells—they were all within that area. He wanted it all to be Detroit," said Motown expert Rick Bueche. In the summer of 1960, Diana Ross asked for a favor from former neighbor Smokey Robinson. Robinson was serving triple duty as a writer, producer, and performer for Gordy's fledgling label, and Diana knew that he could help the girls grab their chance at their big break—or at least a shot at it. But the ascent to fame they hoped for didn't come easily. "They went for an audition when they were still in high school, tenth or eleventh grade. Berry Gordy happened to be in the studio. He heard them and pretty much dismissed them." Suzanne DePasse, a Motown executive from 1968 to1991, agreed, "He basically sent them away and told them to finish school."

At the same time, the Primettes lost their original fourth, Betty McGlown, and Barbara Martin stepped in. With a new voice in the mix, the girl group set out to change Gordy's mind. "They hung around every day," said Rick Bueche, "they were like the mascots. They made themselves known, and they made it clear that you are not going to get rid of them." Diana made an impression on her married boss. According to Randy Taraborrelli, "Eventually, the Primettes did land a job singing background vocals for Mabel John, and many people have said that it was at that recording session that Berry and Diana sort of had this little flirtation going on."

"Berry Gordy liked Diana Ross right away, but what he liked about her wasn't that he was sort of attracted to her as somebody he wanted to date, but he thought that she had this bouncy enthusiasm and sort of a light to her that made her stand out from the rest of the group," offered Gerald Posner, author of *Motown*.

Bueche added, "Berry Gordy was probably the one who saw something special in Diana Ross, because she was definitely the underdog."

On January 15, 1961, Gordy offered the Primettes a contract. The recording deal was a triumph of perseverance for the four girls from the Brewster Projects. Gordy saw the group as young diamonds in the rough. The makeover began immediately with a new name. Admitted Mary Wilson, "We really weren't that thrilled about having to change our name from the Primettes, but what we did was ask our friends, neighbors, church—wherever we were—what they suggested. We got names from everybody." Their new name, the Supremes, actually came from Motown secretary Billy Jean Brown, but the change did not produce results. Their first single, "I Want a Guy," barely made a blip on the radar screen. "Buttered Popcorn" fared no better.

The group was desperate for a spark, and Diana didn't have to look far to find one. Her old neighbor Smokey Robinson was fast becoming Motown's premier writer and performer. Though the nature of their personal relationship might always be unclear, Robinson, Diana, and the Supremes found success when he began to advise the girls, throw songs their way, and regularly work with them. "Diana was probably seventeen years old at the time, and Smokey Robinson was married," said Randy Taraborrelli. "Smokey said they developed an intimacy and they began working in the studio together and who knows how far this intimacy went, but Smokey did say that his wife, Claudette, asked that he and [Diana] stop seeing each other, and, as Smokey put it, they did stop."

The Supremes lost the services of one of Motown's best, but Diana earned a lasting reputation. "Many people felt that this kind of indicated that Diana had maybe a ruthless streak and maybe she would go after somebody's husband in order to get a break," commented Taraborrelli. For seventeen-year-old Diana, the move to Motown notoriety was the beginning of a love-hate relationship. The other Motown acts quickly realized that Diana was serious about her work and was going to do whatever it took to place herself in the center of Motown's growing spotlight. Gerald Posner listed some of the ways that the diva's ruthlessness showed itself: "She would tease [the other members] about the way their bodies were, that they were a little fat. She was always rail-thin. She would tease them about their clothes. They would come up for a show, and they would all agree to wear the same dresses, and [Diana] at the last moment would show up with a different-color dress saying that hers had been ripped. Then she would laugh and say, 'Oh, it's just a mistake,' and they weren't quite sure if she was serious about this or if she was just marking out her territory a little bit more."

Still, Diana was just a kid. In January 1962, she graduated from Cass Technical High School. She was now free to concentrate on music, but the months ahead were bumpy. The group became a trio when Martin dropped out to have a baby. At the same time, poor record sales were starting to worry the Motown brass. "These three girls seemed to have a lot of ability and Diana seemed to have something going for her, but nobody could really figure out what it was," assessed Randy Taraborrelli. For Gordy, one of the problems was obvious. The Supremes didn't have a steady sound or image that made them stand out. Diana, who had been helming primarily light, fun songs ironically soon became the central Supreme because of her unique voice. As Taraborrelli put it, "Diana had the delicate, intricate, sensitive sound that was nasal in pitch and that just kind of cut through that music in a way that it grabbed your attention. Berry saw that, and this did not sit well with Florence." Compared Mary Wilson, "It's like having Aretha Franklin tell her she's got to sing background and she can't sing up front."

The pressure really mounted when Martha and the Vandellas started having one hit after another with "Heatwave," "Come and Get These Memories," and "Quicksand." The songwriters behind these hits were brothers Eddie and Brian Holland and their buddy Lamont Dozier. "H-D-H" quickly became the A-team at

Motown. They were the ticket to the charts. With the Supremes going nowhere, Berry Gordy made a historic decision. In what Bueche called "a last-ditch effort," Gordy asked "H-D-H" to whip up something stellar for his flailing girl group. The young songwriters were game, but they were not impressed by Diana's leads. "They were all in the sky, so to speak, and it gave off a very thin and kind of whiny, nasal sound," Dozier explained. Still, "H-D-H" came through. The Supremes cracked the Top 30 with "When the Lovelight Starts Shining Through His Eyes."

The unexpected success sent shockwaves through Motown. The Supremes were now on the map, and it was clear the king of the label had room for only one queen. "We had the same feeling that you would have if maybe your dad had younger children or took a liking to one of your other siblings. When [Gordy] singled Diana out, I'm sure everybody felt that," Martha Reeves, lead singer of Martha and the Vandellas, said. With Diana singing lead, "H-D-H" wrote a second single for the Supremes, called "Run, Run, Run." The record flopped. Then fate intervened. When another Motown group called the Marvelettes passed on the song "Where Did Our Love Go," it circulated through Motown until it landed in the Supremes' laps.

Ironically, the girls didn't like the song. "They thought it was the worst piece of whatever," commented Lamont Dozier. Producer Eddie Holland refused to give up. "I said, 'This song is a hit. I don't care who sings it as long as they can sing it with a soft voice,' and previously I had heard Diana being recorded in very high keys and I said I knew that Mary Wilson had a soft voice." When he suggested that Wilson sing the song, the executives insisted on Diana, and he acquiesced. But he got more than he bargained for. Diana tried to jazz up "Where Did Our Love Go" with a series of vocal riffs. He put his foot down, and she sulked. To spite him, "she sang the whole song through as dry as she possibly could, and she said, 'Is that what you wanted?'" Holland was unfazed and told Diana it was exactly what he was looking for. "She sang it perfectly."

In the late spring of 1964, the Supremes joined the Dick Clark Cavalcade of Stars Tour. They were listed as "others" on the bill. That changed after "Where Did Our Love Go" was released as a single on June 17, 1964. Described Rick Bueche, "The minute that song hit the streets it was off and running, and while they were touring with Dick Clark they had no idea of the popularity the song was achieving. By the time the tour ended, they were the headlining act." The Supremes left Detroit on a bus and came home by plane. "They came off the plane, man, struttin' with this air," laughed Lamont Dozier. "It was like so funny, but at the same time it was beautiful, too. I mean, to see the success—they had changed. They had arrived." "Where Did Our Love Go" went all the way to number one on the *Billboard* charts. Any doubts about the pecking order in the group were gone forever. Diana Ross was now the face of the Supremes, and the other girls had to accept that fact.

With "Where Did Our Love Go" topping the charts, Motown chief Berry Gordy assigned the songwriting team of Holland-Dozier-Holland to the Supremes full-time. Said Dozier, "Berry definitely wanted us to push it up a notch." And that's exactly what the "H-D-H" team did. The first follow-up, "Baby Love," shot directly to number one. "Come See About Me" reached the top spot just weeks later. "Now whenever they went out, people were after them. They literally would be in a restroom, and people would shove paper under the stalls for an autograph," mentioned Rick Bueche, adding, "they were not accustomed to that, and it had an effect on all of them at that point. I think Diana, of course, loved that attention."

Diana was also loving a different kind of attention. Gordy was now divorced, and the "flirtation" between boss and protégé was getting serious. "Berry became sort of a father figure to her where she didn't really have that kind of father figure at home— somebody that was really encouraging and wanted her to just get out there and do the best she could do," commented Randy Taraborrelli. In December 1964, with a million-selling album under their belts, the Supremes became one of the first Motown acts to appear on the *Ed Sullivan Show*. The experience turned out to be a painful lesson for Diana. The awkward trio wasn't coordinated, choreographed, Diana was "bugging her eyes out," and "nobody knew what to do with them," said Bueche.

But no setback could derail "H-D-H" and the Supremes. "Stop! In the Name of Love" and "Back in My Arms Again" both reached number one in early 1965, bringing their streak to five straight top-selling singles. Diana really began to live a fantasy while she and the Supremes were on tour in Europe. "She became the boss's girl, and they began a romantic relationship," Bueche noted. Added Taraborrelli, "And this is kind of when things started going south for Mary and Florence." Tensions ran high, and "any time there was a dispute between Diana and one of her fellow singers from the Supremes, or another singer in Motown, she had direct access to pick up the telephone and call Gordy directly," said Gerald Posner. "She didn't have to complain to anybody else; Gordy would step in invariably on her side. Everyone knew you couldn't mess with Diana, because she had Gordy in her back pocket."

Still, the other Supremes weren't left completely in the cold. Reasoned Rick Bueche, "If Diana wanted something, they usually got the same thing. Whether they needed clothes or a car, homes, or whatever, what one got, the other one got." In 1965, the three Supremes bought homes on the same block of Buena Vista Street in Detroit. "They would shop until they dropped. They would go out and buy clothes. They were so elated," recalled composer Brian Holland. The Supremes seemed unstoppable, but there was still plenty of work to do.

In April of 1965, Berry Gordy booked the act at the Copacabana, a ritzy New York City supper club. With only three months to prepare, Gordy had to iron out the girls' rough edges. Said Bueche, "He hired Maxine Powell to be their etiquette teacher— to teach them how to stand, how to get in and out of a chair, in and out of a car, and how to be proper ladies." Powell became the director of Motown's in-house finishing school. Like Gordy, Powell thought Diana's act left a lot to be desired. He recounted, "I said, 'No one is going to sit in the audience for two hours to see you perform and you are singing like you are in pain. And we'll also have to work with the mic because I don't want you opening your mouth so wide that it looks like you're going to swallow the mic." He also put a quick stop to Diana's eye-popping routine.

On July 29, 1965, the Supremes opened at the Copacabana. The show was a smash, but the clear hit of the night was the new Diana Ross: cool, suave, and sophisticated. While America was lapping up Diana's new and improved image, "it caused a certain amount of resentment from the other artists at Motown," said Randy Taraborrelli, "because they really didn't view her as the best singer. It wouldn't be until a little bit later on that they would realize that it wasn't about vocal ability as much as it was about superstar quality."

The next step in the makeover came when Diana told a reporter she was now officially going by the name on her birth certificate: Diana Ross. "She and perhaps Berry made a decision that Diana just sounded more glamorous and more sophisticated than Diane," offered Taraborrelli. Gerald Posner added, "It was a big deal to the Supremes, because when they heard that announced first, it wasn't [announced] to them by Diana—their former school friend—it was announced through the Motown publicity machine. They learned of it through the newspapers, and to them, as Mary Wilson described, it was another way that Diana was separating herself from the two of them and from the group itself. The name Diana, however, still has resonance now, noted Taraborrelli, "Today, a lot of people who want to try to keep her in her place and who want to remind us that they knew her back then, they will call her Diana. It's more kind of a slap in the face than anything else, I think. It's just kind of a way not to give her what maybe she deserves."

Berry Gordy revealed another name for his star during a now-famous interview. "The reporter asked, 'Mary, how do you feel about this? Florence, how do you feel about that? Diana, how do you feel?' And Gordy, who was sitting in on the interview, interrupted the reporter and said, 'This one you call Miss Ross,'" described Taraborrelli. It was one more distinction that Wilson and Ballard would grow to resent. Rick Bueche said the new use of "Miss Ross" made her fellow Supremes feel "very disposable" but made the distinction that "it wasn't Diana Ross doing this herself to them. It was a company decision. It still caused a lot of hard feelings. Tensions began to rise, and friendships started going out the window."

For Florence Ballard, the constant spotlight on Diana became too much to bear. Author Mark Bego mentioned, "This is where she started having problems with drinking, with missing shows, with being late for planes, being late for limos, and being late for appearances. I think that she realized it was much bigger than her, and Diana was going to walk away with the stardom of the Supremes." While Ballard's problem centered on excess, Diana had problems of her own on the other end of the spectrum. "She weighed ninety pounds. Many people thought she was anorexic," said Randy Taraborrelli. "She was under a lot of pressure, and for Florence to be unhappy and difficult and perhaps drinking too much was something that Diana wasn't about to tolerate either."

In 1966, the Supremes lost their firm grip on the number one slot. Two consecutive singles finished no higher than number five. In September, Florence Ballard reached her breaking point. "They were rehearsing a song called 'My Favorite Things' for the *Ed Sullivan Show*. By all accounts, Florence's earring just fell off, and Diana happened to step on it as they were doing the dance routines. Florence held her temper until they got into the dressing room with the door closed, but it took three people to get her off of Diana Ross," reported Taraborrelli.

For the first time, Gordy began to contemplate a solo career for Diana, but the Motown chief thought twice before he made that drastic move. Taraborrelli reasoned, "It might have been just Diana that Berry loved, but it wasn't just Diana that the public loved. It was the group, and to pull her out at that point would have been a huge mistake." The Supremes rebounded with two more number one singles, "You Can't Hurry Love" and "You Keep Me Hangin' On," but Ballard's erratic behavior threatened to undermine the new momentum. "For there to be this kind of hostility in the group, for whatever the reason, it just could not be allowed to continue." For Gordy, business was just business, but no one had any idea of the terrible tragedy that lay ahead.

By early 1967, the Supremes were a nonstop hit machine, with ten number one singles in just two and a half years, but jealousy threatened to tear the group to shreds. The constant focus on Diana Ross was driving Florence Ballard to self-destruction. Most of the world assumed Diana was preparing to go solo in 1967, but it wasn't Diana who wound up leaving the group. Ballard began to gain weight, and her drinking was disruptive. She lost her strongest supporter. According to Randy Taraborrelli, "It wasn't just Diana and Berry that sat down and did this. It was Mary, too, who said, 'Florence has got to go,' and it was difficult and heartbreaking for Mary." Regretted Mary Wilson, "I couldn't stand up for her, and I really wanted to." Ultimately, the gig was up for Florence Ballard. She was asked to leave the group once and for all.

Cindy Birdsong, a member of Patti LaBelle and the Bluebelles, was tapped to replace Florence, but the Bluebelles were signed to another label. While Motown worked to buy out Cindy's contract, Ballard was brought back for what she thought was a second chance. "Florence was back, but now she was really kind of pissed off," said Taraborrelli. "She did an engagement at the Copacabana, and Cindy Birdsong was in the audience at Berry's request, and this was a little intimidating." But the final straw came a month later, on June 28. Bueche recounted, "Even though they told her it was going to happen, she actually saw the marquee 'Supremes' come down and then 'Diana Ross & The Supremes' put above it, and she absolutely hit the roof. She just would not have any part of it. When she went on stage drunk in retaliation, she was fired."

By this point, Birdsong was available and waiting in the wings. The change was almost alarmingly quick—"Cindy was sort of walked across the street and put on stage while Florence was on her way to the airport," said Taraborrelli. Ballard was gone for good. Diana Ross and the Supremes was now a reality, and charges of her swelled ego again plagued Diana. "A lot of radio programmers took the name change as being egotistical on Diana Ross's part, and it wasn't even her decision," defended Rick Bueche. Martha Reeves, however, saw a different strategy in play: "There were times when she would not be in the middle or on the side, but a bit of a distance away from the girls, and it was all in an effort to establish her as Diana Ross."

Still, the infusion of fresh talent gave the group a spark. With Birdsong on board, Diana Ross and the Supremes took their stage show to a whole new level. "They got, in my view, even bigger and better than ever, because then they became this sort of fantastic show-business legend. The wigs were bigger, and the dresses were better, and more money was spent than ever," Randy Taraborrelli offered. While the shows were bigger and better, the songs were starting to slip. Songwriters Holland, Dozier, and Holland checked their bank accounts and decided they were being underpaid. In late 1967, the men with the Midas touch walked out the Motown door. The loss was a blow to Diana Ross and the Supremes as well as to Diana's solo aspirations. Said Bueche, "They were lucky to have one number one record a year. Songs like 'The Composer' and 'Forever Came Today' were great songs, but they didn't do much. It was noticeable that the Supremes were falling."

Gordy recruited a group of new producers to give the Motown sound an overhaul. The team of Nickolas Ashford and Valerie Simpson became an instant standout. Reasoned Ashford, "We brought to Motown maybe a different little sound, a little gospel, New York chic sound that they kind of said, 'Hmm, that's interesting.'" Berry Gordy soon began to see the Supremes differently. "In his view, it didn't really matter who was back there as long as

Diana was in front," said Taraborrelli, "and through no fault of their own, Mary and Cindy were then replaced on a lot of music by whoever happened to be walking by, usually the Endetes. And these great songs were coming out, like 'Love Child' and 'Someday We'll Be Together,' which Mary and Cindy really didn't have anything to do with."

Now it was Diana's turn to be unhappy. Said Taraborrelli, "They were splitting the money, if not equally, in a way that was not Diana getting most of it, and she was the star of the group. It was Diana Ross and the Supremes, and from a practical standpoint—and she was a very practical person—this didn't make a lot of sense." But Gordy had a master plan. "Berry Gordy really understood early on that television was a medium that was going to empower and catapult his artists far beyond what the record business could ever do," Suzanne DePasse commented. Added Taraborrelli, "He had, again, Diana in mind to be the woman who would take Motown into the next era, this new period, into the Hollywood years, and he decided that he was going to pull the company out of Detroit and move the whole thing to Los Angeles."

The move to L.A. was gradual, but the impact was immediate. The other Motown artists—and the Motor City itself—were in a state of shock. Shortly before the move was announced, a rowdy young quintet auditioned for Gordy, and the Motown head honcho knew he had found the next big thing. He just needed a clever way to market them. He turned to his best girl, and a showbiz legend was born. "The story was that she saw the Jackson 5 performing, and she discovered them, and she said, 'This is the one, this is the group that is going to take America by storm.' The fact of the matter is that Diana really had nothing to do with the discovering of the Jackson 5," Taraborrelli admitted. Mentioned DePasse, "It was quite the opposite. She was asked by the company of Berry Gordy to present them, and she agreed to help them, and then she kind of got a pie in the face for doing it."

While the popularity of the Jackson 5 soared, Diana Ross and the Supremes struggled. "By the end of '69 it was pretty obvious that the Supremes were no longer going to be instant hit makers. It was time for Diana Ross to go," said Rick Bueche. The end actually came with little fanfare. "People knew what was coming. Ironically, Mary and Cindy were so disposable that they found out from a newspaper article that she actually was leaving." The split was more difficult than Diana expected. Many fans, and some of her Motown colleagues, sniped behind her back. Jean Terrell was picked to take over as lead singer, and the name was changed back to the Supremes, but Diana stayed on the road with the group for a few final concerts. Described Randy Taraborrelli, "Mary and Cindy weren't really speaking to Diana. They had already replaced her, they were already recording with the new girl, and everything that was going on was really pretty much for show."

On January 14, 1970, twenty-five-year-old Diana made her last appearance with the Supremes at the Frontier Hotel in Las Vegas. Described Gerald Posner, "It was an amazing show that night. Everybody who was there said they were spectacular. They put their hearts and souls into it, and the audience knew it, but that was the end of it." When the curtain came down, Diana was on her own. The queen of Motown had to prove herself all over again, and the road ahead was rocky. After her split from the Supremes, Diana went solo in more ways than one. In 1970, her five-year love affair with Motown chief Berry Gordy ended. "Diana was a woman in her mid-twenties who wanted to have children and wanted to raise a family. She had things going on that Berry didn't really have going on in terms of those ideals," explained Taraborrelli. Diana and Gordy remained close friends and focused on their professional relationship.

Diana bought a home in Beverly Hills and began to see another man. According to celebrity photographer Harry Langdon, "his name was Bob Ellis. Bob worked in the mailroom at Jay Bernstein's public relations firm, and I started seeing Bob and Diana out socially. I thought, 'Hmm, this is interesting.'" As she was pairing up socially, Diana prepared to make her professional solo debut. Ashford and Simpson were tapped to produce her first album, and they knew that Motown and the public expected spectacular results. "That was our challenge," said Valerie Simpson, "Diana is leaving the Supremes, and she needs to be supreme. She was the lady of Motown. There was no doubt about that. This was her real stake, and we couldn't fail. It just couldn't fail."

But Diana's first single, "Reach Out and Touch Somebody's Hand," sold a so-so 500,000 copies. Many fans were finding the new Diana hard to swallow. Said *Rolling Stone* editor Anthony DeCurtis, "When a group is together, audiences almost project their own sense of family and friendship onto that group. When they start hearing about bickering and fights and one person goes solo, it's disturbing to them." Ironically, the Supremes were thriving. "The plan backfired," said Bueche. "It was assumed that Diana would go on to immediate success, and the Supremes would have the problem, but they came out with the Supremes first. 'Up the Ladder to the Roof' was a huge hit record. They were selling out. They were having one hit after another."

Diana rebounded with her second release, "Ain't No Mountain High Enough." The song went to number one and earned a GRAMMY nomination. Gordy was anxious to keep the momentum going. Remembered Nickolas Ashford, "After 'Ain't No Mountain' was such an enormous hit, Berry wanted something just like that. So we said, 'Mr. Gordy, we can't just redo the same thing. We're not those kind of writers.'" The follow-up record, *Everything Is Everything,* stumbled. By the end of 1970, Diana's solo career was back at square one. But there was big news to come: Miss Diana Ross was pregnant. On January 20, 1971, the mother-to-be shocked the world when she married Bob Ellis in a Las Vegas wedding chapel.

Diana's new marital status didn't change her life much. Gordy was still in charge. Assessed Randy Taraborrelli, "Bob didn't really stand a chance. He was really in a marriage with two people.

He was in a marriage with Berry and with Diana, and it was really difficult for him to understand the history that Berry and Diana shared." The boss was still passionate about Diana, but now his passion for her was all business. Gordy's priority was finding a film project that could turn his favorite female singer into a movie star. "At the time, there was a lot of cross-pollination between pop, R&B music, and the motion picture business. Today, somebody gets a hit record and suddenly people are running after them for television series and movies, but back then this was a major step," Suzanne DePasse said.

Producer Jay Weston thought he had the perfect fit—a film based on the life of legendary jazz singer Billie Holiday. Berry Gordy wanted no part of this tragic story. "He said, 'Why would I let Diana play a black junkie singer? That's a terrible idea,' and he turned me down flat," said Weston. The producer was convinced that Diana was born to play Holiday. He hired respected director Sidney Furie and approached Berry Gordy again and again. Finally, Weston and Furie convinced the hit maker. Tinseltown snickered when Gordy announced Diana was going to play Holiday in *Lady Sings the Blues*. *Time* magazine senior editor Christopher John Farley mentioned, "She began hearing a lot of rumors, a lot of talk, a lot of critics saying that she can't play this part, that she's an R&B singer, not a jazz singer like Billie Holiday was, that she didn't look like Billie Holiday, so what the heck was she doing playing Billie Holiday?" Added Rick Bueche, "They expected somebody like Diahann Carroll or somebody of a heavier mantle to play that piece."

Everyone involved with the project brought out the big guns to make sure Diana nailed the role and audiences and critics were silenced. Designer Bob Mackie was hired to help Diana disappear into her role: "Most people didn't know what Billie Holiday looked like anyway, so we tried to make it authentic period-wise and make it all work for the audience." But Diana herself worked the hardest to prove her doubters wrong. "I've never seen anybody woodshed like that," said DePasse, "I mean, she studied, she listened. There was one point where she sounded more like Billie Holiday than Billie Holiday."

Production was set to begin in December, but first there was one other pressing engagement. On August 14, 1971, Diana gave birth to a daughter, Rhonda Suzanne. Immediately, the rumor mill began to churn. Rhonda looked nothing like her father, Bob Ellis, and resembled Gordy strongly, noted Taraborrelli. Diana shrugged off the gossip and got to work. The search for her leading man began and ended with a handsome newcomer. Recalled Jay Weston, "We brought Billy Dee Williams in to do a test with Diana. We dressed him in his white suit and white hat, and she did an interplay with him—the dialogue in this scene. Following that, the next afternoon she and I sat in the screening room, and we looked at this test, and I remember Diana scrunching down in her chair and in a little voice she said, 'He's the one.'"

As soon as filming started, everyone on the set could see that Diana was delivering the performance of a lifetime. "She absolutely made herself look horrifying—or not horrifying, but adorable as a little girl with her hair in little tiny braids and little terrible work dresses on and nothing glamorous. She understood that if she did that it would only make the glamorous things work that much better later on," commented Bob Mackie. Behind the scenes, Berry Gordy struggled to keep his pet project afloat. According to Suzanne DePasse, the studio even threatened to pull the plug when money was tight. Gordy dug in his heels, eventually writing a check to claim the film as an independent production, free from the studio execs at Paramount. The gamble paid off. *Lady Sings the Blues* was released on October 12, 1972, and was an instant hit.

Diana missed the premiere. She was about to give birth to her second daughter, Tracee Joy. There was another celebration to come. Diana was nominated for an Academy Award. Gordy was determined to make sure Diana walked off with the Oscar. "He really kind of rammed it down people's throats with a lot of industry ads and a lot of sort of propaganda that 'Diana Ross is Billie Holiday' and 'She is an Academy Award–winning actress' and 'You're going to give her an Academy Award.'" On Oscar night, Liza Minnelli took home the award for *Cabaret*. Berry Gordy's aggressive tactics appeared to have backfired. According to Jay Weston, "It was typical Motown overkill. They wanted her to win, and nothing was going to stop them. In the end, my analysis is—and I think I'm right—that the voters of the Academy rebelled against the pressure and the overkill of the sell." Diana took the Oscar loss hard. At twenty-nine, she was questioning Gordy's dominant role in her life and her career.

Diana burst onto Hollywood's A-list with her portrayal of troubled jazz great Billie Holiday in *Lady Sings the Blues*, but finding the right follow-up film proved easier said than done. She was swamped with film offers after *Lady Sings the Blues*. However, her recording career was limping along. Former Motown executive Suzanne DePasse thought Diana needed new energy and found a spark in an unproven songwriter named Michael Masser. He was told that he needed to "start at the top," since Diana hadn't had a hit in years. He rose to the challenge and composed "Touch Me in the Morning."

The song was complicated and emotional, and so were the recording sessions. "There were a lot of takes and a lot of testy times," said Michael Masser, "but the hotter the fire the stronger the steel. With persistence and with Diana's great talent overcoming everything, her ability to take a chance, not being able to hit a note and go for it again—that's unusual. She might be a little flat in her singing, but it's Diana, and that's what makes her so great. She just went for it." The effort paid off when "Touch Me in the Morning" was released in May of 1973. "We got a number one song, a GRAMMY winner, and, for myself, it was terrific. For Diana, it was a beginning of another stage of her solo career singing ballads."

Now Diana Ross was ready to get back to the silver screen, but Berry Gordy was keeping her under lock and key. Described Jay Weston, "No other producer could have access to her except through Berry, and he didn't want other producers around her." Finally, Gordy decided on *Mahogany*, a star vehicle about a woman who rises from poverty to become a top fashion designer. Veteran filmmaker Tony Richardson was hired to direct. From the get-go, Richardson and Gordy clashed. Just weeks into production, Gordy fired Richardson and took over the director's job himself. Explained DePasse, "One of the things Berry Gordy absolutely understood was how Diana Ross should be directed, and I think that that wasn't happening, so Berry Gordy was the director of *Mahogany*."

The transition between directors was rocky. Gordy had never directed a film before, and *Mahogany* was a high-budget, high-profile project. As Randy Taraborrelli put it, "It was kind of hard enough when he was her manager and her ex-lover, but when he became her director, this was really tough for her." *Mahogany* performed well at the box office, and the theme song "Do You Know Where You're Going To?" became an instant classic, but the critics saw no redeeming value in the film. Farley said that they "didn't get it, didn't like it, didn't want to see black love, didn't want to see Diana Ross in this part, and they really panned it. I think it really hurt her career long-term."

Diana was not happy, especially with Gordy, her longtime manager. Commented Taraborrelli, "She began growing as a woman. She was a very smart, very intelligent, very ambitious, savvy person, and a married woman with her own kids. She really just felt that Berry was sort of keeping her down." Diana retreated into her family life. In November 1975, she gave birth to her third daughter, Chudney Lane. Just months later, in February 1976, the entire Motown family received sad news—Florence Ballard was dead. After leaving the Supremes, Ballard failed to catch on as a solo act. Money problems, depression, and drinking slowly destroyed her until the home on Buena Vista was all she had left. Then it was gone. Ballard managed to get off welfare and started to pull her life together, but then tragedy struck when she was afflicted by a sudden illness and died in the hospital later that week from cardiac arrest. More than two thousand mourners paid their respects at her funeral. Diana was among them.

Disapproving eyes were on the hometown diva as she entered the chapel. "When Diana came into the church, the entire congregation stood up with a big gasp that Diana had come in," Mark Bego described. "People took out their Instamatic cameras and literally took pictures in the church at the funeral—[pictures] of Diana Ross. Diana walked down the aisle, surrounded by bodyguards, and at one point, she swooned—she actually audibly gasped and swooned—only to be caught by bodyguards. It looked absolutely choreographed. I've never seen anything like [it]." Ballard was laid to rest, and Diana was whisked away back to Hollywood and her storybook life. Concluded Bego, "The sad part of this whole funeral was the fact that, even in death, Florence Ballard had to compete with Diana Ross for everybody's attention."

Diana turned thirty-two in 1976, but Motown chief Berry Gordy still treated her like a little girl from the Brewster Projects. "Whatever he said to do, if it was going to make her a star, it could be 'Go stand on your head in the corner,' and she did it. She was a young woman by now. She had three children. She was tired of being someone's puppet," Rick Bueche offered. Diana could not break away from Gordy. She was still under contract to Motown. But Diana could do something about her fading marriage. In June, Diana filed for divorce from Bob Ellis. Randy Taraborrelli speculated, "I think that she misplaced her dissatisfaction with Berry and thought she was dissatisfied with her marriage as well, and she and Bob ended up divorcing. In retrospect I think maybe she regrets it." The marriage ended amicably in March 1977.

For the first time in more than a decade, Diana Ross was single. She threw herself into her career and handpicked a project to put her back on the A-list: a biopic of black entertainment pioneer Josephine Baker. "Diana Ross had actually met Josephine Baker in the past and was sort of obsessed with her," said Christopher John Farley. "She even did whole photo shoots dressed up as Josephine Baker, complete in the sort of scantily clad, topless costumes that Josephine Baker herself used to dress up in on stage." Diana struggled to get the project off the ground.

In the meantime, another opportunity attracted her attention. Motown had acquired the rights to the hit stage musical *The Wiz.* Diana wanted the part of Dorothy. According to Bueche, "She was really bound and determined to play that part. There, again, there is something about the character of Dorothy she identified with, and so she insisted on doing it." Gordy felt casting Diana was a mistake, but, for the first time, he gave in. "He knew it was wrong, but she kept coming back to him," said Gerald Posner, "and of course Hollywood is magic. Suddenly, one of the studios said, 'You know what? Diana Ross in *The Wiz*—we will give you a million dollars for that role if you cast her.' Gordy liked the green and decided it was worthwhile." The part was rewritten for Diana.

The Wiz began production on October 3, 1977. The all-star cast included Richard Pryor as the Wizard and nineteen-year-old Michael Jackson as the Scarecrow. During the shoot, an accident almost ended Diana's acting career. Described Farley, "There's a scene in *The Wiz* where Diana looks into a light that is meant to represent the eyes of the Wizard, and it was a long scene. She was forced to spend a lot of time looking into those lights, and afterward she found that her eyes were not quite right. She went to the doctors, and they thought that her retinas had been damaged." Diana's eyes were burned, but she quickly recovered and finished *The Wiz.*

Her physical pain gave way to emotional distress when the musical was released in 1978. "*The Wiz* was a terrible movie. It just didn't work," scoffed Jay Weston. The film opened to scathing reviews and earned a meager $13 million. Many critics placed the blame squarely on the shoulders of the leading lady. Reasoned Randy Taraborrelli, "Coming after *Lady Sings the Blues* and *Mahogany*, which wasn't as good as *Lady Sings the Blues*, this was really a letdown for a lot of people." Rick Bueche added, "This gave Berry Gordy the chance to say, 'Are you going to listen to me now?'"

Getting back on the charts was no simple task. "In the mid-70s musical styles really began to change. What had been soul music and R&B really rapidly began to become disco, and Diana Ross was having to, in some way, come to terms with that," said Anthony DeCurtis. With her music career floundering, Diana gave Hollywood another try. In early 1979, Warner Bros. searched for a black actress to star opposite Ryan O'Neal in an interracial love story called *The Bodyguard*. Diana wanted the part and O'Neal. She landed both. But the romance and the project collapsed after just a few months.

Ryan O'Neal was bitter, and he took his complaints to the press. "He said that she didn't want to do sex scenes, she didn't want to show her body. He said that she didn't want to sing," reported Taraborrelli, "and worst of all, he said that she didn't want to be black, which was really, really hitting her at the heart of who she is as a person." Diana commented, "My parents raised me past color. I'm really past that, a lot. If I'm in a crowd of people, I don't see that they're black and they're white. I don't see color anymore. I have mixed children. We don't look at things that way. I think the world is going like that. It's just going to be one color."

With *The Bodyguard* fiasco behind her, Diana began a relationship with an unlikely partner: Kiss front man Gene Simmons. Simmons was a notorious womanizer who was just ending a relationship with another diva, Cher. "I think one of the reasons she dated Ryan and Gene Simmons was because she was trying to show Berry Gordy what she was made of and that she could do these kinds of things, and she didn't care what he thought," commented Taraborrelli. Diana also took her music in a new direction. She teamed up with the band Chic and its two rising stars, Bernard Edwards and Nile Rodgers. Rodgers offered, "At the time that we worked with her, it felt that there was a big change going on in her life. This was the last record on her contract, and she wanted to make a statement. She got outside producers and outside writers to do something that was very drastically different from what she had done before."

The album was a landmark and a success for her. The magic touch of the Chic masterminds produced some great hits. "The album with 'Upside Down' and 'I'm Coming Out' on it became maybe her biggest album ever and really put Diana Ross in a whole different world," said Taraborrelli. The timing was perfect. Diana's contract with Motown was set to expire, and lucrative offers from other labels were pouring in. However, would she be willing to walk away from the most important man in her life? Berry Gordy had made her a star, but in late 1980, RCA records offered Diana Ross a seven-year contract worth a whopping $20 million.

"She went to Berry to match it," said Rick Bueche, "and he told her, 'You know I can't match that kind of money. Do you really think you are going to get from them what I gave you—the preferential treatment, the best producers, the best promotion, the movie deals?'" Diana considered her reservations and, according to Taraborrelli, made her decision: "At that point, she said, 'Look, I'm thirty-seven years old. I want to know where my bank accounts are.' She said, 'I want to know who owns my car. Do I own it or is Motown leasing it for me? I want to know.'" Diana expressed these sentiments herself, admitting, "It took that long for me to find out that I could take responsibility for my life and that nobody else was responsible for my successes and failure but me. I could make decisions, and I could say 'Yes' and I could say 'No.'"

Diana Ross shocked Berry Gordy—and the entire music world—by signing with RCA. Remembered Suzanne DePasse, "When I heard that Diana Ross was leaving Motown, not only was I devastated, but I was really concerned about what that was going to do to Berry Gordy." Diana didn't take her decision lightly. According to Michael Masser, she even tried—at his suggestion— to give Gordy a call on her last night at Motown. Despite international phone calls, "she wasn't able to reach Berry Gordy, but she reached out for Berry Gordy." The king and former queen of Motown didn't speak that night—or much at all—after Diana left

Motown. "These were people who had managed to shape popular music not only for the United States and not only shape each other's lives but created a sound for the whole world," commented Anthony DeCurtis, "but the intensity of their involvement often meant a kind of an equally dramatic breakage, and that sort of occurred in that relationship."

Less than a year later, there was another dramatic breakup, with Gene Simmons. "Gene apparently stayed at Cher's home in New York, and Diana thought that perhaps he and Cher had picked up where they left off, and, as it happened, Cher wasn't even there," said Randy Taraborrelli. Diana was giving her whole life a makeover. She left her longtime home in Beverly Hills and moved to a large estate in Connecticut. The diva struggled to sort out her personal life. In the meantime, her RCA career began with a bang. "That's when she goes from what I call diva with a little 'd' to Diva with a capital 'D.' She goes from 'Diana Ross' to 'Call Me Mrs. Ross,'" said Gerald Posner. "It happened before, at Motown, but it became much worse, and that is because at Motown, although Gordy would often intervene for her on her side, he would also come in when her behavior had gone over the line and say, 'Diana, enough.'"

At RCA, Diana quickly came to a painful realization. As Rick Bueche put it, "She began to realize what Berry Gordy had been telling her. At Motown she was the queen. She was the preferred artist. At RCA she was just another recording artist." Although everyone had high expectations, and Diana's reputation was certainly that of a superstar, she did not receive the preferential treatment from her RCA label heads that she received at her former label. Motown was having its own problems. During the 70s, disco and defections crippled the label. By early 1983, Berry Gordy was swimming in a sea of red ink. Record executive Suzanne DePasse devised a plan to jump-start the future by reaching back to the past. "It just seemed like a good idea at the time to celebrate this place that I had grown up in," she explained. Said Bueche of DePasse's plan, "It was her brainchild to have basically almost like a high-school reunion. All the Motown acts—all or most of them—were long gone. She got Mary Wells back. She got Martha Reeves back, and the highlight of the show was supposed to be the reunion of Diana Ross and the Supremes."

The splashy event was titled Motown 25 and scheduled to be a major TV special on NBC. DePasse hit a roadblock when Diana declined to participate. The capital "D" Diva did not have a lot of warm sentiments left for Motown, and she knew the feeling was mutual. Said Taraborrelli, "There were still people at Motown by 1983 who felt that she walked all over them in order to get where she was, when, in fact, what she did was just kind of walked right by them." At the eleventh hour, Diana reluctantly agreed to do the show, but her intuition had been correct. The night began badly and went downhill. Diana, Mary Wilson, and Cindy Birdsong were out of sync from the start. "They just couldn't get their emotional self together," said Nickolas Ashford. "Even when they were singing 'Someday We'll Be Together,' you could feel it."

One incident in particular demonstrated the feuding. "We had told everybody that we were going to bring Mr. Gordy down on stage, and it was a very specific orchestration of how that was supposed to happen," explained DePasse, "but Mary got all excited and started to bring Berry down. What Diana did was just push her microphone down and tell her that we had to do it another way." But the headlines told a very different story. Diana was bashed for "shoving" Wilson. "I have to laugh when I look back on it, because it was so benign. Once again Diana's following the directions that we gave her and asked her to take the lead because it was so appropriate for her to bring Berry on. It just got all blown out of proportion." Motown 25 became the highest-rated musical special in the history of television and earned an Emmy for Outstanding Variety Program. For Diana Ross, the night was a disaster. The Diva needed to do some damage control.

In July of 1983, Diana needed a career boost. She turned to a tried-and-true formula for success. Reasoned Anthony DeCurtis, "Giving a huge concert in Central Park has historically been the kind of thing performers do." The glitzy event was slated to raise $250,000 for a park and playground at the corner of Eighty-first Street and Central Park West, but a sudden rainstorm created a major drama. "She would not leave the stage until she was sure that there wasn't going to be a riot. So there she is with the wind and the rain in her hair, and she's just the greatest diva of all," beamed Randy Taraborrelli.

Triumph turned to controversy when Diana returned for a make-up concert the next day. Taraborrelli explained, "As a result of doing it the second day, the expenses soared and literally doubled. What had been set aside for this children's playground was gone. It had evaporated into the production cost." New York mayor Ed Koch was furious, and the press had a field day, but Diana quickly quieted her critics. The besieged Diva took out her own checkbook and honored the pricey commitment that she had made to the children. Unfortunately, more problems were on the way.

Reports began to surface claiming Diana was a difficult boss. "Many of those who worked for her said that they didn't find they were treated with any respect at all," said Gerald Posner. "She wanted something, and she wanted it then. She wanted it done no matter what it did to their own personal life, and if it wasn't done correctly, she could be quite cutting in the way she dealt with people, even in public." An even lower point came in October 1984, when Diana's mother, Ernestine, died after a two-year battle with cancer. Attorney John Frankenheimer commented, "It was very hard for her. They were very close."

Diana and her three daughters retreated to their Connecticut estate. Once again, Ross seemed adrift, but the Diva was still holding out hope for romance. "I love that idea of marriage," said Diana. "To me, the unit of family is a special part of my life. It was my upbringing, and I'd like very much if I met 'that guy.' That we'd get married and be married for the rest of my life." "That guy" came calling. Described Taraborrelli, "Arne Naess is a Norwegian shipping mogul, and the big story at the time was that, in very Jackie O style, she had come up with her own Aristotle Onassis, and it was a real storybook kind of fantasy." The press and the public loved the fantasy. In reality, the Diva did not need her fiancé's bank account. "People even to this day think that she married him for his money, and that's just not true. Maybe he married her for her money," speculated Taraborrelli. Diana married Naess in Switzerland on February 1, 1986. Designer Bob Mackie called it "quite the fairy-tale wedding with the diamond tiara and the whole works."

Diana was finally receiving some positive press, but that changed in October, when Mary Wilson released her autobiography. *Dreamgirl: My Life as a Supreme* was a huge bestseller. "In that book, I think, more than anywhere else do you see the original Diana Ross who never was kind almost to anybody but herself, who always was a bit of the spoiled brat, who had to be dealt with, who time and time again did things that hurt the other girls and never was concerned about it," said Posner. Wilson justified herself by saying, "I wrote facts about what happened to the Supremes. I tried not to give my opinions about it but only the story of the things we did. In that respect, I said Diana is very competitive and always has been—that's what made her a star."

Once again, Diana was on the defensive. "It was the first time that people really had the validation that they had always expected that Diana Ross was difficult," said Taraborrelli. "Now Mary Wilson, one of the Supremes who would know, was out there saying, 'You know, you ain't heard half of it.'" DeCurtis agreed, "People were ready to believe a lot of the stories that Mary Wilson told, and Diana came off sounding so defensive and high-handed and clueless." With her solo career sputtering and her public image in tatters, Diana laid low. In January 1988, she skipped The Supremes' induction into the Rock and Roll Hall of Fame.

Meanwhile, the newlywed gave birth to two sons over eighteen months and stayed busy at home. Described John Frankenheimer, "Everything had to be worked around her family and her children, and that certainly was the case when she had the boys."

In the music business, Diana Ross was ice-cold by 1988. "As far as a kind of mainstream pop artist, having big hits and being on the radio and commanding that degree of public attention, those days ended pretty much in the early '80s for Diana Ross," assessed DeCurtis. The RCA contract ended, and neither side was eager to renew. "I can't imagine they made their $20 million back, I'll tell you that much," said DeCurtis.

Diana turned to the one man who'd been there at the start: Berry Gordy. Time was healing the rift between the ex-lovers, but Gordy had shocking news—Motown was for sale. "She tried to talk him out of it. She said, 'Look, I'll come back, don't sell it just yet. Stick around a little bit longer,' but his heart was no longer in it," said Rick Bueche. Gordy hit the jackpot when he sold Motown in 1988. The one-time assembly-line worker turned an $800 loan into $61 million.

One of his last acts as head of the label was to make sure Diana got a new record deal and stock in the company. Unfortunately, Diana's 1989 return to Motown wasn't the security blanket she and Gordy had hoped for. Almost thirty years later, the magic and her mentor were gone. Mentioned Bueche, "It was not the same Motown. She was now working for people considerably younger than her who maybe feigned interest in new product, mostly because they were interested in her back catalog." Diana had come full circle. At forty-three, she was just another singer looking for a break at Motown. But Diana and Gordy were not finished with each other yet. There was a secret still left to reveal.

By 1991, the former dynamo had not appeared in a movie in more than ten years. Her once-promising acting career was on the shelf. "I turned down a lot of scripts that I didn't really think were right for me to do," Diana explained. "I thought that if I were to make a film it needs to be something that I really, really like." Then her pet project made it to the small screen without her. A 1991 film about Josephine Baker starring Lynn Whitfield came along and completely passed Diana by without a murmur to her people. "Diana Ross just felt shattered by that, because she felt it was her project," remarked Christopher John Farley. A year later, Diana was scooped again. *The Bodyguard,* a project that began as a vehicle for the diva and Ryan O'Neal, was released with Whitney Houston and Kevin Costner.

In 1993, Diana announced a deal to do three television movies. Diana's first project was as executive producer and star of a drama called *Out of Darkness.* "It was a movie that was by all accounts written very well and had a very demanding part in its center where she played a woman who was a paranoid schizophrenic," described Farley. Diana offered, "My job was not to promote unnecessarily or to mislead but to at least promote a bit of understanding about the illness and what families and clients, as we call them, deal with daily."

Before *Out of Darkness* hit the air, forty-nine-year-old Diana made a startling confession. On October 25, 1993, she appeared on *Oprah* and confirmed that Berry Gordy fathered her daughter Rhonda. "It made sense for her to do it. It coincided with a point in time where Rhonda was of an age where all of that was being discussed more openly and certainly it was becoming more of an issue to be dealt with," said Frankenheimer. People were really talking when *Out of Darkness* premiered in January of 1994. "It got almost universally great reviews. Through-the-roof reviews," Farley commented. Diana was nominated for a Golden Globe.

Her comeback, however, never quite materialized. Motherhood and life seemed to get in the way. Then, in April of 1999, Arne Naess announced on a Norwegian talk show that the marriage was over after thirteen years. "That marriage did work for quite a while. When it ended, it just ended, but a long marriage like that is certainly not a failure," Randy Taraborrelli defended. Regardless of their attempts, said John Frankenheimer, "It was difficult for them to maintain the marriage at the end just because of their schedules and the fact that they lived on different continents for significant portions of the year." Just one month after her separation, Diana appeared with Brandy Norwood in a television movie called *Double Platinum.*

Diana's increasingly bizarre behavior, however, was about to ignite rumors that something was not right. In September, she approached Lil' Kim, decked out in pasties and a risqué outfit, and tweaked the hip-hop star's breast at the MTV Music Awards. Diana "just kind of lost her self-consciousness and got a kick out of seeing one of these young hip-hop stars and how they're presenting themselves to the world," mused Anthony DeCurtis. Just days later, Diana found herself in a tussle with a female security guard at London's Heathrow Airport. As Ross described it, she "felt [the security guard's] hands go down my behind, and they go down your legs, and the side of her hand hit me in my private areas, and that's when I went, 'This is too much, I want to complain.'" Diana "complained" by grabbing the security guard right back. That landed her in hot water with the local police. Diana was detained for several hours. In the end, the authorities did not file charges.

The British tabloids had a field day presenting Diana as an out-of-control diva. She struggled to get a handle on her tarnished public image. In April 2000, Diana was honored by VH-1 as part of their *Tribute to Divas* series. "The word 'diva' really applies to her," said Bob Mackie, "and she likes that. She likes being a diva." Diana added, "If I am a diva, I think I've earned it through the wisdom that I've learned over these years." In true diva fashion, Diana set the music world on its ear when she announced a major tour. "The Return to Love tour initially was going to be the reunion of Diana Ross and the Supremes. It was planned to be the event of the millennium." But the dream collapsed when Mary Wilson rejected Diana's contract offer. Explained Wilson, "I did not take the tour because of money. It was what the money represented to me and to what I supposedly represent to you. I refuse to have my heart and my soul broken."

Cindy Birdsong also declined to join the tour. Diana was forced to move on. She turned to Lynda Laurence and Scherrie Payne, two Supremes from the 1970s who never sang on the same stage with Diana. Once again, Wilson went on the offensive. "She went on a very successful media blitz to let people know that she had been counted out of this," reported Rick Bueche. The tour began on June 14, 2000, at Philadelphia's First Union Spectrum, but many fans, and the media, were not impressed. "All of a sudden the little small blurbs became this huge, massive, negative campaign about our tour," recalled Lynda Laurence. Added Scherrie Payne, "There were some fans who expressed their disappointment openly toward Lynda and myself either on paper or in person at the concerts, but I would have been a fool to say no." After just nine performances, the tour was cancelled. Explained John Frankenheimer, "The economics weren't penciling out. It was a very expensive show. It was scaled to be an arena-level show and had to have almost a sold-out show every night probably to be profitable." The end of the tour was a personal and financial fiasco for Diana, but she was about to face the crisis of her career.

The failure of the Return to Love tour hit her harder than anyone expected. Three years of career and personal disappointments became a heavy burden to bear. In May 2002, the aging idol checked herself into the Promises Rehab Clinic in Malibu, California, to "clear up some personal issues." Randy Taraborrelli speculated, "I think that a lot of things probably contributed to whatever problems that she's had that she's had to go to rehab for, but I think that the Return to Love failure was really pretty chief amongst the problems, right on top of the list."

After several weeks, Diana Ross emerged from rehab, but her troubles weren't over. On December 30, 2002, she was arrested for drunk driving in Arizona. Tests revealed Diana's blood alcohol level was more than twice Arizona's legal limit. On February 9, 2003, Diana was convicted of driving under the influence. She was ordered to spend two days in jail, but Ross ran into more trouble when she served the time near her home in upscale Greenwich, Connecticut. She completed the sentence in three overnight jail visits. Under Arizona law, that didn't count. The judge ordered the diva back to Tucson to serve forty-eight straight hours in the Pima County Jail. He later relented and ruled that Diana had satisfied her sentence requirements.

After decades filled with countless mix-ups, comebacks, splashes, and flops, Diana Ross keeps the world guessing what she will do next and how it will affect her ever-changing image. The architects of the Supremes' indelible sound have all moved on. Motown founder Berry Gordy is long retired. Songwriters Holland, Dozier, and Holland have their own label, H-D-H Records. Mary Wilson tours the world as a solo act. Cindy Birdsong is a minister in Los Angeles. For Diana Ross, however, life after the Supremes has been a series of peaks and valleys. "There's a very interesting, complex, warm human being behind the entertainment icon. It would be good to appreciate that now rather than some time in the distant future," John Frankenheimer commented.

Diana's friends and fans are not willing to count her out just yet. "We all have our problems, you know. We all go through our trials and tribulations, and I'm sure she will prevail," said Holland. Time will tell if Diana makes a comeback. According to Gerald Posner, Diana "hasn't changed with the times. The question is whether she can. That's the difference between Diana Ross continuing to go downhill at this time and ending up nowhere or being able to pull herself back with that great discipline she has and having a second career—smaller than the first one but still a second career." Still, Diana's place in history is already secure. "She's the first black woman artist to me that has been loved totally across the board," said Nickolas Ashford. Suzanne DePasse explained, "Diana Ross was put here to entertain us and to have us sing along to the soundtrack of her life, which is really the soundtrack of our lives."

John Christopher Farley commented, "She made music that was meaningful, that was stylish, that was empowering, and the fact that she could put all those things into her music was really a testament to her abilities as an artist." Despite her pitfalls and public image, Diana Ross originated the idea of superstar. As Randy Taraborrelli put it, "When God created Diana Ross, He probably looked down and said, 'Well, that's the end of that. I can't do any better than that. She's the one.'"

CHAPTER 3

THE DOCTOR IS IN
The Phil McGraw Story

"Self-doubt is not in his vocabulary."

—*Skip Hollandsworth, executive editor,*
Texas Monthly *magazine*

A wife who shops till she drops . . . a husband who plays the ponies . . . a teenage daughter who doesn't give a damn—it's the perfect family storm. So who you gonna call? The man with the plan, Dr. Phil McGraw. But who is this guy? A relationship guru? Or just a "quick fix" artist? Though some see him as an exploiter without much to back it up, others want nothing more than to "get real" with the doctor, said Skip Hollandsworth, executive editor of *Texas Monthly* magazine, "The guy is as glib and fast on his feet as anybody you're ever going to come across." This is the story of plain talk, self-help, and blind ambition. This is the story of Dr. Phil.

From the very beginning, the good doctor knew how to make an entrance. On September 1, 1950, Joseph McGraw was probably the most nervous man in Vinita, Oklahoma. Joe's wife, Jerri, was about to give birth moments before he launched his high school football coaching career. Sophia Dembling, who cowrote the book *The Making of Dr. Phil*, said, "Phil was actually born at kind of an inconvenient time for his dad—fifteen minutes before kickoff for his very first game as a coach." Phillip Calvin McGraw was the second of four kids. While his dad coached football, mom Jerri took care of Phil and his three sisters. In the mid-1980s, Joe gave up sports for a bigger paycheck. "Joe was working as an oil salesman, which was the thing to do around this part of the country. Everybody here jumped on oil. What that meant is that they moved around a lot," said Dembling.

The McGraws left Vinita, went to Colorado, and eventually moved back to Oklahoma. Young Phil grew into a big, strapping kid who loved playing football. He learned an early lesson in psychology when his junior high squad took on a ragtag team from a rival school. "Phil's team of course thought, 'Piece of cake.' Well, they just got their butts kicked. He asked his dad, 'What happened there? Why is it?' and his dad said, 'Well, they just wanted it more than you did,'" said Dembling. "From that, Phil began to understand success and how motivation and urgency are big factors in actually accomplishing what you want to accomplish."

At forty years old, Joe McGraw had some unfulfilled ambitions of his own. In the early 1960s, he quit the oil business and went back to school to study psychology. In 1965, Joe relocated to the Kansas City area to complete an internship. Money was tight, so at first only Joe and his reluctant son made the trip. They moved into a small apartment, and fifteen-year-old Phil enrolled at nearby Shawnee Mission North High School. According to high school girlfriend and ex-wife Debbie Higgins McCall, "He didn't express to me anything about what his dad was doing other than the fact that his dad had uprooted him from Oklahoma City and that he wasn't happy about it." Phil "was not a very committed student," said Sophia Dembling. "He said himself that showing up for school was one of his big problems—that he didn't like to go to school very much."

But the six-foot-four, 175-pound teenager never missed football practice. Some boys played hard. Phil played harder. Phil's high school football teammate Murrell Hayes described, "He would go 110. Some of the other of them may go 75, but Phil would make up for any of his shortcomings by really going after you. He just didn't quit." Phil earned a reputation as a hard-charging player, and he refused to be intimidated. Teammate Hall Burkindine remembered a showdown with Phil over a decision to punt on fourth down. "It escalated to a fistfight. And he's a big man, and he hits hard," he said. "Moral of the story was that I shouldn't have punted. When the fight was over, we both had black eyes, and I think we may have both had broken noses."

Phil had a way with words and soon began thinking about following his dad into the field of psychology. But sixteen-year-old Phil had a more immediate challenge on his hands—getting a date with untouchable Debbie Higgins. "Nobody would ask me out because my brother—I found out—was threatening guys if they asked me out," Debbie laughed. Debbie's brother was no match for the towering jock. Phil made his move. Mused Debbie, "I just remember he came up and asked me if I would go to a dance. I said, 'Sure. Somebody asked me out! Thank you!'" Commented Murrell Hayes, "He picked the top girl in the school. He wasn't taking seconds, you know. She was the head cheerleader."

In 1967, seventeen-year-old Phil kicked off his senior year of high school in style as the starting tackle on the Indians football team and the boyfriend of the head cheerleader. "It seemed like a good relationship was developing," said Debbie Higgins. Phil and his seventeen-year-old girlfriend seemed to be the perfect couple. Said Hall Burkindine, "They treated each other great. It just looked like they were meant for each other." Murrell Hayes mused, "We used to tease him, because we'd always see them together. We started calling them 'Mr. and Mrs. McGraw.'" Debbie herself said that Phil was "so serious. He was easy to tease. You know, if he was inside a window in a store, and I would go outside, and I would do that walk where you act like you're going down the steps and then turn around and come back up—that would embarrass him."

In 1967, Debbie Higgins was named homecoming queen. Meanwhile, Phil McGraw was awarded a football scholarship to the University of Tulsa. Debbie enrolled at Southwest Missouri State, but the couple vowed to keep the fires burning. "I think we just automatically knew that the bond was strong," she said.

While Debbie was flourishing at her school, Phil didn't last long at the University of Tulsa. An eye injury ended his football career, and he dropped out of school after his freshman year. Debbie remained in school, but Phil was now on the move. He stayed for a while in Wichita Falls, Texas, where his dad worked as a psychologist. Phil then took a job selling memberships at a health club in Lubbock, Texas. His MO? No pain, no gain. "Now *that* was intense," said Debbie. "He would take the women in there and shut the door. I don't know what he'd say to them in there, but he would keep them in there a long time. I am sure that he probably got one hundred percent of his sales."

The supersalesman quickly worked his way into management, becoming part owner of the club. Commented Sophia Dembling, "He is brilliant at knowing how to approach people to get what he wants. That's his superskill." But Phil wasn't all work and no play. Debbie remembered, "He kept writing letters and calling, asking me to move there, and at the time, my mom wanted me to make sure I continued on with my college education." Debbie eventually gave in. "The day that I moved to Lubbock, Texas, is when they had three tornadoes. They called it a national disaster. I should have known. Big sign," she said. Despite the bad omen, Debbie decided to stay. The high school sweethearts married on November 27, 1970, in the bride's hometown of Roeland Park, Kansas.

The newlyweds relocated to Topeka, Kansas, where Phil opened another health club. He worked long hours and, according to Debbie, became very demanding. "I would have to call him at the spa and tell him I was leaving and where I was going, and I would have to call the spa to tell him if I was coming to the spa, because he wanted me to come work out," she said. Debbie worked out often and hard. "He wanted me to do bench pressing so it would build up the pectoral muscles—bigger breasts. He wanted longer hair, to make sure I was physically fit, toned. He didn't want me to work, so I spent a lot of time just kind of hanging out, which was kind of hard on a twenty-one-year-old," she remarked.

Too hard, in fact. Debbie quickly tired of being Phil's "arm candy," and the relationship turned sour. "It felt like I was being manipulated and controlled and there was no communication. There was no respect," she said regretfully. "It was the attitude that he couldn't carry on a conversation with me, so he didn't bother. He would tell me I didn't have the mental capacity to carry on a conversation with him, so I didn't." In published interviews, Dr. Phil claims he did talk to his wife. Regardless, in 1973, Debbie filed to end the marriage, citing "irreconcilable differences." In the settlement, Debbie got $500 and their Pontiac Grand Prix, but the pittance didn't matter to her, because, as she put it, she thought, "Do whatever you have to do. Just sign the paper and let me out." With that, the pair split after only three years of marriage.

After fumbling his marriage, Phil tackled new challenges. Members at Phil's Grecian Health Spa continued to pump iron, but not enough money was pumped into the club. In September 1973, Phil suddenly shut the doors of the Topeka facility. He was sued by a local creditor and ordered by the court to pay $3,000. He then put his busted health club business behind him, and turned from barbells to books, from physiology to psychology. In the spring of 1974, Phil enrolled at Midwestern State University in Wichita Falls, Texas. He majored in psychology, and began dating Robin Jameson, a friend of his sister.

Robin and Phil hit it off immediately and got along so well, said Box, because "she's sweet and nurturing and very anxious to please and easy to get along with. So she was really a good balance for that real assertive, aggressive personality that he has." Reported Skip Hollandsworth, "He would always say, and still says this, that he and Robin have never had a fight." The couple married in 1976. Meanwhile, Phil continued to race through college. He entered the University of North Texas, earning his Ph.D. in 1979. The year was about building business and family: Phil and Robin were about to have their first child. Then, Phil joined his dad's psychology practice back in Wichita Falls. Dr. Phil McGraw built up his clientele by courting members of the local country club set. The strategy worked, but Phil sometimes lost patience with his patients. In one of the motivational audiotapes that have cemented his fame and fortune, Phil vented, "They just wanted like a rent-a-friend, and they'd want to sit there and talk to you for six months. There were a lot of times I figured this out in the first hour, and I'd be sitting there saying, 'Okay, here's the problem. You're a jerk.'" Summed up Sophia Dembling, "He didn't like sitting in a room of people who were complaining about their problems."

In 1980, Phil and Robin became the proud parents of a boy they named Jay. Always looking for new opportunities, Phil meanwhile was on a mission to exploit his expertise in psychology. He testified as an expert witness in court and freelanced for several airlines. Phil developed psychological profiles on pilots who were involved in accidents. "He was always exploring other things. He had a biofeedback lab. He would occasionally help his patients with some of the negotiations in their lives that they needed to do," offered Dembling.

Thelma Box, Phil's former business partner and a family friend, witnessed Phil's negotiating skills firsthand. She worked in oil and real estate, and she enlisted McGraw's help in hammering out a new bank loan. "Phil is a master at changing styles. He'll do whatever works. He'll get soft and gentle and sympathetic, or he'll get aggressive and stand up like he's going to come across the table after you," she assessed. In 1984, Box approached Phil with an idea: to combine her business know-how with his forceful personality. "I wanted to pull the strings and have the ideas and have somebody that would get in front of the room and do the part that I felt too shy to do."

The result was a series of seminars called "Pathways," Dr. Phil's first venture into the self-help business. Phil brought his father into the mix, and the three partners rolled up their sleeves. They pulled ideas from a variety of disciplines to create their program. Dr. Phil was a natural performer. He captivated his first audience with an entertaining mix of humor and inspiration. "You could feel the energy in the room. He would get everybody's attention, and he loved that," recalled Thelma Box. As Sophia Dembling noted, the seminars were a runaway success. She described, "They went into it planning to do a couple a year, and they ended up doing one a month. It went very well."

The seminars were going so well, in fact, that attendees eagerly paid up to a thousand dollars a pop to hear Dr. Phil speak. The partnership soon generated more than a million dollars a year. Business was booming, and so was Dr. Phil's ego. One night, a volunteer accidentally flicked on a light switch at the wrong time. Recalled Box, "Phil chewed on him for five minutes, and he was never involved again. It made it difficult to work with Phil." She had another beef. She believed that Dr. Phil took too much credit for the success of the seminars. "I think it's an ego thing with Phil that he needs for people to believe that he's the best in the whole world," she said, "and that he may be the only person in the whole world who can do what he does."

In 1987, Robin McGraw gave birth to their second son, Jordan. With two kids and a hectic schedule, Phil was constantly on the run, but he still found time to relax, sometimes in surprising ways. "One of his favorite things to do was to watch cartoons on Saturday morning," said Box. Phil also never missed the opportunity to further his career. In the late 1980s, two television producers took the "Pathways" seminar. Phil pitched them an idea. "He'd just mention, you know, maybe they can do something with us with television. The next thing I knew, he had them in . . . filming him, talking about the possibility of a show." But the early pilot went nowhere; executives didn't want to pursue it.

By the mid-1980s Dr. Phil had attained star status on the self-help circuit. Phil talked, and audiences listened. But then it was the doctor's turn to get lectured. In 1988, thirty-eight-year-old Dr. Phil found himself in the hot seat. A twenty-three-year-old woman who had been his patient and ultimately an employee filed a complaint with the Texas State Board of Examiners and Psychologists, accusing Dr. Phil of unprofessional conduct. Explained Sophia Dembling, "The charge was a dual relationship, which, within psychology, is inappropriate."

Texas regulations prohibit psychologists from employing current or recent patients. The board of examiners didn't mess around. They ruled that Dr. Phil had violated the professional code of ethics, and imposed strong sanctions, which included retaking his licensing exams and taking ethics, physical, and psychological examinations. In a TV interview, Dr. Phil said he hired the woman as a favor to her parents. Then more trouble: the woman accused Dr. Phil of sexual assault. In a September 2002 *TV Guide* article, the doctor adamantly denied the allegation, claiming he never so much as patted the woman on the back. "He just said that he had jumped into his tennis clothes one day when she was in and out of the office. He just thought that she had taken a very minute incident and blown it up and had not told the truth about it," said Box.

Still, Dr. Phil's life in Wichita Falls was now under a microscope. The state board ordered his practice supervised for twelve months. Dr. Phil again decided to branch out. Thelma Box came up with a clever idea after reading an article about the growing business of jury consulting. "I said, 'Phil, this is something you'd be really good at. I think you could do that.' I knew he wasn't liking what was left of his clinical practice." In 1990, forty-two-year-old Dr. Phil moved to Dallas where he started Courtroom Sciences, Inc. (CSI), with lawyer and friend Gary Dobbs. CSI helped attorneys select jurors and even held mock trials. Said Skip Hollandsworth, "Lawyers also began to depend on him to help come up with the ways to present a case, because the guy is as glib and as fast on his feet as anybody you are ever going to come across."

Word spread quickly, and CSI's client list grew even faster. Dr. Phil traveled to meet with attorneys at corporate giants like Exxon and ABC Television. He charged $400 an hour for his services. CSI billed a whopping $29,000 a day to conduct mock trials. In 1992, Dr. Phil sold his share in the "Pathways" seminar business, catching his partner totally off guard. Grumbled Thelma Box, "He told neither his dad nor me. His dad sat down and talked to me. Actually, his dad cried when he talked to me about it." Then Joe McGraw followed his son out the door, leaving Box out in the cold. "He could have handled that with more integrity than he did."

Phil kept cruising along. Then, in 1996, he collided head-on with destiny. During a show about mad cow disease, Oprah Winfrey vowed to never eat another hamburger. The comment infuriated Texas cattlemen, who filed an $11 million lawsuit claiming Oprah caused beef prices to collapse. The trial was scheduled in Amarillo, Texas, home turf for the cattle industry. Oprah's legal team hired CSI, and Dr. Phil jumped on a plane to Chicago to meet with the queen of television. According to *Texas Monthly* executive editor Hollandsworth, Phil's brusque, no-nonsense demeanor—including a comment that he would leave if Oprah didn't meet with him immediately, charging, "It's not my ass getting sued"—got Oprah's attention and "ushered in the McGraw-Winfrey era."

Dr. Phil knew the deck was stacked against his famous client. He convinced Oprah to fly to Dallas to rehearse for the trial. "And there was McGraw," described Hollandsworth, "constantly helping shape her testimony, shape her appearance . . . and in the process they became fast friends." As the trial got underway in January 1998, a media swarm descended on Amarillo. The media mogul and her entourage settled in at a bed-and-breakfast nicknamed "Camp Oprah." The magnitude of the trial began to shake the star's confidence. Dr. Phil, however, snapped Oprah out of her funk, saying, "This is happening right now, and they're going to come kick your ass if you don't get ready and get prepared."

As Oprah's trial captivated the nation, Dr. Phil's business savvy captivated Oprah. Dembling attributed Dr. Phil's success to his "massive ego . . . because he was not afraid to speak his mind with her at any time, and she probably doesn't get a whole lot of that, because she is so powerful." Phil laid out a battle plan for

Oprah's trial experience, said Hollandsworth. "He began saying, 'You need some strategies about what to do with yourself and how to face the future and how to face conflict.'" Eventually, Phil's tough talk inspired not only Oprah to state her case, but she also encouraged him to state his own. "And as he was talking, she began to say, 'You need to write a book.' And as he continued to talk, she began to say, 'You need to be on my show.'"

Yet Dr. Phil was still largely unknown outside of his inner circle in the Texas-Oklahoma region. Hollandsworth remembered, "When we tried to ask 'Who are you?' he would give us this go-to-hell look. It was a look that would have chilled vodka. I am serious. We thought he was her bodyguard." By the time the trial got in full swing, Dr. Phil had coached Oprah well. She was poised, convincing, and sincere. The trial lasted five and a half weeks, but jurors needed only seven hours to reach a verdict—Oprah had not defamed the cattle industry. Oprah then lavished praise on forty-seven-year-old Dr. Phil, looking into the camera and saying, "This is the man that saved my life," according to Hollandsworth, who continued, "and in that one moment, this obscure suburbanite from Dallas turns into a media celebrity."

Oprah wanted to share Dr. Phil's sage advice with America, but Dr. Phil hated the "touchy-feely" way therapy was practiced on television. According to the doctor himself, "Oprah said, 'Well, you know what? If you don't like the way it's being done, why don't you change it instead of whining about it?'" On April 10, 1998—just two months after the trial—Dr. Phil made his first appearance on *Oprah*. It looked like it would be his last appearance. "His style was so harsh, compared to the sort of loving nurturing that Oprah's viewers were used to, that she got a very bad response," said Sophia Dembling. Skip Hollandsworth agreed that Oprah's demographic was "used to all her other personal-empowerment experts being very cuddly, touchy-feely, using lots of what Dr. Phil would always call 'big, seventy-five-cent words.'"

Just as Dr. Phil sat down with Oprah to help her with her problems, Oprah now sat down with her audience to prepare them for the force and style of Dr. Phil. "She sort of explained him to her audiences and said, 'He's just telling it like it is,'" commented Dembling. "That seemed to turn it around, and very shortly thereafter she said she started getting letters from people, saying, 'I want Dr. Phil to tell me like it is.'" Dr. Phil started appearing with Oprah every Tuesday, delivering his down-home brand of straight talk and folksy sayings. According to *Ventura County Star* features writer Ken Lam Gregory these included, "How did you two run this thing off in the ditch?" or "When Mom ain't happy, ain't nobody happy," and "That dog won't hunt." Oprah's ratings shot up 24 percent whenever McGraw appeared.

Dr. Phil cashed in on his newfound fame, commanding speaking fees of $75,000 a pop. In January 1999, Dr. Phil's first book, *Life Strategies*, rocketed up the *New York Times* bestseller list, but not everyone was digging Dr. Phil's act, including David Letterman. "Letterman has called him everything, from 'some fat boy' to 'some crazed retard,' and shows these little snippets that are hilarious . . . of McGraw making these little one-liners out of context," said Skip Hollandsworth. Letterman's potshots were all in good fun, but many psychologists weren't laughing. They viewed Dr. Phil's approach as nothing but smoke and mirrors. According to psychotherapist Melissa Richman, "He is not doing anything more than identifying a problem and adding entertainment value to that person's problem."

Radio psychologist Dr. Joy Browne was also critical of Dr. Phil's method. "If there was one issue that professionals object to about it is that sort of notion that 'here's a complicated problem, and it's all fixed and now you go away and live your life,'" she criticized. In one of his audiotapes, Dr. Phil defended himself, saying, "I've never been under the impression that we're doing eight-minute cures on television. But I do think that it's a worthy endeavor to be an emotional compass for people and kind of point them down a direction."

Meanwhile, Dr. Phil received a call from Thelma Box, his former business partner. Box ran "Choices," a successful offshoot of the seminar business she started with McGraw fifteen years earlier. She believed Phil still used many of the same techniques they developed together and asked about teaming up again. Though Phil said he would get in touch with her the next time he was in Dallas, Box never received a phone call. "It is a pity that Phil sort of has written Thelma out of his official history," said Sophia Dembling.

But broken alliances and professional sniping did nothing to deter "Philmania." Fans couldn't get enough. Neither could his biggest fan, Oprah Winfrey. On one of his tapes, Phil recalled that on one occasion, "She grabbed me by the arm, came in, and shut the door and said, 'You need to do your own show. It's time.'" The idea was scary yet appealing to Dr. Phil—but only if his family was on board. Phil's son Jay said, "He talked to my mom and my brother and literally gave us the option. It had to be four family members saying yes." The "yes" vote was unanimous. Oprah's company, Harpo Productions, teamed up with Paramount Television and syndication powerhouse King World Productions to develop the new show. But some TV executives questioned Dr. Phil's appeal as a solo act, thinking, as Ken Lam Gregory put it, "How was he going to do without her as a draw, and also without her to soften him?"

On January 26, 2002, the nervous executives gathered at Nashville's Grand Ole Opry to watch Dr. Phil in action. A sell-out crowd of more than four thousand people showed up. At that moment, a new king of syndication started his reign. *Dr. Phil* was picked up by stations in a whopping 97 percent of the country. Buyers were forced to accept one condition: a noncompete clause forbidding *Dr. Phil* from airing opposite *Oprah*. "I think it would be absolutely foolish of me to choose to go head-to-head (a) with my partner and (b) with my sponsor and mentor and the best talk show that's ever been on television," commented Dr. Phil.

Preparing for his one-man show, Phil relocated from Dallas to luxurious Beverly Hills. His family settled into a posh $20,000-a-month mansion. Over at Paramount, Dr. Phil's show struggled to come together, far from Chicago and Oprah's hands-on guidance. "Oprah was this choir figure who would roll her eyes when Phil would get a little too extravagant in his words, or calm him down and make sure the guests were on and off at the right time," said Skip Hollandsworth, "and she was the great facilitator." But in L.A., reports surfaced about behind-the-scenes problems on the new program. Said Sophia Dembling, "Suddenly he was in the position to control the launching of the new show, which is inevitably going to have bumps, and he was perhaps less patient than somebody with experience would have been."

In July 2002, Oprah came to the rescue. She flew to L.A. and delivered a pep talk to Dr. Phil. The *Dr. Phil* show rolled toward its premiere. Studio publicists cranked up the hype, scoring Phil a cover story in *Newsweek* magazine, and that was just the beginning. Recalled Dembling, "He was on *Larry King*, and he was on *Today*, and he was talking to Jane Pauley, and he was everywhere setting this show up." Added Hollandswroth, "He is a driven guy, and he will work seven days a week, and he will put in time in the mornings, in the afternoons, and in the evenings." The hard work paid off. *Dr. Phil* debuted in spectacular fashion on September 16, 2002. The premiere generated the highest ratings for a talk show since Oprah's own kickoff back in 1986, which, Dembling admitted, "took everybody by surprise."

"Self-doubt is not in his vocabulary, and he very much knows how to set a goal and to get there," affirmed Hollandsworth. Any worries that Dr. Phil would stumble without Oprah evaporated as guest after guest received a dose of "What were you thinking?" Dr. Phil admonished his own guests not to be a bully and to "learn something" from their experiences in life. But according to published reports, Dr. Phil himself still had much to learn about treating his underlings. Stories painted the doctor as a stern taskmaster who overworked his people.

"He's harsh. He's hard. There are people who leave his employ with bitterness or with bruises," said Dembling. While many, including Richman, attributed this behavior to Dr. Phil's "narcissistic stuff" and his hunger for power, Dr. Phil laughed off charges of mistreatment during one show. "He made a joke out of it and had one of his people on his crew come out in bandages and so forth," said Ken Lam Gregory, "so he sort of made a joke out of it, saying, 'Do I treat you guys like that?' And he sort of scoffed at it, implying it was just tabloid stuff."

The doctor was "in," and he intended to stay. In December 2002, Phil signed a contract extension through 2006. He celebrated by plunking down $7.5 million for a Beverly Hills mansion. Then he faced off with his toughest critic, agreeing to go toe-to-toe with David Letterman on the *Late Show with David Letterman*. Skip Hollandsworth gave Dr. Phil a lot of credit for his appearance on Letterman, for both putting aside any bad blood and for bringing in sheer numbers. "Not only do the ratings take off in a way that hadn't in Letterman's show for a long time, but Letterman is won over so thoroughly that the next night during the monologue, Letterman does nothing but talk about how wonderful Phil McGraw was to come to New York and appear on the show and swap jokes with Letterman."

In the fall of 2002, *Dr. Phil*, the TV show ended its first season as the number two syndicated talk show, behind Oprah. Viewers clamored for the self-help guru. "A lot of us walk around in a fog and we don't have people around us who ring the bell and try to wake us up and say, 'You're being an idiot,' and that's what McGraw's act is. He shakes us awake," affirmed Hollandsworth. In early 2003, fifty-two-year-old Dr. Phil pounded home his status as America's best-known shrink with two Daytime Emmy nominations, but he struck out when Wayne Brady took home the award for Best Host and ABC's *The View* was voted Best Talk Show.

Dr. Phil, of course, didn't miss a beat following the Emmy snub. In fact, he was ready for prime time. In his professional acting debut, Dr. Phil joined the cast of the popular NBC show *Frasier* to counter Kelsey Grammer's neurotic psychiatrist Frasier Crane, making a great team. "Phil's got a kind of easy quality that loans itself to this kind of a show, actually," remarked Grammer. Sophia Dembling gave Phil credit for his ability to branch out despite other people's perception of him, saying, "You talk to people who knew him in college, and they say, 'Ego.' You talk to people at CSI, and they say, 'Ego.' You talk to people today, they say, 'Ego.' Phil is very confident and, to a degree, he has a reason to be."

Dr. Phil's prescription for success often kept him away from home and family, but with the onset of fame, Phil's priorities seemed to shift. During an interview at Phil's home, Skip Hollandsworth witnessed the change firsthand. "He had a younger son then, who was about thirteen, and he just sort of wandered in and sat down, and what amazed me was that McGraw, despite this demanding schedule that he was keeping, stopped everything and just hung out with his son and waited until his son was ready to leave. So he might be a workaholic, but he shuts down when he has a responsibility with his family."

The man accused of being too controlling in his first marriage has been married to his second wife, Robin, since 1976. "They're best friends, you know, they have a lot of fun together," said their son Jay. "In many ways, they are yin and yang," assessed Hollandsworth. "Phil was this boisterous, brash, tough, articulate guy. Robin can be very feminine, quieter. She chooses her punches." As for Phil's first wife, Debbie, the two met up at their thirty-year high school reunion. The bitter past faded away. Recalled Debbie, "We came over and gave each other a hug. It was just a small talk. I am glad he's happy and successful, and I hope he is happy for me, too."

"I think he is part of a larger picture that says psychology is acceptable. There's no shame in asking for help," evaluated Joy Browne. In September 2003, Dr. Phil's career came full circle. The former-health-club-owner-turned-pop-culture-TV-shrink decided to weigh in on another heavy subject—America's fascination with food—with his latest book, *The Ultimate Weight Solution*. Whatever the problem, Dr. Phil seems to have the answer. His tough-love approach has touched a nerve. Millions of fans are buying his message and heeding his call to "Get real, people!" As Skip Hollandsworth reminded, "He has best-selling books that have been printed in thirty languages. He is on his way to becoming perhaps the best-selling self-help author in American history. He has a show that is watched by 25 million people." Then he summed up, "This is a man that in the strange world of American self-help, where self-help gurus come and go, is really leaving a lasting mark."

CHAPTER 4

AMERICA'S FUNNIEST WOMAN

The Ellen DeGeneres Story

"Yep, I'm gay!"

—*Ellen DeGeneres*

She was the girl next door, with a sassy smile and a very special gift. But when Ellen DeGeneres moved uptown, the neighborhood was never the same again. DeGeneres was the first major television star to come out of the closet and publicly declare that she was gay. While that event—and it was an event—defined Ellen's career, she refused to be tagged as anything but a very funny lady. Making TV history wasn't easy; getting there was even tougher. Tough, talented, tenacious—Ellen is many things to many people, and this is her story.

Ellen was born on January 26, 1958, in Metairie, Louisiana, a suburb of New Orleans. Ellen's dad, Elliott, was an insurance salesman. Her mom, Betty, worked as an administrative assistant. Elliott and Betty were Christian Scientists who raised Ellen and her older brother, Vance, in a strict, middle-class environment. Said friend, celebrated musician, and out lesbian Melissa Etheridge, "I think Ellen had a tough childhood in a way. We all have our own burdens to bear in our childhood." In 1963, the DeGeneres family took a vacation to California that included a trip to Disneyland and a studio tour. Five-year-old Ellen noticed her parents were starstruck, especially her mom. "Ellen's family's reaction to Hollywood impressed Ellen more than Hollywood impressed Ellen," Ellen's biographer Jeff Rovin said. He continued, "She started cracking jokes to amuse people, and that pleased her parents. That was more important than the attention that it got for her."

Elliott's job kept the family moving from neighborhood to neighborhood around New Orleans, and Ellen bounced from school to school. Always the new kid, Ellen found her own way to fit in. Jeff Rovin noted, "Whenever you're uprooted, of course you're gonna feel lost, and humor was her way of connecting with people instantly. If they laugh with you instead of at you, you've got a leg up on that situation." Elliott was a good father and provider, but his wife grew restless. She yearned for something more. "Betty has always been incredibly independent, and I think any time she felt stifled by a place or by a relationship, it was time to move on, without being vindictive or judgmental. She just needed room." Betty and Elliott separated in 1972. Ellen and her mom moved to an apartment on Division Street in Metairie. Melissa Etheridge said, "Coming from a broken home influences one who already has a penchant for comedy to be even funnier." Thirteen-year-old Ellen suddenly discovered her sense of humor also had healing powers. "She was always very observant—a very astute observer," remarked Rovin. "I think that her ability to process information and recycle it as comedy was nurtured very young in her life."

In 1974, Ellen entered Grace King High School. She started hanging out with an older crowd. Rovin described Ellen as a "seeker," saying that she "has always been incredibly curious. That doesn't always translate to aggressive action, but it does translate to observation. So if Ellen was out on her own, it would not be so she could be reckless or party or whatever. It would be so she could explore." In 1975, Ellen's parents divorced. Her mother soon remarried, and later that year the family moved to Atlanta, Texas, a small town near the Arkansas border. According to Rovin, Ellen had serious doubts about her new turf in rural America. "Ellen was, at first, kind of shaken by moving to Atlanta, Texas. It was a real small town and very much a different environment," he recalled from conversations with Ellen. High school friend Debbie Staley described, "The downtown area was a little square, and there was a drugstore on every corner. We would go shopping and go to the little drugstore and have a soda. The bowling alley was the big place. I mean, that was the hot hangout."

Jeff Rovin concluded, however, that ultimately the change provided more material for Ellen's developing comedic style. "The observer in Ellen was fascinated by all of it, even at her young age." Humor became Ellen's not-so-secret weapon. "In school I was funny with people that were close to me. I wasn't the kind of person that stood up and did something loud and obnoxious to get attention," recalled Ellen in an interview. Ellen lived an average life, playing tennis, poring through fashion books at sleepovers with Staley, and singing in the chorus. In her junior year, seventeen-year-old Ellen became close with Ben Heath, a senior and star of the football team, who Staley characterized as "a cutie—cotton-top blond, just a really sweet guy."

While her seemingly perfect, small-town, high school courtship progressed, Ellen began to explore her taboo sexuality by engaging in a secret relationship with one of her best girlfriends. Judy Wieder, editorial director of *The Advocate* and *Out* magazines, pointed out, "Ellen really kind of felt she was gay pretty early. She didn't know what that meant, because she was sort of stranded somewhere." Ellen's mother, Betty, agreed: "She felt a special relationship to girls, but she didn't know what to call it. She had boyfriends, she even had a little, tiny promise ring with a tiny diamond chip." The ring was from Ben, but Ben graduated a year before Ellen and their romance fell apart. "He was older. He went off to college, and she was effectively dumped. That really shook her up," said Rovin.

But Ellen was shaken even more by two other events in 1975. First, a man with close ties to the family made unwanted sexual advances toward her. Wieder emphasized that this experience did not have any part in forming or initiating Ellen's lesbian identity. "It's very important for Ellen and anybody to get across that experiences like that don't make you gay. In fact, Ellen always likes to say, 'If you look at a picture of me when I was ten or eleven, I was wearing a tie,' so it wasn't that, but it was still a very traumatic incident." Ellen desperately wanted to confide in her mother, but when Betty underwent a mastectomy to remove a malignant tumor, Ellen decided to wait, according to Rovin, to protect her mother's health.

At eighteen, in 1976, Ellen graduated from high school, loaded up her yellow VW bug, and left Atlanta, Texas. She drove to New Orleans, where she worked at a variety of jobs: waitress, bartender, law clerk, house painter, and oyster shucker. By day, Ellen lived as a struggling, single, "straight" woman. By night, she hung out at lesbian bars in the French Quarter. Judy Wieder explained the transition from straight life to acceptance of a gay identity, saying, "After a while, it just settles in and you start to admit it. You move away from saying 'I'm not gay.' You move away from saying 'I'm bisexual,' and you just finally say 'I'm gay.'" Journalist Benjamin Morrison added, "Coming out is a process, and it often starts with only one friend." Ellen eventually found a way to come out to her mother. In 1977, nineteen-year-old Ellen joined her family for a vacation in Pass Christian, Mississippi. Ellen asked her mom to take a walk with her on the beach. "I'm in love," Ellen told her mother. "That's great," responded Betty. Ellen then blurted out, "It's with a woman." Recalled Betty, "I was just shocked and stunned, and my mind filled with questions that parents have. First of all, who would take care of her? I worried for her well-being because of society's negative messages. I knew that much even though I was completely ignorant about homosexuality."

Ellen was living with her dad and stepmother at the time. She decided they, too, should know the truth. "She was telling her family that she was gay, and her father married, I think, a religious woman who said, 'That's nice, but you can't come and stay in our house, because of our children,'" summarized Wieder. "It's just so strange to hear the words 'I love you, and I understand what you're telling me. I'll always love you, but you can't live here.' That doesn't compute, and that is just devastating." After that blow, Ellen moved out and into her own apartment in New

Orleans. She found support from her older brother, Vance, who was something of a local celebrity because of his band, the Cold.

Vance's success inspired Ellen to start writing. She filled notebook after notebook with observations of life around her. One day, a friend approached Ellen about a benefit they were planning. "I had never even thought about it. I mean, I'd watched comedians all the time, but I never thought it's something that I can do," said Ellen. Audiences were pleasantly surprised by Ellen's offbeat comedy. Said Benjamin Morrison, "She was a big success, and all of her friends told her she was terrific. Feedback matters." Ellen was bitten by the stand-up bug. She began performing on open-mic nights at local coffeehouses. But Ellen's double life steered her away from the usual comedy fare. Explained Morrison, "She didn't do 'Take my boyfriend, please' jokes, because that was not what was going on in her life. It pushed her into doing comedy of observation that, virtually speaking, nobody her age was doing." Ellen encapsulated her own comedy philosophy in saying, "To take a day-to-day life and everyday experience and then to take it even further is what people can really relate to."

Ellen's passion for stand-up was rivaled only by her new love for a beautiful young woman named Kat Perkoff. Kat wrote poetry and tended bar in the French Quarter. Kat's sister, Rachel Perkoff, described the dynamic between Ellen and Kat, "Ellen is much more clean-cut, and she's from a family that has a fairly religious background. My sister was complicated. She lived on the edge." Ellen's cool demeanor and Kat's fiery spirit sparked a steamy romance. Still, Ellen and Kat often escaped the noisy French Quarter for quieter places. "One of Ellen's fondest memories was when she and Kat were alone in the house. Kat was sitting at her typewriter, typing away, and the wind was blowing in that kind of balmy New Orleans way, and Ellen just felt like they had a home. You know? It felt very satisfying, that connection."

But the bond between Ellen and Kat was broken in the summer of 1979. Ellen moved out when she learned Kat cheated on her. A few nights later, Kat approached Ellen at a local nightclub.

Kat asked if she was planning on returning home with her. Ellen pretended not to hear the question. "They were at a very bad place in their relationship, and Ellen didn't go home with her from a bar and actually they went home separately," recounted Judy Wieder. On her way home, Ellen drove past a horrible accident scene. She had no idea Kat was inside one of the cars. Ellen went to bed unaware that her lover lay dying in a nearby hospital. When Kat's sister told Ellen about the accident, Ellen realized her near miss from the night before. "She felt so guilty that . . . maybe if she had gone with her, maybe this, maybe that, and she went through a very, very hard time about that."

Ellen used the trauma as inspiration for what would become her trademark comedy routine. After the accident, Ellen was wracked with guilt and grief. She moved into a tiny, flea-ridden apartment. Lying on the floor one night, she pictured herself calling God and asking him a question, *Why is Kat no longer around but fleas are?* "She started to talk about these fleas and how absurd it was," said Wieder, "and she sort of went from there and began to turn this sad situation into an absurd situation into a very interesting comedy act. Then she decided in her head that someday she was going to do this routine on a late-night talk show." Not just any talk show would do. Ellen imagined herself performing her routine on *The Tonight Show* with Johnny Carson. Every detail was clear in Ellen's mind, including Johnny's invitation to sit on the couch after her monologue.

In 1981, a comedy wave breaking across the country crashed onto New Orleans. Ellen, who was twenty-three years old at the time, found herself in the right place at the right time. Clyde Abercrombie, comedy club owner and promoter, said, "On Sunday nights, we had an amateur thing that we did where the comedians that we brought in would host for the amateurs, and Ellen started coming in on Sunday-night open mic nights. I thought she had potential." Part of Ellen's potential was that she realized she had to stand out from the droves of comedians. "When you have two thousand comedians talking about McDonald's, you know, you've got to find subject matters that are really, really different, that no-body else is doing. Or you find a subject matter maybe that every-body's doing but you have to find your own slant and do something that nobody else has thought of. That's why you have to write your own material," assessed Ellen.

Despite some initial success and a strong sense of original comedy, Ellen still had a lot to learn about comedy. "In the begin-ning, Ellen wasn't real sure of herself with the audience," said Clyde Abercrombie. "If people heckled her, it kind of put her off her game, but after a while, she got used to the hecklers, and she started listening to all the other comics and how they handled hecklers. Once she got that knack, they didn't bother her again." Within a year, Ellen sharpened her subtle comedy routine to a ra-zor's edge.

Ellen was good, and she quickly grew restless with the New Or-leans club scene. In 1982, Ellen saw in the local paper a story about a comedy competition. The competition held by Showtime—which was, at the time, still an up-and-coming cable channel—was to name "America's Funniest Person." Ellen made a five-minute video-tape of her act and sent it to Showtime. She won the state contest and advanced to the final round. "Soupy Sales, Harvey Korman, and Pee-wee Herman were the three celebrity judges, and not only did Ellen win, but Pee-wee Herman at the time wrote her a fan let-ter, because he thought that much of her," remarked Benjamin Morrison. Winning the competition was huge. In 1983, Showtime sponsored a national tour featuring Ellen, but it wasn't all fun and games.

"I was working in a law firm, and then suddenly I had the title 'The Funniest Person in America,' and had to wear that stupid banner and the crown, and there were enough idiots in the audi-ence that actually believed they were getting ready to see the fun-niest person in America. And they're sitting there, going, 'I don't know. Steve Martin's funny. She's good,'" speculated Ellen. Ac-cording to Morrison, "She also later regretted that it was a little bit of a trial by fire, but Ellen wasn't really ready to be a national headliner." During the tour, Ellen encountered many of the same hecklers she had seen in her first days on the New Orleans night-club scene. She once told the story of her performance in front of a crowd of boisterous marines at a base in the Carolinas. "They were screaming out that they wanted to see body parts. I had no control over them, and I didn't have the experience to know how to handle it. I just dropped the mic and ran off stage, and I was crying." Then, finishing off in typical Ellen style, she quipped, "And to this day I cry when I see marines."

Still, Ellen's training under fire toughened her resolve to make it in a profession dominated by men. "She decided that she really was going to make a career of this, and if she was going to do it, she was going to have to be in San Francisco or Los Angeles. And that's when she decided that she was going to make the move," said Clyde Abercrombie. Ellen picked the City by the Bay, a mecca for stand-up comedy. Manager Bob Fisher described the booming 1980s scene in San Francisco, the "lines of people around the block. It was like the folk music craze in the sixties. You could make a heck of a good living in those days from comedy. If you became a comedy headliner, you were pulling in about $10,000 a month working an hour a night." Tom Sawyer, a San Francisco comedy club owner, agreed: "When Ellen arrived in San Francisco, the scene was at its peak. What we saw in Ellen was one of the most original female comics in the country. The direction she was going was very much her own."

The laid-back San Francisco scene had a liberating effect on Ellen. Bob Fisher remembered Ellen coming to him at the beginning of their manager-client relationship with an important disclosure. She wanted him to know about her sexuality. He responded point-blank, "I don't care if you're gay. I just care if you're funny." From that point forward, Ellen's relationship with Fisher encountered few hitches. In fact, he provided the inspiration for another of her signature bits. "I think I had seen a natural history documentary on television, and I was telling her about how eagles mated. And I said, 'You know these eagles actually

meet a mile up in the air and they start mating, and they stop flying, and they start falling as they mate. And once in a while, they
don't finish mating and hit the ground. That's how committed
they are.'" Fisher's story took flight in Ellen's imagination. She
immediately snapped back, "I don't know about you, but if I'm
one of these two birds, and I'm getting close to the ground, I'd seriously consider faking it."

In 1985, Ellen entered the San Francisco Stand-Up Comedy
Competition, founded by Jon Fox, which Fisher described as "the
entertainment event of the year." Comedian Will Durst, felt that
the competition, in which he had garnered a second-place finish
in his first year, "determined the pecking order. It determined
who got to become a headliner." After a grueling series of elimi-
nation rounds, the competition really heated up. Ellen's top competition, according to comedy club owner Tom Sawyer, was
Sinbad. "They were both totally on their game. Ellen had the
crowd mesmerized and was doing one great joke after another."
But it wasn't enough; Sinbad won. Ellen took home the consola-
tion prize but gained a lot of confidence.

Ellen's success in the competition—even though it was not a
titular victory—opened doors down in Los Angeles. Budd Friedman, owner of the Improv, a famous Los Angeles comedy club,
traveled with his wife up to the competition, and Ellen, the young
upstart, made quite an impression. "We were very impressed with
her unique style, and we encouraged her to come to L.A., where
the big time was," said Friedman. L.A. also had something San
Francisco didn't—TV studios. Ellen told Fisher, "I'm going to be
on television someday, and I'm going to be very famous." Sawyer
summed up, "Ellen left San Francisco because she had accomplished all she could here."

After moving to L.A. in 1985, Ellen, the queen of San Francisco's comedy scene, went looking for a new crown in Hollywood.
Journalist Mick LaSalle speculated, "The reason for someone like
Ellen to leave and go to L.A. is for the pile of gold, the national
reputation and big money." New opportunity abounded, with

television and the club circuit available to hone her comic skills. Also, DeGeneres still wanted to claim her place on Carson's couch. Ellen wasn't exactly an unknown when she arrived in L.A. Still, landing a role on a successful sitcom didn't come easy. Eventually spotted by an NBC talent executive, Ellen secured a development deal with Lorimar, which wanted to create a show for her. She suggested unknown comedian David Spade play her brother, but the men in charge didn't bite.

While Ellen waited for her big break in television, she stayed tight with her friends from the stand-up world. Budd Friedman gave her a spot at the Improv, recounting that "immediately she became a big favorite." Ellen began performing on television specials and headlined clubs nationwide. She often opened for stand-up pro Jay Leno during those days at the Improv. Leno was a frequent guest on *The Tonight Show,* which gave Ellen a connection she had wanted for years. Friedman admitted that "it was very tough for a woman to get on the show in those days. I think Ellen just won [Johnny Carson] over. We used to have auditions every couple of months for him, and we put her up, and she got it." Ellen proudly spoke of the coup, saying, "It was a huge experience, and I had been waiting all my life to do that show." With the chance to make or break her still-developing career, Ellen had to consider carefully how to wow the crowds at home with her comic expertise.

"The scariest moment is when you're behind the curtain, when you have been going to sleep every night and the last thing you hear is the show theme. Right before that curtain opens . . . it's panic!" Ellen described. The opportunity of a lifetime flashing before her, Ellen had five minutes to impress Johnny Carson and millions of TV viewers. The pressure was enormous, but Ellen looked back to some of her darkest moments five years before. Since that time, Ellen had perfected the "phone call to God" routine that her flea-ridden New Orleans apartment inspired. She turned tragedy into triumph after her five-minute bit on Carson, nailing her routine. Johnny did something he'd never done before with any female comedian—he invited Ellen to chat with him after her monologue. Carson complimented her material and her style, and, as Will Durst put it, "anointed" her.

After the success on *The Tonight Show,* industry pros began to pay attention to Ellen. As she had in early '80s San Francisco, Ellen found herself in the right place at the right time in early '90s Hollywood. "Stand-up comedians, the really great ones, had created a worldview, and I think the audience was looking for that point of view," said Dean Valentine, former president of Walt Disney/Touchstone television. Ellen saw the numbers of shows comics were starring in and wanted her own. "Roseanne had a show, and Seinfeld got a show, and so I was waiting to get my own show," she said. Ellen's stand-up success dovetailed with TV's appetite for new faces. On August 27, 1989, thirty-one-year-old Ellen debuted in her first series, *Open House,* where she played a man-hungry receptionist. "It was a tiny part, and I was just happy to get it," said Ellen. She saw the part as a prime opportunity to learn on the job and gain a television audience. Though the show didn't get big ratings, it had a cult following, and Ellen's character was popular. She capitalized on what Valentine called that "sort of archetypal television role of the smart, wise-cracking secretary." According to Benjamin Morrison, "She was very good and very funny—a standout among the people on the show." The show, however, was canceled after its first season.

After a two-year dry spell, Ellen got another bit part on the show *Laurie Hill.* Though her friends thought she was crazy to take another small role, Ellen knew exactly what she was doing. *Laurie Hill* was produced by Neal Marlens and Carol Black, TV powerhouses who also created the hit series *The Wonder Years.* "I thought, I'll just let them see me, and let them get to know me and hope that they will write more and more for me," explained Ellen. But the mix of drama and comedy envisioned by the show's creators never meshed. *Laurie Hill* was axed after five weeks. Marlens and Black, however, had other ideas for Ellen—her own show. Ellen's angling and strong performance skills produced exactly the effect she wanted.

On April 15, 1993, cameras rolled on the pilot episode of *These Friends of Mine*, a sitcom about a bookstore employee named Ellen Morgan and her wacky buddies. Morrison characterized the success of the show by explaining the environment of TV shows at the time. "Sitcom is cookie-cutter land, and producers and writers just keep grinding out the same shows. I think with *These Friends of Mine* there was a certain spark, that something special was going on." When the pilot wrapped, ABC executives liked what they saw. *These Friends of Mine* was put on the front burner for the upcoming season. Ellen had high hopes: "I would like for it to go on and on and on. I'd like to hear the word 'syndication.' That would be a really good word for me, and, oh yeah, 'Here's your check, Ms. DeGeneres.'"

After initial positive reactions to *These Friends of Mine*, Ellen clearly became the focus at ABC. In 1993, network execs gave the green light to the sitcom. Though the show originally focused on a group of quirky friends, Ellen's character quickly took control. The show was, more than anything else, a showcase for Ellen's comic style and personality. "The show was incredibly funny. It was clear that Ellen was a star," said Dean Valentine. ABC ordered thirteen episodes, but midway through production, Neal Marlens and Carol Black abruptly left the series. Valentine explained that stars usually win out during conflicts with producers and networks because "that's who the audience is relating to." Publicly, Ellen and the producers denied any friction.

The series was a breakout. "I don't think that anyone expected the show to do nearly as well as it's doing. I mean, we hoped it would be in the top ten, so when we're up there with *Home Improvement* and *Roseanne*, it's really amazing," said Ellen at the time. Still, the new team of producers wasn't satisfied. The most obvious change in season two was the title. *These Friends of Mine* became *Ellen*. While Ellen explained that show's evolving focus was part of ABC's vision of packaging *Ellen* and *Roseanne* as a night of comic entertainment, Valentine said, "The name change is emblematic of a larger shift under the surface of what the show is about and who was going to be serviced from now on. Was it going to be the executive producers, was it going to be the studio, or was it going to be the star driving the show? The answer, when the name changed, was that it was going to be the star." And the star needed some new playmates. As Arye Gross, Holly Folger, and Maggie Wheeler walked out the door, Joely Fisher came in during season two to play Paige, Ellen's self-obsessed friend. During her reading with Ellen, Fisher noticed an immediate chemistry, which she called "fun at first sight." *Ellen* quickly became a staple of prime-time TV.

After a little retooling, Ellen DeGeneres rode a wave of success during her second season that allowed her to show her diverse talents. The stand-up-comic-turned-sitcom-star penned her first book. As described by Ellen, her book included some of the observational pieces that skyrocketed her to fame. "There's a little bit of my stand-up in these. It's mostly just kind of stories and daily affirmations, a recipe for French toast, a dance lesson," she said. *My Point . . . and I Do Have One* landed at the top of the national bestseller lists. A short time later, *Ellen* kicked off its third season. By spring 1996, the show was a ratings winner, finishing first in its time slot. During hiatus, Ellen capitalized on her success, starring in the offbeat comedy *Mr. Wrong*. The big-screen role was tailor-made for Ellen's gender-blender style. As Ellen herself explained, "I don't fit into the certain mold of the romantic comedies today. Although the movie is very romantic, and it seems very much a love story, things start to go wrong." The film flopped.

Undaunted, Ellen returned for season four of her sitcom with something much bigger on her mind. She confided in comedienne and film actress Kathy Najimy, who guest-starred on the show. Najimy remembered, "For some reason, when I first arrived on set, we just had this connection, and we went into her trailer and sat down on the couch and immediately started talking about her sexuality and how she hadn't come out yet, her concerns about it, what people were expecting of her, and what she felt comfortable doing." Melissa Etheridge commented, "It was an interesting time in the early nineties. There was myself, k.d. lang, Rosie O'Donnell, and Ellen DeGeneres. We all hung around in the same circles and talked many late nights. k.d. was the first who came out. k.d. and I just became insufferable. You couldn't talk to us without us saying, 'Everyone must come out'—it was our job."

However, Ellen DeGeneres was still uncertain about how to behave as a closeted lesbian in Hollywood. "Ellen never denied that she was gay. She just wasn't going to say the words, and she certainly wasn't going to converse about it," explained Judy Wieder. After years of staying quiet, Ellen made the decision to come out. She consulted with a group of friends, including Etheridge, about finally incorporating her sexuality into *Ellen*. "I specifically remember the dinner where she said, 'I'm coming out, and I'm going to do it on the show,'" said Etheridge. "I tried to tell her, 'You know what? It's going to be insane.'"

DeGeneres discussed her plan with Valentine, then the president of Disney-owned Touchstone Television. "Ellen informed me that she wanted to come out, and that was my first inkling about it," he recalled. "I thought all hell would break loose inside of the Walt Disney company, which it sort of did, and that all hell would break loose inside of ABC, which it sort of did." Before the season began, Ellen dropped some hints for the fans. "Ellen's world is kind of crumbling, and you don't really see it yet, but this whole season there's going to be a lot of things that I've, uh, that the character has sort of just taken for granted that will always be, and everything changes," she said in a season preview interview. She continued, "It will be interesting to see how the character responds to that and the changes that it takes her through, because I think when your world changes around you, it changes you, and you start seeing things differently."

"She was on her own path. She knew that to truly be comfortable in one's own success one needs to be truthful to herself. And you really can't take on the success and stand in it unless you feel like you've been truthful," commented Etheridge. Ellen had indeed begun to see things differently; so differently, in fact, that she took a renegade path and butted heads with the network to put this groundbreaking new storyline on prime-time television. Dean Valentine discussed the conflict between Ellen and hesitant network executives. "Various people said no, and she just kept saying that that was unacceptable, so I didn't think that anybody would have any luck in stopping this from happening, short of firing Ellen or shutting down the show, and that I didn't think was going to happen." In January 1997, executives at Disney and ABC finally gave DeGeneres their blessings.

As thirty-nine-year-old Ellen and her sitcom character prepared to set the record straight, the hush-hush coming-out party wasn't so hush-hush. Wieder explained, "There was a leak. It was in *Variety*, and it was in the *Hollywood Reporter*, and suddenly we were all reading about the fact that Ellen's character was going to come out." This surprise publicity gave Ellen a bit of a shock but also signaled an occasion to speak about her life candidly. "It really was a huge jump for me when it leaked out that my character was going to come out on the show. And then all the speculation started. I remember turning on the talk radio and listening to everyone talking about me," she said. Week after week during season four, Ellen and her writers fueled the fire with gay-inspired gags. Cited Benjamin Morrison, "There was one episode, I think, when she was seeing a psychiatrist. There are a number of dolls representing a family unit, which are the mother, the father, and the two children. She throws the father away in the scene and says something like 'We're not going to be needing that.'" DeGeneres had even more fun teasing viewers on the talk-show circuit. Kathy Najimy remembered, "I know she went on the Rosie O'Donnell show and said, 'I've got something to tell you. I'm Lebanese,' and everyone laughed."

In March 1997, Ellen appeared at a gay-and-lesbian awards ceremony honoring singer k.d. lang. Ellen wowed the audience with her typically self-deprecating humor that would also define her upcoming "out" episode. She joked, "I absolutely adore her, and we've been friends for six years, and I think I was as surprised as anyone when I found two days ago that she is gay. And I thought to myself, 'I should have seen the signs.'" Meanwhile, Ellen kept things loose on the set of her sitcom. Joely Fisher applauded her unabated spirit during this contentious time. "She made the cast laugh. She made the crew feel comfortable. She was waging battles in her own private life, and in her own decision-making process. I think that we all sort of witnessed it and were taken on a wild ride and were along for the journey," she recalled. Morrison was more specific about the pressures surrounding Ellen during this period, mentioning "the weight of a half an hour of prime-time television and all of the people, all of the paychecks involved in it. And she can make a bad decision, but she can't really make a deadly decision."

Filming of the star-filled, controversial coming-out show—codenamed "The Puppy Episode"—began on March 14, 1997. It was scheduled to air as the season finale six weeks later, and the atmosphere was festive among cast members. Said Melissa Etheridge, "All of her friends wanted to be a part of it, so everyone— you know, Demi Moore and Oprah Winfrey and just everyone was in this episode." Also included were Etheridge, k.d. lang, and Laura Dern, whose character inspires Ellen Morgan (DeGeneres's on-screen persona) to finally come out. Kathy Najimy, too, took part in the episode: "It was very important for me to be there and, oh my gosh, I was in New York and missed the flight and had to get another flight. I literally ran onto the set as they said 'Action.'"

But the light-hearted atmosphere quickly turned deadly serious. "There was a bomb scare. They actually all had to leave. That was an early kind of incident that people don't even think about," accounted Judy Wieder, who elaborated, "that you are in danger if you are a gay person, and you are popular and you are trying to say it's a good thing for coming out and hoping others are going to come out." Dean Valentine, in many ways a fringe figure as a network executive, also suffered from his connection to the show. "I'd gotten personal death threats. I had to have armed detectives in front of my house."

Stepping back from the chaos swirling around her and her coming-out episode, Ellen blew off steam with several hundred other celebrities at the *Vanity Fair* Oscar party on March 24, 1997. She didn't realize that this event would ignite another media storm. At the party was up-and-coming actress Anne Heche, and the connection between the two was electric. "I think it was one of those sort of movie moments where they saw each other across the room and, you know, firecrackers went off and slow motion happened," said Kathy Najimy. Heche had dated some high-profile actors, including comedian Steve Martin. Joely Fisher, who worked with Heche before landing the part on *Ellen*, realized that the pair would be subject to a lot of media attention, "I thought, 'Be careful,'" she said. Just days after Ellen and Anne met, *Time* magazine revealed what most Hollywood insiders already knew, with its cover featuring Ellen, with the headline, "Yep, I'm Gay."

Ellen's coming out had turned into a media frenzy. Explains Wieder, whose magazine, *The Advocate*, has reported many ambitious and historic coming-out experiences, "There was a time that people would never come out anywhere but in *The Advocate*, because nobody else would either say the word or was interested in that kind of story. You *had* to come out in *The Advocate*. Here, *Time* magazine was doing this story, because they knew this was going to be a real event." Morrison, himself an out journalist, admitted to underestimating the impact of Ellen's on-air coming-out party. "In gay circles, we hardly even understood then how one of a kind that was and what a big deal it was." Even though Ellen was besieged by naysayers, she took more steps to showing her sexuality to the public. Ellen and Anne turned heads and made headlines at the White House on April 26, 1997, when they attended a function hosted by President Bill Clinton, together.

The controversy surrounding "The Puppy Episode" turned ugly when Reverend Jerry Fallwell referred to Ellen as "Ellen De-Generate." Several national advertisers pulled their ads from the show, but Ellen stood behind the episode. The excitement hit fever pitch Wednesday, April 30, 1997, at 8:00 P.M., as ABC aired "The Puppy Episode" and Ellen's character, Ellen Morgan, boldly broadcast her orientation to the world. Fisher described the bittersweet moment of Ellen's comic coming-out onscreen: "She says to Laura Dern's character, 'Why can't I say the word? Why can't I say the word?' And I saw this, and it was so real. It was so honest." Not only did the show perform to high expectations, but according to cast member Dave Higgins (the show's smart-mouthed coffee server, Joe), "It met the challenge of the promotion and all the press it was receiving. I think the show stood up to the challenge and was very funny." Dean Valentine thought that the dramatic and comedic success proved "cathartic for Ellen, and liberating, and I think all of us had a sense of having watched something really unique."

The hopes pinned on the success of Ellen's national coming-out were also much bigger than her own career, argued Benjamin Morrison. "In the circles I run in, it was better than any of us could have dreamed of. And it was terrifically funny. This came at a period, I certainly can't say after AIDS but when 'gay' and 'AIDS' were very much one and the same. In a period that 'gay' was taken as being some kind of death sentence, for people to be able to laugh and have a good time and to have something, that was nice." Said Joely Fisher, "It just felt like we were doing something that was important. We were changing television." DeGeneres herself commented about the importance of her transition to "out" entertainer. "I truly, truly believe that years from now everyone will look back and see what an important show this is. It's something that will be a watermark for everyone in history, and I'm proud of that," she declared.

The episode was one of the most watched TV shows of all time. Morrison pointed out the irony that even those who fiercely resisted the show contributed to its ratings surge. "Everybody watched. They watched to confirm that she was the evil, terrible [bleep] that they'd heard about. Or they watched because they were curious, but it was, as NBC likes to say, 'must-see television.'" Despite some harsh reactions, Ellen was rewarded by an overwhelming response from her fans. "I got a letter from a seventy-six-year-old lesbian, saying, 'I cannot believe this is happening in my lifetime.' And then I get letters from kids that aren't gay but like me and like the show, so that feels really good. That's an accomplishment that if the show goes on, even if it doesn't go on, I've done something," she said proudly.

While doubters and haters gathered on the sidelines, Ellen's friends and family, and her new lover, Anne Heche, supported her in private and public ways. Kathy Najimy pondered the absurdity of a certain shift in popularity that Ellen experienced after her coming out. "You had to love Ellen," she said. "There was nothing not to love about her. And then because she said 'I'm gay,' you can't change and go, 'Well, now I hate you.'" Anne Heche, too, supported her new flame without wavering. "I have seen what happens when you do not tell the truth, and I didn't ever want that to happen to me. Certainly to support Ellen I was going to tell the truth about our relationship, and I, in my naïveté, didn't understand that it would cause such a ruckus! You know, it was like, 'I'm in love!'"

Ellen's mom also rallied behind her daughter. At age sixty-seven, Betty DeGeneres became the spokesperson for the National Coming Out Project. Like many others, Betty saw her daughter's out persona in terms of the importance it would have for gays across the nation. "Generally, when a young person discovers that they're gay or begins to question their sexuality, it takes them time to grapple with it and accept it and themselves, because they are being bombarded with the idea that you can't be that way and that's wrong." Ellen beamed when describing her mom's acceptance and service work, saying, "When you think about the teen suicides and the gay bashing, the people that are beaten up and kicked out of their families, and to have a mom like this not only to accept me and love me but to come out and be this spokesperson and travel. I'm so proud of her, I can't tell you." Backed by loved ones, fans, and most TV critics, Ellen was clearly the woman of the hour.

But Ellen's groundbreaking episode was a nightmare for network executives. "My thoughts were that it was going to be a very exceptionally difficult act to follow. There are not a lot of places to go really, once you've gone there," conceded Dean Valentine. Kathy Najimy, a veteran of TV shows like *Veronica's Closet*, also understood that "the networks and the suits aren't really behind anything that's not proven and that's not going to make them a lot of money and high ratings." Turning back was not an option. Going forward was a minefield. "Right after, there was an enormous amount of darkness. Nobody was really sure what was going to happen," described costar insider Fisher.

In the spring of 1997, Ellen was also gushing over her new squeeze. According to Ellen's assistant Craig Peralta, "I think they were both very much in love. They weren't playing at something. It was a very true bond of love that they experienced." On May 13, 1997, *Ellen* was renewed for a fifth season, but DeGeneres reportedly had mixed feelings about continuing the series. "I think everybody agreed it would be a bad idea to stop the show last season, because we did something huge and then to not follow through would have been kind of cruel," she said at the time. Ellen wanted her show to build on "The Puppy Episode" by fully exploring the life of a lesbian woman, but network executives balked. Ellen countered with her trademark wit. "I would like to really focus on reality. What it's like to be a single gay woman. It will be me in bars every week. That's what Disney wants to see. It's just me cruising women every single week," she deadpanned in interviews.

The brass at Disney weren't laughing, but members of the TV

Academy got the joke. On September 14, 1997, Ellen DeGeneres won an Emmy Award for Outstanding Writing in a Comedy Series. Commented Najimy, it was "a reaffirmation that there were lots, lots, lots more people who were so proud of her and thankful than there were people who didn't understand it and were bigots." Ellen, too, found personal affirmation from the Emmy win, saying that "it makes me feel like I'm accepted in this business. I've never even felt like I was accepted, because I knew people knew that I was gay. That was a really hard thing, to feel like an outsider, and now, for the Academy to do this, I feel it's a nod of respect."

Ellen acknowledged the double edge of such volatile success. "If the show does well, suddenly everybody is going to get behind the show and say, 'It's the greatest show, isn't it?' But if the show isn't doing that well, they'll say, 'Well, we gave it a shot.'" Benjamin Morrison described, "This is a lady who has created controversy bordering on pandemonium about what she has done, and I think there wasn't a way to comfortably present that to an all-American audience." Reasoned Dean Valentine, "The show fundamentally has to become a show about a woman who's having gay relationships. And that, I think, was something that ABC had tremendous issues with." But Ellen was game to try anyway. Writers on the series cooked up a variety of storylines, each with an obvious gay theme. Season five of *Ellen* kicked off on September 24, 1998.

Ellen quickly found that there were limits to showing an on-screen lesbian relationship. She was flabbergasted, imploring, "We're not asking to be in bed together, we're not asking to do— we're just trying to show that there is affection. What's more important, to promote promiscuity or to promote monogamy in a committed relationship? Look at all of us. I mean there's no one normal way to raise a kid. It takes a village, and if you've been to the village, it's chockful of gay people!" Judy Wieder saw in Ellen's character a bit of her desire to be open about her off-screen reality. "She was full of this energy, this joy, and this excitement. She was also in love, and she wanted her character to have some kind of a love interest. So this was all coming together." Unfortunately for Ellen, the show became less well received, and even loyal viewers began changing the channel, shutting her and her positive message off. "Some gay people didn't think it was funny, and they were embarassed because they were afraid other people weren't going to think it was funny. It was a very weird situation, and her ratings went down," recalled Wieder.

The show fell into a downward spiral. Even Ellen expressed serious doubts. "I think the network is very, very nervous about the show. So, if they're nervous, I don't know where we can go next year. So, let the show go on," she said with resignation. Wieder saw the network's lack of promotion as contributing to viewers' increased nervousness: "When the network stopped publicizing it, that compounded everything, and they began putting signs in front of the show that were saying, 'Take care, if you watch this you're going to all turn to stone.'" Ratings continued to slide, and on April 24, 1998, *Ellen* was canceled after 109 episodes.

Most successful sitcoms end their run with a mix of joy and tears, but there was no celebration that day on the set of *Ellen*. "Nobody came down from the office and congratulated us . . . it was treated with a lack of respect," said Joely Fisher. Agreed Judy Wieder, "They did not decide to save it. They decided to kill. That certainly took Ellen down." Melissa Etheridge suggested that the end of *Ellen* came primarily because the show no longer fit into ABC's prescribed ideas for it and for television generally. "ABC and Disney wanted a funny little sitcom, and it wasn't anymore. It was a groundbreaking, earth-shattering, important sitcom." The same month as her show's cancellation, Ellen was honored by a gay youth organization. The now-defunct sitcom's star was hailed as a lifesaver, but her private wounds cut deep. At the ceremony, Ellen took the podium with passion. "As I get attacked or criticized, or as the show is canceled, the thing that makes me hold on is knowing that I've saved one life," she said, "and when a kid is thinking they have to kill themselves because of who they are and because of who they love, something is wrong with our priorities."

Ellen's speech came from a very personal place. "She had been caught up in a whirlwind, not just the coming out on *Ellen*, but the whirlwind around the media speculation about her relationship. And I think she needed some time to really digest it," said her assistant Craig Peralta. For the next few months, Ellen kept a low profile. Then, in the summer of 1998, she accepted a role in the movie *EdTV*. Forty-year-old Ellen played the producer of a reality series who documented the minute-by-minute life of a guy named Ed. Matthew McConaughey starred in the title role, but Ellen certainly related to the plight of a character living in a fishbowl: "I actually was like Ed, like, 'Yeah, I'll tell you everything, you want to come into my house?' . . . And then it was like, now having a little time and distance and perspective on it, now it's like, 'Whoops! Maybe I should have had some boundaries.'" People close to Ellen felt that she gained some wisdom from going through the media gauntlet. "I saw my friend in a lot of pain," said Melissa Etheridge, "and it was a very difficult time. I also saw her pull herself up, get through it, walk through it, go on, and do what she loves."

Ellen DeGeneres kept on working. She hosted the VH-1 Fashion Awards in October 1998, then took a supporting role in the romantic comedy *The Love Letter*, but the press was more interested in Ellen's relationship with Anne Heche. "There was no way that the media feeding-frenzy was not going to go nuts over Ellen's private life," said Benjamin Morrison. The relationship gave Ellen a chance to work with Anne as they took on artistic projects together. In March 2000, Ellen starred in one of three vignettes in the HBO movie *If These Walls Could Talk 2*. Spanning three generations of lesbian experience, Ellen's story featured Sharon Stone. In the segment, Ellen and Stone played two women trying to have a child. Ellen's real life costar, Heche, served as the film's writer and director.

That summer Ellen hit the road for a national stand-up tour. The finale was taped for an HBO special, which aired in August 2000 and was a huge success, according to Peralta. On August 3,

2000, Ellen and Anne appeared together at the premiere of Heche's Showtime drama *One Kill*. They were all smiles and seemed happy, but two weeks later, the couple issued a joint statement that their three-and-a-half-year relationship was over. It was another tough blow for Ellen. Said Kathy Najimy, "The breakup between Ellen and Anne had been sort of a long time coming. You can glean that there were some things that would make it hard to have a relationship between them, and I think, ultimately, it was the best thing that they separated."

Adding insult to injury, the day after her much-publicized breakup with Ellen, a dazed and confused Heche was picked up by sheriff's deputies at a farmhouse near Fresno, California. According to a police report obtained by NBC affiliate KSEE-TV, Heche told deputies that she was God and was going to take everyone back to heaven with her. Heche was brought to a nearby hospital for observation and released the same day. Two weeks later, in an interview with Barbara Walters, Heche announced that she was in love—with a man. Anne's new flame was a twenty-six-year-old cameraman she met during the filming of Ellen's HBO special. "It came out of left field," said Craig Peralta, "and it was a very tough time. Ellen was devastated, and rightfully so." However, according to Judy Wieder, the relationship and its demise ultimately helped Ellen. "This was the first time she had loved like that. Now that she got a glimpse of love, she understood how she would have to take care of it now. So there was a lot of growth for Ellen in the breakup. Also, a lot of heartache."

Ellen went back to work developing a new sitcom for CBS. The series was called *The Ellen Show*. Ellen mused, "They can call it anything they want. But I think *The Helen Hunt Show* would get a lot more viewers, personally, I do. But I guess that's misleading." The show again centered on a character named Ellen, but this time she was a former dot-commer who returned to her hometown to live with her mother and sister after the failure of her company. Ellen wisely avoided specific topics or themes about her sexuality. "It's not focused on my sexuality this time around," she asserted. "We decided to focus on everything but. I'm gay on the show, so we're not dodging it." Despite the change in focus, viewers didn't respond. Ratings for *The Ellen Show* were disappointing.

Meanwhile, Ellen prepared to host the Emmy Awards, scheduled for mid-September 2001. On September 11, 2001, everything changed. The Emmy broadcast was postponed and rescheduled twice. The show finally aired on November 4, 2001. Ellen didn't dwell on the tragic circumstances surrounding the postponed show, but again demonstrated the healing powers of comedy. "She said all the things that needed to be said. She made it feel okay to everybody to be in that room and to laugh. We were in a country that didn't know when it would be all right to laugh again," said Craig Peralta. Moreover, Ellen poked fun at other news by wearing a dress imitating the swan outfit Björk wore to the Oscars earlier that year. "I don't know if it's appropriate, but I planned on wearing it when we were going to do the original Emmys in September. Everybody knows that it's fine to wear swan in September," she said with a straight face, then asking, "but is it okay to wear it after September? I don't know. I know it's duck after October, goose before November."

People loved and lauded Ellen's approach. Said Peralta, "She offered us humor and pathos and joy and made us realize that life goes on, without pointing a finger and saying, 'We've got to pull ourselves up.' There was a great sense of comfort that she offered that night, and I think that truly turned her career around." Jeff Rovin, Ellen's biographer, agreed, "Hosting the Emmys probably was one of the most instrumental things in bringing her back into the mainstream as 'Ellen.' Not as 'Ellen, the gay activist, partner of Anne Heche.' She was able to just be herself again."

In November 2001, just as Ellen was scoring high marks for her work as host of the Emmys, her sitcom was in jeopardy. Less than three months after the awards ceremony, *The Ellen Show* was unceremoniously cancelled. Understandable, in light of what television executive Dean Valentine sees as Ellen's particular strength. "Scripted material," he reasoned, "tends to dampen a lot of what makes Ellen unique." Ellen rebounded once again. She returned to her stand-up roots, embarking on a thirty-five-city tour. She also began writing her second book, though TV remained on her mind and she began to consider doing a talk show. Not everyone was as enthusiastic about Ellen's idea of hosting a talk show. Kathy Najimy said, "When she first told me she was considering a talk show, I thought, 'Oh no,' because that's what people do when they're sort of done doing other things." Craig Peralta also noted that he considered the talk show idea a risky endeavor. "There are so many skeletons behind you, of talk show hosts that have not made it." To which she responded, "Why not a talk show?" Peralta then realized, "She's going to bring to this talk show what she brings to anything she does, and that's her God-given innate humor that nobody else has. Nobody in this business has her voice."

In 2001, Pixar studios reeled in Ellen to voice a scatterbrained blue fish named Dory in *Finding Nemo*. Ellen drew on real-life experience to make a big splash with her character. "There was a woman that lived next door to me that used to do yoga to whale albums," she explained. "At the time, it was really annoying, but then all of a sudden I could use it. They asked me to speak whale, and I realized as I was speaking whale that I got it from hearing this woman do yoga, listening to whale albums." Audiences were passionate—*Finding Nemo* pulled in $340 million at the box office, becoming the top-grossing animated film of all time. Ellen was back, and TV executives began pounding on her door.

This time Ellen insisted on calling the shots. "She wanted to do a smart, funny show in the daytime, for women who were at home and wanted to laugh and wanted to learn and wanted to be informed," recalled Mary Connelly, executive producer of Ellen's talk show. Dean Valentine credited Ellen's "tremendous empathy" for her ability to connect with viewers and successfully host a talk show. Connelly also drew attention to the fact that "it felt really right to her. As a young comedian who got a shot on *The Tonight*

Show and was the first woman to be called over on her first appearance to sit on the couch with Johnny, I don't think you can have that experience and not be touched by it." At age forty-five, Ellen was finally able to do what she does best: be herself.

In the summer of 2003, Ellen taped the debut episode of her daytime talkfest, *The Ellen DeGeneres Show*. "She's working so hard, and she's thrilled at what she's doing. She knows there are things to tweak and there's growth," commented Craig Peralta. Mary Connelly agreed, "We think we are doing a good show, and I only think we will get better at everything we do."

When, on September 8, 2003, *The Ellen DeGeneres Show* premiered, critics and fans loved Ellen's fresh approach. Politics were out, so was pandering to celebrities. Instead, as close friends and average fans quickly noticed, Ellen's show incorporated her natural talents to connect celebrities and viewers. "Ellen's greatest strength, ultimately, is who Ellen is," said Valentine. "[H]er comedy in the end is not really based on being gay or even being female. It's based on looking at life and its absurdities and its humiliations." Benjamin Morrison also remarked that her skills in interviews lie in how her "completely laid-back" personality "charms and disarms her guests." Ellen's talk show was hot, and this time there was no backlash from advertisers. With good reviews and good ratings, the chance for disappointment seemed distant. "I think she's going to do this talk show for the rest of her career," commented Peralta. Valentine added, "In Hollywood, success just generates more and more opportunities. I think Oprah is a perfectly good example of what that is. I wouldn't be surprised to see *Ellen* magazine one day."

With universal praise for her show, Ellen also saw love reenter the picture. Ellen went public about her romance with actress and photographer Alexandra Hedison. The couple had a good relationship, which Valentine attributed to Ellen's matured sense of self. "I think she's much more at peace with who she is and with her life than she was during those crazy, intense moments, and she just seems like a much happier person in every way," he commented. This peace with herself, in turn, allowed Ellen to now approach her lesbian identity from a much more effective angle. "Ellen is an activist through example. She's someone who says, 'Hey, this is who I am. I can't stand being who you thought I was anymore, and I have to be true to myself,'" affirmed Sawyer. In 2004, though, Ellen's six-year relationship with Hedison ended. On the red carpet of the 2005 Golden Globes, Ellen introduced the world to her new girlfriend, actress Portia de Rossi.

Comedian, actress, activist, talk-show host—Ellen DeGeneres blazed bold new trails wherever she went and will likely continue to do so for years to come. "The greatness of Ellen is that the controversy is such a small part of the whole. The controversy is now a blip," said actor and producer Henry Winkler. "I'll tell you what the future holds for Ellen," he concluded. "Whatever she visualizes, whatever she wants to do. This is not a flash in the pan. This is not a woman who pretends to be what she says she is. She's out there. She's the real deal."

CHAPTER 5

HER MOTHER'S DAUGHTER

The Liza Minnelli Story

"She was the most glittering, dazzling star there was. Bar none."

—*Michael Musto, New York gossip columnist*

Liza Minnelli made headlines the day she was born. Her mother was a legend, a haunted superstar who left her daughter a dark legacy. She was pampered by her father, a brilliant filmmaker who battled to keep his own personal life private. Liza inherited privilege, fame, and unbelievable talent. But all she really wanted was love, and her desperate search to find it made the rest of her roller-coaster life a never-ending cycle of honors and heartbreaks, smash hits and embarrassing flops, total wipeouts and impossible comebacks. In her incredible life, Liza has conquered Hollywood, Broadway, drugs, alcohol, weight gain, and terrifying bouts of emotional and physical pain. She's more provocative and outrageous than any cabaret, and this is her story.

For Liza, the "arena" was always larger than life, and stardom was the singer's birthright. In 1943, her superstar mother, Judy Garland, married esteemed director Vincente Minnelli. According to James Spada, biographer and author of *Judy and Liza*, "Vincente was a very quiet, very sensitive man—a lover of beauty, a sophisticate. He wasn't the kind of man Judy needed to keep her in control." He also wasn't the kind of man many people expected her to marry. According to biographer Gerald Clarke, who wrote *Get Happy*, about Judy's life, "People suggested that maybe he wasn't the right man for her, and Judy said, 'No, he's not homosexual. It's just his artistic temperament,' and so they got married. They had a child, Liza."

Liza May Minnelli was born on March 12, 1946. The Hollywood baby instantly stole the spotlight. Spada noted, "Liza Minnelli's childhood, publicly at least, sounds like a fairy tale. The first person to visit her mother in the hospital after she was born was Frank Sinatra. Fred Astaire and Gene Kelly would dance in their living room." Liza's own recollections of her childhood are full of glitz and glamour. "When you lived in Hollywood, everybody did the same thing, and everybody's kid was my friend," she said. "I knew the Bogart kids. It was a factory town. These people that I knew, they were the neighbors. Fred Astaire was a neighbor, that's all, a friend of my mother and my father. When we moved and started to travel, when Mama did concerts, I suddenly realized who these people were. I got very impressed with myself. I thought, 'My God, I know all these people.'"

"She appeared in her first movie at the age of two. It was *In the Good Ol' Summertime,* which was one of her mother's films," said James Spada. But life off-camera wasn't always sunny for Judy's daughter. By the age of five, Liza was already the caretaker of her drug-abusing mother. "Living with Judy Garland must have been like living with Dr. Jekyll. You never knew when Mr. Hyde was going to show up. Judy Garland adored her children, and she would go days helping them with their homework, just taking care of them, loving them to death. And then her mood—because of the drugs that she was taking—would switch entirely, and she would scream at them. Liza said that there was nothing worse than the sound of her mother's voice when she was angry."

Besides coping with Judy's erratic behavior, Liza had to deal with inevitable gossip about her famous family. "Liza says that there were always rumors floating around her father, her grandfather, everybody in her family. She refuses to confirm any of them. She says that she thinks because her father, Vincente Minnelli, was an artist, and he looked a certain way, that people assumed he was gay, and that she did not know him as a gay man or a bisexual man," offered Judy Wieder, editorial director of *The Advocate*. Liza just knew Minnelli as the father she adored. Unfortunately,

Judy's affection for Vincente didn't last. The diva and the director split up in 1951, just two weeks after Liza's fifth birthday. "Liza was very unhappy when her parents divorced. They were now two households, and her custody was given half to Vincente and half to Judy," said Spada, "and when Vincente remarried and had another child, she felt she was an extra wheel when she would be with him."

In 1952, Judy married producer Sid Luft. The couple had two children, Lorna and Joey. Liza's father also had another daughter, Christiane, but he never stopped doting on Liza. She recalled with glee, "For Christmas each year, he would give me five costumes, and they could be anything I wanted. They were usually costumes from his movies. I was really young, but I had these costumes, and I would dance on the lawn and hope somebody would give me money. It was insane but it was wonderful!" Liza's former boyfriend, musical arranger Billy Stritch, added, "I remember Liza telling me at one point the first thing that she really ever decided she wanted to do was be a professional ice-skater. That would have been a totally different turn, and she was into dancing. So her mother, picking up on that, thought, 'Liza's the dancer and Lorna's the singer.'" Said James Spada, "Judy was not very encouraging of Liza's singing. She said after one of Liza's performances, to a friend, 'My God, her voice is like chalk on a blackboard.'"

Judy's scathing criticism didn't hold Liza back. On April 24, 1959, the thirteen-year-old sang a duet with family friend Gene Kelly on a TV special. An article about Liza's performance got everything right but her name. "In the story they called her Lisa Minnelli rather than Liza Minnelli, because Liza's an unusual name. Years later she did a special called *Liza with a Z* with Kander and Ebb, and it became one of her trademarks," said Spada.

As a teenager, Liza bounced back and forth between her divorced parents. The time she spent with her father was calm and comforting, but living with her mother was an entirely different matter. Liza spent her early teenage years mothering her own mother, running the household, hiring staff and paying bills. Said Spada, "One of her jobs was to take Judy's sleeping pills and replace half of them with sugar so that it would be less likely that Judy would overdose. When Judy was on drugs or sick or just in a snit in her bedroom for three days, Liza would have to get her younger siblings off to school and make their lunch and just be the mother figure in the house."

The days and nights were frenetic and filled with turmoil. "One story has Liza and Joey and Lorna and Judy sneaking out of a hotel wearing five layers of clothing so they wouldn't have to carry any luggage and the hotel wouldn't know that they were skipping out on the bill," reported Spada. "The lifestyle with Vincente was so different than the lifestyle with Judy—it was very schizophrenic for Liza."

When she was sober, however, Judy was a very strict parent. In 1960, she sent Liza to a boarding school in France. After one unhappy semester, Liza returned to Judy's home in suburban New York to attend Scarsdale High School. That fall, fifteen-year-old Liza won the lead in the school's production of *The Diary of Anne Frank*. Liza felt safe on stage, but, among her acting buddies, she wasn't always secure. Louis Briganti, a classmate who played Otto Frank, commented, "Liza was really trying to fit in and trying to be one of the girls. In one of the breaks in rehearsal for the play, one of the girls asked, 'How is it to be the daughter of a great star?' and Liza said, 'Oh, I've learned a lot of great things from my mother.' The girl said, 'Really, like what?' and Liza answered, 'Like how to ditch a man.' I think that made them really all kind of uneasy." There were more uneasy moments ahead for the daughter of Judy Garland.

In 1961, fifteen-year-old Liza was already a star, at least at Scarsdale High. The teenager knew that she could make audiences love her. Making her mother love her, however, was a different story. Liza was more determined than ever to win the affection and support of her pill-popping, superdiva mother. Liza conspired with friend and future composer Marvin Hamlisch, and they came up with a unique way to reveal her desire to follow in her mother's footsteps. Said Hamlisch, "I wrote four songs for her, and we went and recorded them in a little studio. And now we go to this famous Christmas party of Judy's, and Liza says, 'Now I'd like to give you my present,' and she just sits down, and we put these records on. And everyone is, like, spellbound. After we did the records, Judy asked her could she do it live, and there I was, and we did it live."

Judy was impressed, but she urged her oldest daughter to stay in school. "I wanted to go to New York and be a dancer and be in Broadway shows," said Liza, "and I just loved that idea. So I asked if I could go, and Mama said, 'What are you going to sing for these auditions? Not any of my songs, I hope.'" In December 1962, the sixteen-year-old performer dropped out of high school to pursue acting full-time. Her mother wasn't happy. "Judy had said, 'That's fine. I won't stand in your way, but don't expect any financial help from me. If you're going to make it, you're going to make it on your own,'" wrote James Spada. Liza moved to New York City in 1963. The teenager's showbiz pedigree opened doors for her. "Her first big break in an off-Broadway play called *Best Foot Forward* actually came purely because she was Judy Garland's daughter." The play's director, Danny Daniels, credited Liza's ability—not her DNA—with winning her the lead role in his musical: "She has a very individualistic style when she sings. Her singing is Liza's. It's not anybody else's. The critics, as a matter of fact, said that one of the reasons to go see the show was to have the memory of seeing the beginnings of a star."

One seat was empty opening night—Judy's. "The official version was that she was ill, but someone in the company heard Liza on the telephone during intermission saying, 'Mama, how could you have thought it was tomorrow night? I kept telling you it was tonight,'" said Spada. Liza's neglectful mother showed support in other ways. Judy invited her daughter to perform on two episodes of *The Judy Garland Show*. The programs aired on CBS in the winter of 1963. George Schlatter, who produced the series, re-called, "I think it was the first time she'd appeared on American television with her mom. It was exciting to see these two women together." The following year, Liza reluctantly agreed to perform with her mother in London. According to Spada, when Judy—who thought she was too weak to perform an entire show alone—pitched the idea to Liza, the rising star declined. When Judy went ahead and announced the show as a mother-daughter affair, the tickets sold out in twelve hours, and Liza had no choice.

The premiere of the live family affair revealed a problem between the two generations of superstars. "The show itself is really a fascinating study in psychodynamics," remarked James Spada, "because initially Judy is very sweet toward Liza and very motherly. But as the show went on, it was clear that Liza was stealing the show. She was in better voice than Judy. She was more energetic than Judy. She was like a younger, fresher version of Judy." Actor Ken Howard witnessed the memorable performance and agreed, "Liza watched her mother kind of turn from loving, supportive mother to the competitorlike, 'Now wait a minute, honey.'" Spada continued, "Liza said she was pretty scared during the concert, because she had not seen that side of her mother before." According to Billy Stritch, "I don't think her mother really took her seriously as a singer until the night they were onstage at the Palladium together and Liza stopped the show over and over and over again. Liza says that she went from being the little girl to being competition onstage in the space of an hour and a half." For Liza, it was "a lifetime of therapy in one night," according to Stritch.

When the curtain dropped, Judy morphed back from competitor to mother. Backstage, she introduced Liza to a young man she met while traveling in Hong Kong. Peter Allen was a twenty-year-old singer from Australia. While she was now officially a pro on stage, eighteen-year-old Liza was still taking cues from her mom in her love life. In the fall of 1964, Judy advised Liza to give all her love to Peter.

Peter and Liza hit it off immediately. Minnelli's friend *Hollywood Reporter* columnist Robert Osborne described, "He was young. You could see where there would be an attraction. And he absolutely adored her." Said Marvin Hamlisch, "Peter was a fabulous guy, and I loved him a lot. I think again she was drawn to a person who was, first of all, a very kind, very sweet man." Peter Allen supplied the warmth and attention Liza so desperately craved. "They hit it off extremely well, and within a couple of weeks, they were engaged to be married," said James Spada. Liza and Peter shared a lot of the same interests, music and partying among them, but one of their shared interests was also Peter's darkest secret—a secret Liza didn't necessarily know about: Peter's preference for men. "A reporter once asked Liza about her sex life with Peter Allen, and she refused to answer the question but would say only that that was one of her demons."

If Liza and Peter weren't a match sexually, then at least he served as an emotional anchor when Liza needed stability. Liza did know that she needed someone to help distance her from her manipulative mother. Said Judy Wieder, "He was so important to her because he helped her break away from Judy at a time that was really important for her to try to find a way to leave her mother."

"There was no question that this girl was on her way. It was just a question of putting it all together and a little bit of time," characterized Hamlisch. It didn't even take a little bit of time before Liza got the break she'd dreamed of. In 1965, Liza won the lead in the Broadway musical *Flora, the Red Menace*. Broadway's newest star was determined not to be just another Hollywood princess. Her costar Louis Guss affirmed, "She worked her butt off. There was nothing temperamental about her or that she was Judy Garland's daughter." Another of the show's stars, Diane McAfee, mentioned that she "was walking past her [Liza's] little place on the dressing table and her address book was open, and I just glanced at it, and it said 'Mama.' I thought, Mama? Mama is Judy Garland." George Schlatter laughed, "How do you call Judy

Garland 'Mommy,' you know? She always wanted her mom's approval and, for the most part, got it—when Judy was paying attention."

Judy paid attention and stayed sober long enough to attend the opening night of her daughter's first Broadway show. In the presence of her mother, Liza was always Judy's daughter, but theater critics recognized that Liza had star power of her own. For Marvin Hamlisch, "Everyone in the audience knew this was a star. It was just a question of when." In June 1965, Liza won a Tony Award for her performance in *Flora, the Red Menace*. At age nineteen, she became the youngest woman ever to receive the honor as Broadway's Best Actress. While Liza's star was on the rise, her mother's was plummeting fast. "Judy was in the middle of an inexorable decline in the late sixties," said James Spada, due to "drugs, money problems, canceled concerts, and poorly performed concerts." Liza was often the only one to look after—and often protect—Judy's other children from their mother.

In 1967, nine days before her twenty-first birthday, Liza Minnelli found some peace. She married Peter Allen in a simple ceremony in New York City. The couple's honeymoon didn't last long. They were swept into Judy's never-ending drama. "It really became more and more difficult for Liza to deal with Judy, and she wouldn't answer the phone. She would let her husband, Peter Allen, answer the phone just in case it was Judy," said Spada. Liza and Peter often came to the rescue. They became surrogate parents to Liza's sister and brother, Lorna and Joey. Besides taking care of the family, Liza managed to keep her career on track.

The singer's success on Broadway provided her with new opportunities, including her first film role. Liza starred opposite Albert Finney in the 1967 drama *Charlie Bubbles*. Though *Charlie Bubbles* barely made a ripple, her next film, *The Sterile Cuckoo*, made a big splash. "She played a college girl who was desperate for love—kind of quirky, kooky, and just a sponge for any kind of affection—and it's very much like Liza Minnelli herself," assessed Spada. Commented actress Sally Kirkland, "She's not afraid to wear her heart on her sleeve and to let the insecurities be there." Liza's impressive performance in the 1969 drama won her an Oscar nomination, but Liza didn't take home the gold. Still, rave reviews kept the offers coming. The following year she landed a part in the comedy-drama *Tell Me That You Love Me, Junie Moon*.

Liza's family life, with all its flaws and magic, was forever changed on June 22, 1969. Recounted James Spada, "Peter Allen went into Liza's bedroom and she could tell just by the look on his face that something terrible had happened, and she said, 'It was my first thought that my father had died, because my mother seemed indestructible to me. I never imagined her ever dying.'" But Judy Garland was dead. At the age of forty-seven, she passed away in a London hotel room. An autopsy revealed that Judy took the equivalent of ten sleeping pills and died from "barbiturate poisoning." The coroner ruled her death an "accidental overdose." With Judy gone, Liza tried to carry on, but the death of her mother left a void no drug or man could fill.

When Judy died, she left her fans music and memories and her daughter a mountain of debt and a hole in her heart. Liza tied up all the loose ends in her mother's life, including repaying nearly $200,000 Judy reportedly owed creditors, colleagues, and friends. "My first introduction to Liza and who she was and her work ethic and personality was watching her deal with all the funeral arrangements and manage all this at twenty-three," commented Ken Howard. Liza may have struggled with the huge debt her mother left behind, but she struggled more with losing her mother. "The thing that you have to understand about Liza and Judy is that Liza adored Judy. She needed Judy to love her," said Spada. "She said once, 'Millions of people loved my mother, and they never even met her. Can you imagine how I feel?'"

The day after her mother's funeral, Liza returned to the set of *Tell Me That You Love Me, Junie Moon*. Her mother was never far from her thoughts. Liza numbed her grief with Valium, following in her mother's footsteps in the worst way. "She was also not looking at the harm that it was doing her," said Judy Wieder, "and the fact that she was not taking care of her own emotional life. So she, too, was trying to fill some of this emptiness and some of the psychic pain with drugs. So she fell into some of the patterns that her mother fell into." On the set of *Junie Moon*, Liza became friends with the costume designer, Roy Halston. He gave her confidence, comfort, and her signature style. Under his watchful eye, Liza blossomed from a gawky girl to a sophisticated star who wasn't afraid to show her sassy side.

But just as she was coming into her own womanhood, Liza Minnelli also made an unexpected and unfortunate discovery about her husband. "Liza told me that it was a very unhappy occurrence that led her to finding out that Peter Allen was gay," said Wieder. "She came home and walked in and found him in bed with another man, and it was heartbreaking to her—and very confusing to her." In April 1970, Liza and Peter separated. The couple eventually divorced. Liza didn't dwell on her broken marriage. Instead, she toured with a lounge act, winning rave reviews with every performance.

In the summer of 1971, the actress landed a role that she desperately wanted. The twenty-five-year-old traveled to Germany to film the musical *Cabaret*. "*Cabaret* was one of those magical combinations of vehicle and talent," said James Spada. Cy Feuer, the movie's producer, commented, "She was perfectly cast for it, and she enhanced it. She just understood Sally Bowles. She kind of is Sally Bowles." Liza described her character as being "like a lot of people I'd met who really threw themselves into the moment and really didn't care about the future very much."

Cabaret premiered in February 1972. The reviews were outstanding, but it was Liza's performance of the film's signature song that caught everyone's attention. The moment she turned "Cabaret" into her own personal anthem was the moment Judy's daughter officially arrived. "When the film was released, it was one of those rare moments in show business where you felt that a star was being born before your eyes. She was on the cover of *Time* and *Newsweek* in the same week, which is very unusual," said Spada. In January 1973, Liza won the Golden Globe for her performance in *Cabaret*.

Two months later, she went to the Oscars. *Cabaret* was nominated for ten Academy Awards, including Best Actress. Liza's father was in the audience along with his fourth wife, Lee, who said that Vincente "rose five feet in his seat" when Liza's name was announced. Described Liza, "My father screamed so loud in my ear, I couldn't hear out of it for two days. Then he started to cry, and I realized how much it meant to him—that the union with my mother produced a lineage that would continue." That night, Liza surpassed the success of her legendary mother. Though Judy had earned a "Juvenile" Academy Award for her role in *The Wizard of Oz*, she never won the Oscar for Best Actress.

"She was the queen. She was the seventies," characterized Liza's friend, illustrator Joe Eula. With an Oscar to her name, Liza was a bona fide movie star. She returned to New York triumphant and ready to take on Broadway once again with her show *Liza with a Z*. The magic continued when *Liza with a Z* moved on to the small screen. It was her first television special. "The absolute high point of Liza's career was 1972," assessed Michael Musto. "She won the Oscar for *Cabaret*. She won Emmys for *Liza with a Z*. She had conquered all the media, and she was the most glittering, dazzling star there was. Bar none." In hindsight, James Spada said, "But if her mother's life is any lesson to us, the high points always seem to be followed by very low points."

In 1973, the twenty-seven-year-old entertainer took her show *Liza with a Z* on the road. Bobby Keller, the saxophone player in Minnelli's band, said, "The relationship with Liza and the orchestra was the best that I've had with any performer, and I've worked with just about everybody. She just loves musicians, and she loves to have a great time." He then added, "She wanted to do something special for us, so she did an outrageous thing. She hired two party girls to travel with us for a weekend with some extracurricular activities—and I'll leave it there." This very wild side was on display at New York City's most outrageous disco. According to friend and Kiss front man Gene Simmons, "Studio 54 was a very strange place, because all the celebrities would want to go there because there was a special door policy. Literally, Jackie Onassis didn't get in one night. The king of Jordan didn't get in one night. It was whoever the owner Steve Rubell and the other owners of Studio 54 allowed to get in. Because of that, it was highly prized." Liza and her best friend, forty-one-year-old fashion designer Halston, were playmates on the prowl. Said Eula, "They drank and drugged and carried on like two absolute seventies characters. And didn't everybody?"

When Liza wasn't doing the town, she was trying to find Mr. Right—or at least a reasonable facsimile. In 1973, Liza was briefly engaged to fellow Hollywood baby Desi Arnaz Jr., who was seven years younger than she. "Oh, they were a couple wild as the wind. He was so darling. He was very attractive, like all Latin men are. We all loved Desi," said Liza's stepmother, Lee. But the pair broke up when Liza fell madly in love with forty-four-year-old actor Peter Sellers. Unfortunately, their May–December romance flamed out in less than a month. Liza briefly reconciled with Desi Jr., but that return engagement had a very short run.

Love soon followed when she met Jack Haley Jr., the son of the man who played the Tin Man in *The Wizard of Oz*. According to longtime friend and confidante Lynn Wyatt, "Jack was very caring of Liza, and she has always respected men that have talent, and of course he was very talented." James Spada recounted, "Liza and Jack met when she was doing *That's Entertainment*, and he showed her the footage that they had compiled. She saw the footage of herself as a two-year-old in *In the Good Ol' Summertime*, and she saw her mother singing and dancing, and she saw the productions that her father directed. She had to leave the theater several times, because she was just in tears. It was a very emotional experience for her, and it just forged a bond between them that grew into love." Dorothy's daughter married the Tin Man's son on September 6, 1974.

Secure on the home front—at least for the time being—twenty-eight-year-old Liza concentrated on her career. That year, she costarred in a quirky love story with Gene Hackman and Burt Reynolds. "*Lucky Lady* was not a hit. People thought it was fairly boring and that Liza was miscast," said Spada, "and it was her first movie after *Cabaret*. So it was an important film to try to keep that alive, and that didn't happen." In 1976, Liza wanted to work with a filmmaker she could love, her father—seventy-three-year-old Vincente Minnelli. The film called *A Matter of Time* was, according to Michael Musto, "one of the possibly worst movies ever made. Ingrid Bergman overacts as this kind of demented countess. Liza isn't quite right for the part that she's playing, and it's not funny, it's not dramatic, it's not anything. And you kind of wonder, is this really the Vincente Minnelli that made *Gigi*? What happened?"

Desperate for a hit, Liza Minnelli jumped at the chance to star in *New York, New York*, a production reminiscent of the classic MGM musicals. The 1977 film was an experiment for acclaimed New York director Martin Scorsese. He cast Liza as a big-band singer who falls in love with a saxophonist played by Robert De Niro. Rumors about an on-set extramarital romance between Liza and Scorsese circulated, as did rumors concerning her escalating drug use. In his published diaries, famed pop artist Andy Warhol wrote that, during the seventies, Liza often indulged in cocaine, Valium, and Quaaludes. Meanwhile, the ambitious musical went $2 million over budget and was four hours long. MGM Studios forced Scorsese to slash eighty-five minutes from the film.

Despite the director's last-ditch efforts, the movie opened on June 21, 1977, to negative reviews, including one headline that read, "Is *New York, New York* a Last Stand for Liza, De Niro and Scorsese?" Mentioned James Spada, "When they showed Liza singing 'New York, New York' at the end of the movie, it was absolutely eerie how much like her mother she was, and it was really the first time that people started to say, 'My God, she's turning into Judy Garland.'" Even though she was the Queen of the Disco Age, three failed films, a flailing marriage, and too many nights out made Liza realize that she needed to get her act together. In 1977, the thirty-one-year-old entertainer returned to Broadway in the musical *The Act*. Liza demanded that Martin Scorsese direct the show. Scorsese, who had no theater experience, seemed out of place during rehearsals and bowed out. Liza had a meltdown. "She was very upset when Marty withdrew, and we said, 'Liza, it's the best thing ever happened to the show and to you. You're going to have to appear on Broadway, and you need a director,'" recalled Cy Feuer, Liza's *Cabaret* producer. Despite a new director, Musto said, "it was a mediocre result only carried by Liza. Her star quality saved every minute of it, and she won another Tony Award."

Liza Minnelli's talent and charisma kept her in the spotlight, but behind the velvet curtain, the singer's personal life was a mess. Liza was estranged from her second husband. Love found Liza—or the other way around—again. According to her stepmother, "Liza was in New York doing a show, and Baryshnikov fell madly in love with her. He was always in her dressing room, night and day, and Jack called up Mr. Minnelli and he says, 'I'm sorry, I'm going to have to divorce Liza.'" On February 24, 1978, Liza and Jack Haley legally separated, and while the relationship with Mikhail Baryshnikov wasn't long-term, Minnelli didn't stay single for long. She soon met a sculptor named Mark Gero. Liza was crazy about her new boyfriend despite her father's reservations. "He was like a man that's here today and gone tomorrow, you know. You couldn't depend on him," characterized Lee Minnelli.

Liza didn't listen to Daddy. The couple married on December 4, 1979. Thirty-four-year-old Liza welcomed twenty-seven-year-old Gero into her apartment on Manhattan's Upper East Side. With her romantic life again stabilized, she was ready to get back on Hollywood's A-list. In the spring of 1980, Liza was offered a role in the comedy *Arthur* opposite Dudley Moore. According to longtime friend Robert Osborne, she was initially unsatisfied playing second banana to the diminutive comedian. "If you're playing secondary roles, it's very hard to get a leading role again. Anyway, it turned out to be such a great hit that she got a lot of the credit for it, and one of the reasons the film works so well was because Liza was in it. She brought that unique personality of hers to that part." For the first time since *Cabaret,* a movie with Liza in it was a hit.

At the same time, thirty-five-year-old Liza was enjoying professional success and moving toward calm in many areas of her life, she was living on the edge in a lot of ways, too. "Liza was ripe" with the smell of vodka, remembered Joe Eula. Liza herself admitted, "I just was sick all the time, and yet I didn't stop drinking. Mostly it was a combination of prescription drugs like Valium and a sleeping pill." Liza was an alcoholic and hooked on Valium, but, like her famous mother, she was hooked on to something else far more addictive than drugs. "Judy Garland had a tremendous need to perform," said James Spada, "a tremendous need to feel the love of an audience and the love of individuals. Liza is the same way. She's really a sponge for affection. She wants people to like her, really, really desperately."

In 1984, Liza hoped to win approval from critics and fans in the Broadway musical *The Rink.* The saga about a daughter who confronts her past also starred longtime family friend and Tony winner Chita Rivera as Liza's character's mother. Rivera revealed, "So much was going through both of our heads, but we had to blank it out as much as we could. I certainly didn't feel like Judy Garland, but we delved into our own lives, pulled it up, and it worked beautiful for the scene." When she took the stage to accept a Tony Award for her performance in *The Rink,* Rivera made a regrettable oversight when she forgot to thank Liza. Liza, however, may have been too distracted to notice her costar's faux pas. The pressure of performing eight shows a week combined with her heavy drug use turned Liza into a walking zombie. Scott Ellis, who played Liza's boyfriend in the show, remarked, "Once she started missing shows, you went, 'Okay, something's wrong.' She would come back, and she wouldn't sound as well as she did before. So you knew something was wrong."

On July 15, 1984, thirty-eight-year-old Liza finally hit bottom. The singer's family knew she needed help. Liza's half sister, Lorna Luft, checked her into the Betty Ford Clinic in Palm Springs, California. Vincente Minnelli couldn't help but compare his daughter's struggles with those of her mother, his first wife. "It was heartbreaking," said Lee Minnelli. "He came to me with tears in his eyes, bless him. He said, 'I had to go through this with Judy, and now I'm going through it with Liza.' We'd go and visit her on weekends, and she said, 'Daddy, this will never happen again, ever, ever, ever.'" After seven weeks of detox, Liza returned to New York. Liza was hopeful but aware of her family legacy. "I was busted since I was slapped on the buns," she said, "and it runs in my family way back. There are people who have a drinking problem, and there are people who have alcoholism . . . I don't want to sound like I am preaching, because preaching doesn't work. People did it to me for years, and it didn't stop me. What worked was finding the light and listening to a group of people who had been through what I had been through."

In 1985, Liza Minnelli was ready for a fresh start. Her first role out of rehab was the TV movie *A Time to Live*. She won a Golden Globe for her performance as the mother of a terminally ill child. Liza was back again. Part of her return to normal was due to the fact that she "got in touch with a lot of her friends that she really felt she had to apologize to," said Chita Rivera, "and I remember over lunch when she did that. She did not have to apologize to me, as far as I was concerned."

While Liza tried to get her life back on track, she received some terrible news. On July 25, 1985, her father, eighty-one-year-old Vincent Minnelli, died of heart failure. Confirmed James Spada, "Liza was very devastated when her father died. Liza adored her father, and they stayed as close as was possible with the craziness that life with Judy could create." Liza herself remembered a sentimental and touching moment that she shared with her father at the end. "It was the last thing he said to me," she said. "I said, 'Daddy, I want to thank you for everything that you've given to me,' and he looked at me with such love, and he said, 'My darling, you haven't scratched the surface yet.'"

Liza coped with her loss by returning to work. On May 28, 1987, the entertainer walked on stage at Carnegie Hall and gave a knock-out one-woman concert. The following spring, forty-two-year-old Liza was swinging to a different tune. She filled in for Dean Martin during the Rat Pack's reunion tour, "The Ultimate Event." The show was great, but Liza wasn't interested in becoming a musical relic.

In 1989, she made a daring move and recorded an album with the British pop duo the Pet Shop Boys. Kiss's Gene Simmons got her the gig. "It was a big uphill battle, because there was a preconceived notion about Liza and sort of a Kander and Ebb Broadway-esque style of singing, which was not very commercial. She had to literally sing differently, tone down the vibrato and sing very commercial-based music—which, by the way, I thought she did terrifically," he said. Liza's new sound was a hit in Europe, but fans in the United States didn't bite. Fans also weren't hungry for Liza's latest movies. The 1990 films *Arthur 2* and *Rent-a-Cop* both tanked at the box office.

Liza wasn't scoring at home, either. Her eleven-year marriage to Mark Gero was falling apart. She suffered numerous miscarriages, which put a terrible strain on the relationship. Furthermore, Gero had a hard time living life as "Mr. Minnelli." Said Joe Eula, "She was terribly supportive, but none of us ever knew who Mark was. And his work was so—that's a terrible thing to say—I ain't gonna say second-rate, but it was . . . She was supportive of it. It just didn't work. Nor did the marriage." Liza and Mark separated in 1990.

Sadly, that wasn't the only loss Liza Minnelli endured that year. She also lost her favorite friend and designer, Halston, whom Judy Wieder described as "a great sort of protecting figure for her—almost a father figure in certain ways. When he died of AIDS, she lost her mind over that. She just completely didn't expect that to happen." By the age of forty-six, Liza had buried her mother and father, battled addiction, and survived the death of her best friend. In June 1992, she suffered another blow—the death of her first husband and longtime friend, forty-eight-year-old singer and songwriter Peter Allen. Though Peter claimed he had throat cancer, Liza instantly knew that he was covering for the truth: Peter had AIDS.

"When Peter Allen died, I was with her that day," described Billy Stritch, "and I was the one that told her. I remember being in the back of the car . . . and I just held her and grabbed her hands, and I said, 'I've got some bad news for you.' And she said, 'It's Peter.' I said, 'Yeah, it's Peter. He died this morning.'" Said Wieder, "In the end, she was very there for him. She helped to let him go and let him succumb to AIDS and know that she forgave him in a certain way that he needed to feel." Liza was always a model of dignity when faced with tragedy, but her strength and sobriety were about to be tested.

In 1992, Liza picked herself up and returned to the one place she felt safe, the stage. At Radio City Musical Hall, the forty-six-year-old singer gave a rousing tribute to her mother and father titled "Liza Live from Radio City Music Hall." Reminisced Stritch, "There wasn't a dry eye. The lights went up in the house and people were sobbing—especially women. There was so much love within it, and it ended with how Vincente gave her her dreams, gave her the wings." Liza affirmed, "He gave me courage. He gave me a sense of fantasy, a sense of possibility. I've always said that my mother gave me my drive, but my father gave me my dreams."

Years of hard living, however, started to catch up with Liza Minnelli. In 1994, the performer underwent the first of two hip replacements. The forty-eight-year-old was approaching middle age, and it wasn't pretty. "I suffered with this pain of degenerative arthritis for ten years, and I never told anybody, because I was ashamed of it," she said. "I don't know why—you start lying. People say in the airports, 'What's the matter with your leg?,' and you say, 'New shoes!'" Liza's convalescence was slow and agonizing. After a three-year absence, she was eager to return to Broadway.

Now fifty-one years old, Liza agreed to fill in for an exhausted Julie Andrews in the musical *Victor/Victoria*. Audiences loved having Liza back, but the critics weren't so kind. They felt the actress couldn't pull off playing a man. "Liza never lost her Liza image, no matter how you'd try to slice that," said Joe Eula, "and she's never going to come out a guy." Billy Stritch agreed, calling it "one of the worst decisions she ever made."

In particular, Liza had conflicts with costar Tony Roberts. "Tony likes to do it the same every night and make it appear as if it's happening for the very first time. Liza likes to keep it loose and just do something a little bit different every night, and they probably didn't always work it out," commented Ken Land, another cast member. Citing illness, Roberts left the cast of *Victor/Victoria*. Within a few weeks, Liza's usually tireless voice left her as well. Said Stritch, "She hadn't had the proper vocal training to know how to place her voice—and it would happen to anybody. By the end of like the third week, she wasn't able to talk."

Liza's throat operation in 1997 was just one of several surgeries that she endured that year. The entertainer also went under the knife to repair a damaged knee, and she had a second hip operation. Her health situation, said Michael Musto, became "more and more vulnerable." With all of her medical problems, Liza found relief with some old, familiar friends. "She couldn't walk. She couldn't talk, and she was drinking way, way more than anybody knew, and taking a lot of pills," commented Eula.

By 1999, fifty-three-year-old Liza was once again determined to chase her devils away with work. She mentioned that she was "so bored up in the hospital" that she began to watch all of her father's films. She continued, "As I was watching them, I thought, 'Wait a minute, this is terrific! Somebody's gotta do something about this!'" And she did. That year, Liza Minnelli staged an evening of song and dance to celebrate her father's legacy. Alec

Timerman, a dancer in the show, remembered the intense pressure weighing down on Liza. "When they were putting together *Minnelli on Minnelli,* Liza was sort of pushed by this time constraint to 'Get ready now!'" he said, "and, you know, the body heals at the rate that it heals, and there's nothing you can really do about that."

"It was terrifying! It was really frightening. I've never been frightened before, and I was frightened that night. Then I thought, 'Buckle down, just do it. Concentrate like a bastard and keep going,'" mused Liza herself about her opening night in the show. Her star power may have shone through onstage, but she had a huge obstacle to contend with in the form of her physical capability. Alec Timerman noted, "She's got that Broadway sell face, and as soon as the curtain came down, she reached for the first person closest to her, which happened to be me, and she just kind of grabbed a hold of my shoulder, and I would physically have to walk her back to her dressing room."

Despite Liza's poor health, she began what was supposed to be her yearlong tour with *Minnelli on Minnelli.* After one month, the show was canceled due to her illness. Liza's body failed her. It was one obstacle she couldn't overcome. "She wanted this to work, more than anybody," said Timerman. "This was so critically important to her, and the tragedy of it falling apart is that she worked so hard." Depressed, Liza let her weight balloon. She retreated to South Florida to rest, but on October 8, 2000, paramedics found her semiconscious on the floor of her waterfront home in Fort Lauderdale. Her symptoms suggested that she had suffered a stroke, but Minnelli was later diagnosed with viral encephalitis, a sometimes-deadly inflammation of the brain. "Brain encephalitis was no fun," stated Liza. "Being told I couldn't walk or talk ever again in my life was no fun. But I did."

The dawn of a new millennium found Liza plunging into a personal hell. The actress spent the year 2000 recovering from more ailments than most people suffer in a lifetime. She endured knee surgery, hip replacement, a vocal cord operation, and viral encephalitis—not to mention her battles with weight, alcohol abuse, and drug addiction. But Liza seemed to have more lives than a cat. At age fifty-four, Liza had already lived longer than her mother Judy. Liza's friends were rooting for the actress, but they weren't holding out much hope. "She was fragile. She would perspire. She would be nervous," said gossip columnist Cindy Adams. "I took her to a friend's house for dinner, and they told me, while I was in another room, that she was drinking a glass of wine—and she wasn't supposed to—and then she would sit there and drink milk and eat Oreo cookies. So she didn't have a hold of her compulsions at the time."

In the summer of 2001, Liza was off the celebrity radar. That August, the singer got an unexpected opportunity she couldn't afford to pass up. Producer David Gest was planning a major event at Madison Square Garden to celebrate the career of his friend Michael Jackson. The forty-seven-year-old impresario wanted Liza on the marquee, but he wasn't sure she still had the magic. Recounted Michael Musto, "He felt he had to audition for her, so he sent someone to her apartment to try her out, and they reported, 'It's the old Liza again. She can still sing. She can still hit the high notes. She can stand up. She can do it all.'" On September 7, 2001, Liza joined an all-star lineup to pay tribute to the King of Pop. But when Liza Minnelli appeared on stage, her fans were shocked. She was overweight and almost unrecognizable. And the press was brutal.

But one person still saw a glimmer of the old Liza with a "Z." David Gest decided to make the fifty-five-year-old diva his next project. It didn't take long before the couple's relationship became more than just work. "She told me on the phone," Chita Rivera laughed, "she said 'my boyfriend,' and I said, 'Hold it a minute, Liza. How long have you known him?' I can't remember how long she said, but I heard the excitement in her voice." Over the next few weeks, David became Liza's Svengali, lover, and nurse. "I did not believe that there was going to be this wonderful, mad love affair. I was just grateful that somebody was taking hold, because Liza needed somebody to take hold—that's what David's done," commented Cindy Adams.

Under David's fierce direction, Liza got down to business. She lost more than thirty pounds and started looking like her old self. "She has a piece of toast and yogurt for breakfast. She has a piece of fish for lunch," accounted Adams. "It's very carefully measured. If she ever has a relapse on drugs or alcohol, he says he will be finished with her." After a two-month romance, the couple decided to tie the knot. Over Thanksgiving 2001, David and Liza announced their engagement. David wasn't shy about showing off his fiancée. The press couldn't get enough of this Hollywood-style fairy tale. The wedding promised to be the event of the year. "When Liza went on *Larry King Live* and said, 'Well, gee, I don't know how this thing just blew up so big,' it's like, well, it blew up so big because you hired a publicist to flaunt it for weeks and weeks and weeks," said Michael Musto.

On March 16, 2002, four days after Liza's birthday, Liza, David, and 1,100 of their closest friends gathered to celebrate their union. The ceremony was held in New York City's Marble Collegiate Church. With metal detectors at every door, it was a wedding of epic proportions that defied reality and reportedly cost the couple nearly three million dollars. David and Liza made sure not a moment was missed. Joe Eula described the church scene as "transformed into Hawaii with dripping orchids and bouquets on every single pew." Fans and star-watchers gathered on Fifth Avenue outside the church. They hoped to get a glimpse of the celebrity guests and the thirty-member bridal party, which included best man Michael Jackson.

Guests applauded as Liza Minnelli marched down the aisle for the fourth time. The star still wore white—a one-of-a-kind gown designed by Bob Mackie. The dress had, said Eula, "a skinny train that went all the way to the back of the theater . . . or the church, excuse me." The reception was held in the ballroom at a hotel in downtown Manhattan. Guests were treated to filet mignon, all the Godiva chocolate they could eat, and a six-foot-high wedding cake. Said Chita Rivera, "The champagne, the wine, the food, and the music . . . It was like the biggest bang, the biggest party, the most fun party you could go to."

When fifty-six-year-old Liza married forty-eight-year-old David Gest, she got a ring, the wedding of the year, and a husband and manager rolled into one. For the once down-and-out singer, it all seemed too good to be true. Friends were thrilled for Liza, but as the singer embarked on her new life, some of her old pals were left behind. Remarked Cindy Adams, "That David has isolated Liza is something that we have all heard. This is not uncommon with stars. Has he gotten rid of the people that maybe in his head were not good for her? Yes. He is her entire world. Her entire family." Still, David couldn't shield either of them from the rumors surrounding their marriage. The tabloids pounced on the story that the union was a sham, suggesting he was gay. Liza and David thought the whole matter was silly.

On March 20, 2002, the couple appeared on *Larry King Live*, and, when asked about rumors of David's sexuality, the blushing groom simply said, "I guess it sells papers. I mean, I know who I am. That's the most important thing." He later went on to say, "I think we're going to beat the odds," and "We'll die in each other's arms." Affirmed Chita Rivera, "David is so funny, and he's such a good friend, and he loves Liza. I've never seen her happier." Scott Ellis, Liza's costar in *The Rink*, said, "If she's found somebody who loves her and she loves him, that is great. And the fact that he's a producer and wants to help her career—great."

In April of 2002, Liza took her remodeled self for a test drive. That month, the singer kicked off her new tour, Liza's Back, with a concert at London's Royal Albert Hall. When she walked onstage, fans and critics couldn't believe their eyes or ears. "The London show was a huge success," said actress Marisa Berenson. "I mean, she got a standing ovation every night, and it was, you know, rave reviews." But the buzz surrounding Liza was about to turn sour. For forty years, Liza's ninety-five-year-old stepmother Lee lived in the Beverly Hills mansion she once shared with Liza's late father, Vincente Minnelli. In the director's will, he provided that his widow could live there for the rest of her life, then the house would be turned over to Liza. But Liza wanted to sell the six-bedroom home. In 1988, two years after Vincente's death, Lee and Liza entered into an agreement that allowed Liza to sell the house during Lee's lifetime as long as Liza provided Lee with alternative housing. By 2002, Liza was ready to put the house on the market, and her stepmother wasn't happy.

The actress was prepared to move her stepmother into a condominium near Beverly Hills, but Lee didn't want to leave the place she called home for forty years. In April 2002, a lawsuit was filed on behalf of Lee Minnelli, claiming breach of contract, infliction of emotional distress, and elder abuse. Liza denied all of the allegations against her. In a court hearing that May, Lee said that although she did not want to leave her house, she also didn't want to sue her stepdaughter. Consequently, the lawsuit was dismissed. In May 2002, Liza arrived in Los Angeles with her husband. The couple invited Liza's stepmother to a family dinner. The women reconciled their differences.

Liza Minnelli had kicked off her fifty-sixth year at the center of a three-ring media circus. The actress's every move was scrutinized and played out for public consumption. It was unclear whether the spotlight could bring her lasting happiness. Minnelli's latest tour, *Liza's Back*, brought her back into the city that never sleeps. In May 2002, she began her concert series in front of a sold-out crowd at the Beacon Theater in New York City. According to Liza's *Cabaret* cohort Joel Grey, it was "one of the greatest performers in the world doing what she does best." The rave reviews were welcomed by Liza, and by David Gest, who got double billing as Liza's husband and producer. For those fans who couldn't see the show, she recorded a live album of her performance. It was her first recording in three years.

"I'm so proud of it," Liza said. "I have never really been able to say that before. There was no going in and like fixing and doing it over. That was it. You know, I had to be that way at that moment."

The Liza phenomenon was happening all over again. In July 2002, she and David decided to give the Osbournes a run for their money. The couple signed a deal with VH-1 to star in their own reality series. "Ours is more a musical show about a showbiz couple, and it's reality in that it's real, but it's really a musical show," explained Gest. In October 2002, plans for the heavily promoted cable reality show *Liza and David* suddenly collapsed. Executives blamed production disputes on Liza's husband-producer while still expressing praise for her at the same time. On December 12, 2002, David Gest filed a million-dollar lawsuit against MTV Networks, which owns VH-1, for breach of contract and defamation. This time, he was in the headlines for fighting allegations that he was a control freak. "We lived up to our part of the contract. We were willing to do the show and are still willing to do the show, and the footage speaks for itself," he defended. MTV responded to Gest with its own multimillion-dollar countersuit that same month. In September 2003, both he and MTV dropped their lawsuits. Gest and VH-1 said in a joint statement that they had "amicably resolved their differences and withdrawn their respective lawsuits." No public disclosure was made on the terms of the settlement, if any.

Despite the controversy, the couple seemed happy. They even planned to adopt a three-year-old girl. But the headlines never let up. Handling the press wasn't easy. "They are going to write what they are going to write. We can't stop it," David Gest commented. "You know, today they wrote ridiculous things, I heard from people, and I just laugh it off because my wife is in the best shape she's ever been. She is sober. She is not drinking. She is preaching to the choir why not to drink, and regardless of whatever people say—make up—she is leading the fight for AA all over the world, and she is a great representative." On December 18, 2002, Liza Minnelli headlined at New York's Madison Square Garden in the extravaganza *Miracle on 34th Street*.

David Gest was right when he predicted the tabloids would continue to "write what they want to write." Despite Liza's optimism that he might be her lasting, lifelong love, the couple endured a nasty split when she filed for divorce in October 2003.

But for Liza Minnelli, the party is far from over. Four divorces and a barrage of bad press later, she's still standing, and all these setbacks are just bumps along the road. "She's had all these numerous horrendous things happen to her that if one of these things happened to one person, they'd be devastated already. Yet she keeps recovering and recovering," praised friend Lynn Wyatt. Liza has proven time and time again that she's a pro and a survivor. "I think part of Liza's story can be a cautionary tale—things to avoid. But it can always be an inspirational tale—the ways to survive, the ways to keep going despite the pitfalls, despite the tragedies. Just keep on going," summed up Michael Musto. So what's next for the legendary Liza? As she put it, to "go in my sobriety to serenity and all kind of things that I haven't had a lot of time for before. I would like to look at the sunset every night."

CHAPTER 6

LONE STAR STUNNER

The Anna Nicole Smith Story

"She was like, in many ways, the American Dream."

—*John Casablancas, founder, Elite Model Management*

S he was a big girl with big dreams, dreams so big even Texas couldn't hold her. She dreamed of getting out and going far. But did Anna Nicole Smith go too far? She was a poor teenager who went from fry cook to stripper to worldwide sex symbol. Plastic surgeons changed her body. A fashion mogul changed her name. Image builders rewrote her past and created an international icon of sex and style. Blessed with a stunning face, flawless skin, and traffic-stopping curves, Anna was also cursed with an appetite for sex, drugs, money, and, above all, trouble. Anna Nicole lived out her dreams. It was reality she couldn't deal with.

Who would have thought this small-town firecracker could soar to the top and crash to the depths of addiction and despair? On the way, Anna left behind a trail of broken hearts, including former boyfriend and bodyguard Clay Spires, who said he and Anna "loved hard. We played hard. We partied hard. And we fought hard." She captured the heart of elderly, multimillionaire J. Howard Marshall and became a widow, which embroiled her in a fierce contest for the Marshall estate with Marshall's son Pierce. Anna busted past the city limits of Mexia, Texas, and the walls of Gigi's Cabaret, popped out of the pages of *Playboy* and off billboards in Times Square. She was and still is a girl who cannot be tamed, and this is her story.

"I'm from a really small town. I have a really big family, but we grew up poor. I grew up on pinto beans and potatoes," said Anna

Nicole Smith. That small town was Mexia, Texas, population 7,000, which Anna claims as her home. Others, like Bob Wright of the *Mexia Daily News*, offer a different story. "Anna Nicole has probably claimed Mexia a little more than Mexia's claimed her, because" the rags-to-riches, small-town girl story is "just a little bit more poignant." Born in Houston, Anna (originally named Vickie Lynn Hogan on November 28, 1967) often stayed in Mexia with her aunt Elaine Tabers during her parents' divorce. She was a tomboy, "one of those girls that did not like to brush her hair," according to Tabers, but Anna had dreams of being in the spotlight. "She always wanted to be the center of attention, and when she was younger, I remember her telling us that she was going to be a movie star, and I didn't realize how true it could have been."

For the sixteen-year-old who would become America's newest glamazon—standing five feet eleven inches tall, and recapturing the brand of beauty of Marilyn Monroe and Jayne Mansfield—the road to celebrity was bumpy from the start. Anna's mother, Vergie, worked as a deputy sheriff. She was a no-nonsense lady, and she employed stiff rules at home. However, discipline and Anna didn't mix well, and she and her mother clashed. "Her and her mother had a disagreement, and she decided that the grass was greener on the other side, I guess. So she came to live with me," said Elaine Tabers.

Despite her thirst for fame, Anna's cousin Melinda Beall said, "In high school, nobody ever really paid attention to her," adding, "and she didn't like it." If they didn't like Vickie Hogan, the teenage Anna reasoned, maybe they'd like someone else. For her 1985 yearbook photo, she called herself Nikki Hart, linking her favorite nickname with the last name of her mother's second husband. The photo was shot when she was a sophomore. The next year, Anna dropped out of school. Uneducated and untrained, Anna took a job as a fry cook at Jim's Krispy Fried Chicken. Beall remembered, "She helped us. She worked. She was great, just like a sister. We'd kill for her chicken." Anna's bid for attention paid off in unexpected ways, and at seventeen, she fell for sixteen-year-old coworker Billy Smith. They were married, and nine months later Anna gave birth to a son, Daniel. Little Danny was not a healthy baby, according to Joe Thompson, who was married to Anna's mother at the time. "When he was six weeks old, he had a pretty bad bout, and he was in the hospital and suffered a lot of dehydration," which did not help the state of Anna's already failing marriage.

By the time she was nineteen, Anna was a divorcée and a single mom. "She moved in with us and just stayed in the trailer where we were living," said Joe Thompson. High school dropout, Anna worked at a series of minimum-wage jobs, struggling to make ends meet and to support her baby. "I worked at Wal-Mart. I've had jobs like Red Lobster and just little jobs," she said. While Elaine Tabers recalled, "I don't think she was making enough to actually get a place of her own," Anna was casually mentioning unreasonably big tips to her parents. Thompson remembered, "One day she was telling Vergie and I about the tips that she was making. She said that she'd made $300 in tips in a day. And I was telling Vergie that I know a lot of Red Lobster employees, but they don't make that kind of money." In reality, Anna had earned her big tips dancing at a topless club, an occupation she could not hide forever from her mother, the cop.

"I remember the day I came home from work and I opened the door to the house, and I could hear Vergie crying, I mean, just wailing," said Thompson. "And I didn't know what was going on. I come in the house. It ended up, she told me, that her and another deputy had gone to this place and had found Vickie in there and just literally almost drug her out and brought her home." Trying to defuse the situation, Thompson "kind of joked about it a little bit. I says, 'What do you want me to do? What can I do? You want me to go handcuff her to the bed? You know, she's a grown girl. She's going to do what she want to do.'" Attributing Anna's indiscretions to her unstable family life, Tabers said, "When I found out, I was shocked, because, you know, it just wasn't anything that was acceptable, and then, you know, I had to realize how desperate Vickie was, because I know what her upbringing had been."

Anna continued to bump and grind at topless clubs like Gigi's Cabaret. Regular cabaret-goer Bob Ferguson noted, "She was taller and had a little bit more of a big butt, and she didn't really feel secure with herself." Smith found that security in a makeover. Anna restyled her hair, changed her dance name to Robyn, and enlarged her bust size with the help of a plastic surgeon. Former coworker Ava Dawn said, "Quite honestly, after the first surgery, I didn't really know that she had had an augmentation, but she was average size, still blond, still beautiful. She always had a very beautiful face." Anna's smoke and mirrors were set up early, Ferguson said, "She informed everybody that her breasts were Texas-corn-fed, but everybody here knew they were silicone-fed."

While Anna spent her nights teasing strip-club patrons, family members took care of her five-year-old son. Claimed Joe Thompson, "I raised Danny from the time he was six weeks old. Me and his Memaw, as he called Vergie, practically had him the whole time. He would go to stay with Vickie during the day, but it started getting dark, and he would call us on the phone and say, 'Memaw, I got to come home.'" In 1990, Anna began dating a personal trainer named Clay Spires. The couple moved in together and lived in a small apartment in Houston. Her son stayed with his grandparents. During that time, Anna's profitable stripping career allowed the couple to feed their appetite for excess. Said Spires, "At the parties we used to have at our apartment, I should have charged rent for the things that went on in the back bedrooms. I could have made a lot of money if I had." He continued, "We all went by animal names, so they used to call this place the Zoo. I was the Wolf, and Anna was the White Panther. We'd have parties up to three or four in the morning. The alcohol flowed freely. People got a little crazy."

Excessive with her partying, her career, and her body, Smith was arrested three times for drunk driving between 1989 and 1990. She underwent another breast enlargement in 1990, but complications arose in all sectors of her life. The day after her surgery, she developed a severe fever, and the doctor told her she had an infection. Said Clay Spires, "They had to remove the actual sac of the breast, so she went three weeks with just one breast. Of course, you can imagine the psychological trauma of that happening." Anna's health problems didn't slow her down, though. For the voluptuous Texan, too much was never enough. Said fellow dancer Pamela Ann, "One thing that I can remember about her most was the day she got fired, and I'm sure she probably won't like hearing this, but she fell off the stage, and it was kind of a joke around here for quite a lot of years." In 1991, after four years of chaos and craziness on the Houston topless circuit, Anna was among the best-known and best-paid strippers in the area. Her fast-lane lifestyle was zooming full speed ahead.

Before she ended her tenure at Gigi's Cabaret, Anna also gained the attention of a much older oil tycoon named J. Howard Marshall. According to Marshall family attorney Don Jackson, "Mr. Marshall was a remarkable and a fascinating man in character. He was born in 1905 in Philadelphia to a Quaker family, attended Quaker high school and Quaker college, and then from there went on to Yale law school." By 1952, the Yankee blueblood settled in Texas, where he made his fortune in the oil business. Marshall was known as a wheeler and dealer and became a self-made millionaire by the age of forty-seven. Married twice, with two sons, the Texas oilman liked the company of women, especially a flamboyant stripper by the name of Lady Walker, who set the gold standard for later mistresses, like Anna. Marshall and Lady Walker met in 1982. By all reports, the brunette was a colorful character on the Houston social scene, and the two were often seen dining together at posh locales around town. Cars and jewelry were among the many lavish gifts Marshall reportedly gave his mistress. Said Houston gossip columnist Betty Parish, "I heard from waiters that one day at lunch, they saw Mr. Marshall hand her a check for $1 million."

Anna and Marshall's relationship was forged from tragedy. In

1991, in the span of a month, the millionaire lost his second wife to Alzheimer's, and his mistress died unexpectedly from a congenital brain defect during plastic surgery. Marshall was devastated and lonely. One afternoon, the oil tycoon's driver tried to cheer his boss up by taking him to Gigi's strip club. Anna was dancing, and Marshall was mesmerized. The unlikely pair hit it off immediately. Recounted Clay Spires, "We were living together when she first met Mr. Marshall, and the next day he wanted to take her on a shopping spree at the Galleria, and she asked me if that would be all right. At that time in our relationship I didn't feel threatened by that at all." Anna continued dating Spires but developed a close relationship with her new sugar daddy. "I can hear Mr. Marshall saying, 'Honey, you're the light of my life.' She never went back to stripping, because he took care of her from that point on," said Elaine Tabers.

Living in the lap of luxury suited Anna, but the price was an escalating affair with Marshall, who was more than sixty years her senior. Marshall reportedly first asked Anna to marry him in 1992. Anna turned down the offer more than once. Tabers claimed Anna had good intentions: "She'd say, 'I don't want them to think that I'm marrying you for your money, because I want them to know that I love you and you love me, and I don't want them to think it's just the money,'" adding that Anna would also assert, "I want to have my own career. I want to be established." The buxom blonde was definitely determined to make a name for herself.

When Clay Spires showed Anna an ad looking for *Playboy* models, her eyes lit up. "She was excited at the start with it and wanted to do it, but after canceling two appointments, she was ready to back out of a third," he recalled. "Basically, we pulled her out of bed, got her dressed, put her in the car, and brought her to the audition." Photographer Eric Redding and his stylist wife D'Eva had placed the ad. Eric said, "She was very nervous, and she was shaking. I talked to her for thirty minutes and helped her fill out her bio and all that. She was holding on to my hand, sweating to death and trembling." However, D'Eva was certain from the start that she and Eric had found their first centerfold. She remembered, "I said, 'Once we send this photo off, that's it. They are going to love her face.' It didn't matter about the body." D'Eva was right. Within days, a *Playboy* editor called the Reddings and asked them to shoot a full-scale test with Anna. To capitalize on Anna's "natural" talent, they found an outdoor location. D'Eva offered, "When we started with her, she was really a natural. I mean, the light was beautiful. Her hair, her skin—it all started working, and we all knew it. It was just incredible. She was just magic." The Redding's experience with Anna led them to later author a book about her, called *Great Big Beautiful Doll*.

Following the test shoot, Anna was flown to Los Angeles for more photos. *Playboy* executives loved Anna's look and commissioned a shoot for the magazine. Anna made the March 1992 cover, posing as a debutante—quite a stretch from selling fried chicken. Two months later, Anna was featured as Miss May 1992, "The Lone Star Stunner." In less than a year, Anna Nicole Smith (still under the Vickie Lynn Hogan moniker) hopped from stripper to *Playboy* superstar. The photos grabbed the attention of powerful image shapers who could turn her into a fashion phenomenon around the world. After seeing Anna in the May issue, Paul Marciano, head of the Guess? clothing empire, considered making her the model in a groundbreaking ad campaign for Guess? Jeans. Marciano made Anna no promises but flew to Texas to meet her and introduced her to the Guess? line by buying her some clothes at the local shopping mall. Before meeting Marciano, Anna had never heard of Guess? clothing.

Paul Marciano found his newest Guess? pinup girl in *Playboy*'s cover girl. He changed her name from Vickie Lynn Hogan to Anna Nicole Smith and gave her a makeover by Hollywood stylist Laurent DeFourg. DeFourg envisioned an image informed by retro glamour. "I decided she would be beautiful with some kind of like Jayne Mansfield feeling, because, I mean, I think she looked like Jayne Mansfield and Marilyn Monroe, these pinups from the fifties. We did one shot in the salon with a famous photographer. Then they used that picture all over the campaign for the beginning of Guess?" In early 1993, the Guess? campaign exploded overnight. The ads placed Anna at the peak of the high-fashion pyramid. She even landed an agent at Elite, the prestigious New York City modeling agency run by John Casablancas. Casablancas himself described Anna as "in many ways, the American dream, which was contrary to everything in modeling at the time."

Anna made an immediate impression. Stylist Gareth Green said, "As a supermodel, let's face it, she wasn't the stereotype: six feet tall, beanpole, plain-faced supermodel. She was a *full-fledged woman*." Public relations guru David Granoff said, "She'd bring her Marilyn Monroe tapes along, and she'd play 'Diamonds Are a Girl's Best Friend,' boogie down, and just get into the whole thing." In 1993, Hugh Hefner awarded Anna *Playboy*'s highest honor, naming her "Playmate of the Year." Anna's resemblance to Marilyn Monroe was one reason she was chosen. "Whether it's charisma or light or love, there's a light that shines from her," offered Green. "She had it all." There was no stopping Anna Nicole Smith.

But as Anna's biggest dreams were being fulfilled, those closest to her were left behind. "We broke up once she started doing a lot of traveling with *Playboy* and with her Guess? promotional tours," said Clay Spires. "Her behavior changed, and we had a lot of problems. I just couldn't deal with men calling all the time." Smith jetted across the country for publicity appearances and photo shoots. Anna also made brief stops in Houston to visit J. Howard Marshall. As the model's popularity soared, Anna's seven-year-old son Daniel was exposed to his mother's new lifestyle. Some, like Eric Redding, were uncomfortable: "Anna would run around nude in front of her son, and she thought that it was a natural thing for your children to see their parents nude." He cited an example in 1991, when she gave nude test Polaroids to Daniel and said, "Look, Mommy's going to be in *Playboy*!" When

Redding suggested that wasn't good for a little boy, Anna retorted, "It's a natural thing. It's normal. Let him do it." Anna's family in Texas began to see the last signs of Vickie Lynn Hogan slipping away.

For a while, some of Anna's newfound fortune found its way to cousin Melinda Beall and Anna's relatives in Mexia. Said Beall, "She helped us with the bills, and at one point, when my mom needed a car, Anna bought her that car." In return, Anna made certain demands, and her hard-up family eventually complied. Beall said that Anna requested that she and Beall's mother show their love for Anna by getting tattoos of her face on their bodies. Aunt Kay and Melinda both gave in to Anna's peer pressure to get a tattoo dedicated to her. Despite her family's devotion, Anna did not contact Melinda or her Mexia family for years. Said Melinda, "I wish she would come home and visit us or something. I'd really like to see her." But Mexia was a long way from the limelight Anna always craved.

In 1993, at the peak of her popularity, twenty-six-year-old Anna was more than a model. Adoring fans worshipped her like a voluptuous goddess of sex and celebrity. Gareth Green saw the phenomenon firsthand during a New York rooftop shoot. "Toward the middle to the end of the shoot, we looked up," he said, "and in every single window, there's people hanging out and then they start screaming. They're chanting her name." On more distant shores, a near riot by fans at a Hong Kong mall led to a frantic late-night call to Anna's publicist, David Granoff. "I pick up the phone and she said, 'David, you're never going to believe it,' and she said how windowpanes are being broken, people are being hurt trying just to touch her, and ripping her clothes." With so much hype and high energy around her, Hollywood was eager to test Anna's box office appeal and see if she could put the same excitement on the screen.

In 1993, Anna's small role in *The Hudsucker Proxy* led to a bigger part in *Naked Gun 33⅓*. But as the model's film career was taking off, signs of trouble were starting to surface. According to

Granoff, "I felt that she was experiencing some inner turmoil. She didn't seem as happy as she should." He reasoned, "Basically, coming from nothing and then becoming one of the most sensational women in the world, being written about, covered, photographed, invited to parties, and so forth. It was very difficult to come from zero and go to ten, which is what she did." Elaine Tabers agreed, "You couldn't go out in the yard of Anna's house, because people were coming, popping over the fence, and taking pictures."

As quickly as Anna's dream life came together, her world started to crumble. The model struggled with juggling a career and caring for her son, Daniel. To help ease the stress, Anna hired a nanny, Maria Cerrato. After working for Anna for five months in 1993, she quit abruptly one evening. According to legal documents, she allegedly tried to take Daniel with her. Police were called to intervene. Five months later, Cerrato's attorney sent a letter claiming that Anna sexually assaulted the nanny in a hotel room during a trip to Las Vegas. Cerrato demanded $2 million, but Smith fired back by suing Cerrato for slander and accusing her of the attempted kidnapping of Daniel. Countersuing, Cerrato retaliated with a suit claiming sexual harassment, assault, and wrongful termination. Less than two weeks later, Anna was rushed from the Peninsula Hotel in Beverly Hills to Los Angeles' Cedars-Sinai Medical Center. Police reports stated that she and a man named Daniel Ross, her companion at the hotel, overdosed on tequila and prescription pills. Anna spent three days in the hospital. The double-barreled blast of bad publicity sent her modeling career into a tailspin. Then, in August 1994, *New York* magazine ran an unflattering cover of Anna. The model sued, saying the photo made her look like a cream puff. The suit was later settled out of court. Guess? chief Paul Marciano cut all ties to the model, and Anna's modeling agency couldn't book her on jobs. Summarized John Casablancas, "I think we got a good amount of results from Anna but not for very long."

In late 1994, a new face appeared in Anna's entourage, a bodyguard named Pierre deJean. Many close to Anna saw this as one more sign that her fortunes were fading. Tabers said, "I did not like that man." Pierre had charm, but he also had a criminal record. During their short-lived professional relationship, deJean claimed not only to be Anna's bodyguard but also her lover, which she denied.

With her modeling career in shambles, and her personal life in turmoil, the one constant was her relationship with J. Howard Marshall. The pair frequently spoke on the phone, and he supported her financially. "Anna cared about Mr. Marshall," commented Clay Spires. "She cared about him in a way that you and I would care about our grandfather or grandmother. There's no doubt that she had feelings for him."

"J. Howard Marshall probably would have given the shirt off his back for anyone that he actually cared about, and he did care about Anna very much, and he cared about her son," speculated Eric Redding. "But to say she cared back? No. It was more like a grandfather, not like a lover or a husband."

After seeing each other on and off for almost four years, Anna Nicole Smith and J. Howard Marshall decided to tie the knot. Even though the engagement raised a few eyebrows, those closest to the pair believed their affection for each other was genuine. Or at least genuinely beneficial. Said Elaine Tabers, "I think it was like a mutual agreement: beauty for money, money for beauty. I mean, not to say that they didn't love each other, but there was an understanding between them."

In a less-than-romantic, spur-of-the-moment wedding, Anna and Howard arranged a ceremony at the White Dove Chapel in Houston. On June 27, 1994, Aunt Elaine helped calm Anna's prewedding jitters. She claimed Anna doubted her ability to go through with the wedding, but ultimately wrote off her cold feet, saying, "I'm just nervous." Marshall was less apprehensive about the nuptials. Tabers remembered him saying, "I can't believe she wanted to marry me." The bride wore a 22-carat diamond ring on her finger. At twenty-seven years old, she was sixty-two years younger than her groom.

Immediately after the ceremony, Anna took off on a modeling assignment, accompanied by bodyguard Pierre deJean. Marshall was left alone on his wedding night. Recalled Eric Redding, "Anna had told J. Howard Marshall that she had a photo shoot in Greece immediately following the ceremony. So she left him right there at the chapel in his wheelchair." Tabers corroborated, "He had tears in his eyes, because, I think, he wanted to spend more time with her. He wanted to spend more quality time with her than just the wedding."

Regardless of the bumpy start, J. Howard's affection for Anna did not waver, and he continued to shower her with gifts. Over the next year, Anna and Marshall never lived together. Still, the older man spoiled his new wife by buying her homes in Texas and California as well as many other luxuries. According to Tabers, "She had a Mercedes. She had a ranch. He bought that and paid cash for it—all the furnishings, three Arabian horses, a Ford Duley, motorcycles, four-wheelers . . ." Although Marshall reportedly discussed a prenuptial agreement with his lawyers, the documents were never finalized. Marshall's attorney said, "He had intended to have these prenuptial agreements signed before he married Anna Nicole Smith if that day ever came. He got married, and there was no prenuptial agreement executed, so he called and wanted to know what we could do to achieve the same benefits and the same effects that the prenuptial agreement would have accomplished." Marshall's attorneys told him the best option would be to make his will irrevocable, meaning Marshall could make no further changes to the document. Two weeks after marrying Anna, Marshall finalized his will. Anna was not named in the document.

J. Howard Marshall's new bride knew nothing about these arrangements as they were made. Smith had her own issues to worry about. In late 1994, she was reportedly hospitalized once again for a problem with one of her breast implants. Although medical records were sealed, Spires said Anna had chronic trouble with her implants. "She developed such pain and such an infection once again. It would swell up so much it would almost touch her chin. She had to be helped in and out of bed even to get up and use the restroom." Anna's doctors prescribed pain medication, which, Clay Spires claimed, began to take a toll on her behavior. "Basically, due to her problems from cosmetic surgeries, she developed a pattern of mixing and matching different types of prescription drugs. And that, of course, affected her behavior patterns."

After recovering, Anna focused on her professional life. But by 1995, just two years after being named "Playmate of the Year," Anna couldn't find work. While her career stalled, her social life was going full-speed ahead. "Generally, she was, you know, just having too good a time, and I think that was her problem," offered David Granoff. Anna's partying helped spark a noticeable weight gain. Said Spires, "She just pushed everything to an extreme. She did that in the little things in her life. She did that in the big things. She did that in her eating habits. She did that in going out and drinking." Eric Redding thought that Anna's state of mind also contributed to her extreme behavior. "She got depressed and started drinking more, and she started doing more medication. Plus, she's a late-night binge eater. She loves to eat at midnight, things like Taco Bell and Burger King. Because she ate late at night, she would put on weight. I mean, she was eighty to a hundred pounds overweight." Following her weight gain, Smith could no longer pose in couture fashion.

Instead, Anna modeled clothing for Lane Bryant, a clothing store chain for full-figured women. In 1995, with few options, she made two low-budget films, neither of which boded well for her prospects as an actress. Anna played a helicopter pilot in the straight-to-video movie *Skyscraper*. Richard Steinmetz, her costar in the film, admitted, "The acting is on a certain level. I mean, you're not talking Shakespeare or Chekhov or anything like that." About her next movie, *To the Limit*, Anna commented, "Filming was wonderful. The adrenaline was pumping, and I was raring to go, and I'm chasing cars and people are knocking me out. We're having a wonderful time. It's going to be a brilliant movie." The movie was not well received, and also went direct to video.

Despite her career problems, Anna Nicole Smith still made headlines. A spat with Pierre deJean led to a bitter split. On December 12, 1994, police were called to her Los Angeles home after deJean repeatedly tried to contact her. Anna then asked Clay Spires to act as her new bodyguard. About deJean, Spires said, "He would call thirty or forty times a day. He would come to the house and hop the fence and set off the alarms two or three times a day just to irritate her. She feared for her life. We probably had anywhere from eight to ten guns in the house at any time." He continued, "Basically, all he was trying to do was cause conflict and problems in her life because of the relationship that they had had before." Anna got a restraining order to keep deJean away, but she was convinced that she lost work because of the blizzard of bad publicity. By 1995, she was in personal hell, but even worse times lay ahead. The health of Anna's ninety-year-old husband was fading as fast as her career.

Anna's high-speed, no-limits, party lifestyle pushed her body to the breaking point. In the spring of 1995, the former Playmate was reportedly hospitalized for depression. Said Elaine Tabers, "She stayed depressed. I mean, she cried a lot. I don't know if it was her job or always being in the press no matter where she went, no matter what she did." As Anna battled emotional problems, husband J. Howard Marshall continued to deteriorate. He was hospitalized with pneumonia. His son Pierce worried about his ailing father. According to Marshall family attorney Don Jackson, "Mr. Marshall became sick to the point where he needed somebody to make healthcare decisions for him. Pierce filed a petition to be appointed guardian so that he could be there to make those healthcare decisions and to look after his father."

But Anna believed that, as J. Howard Marshall's wife, she should be her husband's guardian. The former stripper filed a separate petition for guardianship. During this time, Anna claimed that Pierce hired guards who would not leave her alone with her husband. Attorney Glenn Johnson was appointed by a judge to evaluate J. Howard's need for a guardian. Johnson remembered, "I wanted to meet with Mr. Marshall and Anna Nicole Smith in private, just the three of us. I still couldn't get the guard to leave the room, and that was after we succeeded in ultimately getting into the house. So I think they were there at Pierce Marshall's instructions to assist in enforcing this very strict visitation."

Smith also claimed Pierce cut her off completely from the monthly allowance she received from Howard. Anna was accustomed to having her bills paid by her husband's company, Marshall Petroleum Industries, also known as MPI. However, new ownership at MPI issued a direct hit to her wallet. Said Jackson, "Pierce, who at that time was president of MPI, had to take over things. The staff at MPI had been burdened with having to pay her bills, which were sometimes huge, especially credit card bills."

After Pierce's hands-off policy took effect, Anna became desperate. She alleged that his actions resulted in her utilities being turned off. Pierce's lawyers denied those claims. "There was never a month during the entire time of the marriage where her account, where her personal bank accounts, had less than $50,000 in them," said Don Jackson. "Why in the world would your utilities be cut off if you've got $50,000 or more, sometimes hundreds of thousands of dollars, in the bank to write a check on?" On August 2, 1995, Anna appeared on *The Howard Stern Show* and explained her feelings for her husband. "It's appreciation for him getting me out of the gutter, for him helping me and my son," she reasoned. To which Stern asked, "It's more like a medical thing?" and she responded, "I love him. I love him for it." Howard Stern wasn't convinced, asking, "Really?" Anna Nicole Smith simply responded, "I would never marry anybody unless something had happened to him."

According to Anna's former manager, Joyce Wagner, "She told me how much she loved him. She has a tattoo in a private place with 'Papa' on it, which was her nickname for him. And she had a photo by her bed." Likewise, J. Howard Marshall kept a photo of Anna close by his bed. Remembered Clay Spires, "He had a large, wall-size picture of Anna in one of her Guess? shots on the wall at the end of his bed so he could look at it when he woke up in the morning and when he went to sleep at night." When Anna visited her elderly husband, she had a special way of comforting him. "She would baby-talk to J. Howard Marshall, and that's what would really send him off, and she learned that from her topless dancing days," remembered Eric Redding. "She'd go, 'Oh, hey, Howy,' and she had this little soft voice. He liked it."

Even though Anna didn't see her husband often, Marshall was in her thoughts. In 1995, when a reporter asked Anna, "If you were stranded on a desert island, who would you want to be with?" The glamour girl was true to her husband, saying, "Let me think, probably right now, right now I would want my husband there with me because he's not feeling too well." By July 1995, J. Howard's health situation was grave. His private nurse, Letitia Hunt, recalled, "Mr. Marshall had been ill for a while. He was ill the entire time for the last four or five months of his life." Don Jackson agreed, "He was in a very weakened physical condition. He had good days and bad days."

During the five months Letitia Hunt cared for Marshall, she rarely saw Anna. The couples' contact consisted mainly of phone conversations. Said Hunt, "He wanted to talk to her any time that she called, and so, he was happy to see her when she came. I only saw her the two times, but he was happy to see her." J. Howard's nurses were under strict orders not to leave Anna alone with her husband. According to *Houston Chronicle* reporter Bill Murphy, "Sometimes Anna would feed him things that he shouldn't be fed.

There was an incident involving chicken soup, and he began choking, and he ended up in the hospital." Hunt said, "I think there was a fear that Mr. Marshall might be hurt [by her] in some way." During Marshall's last days, Anna was at her Los Angeles home. "The whole month of July, before he died, she was there, even the last week. He was in the hospital, and the last day I was beside his bed when he took his last breath. That should have been her to experience those times with him," said Hunt.

On August 4, 1995, J. Howard Marshall II died in Houston. Anna was in a limousine in Los Angeles when she received the news. Even before Marshall's body was buried, the three-way tug-of-war over his money began, proving as Anna herself has said that "marrying into money was not a good thing for me." On one side was Marshall's younger son, Pierce. On another side was his wife of fourteen months, Anna Nicole Smith. Lastly, Marshall's elder, estranged son, Howard Jr., staked his claim. The lawsuit would be the biggest fight in Texas since the Alamo. After J. Howard Marshall's death, Pierce planned to have his father cremated in keeping with the family's Quaker beliefs. But J. Howard's grieving widow had other plans.

Said Eric Redding, "Anna wanted to have J. Howard Marshall brought out to her ranch, have him put out by the pool, and have a party, and everyone to come pay their last respects. Of course, that didn't go over so well with Pierce, so they had two separate ceremonies." At Anna's service, she shocked fellow mourners by wearing a low-cut white dress and a veil. She honored her late husband by singing "Wind Beneath My Wings" while her small dog roamed the aisles. Letitia Hunt described the scene: "The little dog was running around the coffin, you know, and she sang. There was somebody with a white grand piano, chandeliers, rings on every finger," emphasizing, "it was hilarious. It was like Liberace, and then she ran out real dramatically during the end of the funeral." A few days later, Pierce Marshall held another service for his father. That memorial was a stark contrast to Anna's wild shindig. Said Hunt, "The people who were close to Mr. Marshall during the years came to Pierce's ceremony and made comments about his father. It was really about Mr. Marshall. I think her ceremony was more about her."

But Anna and Pierce still couldn't agree on how to inter the body, so they turned to a Houston court for help. Marshall family attorney, Jeff Chambers, said, "She said that she had converted to Catholicism and that Catholicism did not allow cremation. It had always been Mr. Marshall's intent to be cremated, and the family wanted to see his wishes carried out. She waged a battle, and the judge, in Solomon-esque fashion, split the ashes between them." For Anna and Pierce Marshall, splitting the ashes was one thing. Splitting millions of dollars was another matter. Said Chambers, "Pierce did a simple thing that you have to do when someone dies. He filed the will for probate. In return, he got two will contests, one from Anna and one from the disinherited brother." Pierce was confident he was entitled to the entire estate. According to Pierce, J. Howard disinherited his other son, J. Howard Marshall Jr., who was exiled from the family after he allegedly betrayed his father in a corporate takeover attempt. Pierce claimed that from then on, Howard Jr. was left out of the will. Don Jackson affirmed, "Mr. Marshall specifically included a provision that said, 'I am intentionally disinheriting J. Howard Marshall III, and I intend for him and his issue to receive nothing from my estate.' It was very clear."

Perhaps a more legitimate contest to the will came from Anna, who claimed that J. Howard Marshall promised her that, if she married him, he would give her half of everything he owned. After her husband's death, however, Anna learned of the new will and claimed Pierce was up to no good. Pierce said that the decision had been his father's, and the action merely finalized already existing estate plans which had been set long before Anna came into the picture. Pierce Marshall's public relations representative David Margulies said, "In Texas, getting married doesn't give you half. Mr. Marshall put his stock—which was the bulk of his wealth—in a separate property trust years and years ago, when she was probably still eight or nine years old, and she wasn't going to get that whether they got married or not."

The fight over J. Howard Marshall's estate created an unusual alliance between Anna and Marshall's estranged son, noted Bill Murphy. "She joined with J. Howard Marshall III, suing Pierce Marshall, and both of them say essentially the same thing—that Pierce Marshall blocked them from collecting inheritances." Anna hired Houston attorney Diana Marshall (no relation to the Marshall family). In August of 1995, Diana Marshall implied to a reporter that Pierce had manipulated his elderly father into making the last-minute will change. Said Pierce's attorney Jeff Chambers, "The comments of Ms. Smith's attorney in the *Houston Chronicle* implied that Mr. Marshall couldn't read when a blizzard of documents were put in front of him and that the blizzard of documents had given control of his fortune to Pierce Marshall solely." Pierce sued Anna's lawyers for defamation, but that was just the beginning of Anna's legal woes.

The trouble with her former nanny, Maria Cerrato, was still brewing in the courts. On September 29, 1995, a Los Angeles judge awarded Cerrato $800,000 because of Anna's repeated failure to participate in the legal process. Anna was buckling under the pressure. Over the years, former boyfriend Clay Spires witnessed Anna's depression and use of painkillers, including a time when Anna thought a photo of Marilyn Monroe had come to life. Recounted Spires, "[She thought] it was trying to suck her into it, and she was seeing devils again. She was given . . . a Christian handbook, and was singing songs like 'Onward, Christian Soldiers,' trying to keep all these devils from coming and getting her." Redding agreed with Anna's closest friends who were concerned about her use of painkillers and booze to cope with the pressures in her life, saying, "She was taking probably twelve to fifteen prescription medications there back in the midnineties and, on top of that, drinking champagne, vodka, whatever it was. It took a lot to make her feel good."

In November 1995, Anna Nicole Smith was rushed to St.

Joseph's Hospital in Los Angeles. Her publicist said that prescription painkillers were the cause. Her attorney Diana Marshall did some creative damage control, announcing: "She has in the past had situations where migraine headaches would evolve into something that resembled a seizure, and she was under doctor's orders to go to the hospital immediately if that occurred." After being released from the hospital, Anna immediately checked into the Betty Ford Center.

Her problems continued to escalate. In January 1996, Anna filed for bankruptcy in Los Angeles. She claimed she was broke and that Pierce Marshall had cut her off from any family money, and found the ammunition to fire back at the stepson who had kicked her to the curb. "She countersued Pierce Marshall in bankruptcy court, saying, 'I'm bankrupt because of you, Pierce. I'm bankrupt because you prevented me from getting half the estate. That's what my late husband, J. Howard Marshall II, promised me. He said I would get half of what he had, and the reason why I'm now in bankruptcy court is because of you, mean old Pierce,'" reported Bill Murphy.

The bankruptcy court judge, Samuel Bufford, decided that, in order to resolve Anna's financial problems, he needed to examine her deceased husband's estate plans. "Now, the question is, Why should a bankruptcy court hear a probate matter, an inheritance matter?" asked Murphy. "They're always ultimately heard in state probate court, and so he ultimately says, 'I do have jurisdictional grounds. This guy Pierce voluntarily came into my court and allowed me to assert jurisdiction over this case.'"

While Anna's legal soap opera played out, her career and personal life continued to deteriorate. "She wasn't America's sex symbol anymore, and she was very heavy," offered Eric Redding. "But she didn't want to admit it. She was in denial. I mean, everyone kept confronting her to lose the weight, but she didn't even think she was overweight." Writer Joyce Wagner, who eventually became Anna's manager, thought Anna's life would make an interesting book and requested a meeting with her. Wagner remembered, "My first impression of her was, This is unbelievable. The woman was heavyset, slovenly, no makeup. She walked in, sort of schlepping her feet." Although the book deal never panned out, Wagner was intrigued by the possibility of helping twenty-nine-year-old Anna regain her former glory.

"She was extremely depressed, and she was engaged in a battle that she saw as the battle of her life with her ninety-year-old late husband's son over a lot of money. She felt persecuted and besieged," said Wagner. "She had lain in her house in Bel Air and popped bonbons for months. She said to me, with her little-girl voice, 'I just prayed to God that I'd get a second chance, because I know that I made a lot of mistakes. I did it wrong, and I'd give anything to have another chance to do it right.'" Joyce Wagner offered to act as Anna's new manager, which Anna gladly accepted. "We started working on goals such as losing weight, not drinking, staying at the house, and not talking to the tabloids," said Wagner. But just as Anna's life was on the upswing, the former model slipped again.

"She was looking great. Everything was positive," commented Wagner. "We had a contract for the European market, which would have paid her a great deal of money, and all of a sudden she announced one day she was going to Europe under mysterious circumstances. She didn't want to tell me what it was about, who was booking it—nothing." Anna did press interviews that were not approved by Wagner, and the manager-client relationship between the two women ended abruptly. "She destroyed almost every relationship she ever had, including the one with *Playboy*. She destroyed the relationship she had with Guess? Jeans. There have been a number of good people—and I like to include myself in that group—who have sincerely tried to be of assistance and help her. And she has wound up driving a stake through their hearts and never realizing that it's her. It's her."

During the two years following J. Howard Marshall's death, Anna Nicole Smith fell into a deep depression, binging on fast food and alcohol. Determined to get in shape both emotionally and physically, Anna went on a successful crash diet. In December 1997, E! Entertainment Television awarded Anna a Golden Hanger Award for Biggest Fashion Breakthrough for 1997. Said she, "It's the first thing I've ever won from Hollywood, so it's my Oscar. I'm shaking. I'm so excited."

A few months later, Anna was in trouble once again. The fiery blonde was arrested at the Beverly Hills Hotel for allegedly assaulting a hotel employee. However, the district attorney's office dropped the charges due to lack of evidence. Despite Anna's public relations problems, the onetime model still had her adoring fans. In April 1998, she was crowned Miss Republic of Cuervo Gold. Reps for the liquor company said that Anna's party spirit won them over. Anna made headlines again in the summer of 1998, with the release of a steamy video titled *Anna Nicole: Exposed*, which Anna described as "Well, a typical day in the life of Anna Nicole Smith." By late 1998, Anna said she was tired of constantly being the target of bad press. She fought back and started SASS, Stars Against Scandals, an organization designed to help celebrities embroiled in high-profile mishaps. "Stars Against Scandals, with an extra 's' included, was formed because there seems to be so, so many scandals," Anna explained. "Our goal is simple: to defend the honor of the celebrities and politicians who have been dragged through the mud, those who have gone from the White House to the Walk of Fame to the Nowhere Hall of Shame."

Still, the bad press surrounding Anna continued unabated. Later that month, Pierce Marshall's defamation lawsuit against Anna's attorney Diana Marshall went to trial. On August 14, 1998, the jury announced the decision. Reported Pierce's attorney Jeff Chambers, "The jury found in our favor, found that Pierce Marshall had been libeled and slandered, and awarded him eight and a half million dollars." The bad blood between Anna and Pierce was far from over. The big showdown was yet to come. In October 1999, Anna and Pierce squared off in a Los Angeles bankruptcy court. The press couldn't wait to catch the latest word from the weepy widow. Asked one reporter, "Where are you getting all your emotional strength through all this?" Anna responded, "Oh, Lord up above." Los Angeles reporter and legal analyst Manny Medrano remembered, "When Anna Nicole Smith would arrive and depart from the federal courthouse, you would have thought it was the president of the United States, because of the media coverage."

Medrano hailed Anna's chutzpah: "No matter how tough the cross-examination by Pierce's lawyers, she stuck to her guns. The accusations that were flying back and forth from both sides, I mean, there was a lot of venom there. So you put that whole ball together, and it made for some incredible court action." Anna's attorney Philip Boesch appeared confident. "The writings that we showed the judge and that we're introducing as evidence are confirmation of written instructions to Howard's lawyers to make sure that Vickie receives half the appreciation of his assets." The question the court grappled with was whether Pierce interfered with any inheritance Anna might be entitled to, an estimated half billion dollars. After the trial, the bankruptcy judge Samuel Bufford delayed his ruling to avoid influencing the Houston probate proceeding, which wasn't scheduled to start for another year.

Plus-size clothing manufacturer Lane Bryant took advantage of their model's high profile. In August 2000, Anna appeared, larger than life, on a Lane Bryant billboard in Times Square. "I want to be a leader, not a follower, for full-figured women," said Anna at the time, "and I love Lane Bryant. I've had a history with them, and they've always been good to me." On September 27, 2000, Anna was ready for round two of her legal battle with the Marshall family. The jet-set model was ushered into the Houston probate court. "On the day the trial started, Anna looked like a goddess," recalled Eric Redding. "She was dressed all in black. Her hair was immaculate. Her makeup was immaculate. She looked beautiful. On a scale of one to ten, she was definitely an eleven or a twelve, and any time she walked into the courtroom, everybody was mesmerized by her." Juror Regina Mitchell described her initial reaction to Anna, saying, "In the beginning, when I saw her, I thought she was just so beautiful, and I thought, 'You know, everybody deserves something. If they're trying to do her wrong, then let's see what's going on, and it's her word against theirs. Let's see what they've got.'"

Redding analyzed Pierce's stern, traditional appearance in those first days of the trial. "Pierce Marshall came in looking like the bad guy. A lot of people perceived him as being a money-hungry son." J. Howard Jr. and Anna said that they both received verbal promises from J. Howard Sr. that they would inherit part of his estate. Then, two days into the Houston trial, Los Angeles bankruptcy judge Samuel Bufford dropped a bombshell. Despite his promise to delay his ruling, Bufford awarded Anna a staggering $475 million, saying she was deprived of her late husband's estate. Summed up Manny Medrano, "He concluded that Anna Nicole Smith had an expectation of an inheritance and that Pierce Marshall interfered with that. It was on that basis that he awarded this enormous award to Anna Nicole Smith." Pierce and his attorneys were stunned and outraged. "I'm shocked that a judge would issue an order that would create any publicity while a jury's being picked over the same matter," groused Pierce Marshall's attorney Rusty Hardin.

Houston judge Mike Wood tried to shield his court from the Los Angeles decision and move forward with the probate trial. On October 2, Anna's attorney Tom Cunningham made his opening statement. Cunnigham appealed to the jury's basic notions of right and wrong within the bonds of marital fidelity. "Mrs. Marshall says, and she will tell you from the witness stand herself, 'He told me he loved me, that he wanted to marry me, that he wanted to take care of me and my son and give us security, and he promised me half of everything that he had, that he wanted to always take care of me.'" Cunningham then pointed the finger at Pierce Marshall: "We're going to see that Mr. Pierce Marshall suggested his motive was to take care of Mrs. Marshall up until J. Howard Marshall II died and then throw her into the gutter." Rusty

Hardin fired back: "Keep in mind what this case is about. These two people say they had oral agreements with J. Howard Marshall II that he didn't put in writing, that they have no witnesses for, and that they have no evidence for. This is not a woman who loved him, I would suggest, but a woman who took tremendous advantage of him."

Pierce Marshall was first on the stand. Detailed Eric Redding, "He was very calm, cool, and collected. He knew what the facts were, and he came across very well to the jury." In early October, Anna came to court with her left arm heavily bandaged. Smith's attorney said she dropped a dumbbell on her wrist while working out. "She seemed to be in a lot of pain, to the point where she had to lie down during one of the breaks," recalled Regina Mitchell. "She would come for like a week, and then you might not see her for another two or three weeks, so we didn't know when Vickie was going to show up. It was her case, but she wasn't going to be there." On October 10, 2000, Anna was admitted into the hospital. Smith asked for and received the powerful pain medications morphine, Dilaudid, and Demerol. Some thought Anna's two-week hospital stay was all an act. Pierce hired neurologist Dr. Stanton Moldovan to examine Anna. At the time, Dr. Moldovan concluded, "There is no reason for her to be on intravenous narcotic treatment. She probably didn't need to be in the hospital beyond the first day." Redding also withheld sympathy for the beleaguered Anna. "Yes, her wrist was sprained," he conceded, "but it would be like if you broke your leg. You would still go to work. She just didn't want to be there."

Then, on January 5, 2001, in a stunning turnaround, Anna announced she was pulling out of the probate trial. According to Anna's attorneys, there was no need to continue with the Texas proceedings after the California judge awarded her $475 million. But Pierce Marshall and his lawyers weren't about to let Anna off the hook. They rushed to serve her with a subpoena before she bolted out of town. "She comes in this horrible Versace outfit and prances down and holds a new conference, shows up in a limo and says, 'I'm out of here. I won,'" Pierce's right-hand PR man, David Margulies, scoffed. "And we had a process server there waiting for her, because, if she left the state, there was a concern she was never coming back. So she's walking there with her huge entourage, and the cameras are on her, and this lady walks up to her and gives her this paper, and Anna looks like she's going to autograph the paper, saying, 'Oh, a fan.' And then she figures out that it's a subpoena."

According to *Houston Chronicle* reporter Bill Murphy, "She wasn't able to drop out of the case completely, because Pierce Marshall had a countersuit against her. Because she dropped her claim against Pierce Marshall, her side didn't put on much of a case." In late January, Anna Nicole Smith took the stand. A ripple of excitement spread through the courtroom. She began by stating her position. "My understanding was that my husband told me that I would have half of everything that he had once we were married, and I believed that," she said. "I believed him. I believed my husband. He wouldn't lie to me. He loved me."

Recalled Pierce's attorney Jeff Chambers, "Anna Nicole Smith kept repeating over and over on the stand that she was promised half of J. Howard Marshall II's fortune. Every document in the case is to the contrary. Every will that was done before and after that fact gave everything to Pierce." Murphy summarized: "One of the main points that Pierce Marshall brought out was there was never anyone besides Anna Nicole Smith who heard Marshall II say that he wanted her to get half the estate. She's the only one who can back up that statement." Anna was questioned for six days as Pierce's team of lawyers tried to destroy her credibility.

Bill Murphy watched as Anna's argument gradually deteriorated. "She began to make accusations from the stand that no one had heard before and that were so incredibly serious that it shocked the courtroom. She accused Pierce Marshall of trying to have her electrocuted. She accused Pierce of possibly getting an anesthesiologist to kill Lady Walker, and then she also accused Pierce of killing his father." Judge Wood responded immediately to Anna's claims. "The judge stopped the trial and said to her attorneys, 'You need to go out and explain to her what perjury means,' and then she came back, and she was better coached. All of a sudden, it was her opinion, as opposed to something that happened," offered David Margulies.

Anna's poor memory for dates and events appeared to frustrate Hardin, among others. Said juror Regina Mitchell, "It got to the point where he would ask her the question three or four times, and then she would look at him like this is the first time she ever saw him and ask him to repeat the question again." Nevertheless, Rusty Hardin stuck to his no-nonsense approach, asking Anna, "Ma'am, do you think that you're accountable or that you should be held accountable for anything you do or say?" Anna was unfazed, "Not if it's legal mumbo jumbo that I don't understand." Juror Regina Mitchell, who had once been sympathetic to Anna, quickly lost patience with her yokel posturing. "She always kind of fell back on that 'Oh, I'm a poor girl from Mexia, and I only have a ninth-grade education, so don't yell at me because I'm not real smart' thing," she said.

The exchanges between Anna and Hardin frequently became heated. Hardin's questions were often pointed, as when he asked, "Have you been taking new acting lessons?" Anna retorted, "Screw you, Rusty." Throughout the trial, Anna held a small, framed photo of her late husband. "She kept it next to her the whole time," recalled Eric Redding, "and I really found it kind of comical. At times she would appear to be talking to it." Hardin even asked her about her private conversations with the photo, but she responded that these moments were none of his business.

As the trial proceeded, Anna's credibility was attacked both by Pierce's hotshot attorneys and by her own actions. She transformed, as Margulies put it, from Marilyn Monroe to "a really mean Elly Mae" [Clampett, from the *Beverly Hillbillies*]. During the course of the trial, Anna took a break to model in a plus-size fashion show. Publicity about her offstage antics with comedian Roseanne Barr didn't help her case. Back in the courtroom, Anna struggled to stay focused and confident. Like many others, Elaine Tabers noticed a change in Anna. "The first couple of days she really looked good, and then toward the end it was like she was losing it," she remembered. Eric Redding also noted this shift: "After a little while, you could tell that her demeanor changed. She looked like either she was taking some kind of prescription drugs or something during breaks, because you'd see her in these highs and lows." "In the beginning she was dressed so beautifully. That only lasted for like two or three weeks," offered Regina Mitchell, who drew attention to one of Anna's outfits, which consisted of "this green shirt and this big purple belt from the eighties, with her hair all curly with a big purple bow on top." Mitchell remembered thinking, "She looks like an elf on crack. What is going on with her look?"

Pierce Marshall's camp tried to hammer home the claim that Anna Nicole Smith took advantage of her husband's generosity. When Rusty Hardin asked how Anna managed to spend $5,000 a week in cash, she stumbled, "Well, I'm a very—I don't know how to say this . . . I would go to premieres like every week. You have to buy a formal gown, I mean, gowns are like—I mean you buy gowns—they're, like, thirty thousand dollars. You got to buy gowns and shoes, pay for hair and makeup. I mean, it's very expensive to be me. I mean, it's terrible the things that have to be done to be me." Anna claimed that her husband wanted to give her money, but Pierce interfered. "Well, he told me that Pierce would only give him a hundred thousand dollars for my Christmas," she grumbled. Hardin asked, "Mrs. Marshall, what kind of world is it when people start talking about *only* one hundred thousand dollars for Christmas?" Anna's lawyers were quick to swoop down, "That's argumentative, we object." Anna replied, saying, "My husband spent hundreds of thousands of dollars on me—a hundred thousand dollars was not a lot of money to me. My husband just threw money at me. You don't understand."

On February 14, Anna Nicole Smith arrived at court clad in a pink shirt that seemed to say it all. She explained, "It says

SPOILED, and it's Valentine's Day, and my husband always spoils me on Valentine's day so . . ." Things went from bad to worse for Anna Nicole when J. Howard Marshall's nurse Letitia Hunt took the stand. Hunt described an exchange she witnessed between Anna and her elderly husband. "Now, you have to picture this," said Hunt. "This is a man who is ill, and he's sitting in a chair. He is frail, and this is a woman with her shirt up. She would turn the tape recorder on and off, and she would hold it to his mouth. 'Now, honey, I want you to tell the judge that you want your wife to be taken care of.'"

The hits continued to rain down on Anna when Marshall's former housekeeper, Ada Estes, testified that she believed Anna and her former boyfriend Clay Spires slept together in J. Howard Marshall's house while the ill man was hospitalized. Anna's behavior appalled those close to J. Howard. "No one had any problem with this relationship in terms of their age difference," offered David Margulies. He reasons that people were put off by Anna's hot-and-cold, opportunistic behavior. "What they were so upset about is that she was so cruel to him. She wouldn't call him back. She wouldn't show up. There were tapes played of her saying, "I'll be there," and then showing up very late and creating a scene, saying, "They're throwing me out," when all they were asking her to do was leave for a few minutes so they could take care of Mr. Marshall and change his linens," he offered. Like many, Mitchell found it "completely sad" that Marshall felt abandoned by his wife during the last months of his life.

Closing arguments began on March 2, 2001. After five and a half months, the battle over J. Howard Marshall's megabucks came to an end. Somebody was going to walk out of the courtroom with a lot of money, and somebody else was leaving empty-handed. Even though Anna dropped out of the Houston probate trial, the jury was asked to consider one key question, number sixty-six on the long list the twelve jurors were asked to consider. The question asked, point-blank, Did Anna have an agreement with J. Howard

Marshall that he would give her half of his property? Lee Ware, one of Pierce's attorneys, summed up, "I think that the verdict with respect to Anna Nicole Smith has great significance in that the jury found that she had no interest, had never been made a promise, and had no claim upon her deceased husband's estate." Even Anna's aunt Elaine Tabers agreed with the Texas jury. "He wanted her to be taken care of. I do know that. He didn't want her to want for anything, but as far as half—I don't know about that," she reasoned. The jury also denied Howard Jr.'s claim that his father promised him part of the estate. It was, according to Mitchell, "a family divided."

In mid-July 2001, probate judge Mike Wood leveled another blow to Anna Nicole Smith, ordering her to pay $541,000 in legal fees to Pierce Marshall. For Anna, however, the Houston trial wasn't the end of the story. There was still the matter of the bankruptcy judge's ruling in Los Angeles. "You have two separate cases in two different states, and both have very strong legal legs," offered legal analyst Manny Medrano. "That Texas probate jury spoke unequivocally and loudly. They said, 'The only heir to that estate is Pierce Marshall.' A California judge, a federal judge no less, says that Anna Nicole Smith is entitled to half a billion dollars. It's going to be an appeals judge, an appeals court, that will finally decide all these issues." In May 2001, Pierce Marshall marched into a federal court in Santa Ana, California, to appeal the bankruptcy court's $475 million award to Anna. In a stunning ruling, appellate judge David O. Carter overturned the lower court's half-billion-dollar award to the former model. Judge Carter planned to review all the evidence in a new trial. On March 7, 2002, the court decided Anna deserved a portion of her late husband's fortune, and Carter awarded her $88.5 million. Anna was understandably happy with the ruling. She wasn't counting her millions yet, but she could almost taste victory. "Court's over," she said, "time for me to get out and play!" Pierce appealed that decision.

In the spring of 2002, E! Entertainment Television decided to make Anna Nicole Smith the focus of another drama—a reality TV show about her life. The star got the news from her attorney Howard K. Stern. "He told me they wanted to do a reality show with me," she recalled. Always up for a new wild ride, she had said, "Okay, let's go!" And they did. Throughout the summer of 2002, E!'s cameras shadowed Anna on a daily basis. By August, the miles of videotape were turned into *The Anna Nicole Show*.

For the popular model, having her own TV show meant launching a whole new image outside the courtroom. In 2003, Anna became the spokesperson for TrimSpa, a popular diet aid. By 2004, fabulous Anna had shed a whopping sixty-nine pounds. She began to resemble that shapely southern centerfold from way back when.

By the end of 2004, Anna's courtroom woes returned. On December 30, an appeals court threw out the Texas probate court's previous decision to award Anna $88.5 million from the J. Howard Marshall estate. Pierce Marshall issued a statement, saying, "After nine years of litigation, I'm very pleased by the judgment issued by the 9th Circuit upholding my father's wishes regarding disposition of his assets." But Anna and her lawyer Howard K. Stern fired back with their own statement, insisting that Pierce used fraudulent measures to secure the dismissal and promising that they planned to fight for Anna's money until the bitter end. The once-shy Texas dynamo was back in the spotlight again.

Vickie Lynn Hogan, Nikki Hart, Robyn, Anna Nicole Smith, Mrs. J. Howard Marshall—she's had many names, but one fact remains: Anna still struggles to overcome her self-destructive tendencies. Nevertheless, she possesses a relentless will to succeed, and, this time, she just might pull it off. Former boyfriend Clay Spires values Anna's ability to bounce back and pursue her dreams, saying, "No matter what other people think, she took a goal, and she worked very hard to make that come true." But Anna paid a price. "If you had known her ten years ago, she was sweet, down-to-earth, very, very sexy," commented Eric Redding with some sadness. "You see her now, ten years later, she's still sexy, but now she's got that hard look." In the words of Elite Model Management founder John Casablancas, who once described Anna as a version of the American dream, "She's a young woman, why not? Here in America, anything's possible."

CHAPTER 7

I DID IT, I LIKED IT, SO WHAT?

The Ginger Lynn Story

"This is a girl that loves sex.
She's an Olympic athlete when it comes to sex."

—Suze Randall, photographer

If you don't know who she is, you were probably good in the 1980s. Almost twenty years ago, Ginger Lynn was the queen of adult films—an actress who did whatever it took to be a star. Fueled by cocaine, booze, and raw ambition, she had the world at her feet. But when she tried to conquer mainstream Hollywood, doors slammed in her face because of her past. Then she landed in a detention center. From her violent childhood to her lifelong battle with addiction, from the XXX superstar that helped her become a legend to the celebrities who became her friends and lovers, from sex all day and all night in her professional life to her struggles to become a mother, this is the story of a woman who knows what she wants and refuses to apologize. Her name is Ginger Lynn, and this is her story.

Ginger Lynn Allen was born on December 14, 1962, in Rockford, Illinois, an industrial town eighty miles northwest of Chicago. Ginger's seventeen-year-old father, Wayne, was a mechanic at the local air force base. Her nineteen-year-old mother, Marilyn, worked as a switchboard operator. "My mother was abused as a child, and I was conceived—in my opinion—as a device to get my father to marry my mother," Ginger explained. Wayne was a reluctant new parent at first. "He liked to have fun. He liked to gamble. He liked to drink. He liked to go to bars. He liked to play pool. He liked to play darts. He was gone a lot." Money was tight in the Allen household. To make ends meet, the young family moved in with Wayne's parents, Evelyn and Robert Allen. In 1965, Ginger's family found a place of their own.

Two years later, in September 1967, Marilyn and Wayne had a second child, Keri, but Wayne wasn't much help. "I would guess that there were times my father may not have been faithful," Ginger speculated, "and I think that eventually my mother just got tired of it. She was lonely." As she put it, "My father running around and doing the things that he did made it even more difficult for my mother, and she had her own insecurities and her own fears and her own anger, and they were all just taken out on me." In 1968, Wayne and Marilyn separated. Wayne moved back into his parents' house. As alleged in court documents submitted on Ginger's behalf, even though her father had not been a big part of her life, when he left, no one remained in Ginger's house to protect her. Ginger claimed, "I grew up being told that I was homely, I was ugly, I was evil, I was going to burn in hell, I was a cheater, a liar, I was going to turn out just like my father, who I thought was fabulous. Everything that I did was wrong. I could do no right."

Ginger's mother made her come home right after school. Marilyn didn't allow any of Ginger's friends in the house. Soon, the seven-year-old girl began to retreat. She revealed, "I had a pretend playmate that I played with and talked to, and she would listen to me when I was sad and lonely." Since the house was off limits to Ginger's friends, the youngster turned the backyard into her play area. "I would put on plays in my garage and get all the neighborhood children to be in them," she recounted, "and we would charge people a dime to come see us dance and sing. We used to dance to 'Mr. Bojangles' and wear all the little raggy clothes."

But not even Ginger's fantasies eased her anger toward her mother. "I remember drying the dishes, and I would have the knife, and I would want to kill my mom because she was always telling me, 'You're gonna end up here, and we're gonna put you away, and you're gonna be in a reform school, and you're gonna end up in jail'—just all these things, and everything was so cruel," she admitted. By 1973, Marilyn and Wayne filed for divorce after a five-year separation. Ginger and her sister, Keri, remained in their mother's custody. A year later, twelve-year-old Ginger took desperate measures. She swallowed more than a dozen of her mother's prescription sleeping pills. According to court documents, Ginger said Marilyn ignored her while Ginger spent the next four days semiconscious. "I wasn't looking for attention. I wasn't looking for approval," she said. "I wanted to die. I was afraid that I would kill my mother. I was afraid of what I was going to do."

Ginger recovered, but for the next year her life continued to be a living hell. On a summer night in 1976, thirteen-year-old Ginger and her mother clashed one last time. Ginger described, "I remember the belt coming down on my back just over and over and over, and I didn't cry. I stopped crying a long time before that, and I just turned around and on one of those downswings I grabbed the belt and put it around her neck, and I was pulling as the phone rang. It was my grandfather." Ginger began screaming at the top of her lungs. "He was there within probably sixty seconds, and that was the last night that I lived there." Ginger was reunited with her father who still lived with his parents.

With her grandparents, Ginger Allen felt safe. "They played the role of her parents most of the time she was young. They did most of the care and watched over her," childhood friend Patte Hamilton observed. For Ginger, her grandparents "represented love, honesty, friendship. They were my best friends. They were everything."

But Ginger didn't tell her grandparents everything. By now, she regularly drank alcohol and smoked marijuana. Ginger, who "had a crush on a boy since I was nine," also became sexually active. "I was thirteen years old, and I had sex for the first time. We used a condom, and it broke, and I became pregnant at thirteen." Ginger decided to get an abortion. As she put it, "Abortions were not something that anybody did. I said, 'I will be dead if you don't do this,' and I talked him into doing it." After the abortion, Ginger continued her wild ways. "Her grandparents were very good role models for her, but at the same time I think that she probably didn't have too many restrictions on her," said Patte Hamilton. As Ginger recalled, "I was out of control and getting crazy. I met a guy and stayed with him for three days."

In the spring of 1979, Ginger broke up with the boy who got her pregnant. Soon after, she met Robert Salamone at a gas station. She was pumping gas to earn extra bucks. "This guy pulls up one day on a Harley, and I asked him out," she said. "It was the perfect boyfriend. Somebody who's five years older than me. He's twenty-one. I'm still in high school." Though Ginger was by no means inexperienced for her age, Salamone introduced her to a new group of people who partied regularly. Ginger continued, "I started hanging out with a whole different crowd. We would take tractors and attach flatbed trailers to them, cover them with hay, put a barrel of beer in the back and just go down the country roads from bar to bar and play pool and dance." Ginger Allen graduated from Rockford West High in the spring of 1980. A few weeks later, she split up with Salamone.

In June, Ginger's dad Wayne married his longtime fiancée, Sandy Proctor, a divorcée with two children. According to Ginger's stepbrother, Keith Proctor, "We moved in with Ginger and her father and his parents, and suddenly there were seven of us." Ginger wasn't happy about her new extended family. "It was hard for her. It was hard for everyone. She lived there in the house with us for a while." Added Ginger, "At this point in time I was working at a place called Playback, and we sold stereos. My girlfriend Julie worked there, and she said, 'Oh, I've got a roommate and we have enough room. Come and move in with us.'" And she did. Ginger Allen, then seventeen years old, also found a new boyfriend with a dark past. "I thought he was the coolest guy I'd ever met. He'd been in prison. He was a drug dealer. It was like all the bad people are who I wanted to be with and where I wanted to be, so I told my girlfriend Julie that I found a boyfriend, and I'm moving in.'"

By 1980, Ginger was headed for trouble. She was hooked on alcohol and lived with a drug-dealing boyfriend. She knew she had to change her ways, and she had to do it fast. In 1981, Ginger's grandparents moved to Lucerne Valley, California, and asked Ginger to come out West with them. "I decided that I was madly in love, and I wasn't going," she said. But Ginger's relationship with her druggie boyfriend deteriorated. One night, "I walked into my bathroom, and I found a guy shooting up on the toilet. I had never seen needles. It wasn't a place that I wanted to be." After that revealing incident, Ginger left her drug-dealing lover behind and found a new boyfriend with a hot new car.

In September 1982, Ginger received a call from her grandmother. Evelyn had bad news: Ginger's grandfather suffered a massive heart attack. "I was told that if anyone could make him want to live, it was me, so I flew out," she said. "I had a suitcase, and my grandmother had parked their fifth-wheel trailer in a little trailer park outside of Loma Linda." Evelyn and Ginger spent every waking hour taking care of Robert Allen. "That was very difficult for her, having to deal with it. Suddenly being twenty years old and having to be the person who was taking care of her dying grandfather," said Sandy Proctor.

In November 1982, Robert Allen passed away. Ginger was devastated. "When my grandpa died, it was like a part of me was gone. He was the one person who always believed in me no matter what. My poppy believed in me, and he was the only one who had always, always been there. And I think I got angry that he wasn't there anymore, and I decided I was never going to let anybody in like that again, and I was never going to love anybody like that again." Despite her grief, Ginger did her best to assist Evelyn. Evelyn decided to move back to Illinois, but Ginger wanted to stay in California. After her grandfather's funeral, Ginger packed up and broke the news that she was moving in with her boyfriend with the hot car.

A few days later, Ginger returned to California. "So I was living in this trailer, literally, in a trailer park in Loma Linda. I started working at the Musicland Store, and I thought, 'I live in California. This is really going to be cool and easy and fun.'" Ginger soon found that her job was more demanding than she expected. "I became a troubleshooter, so I went from store to store, getting them back into shape, restocking the stores, hiring new crews, and getting the store from the red into the black. I was working seventy, eighty hours a week." By 1983, she had enough of Loma Linda. She packed up again and moved to Huntington Beach, thirty-six miles south of Los Angeles. She found an apartment and worked at a music store in the local mall.

A few weeks later, Ginger's boyfriend showed up in his Corvette with no job and lots of car payments. "So I'm supporting myself and paying his car payments. I decided that I would look in the paper and see if I could find some other work. The first ad I saw, it was to go and dance at bachelor parties." With her boyfriend along for protection, Ginger reported to work. The party wasn't exactly what she anticipated. "I walk in, and I hadn't thought this through. It was all men. I'm the only girl. They want me naked, and I couldn't do it. I ran out. I grabbed the music. It was horrible." But Ginger Allen didn't give up.

For her next job, said Ginger, "I found an ad that said, 'Figure Models Wanted, five hundred to five thousand dollars per day.' I called the number, and a man by the name of Jim South said, 'Come on up.'" Jim South was the owner of World Modeling, a Los Angeles talent agency that specialized in finding figure models. "We explain to people when they call, mostly girls, that nudity is required," he noted. Ginger continued, "I walked into his office with the paneled walls and the shag carpeting, and this man with big sideburns with kind of a southern accent and a pompadour look. There were these pictures on the wall, and they were of these beautiful, naked girls." South described, "She was a little nervous at first, of course, like most people are, but she seemed like she caught on pretty quick." Explained Ginger, "I'd never thought of myself as pretty, and I'd never thought of myself as sexy, but I looked up at these girls and I thought, 'Well, I can do that.'"

Jim South instantly knew he had a winner. He wasted no time and called his friend, former *Playboy* centerfold-turned-photographer Suze Randall. "We obviously shot her as fast as possible, trying to beat all the other guys to it. One does a whole variety of shoots just to try to get the mood of the girl," Randall explained. Summed up Randall, "I mean, she was such a hot little tamale, just naturally very, very sexual and very, very pretty."

In September 1983, Ginger posed for her first cover spread for a men's magazine called *Cheri*. She was excited, but back in her hometown of Rockford her friends couldn't believe their eyes. Robert Salamone remembered, "A friend of mine came to my house and threw this porno magazine on the table, and it was like, 'Did you see who's in this?' and he opened up the page. He says, 'Didn't you date that girl?' And it was actually a little baffling at first, because of the hair and the makeup. I was like, 'Oh my God. Yeah, I guess I did.'" Meanwhile, Ginger had to make a decision. "My agent Jim sent me from one photo shoot to the next, and I was working every day. I was still working at Musicland, and I remember going to Jim and saying, 'If I'm going to quit my real job, I need to know if I'm going to make two thousand dollars a month, or I can't quit." Jim South quickly put Ginger's mind at ease, assuring her that $2,000 a month would not be a problem. But before Ginger could become a superstar in the business, she had to take the next step—acting.

Said Jim South, "Most of the girls that start with us, their primary interest is getting into magazines and doing just the nude modeling. Then, as they meet a lot of nice people in the industry, they feel like they could take a chance doing movies." Ginger recalled a different entrée into the adult-film world: "My agent said to me one day, 'There's some people who would like you to do a commercial,' and I'm thinking, 'Yes, it's toothpaste! I've really made it now,' and I didn't know that 'commercial' meant adult, that it meant porn—it meant sex on camera. When he told me what it meant, I was insulted."

South knew Ginger was too good to lose. "Most of the people that used Ginger, if not all, wanted to reuse her and reuse her, and that's the sign of somebody that can become a superstar in the adult business," he assessed. Ginger became more and more curious about the porn industry. After meeting one particularly friendly actress, who compared acting in adult films to meeting, flirting, and hooking up with a guy at a party, Ginger's interest was piqued: "I went back to my agent's office and said, 'Okay, I'm going to do it. I want to pick my own partners. I want to make sure I like the script. I want a thousand dollars per scene, and I'm only doing certain things.'" South told Ginger her demands were unreasonable. "So he says I'll never work, and he was laughing at me," she said.

Fate intervened, and Ginger soon got a chance to make her debut. Svetlana, the Gong Girl on *The Gong Show*, and her husband were looking for a first-time performer to appear in two features. They agreed to Ginger's rules. Before production began, South asked Ginger to make a pair of "loops"—short, hardcore silent movies. In the first one, Ginger was paired with future adult-film legend Tom Byron. "I was still fairly new in the business back then, too," said Byron, "so I was kind of learning my way into the business and whatnot. She made me feel really comfortable." Ginger found the work less difficult than she expected, since Byron was cute and all she had to do to succeed in a silent film was take direction. About Ginger's presence, Byron continued, "The thing that was kind of surprising is that she wasn't timid. It was kind of weird, especially back then, that she wasn't afraid to be, you know, a sexual being."

Ginger's second loop teamed her with another adult-film superstar-in-the-making, Ron Jeremy. According to Jeremy, "I'm going, 'Good Lord! This girl's adorable and so sweet and innocent.' I'm saying, 'Are you sure you didn't stumble into the wrong door? Honey, you know this is an adult movie here.'" Ginger was not as smitten with Jeremy. "I'm looking at him, and I'm thinking, 'Okay, I would never in a million years have sex with this man, but if I can do it with this guy—not look at him, just feel the pleasure and get through this—then I can do anything. Then I know I'll be able to handle the lead in this film.' And that's what I did."

In December 1983, filming began in Hawaii on *Surrender in Paradise*, Ginger's first adult feature. The movie introduced Ginger along with a bevy of beautiful women marooned on an island with a man. On the first day of shooting, Ginger was speechless. "Every time I'm supposed to say my dialogue, I see this microphone, and I start to laugh. I can't talk. We shoot this scene probably twenty times. I can't do it. I can have sex on camera. I'm not going to talk," she described. Ginger soon got over her jitters. She also turned twenty-one on location. When the project was finished, she began her second film in Hawaii, *Hanky Panky*. The movie reunited Ginger with Ron Jeremy, who was excited to see the newbie again. He commented, "Life just gets no better than this."

The work was easy for Ginger Allen. Acting brought back memories of her childhood. "It was just playing in the garage again. It was dancing to 'Mr. Bojangles.' It was being somebody else," she explained. Throughout 1984, Ginger's adult-film career took off. Her girl-next-door appeal brought offers from the industry's top producers, including Suze Randall. "I probably was part of the beginning for her making adult movies because we were making something called *Suze's Centerfolds* at the time, and we were making X-rated movies," she said. "We spent quite a lot of money and we took a lot of pride in our work, and we thought we had wonderful scripts, and of course we didn't realize people just want to have a wonderful, hot sex scene without the trappings. But in those days, we were trying very hard to be filmmakers."

Word of Ginger's new career soon reached Rockford. Ginger tried to soften the news by telling childhood friend Patte Hamilton about her nude modeling. Hamilton was stunned. "I, for the life of me, could have never, ever imagined what she was going to say. What else could there be? And she told me about the adult films and we said our good-byes, and I just kind of got used to the idea, and the word was getting around town." Ginger's father found out from a stranger who sat beside him in a bar. Wayne immediately called his daughter. Ginger described the conversation: "The words that came out of his mouth make a truck driver look like a saint. He was furious, and he told me not to come home for Christmas, that I was disowned, not to speak to my younger brothers or sisters. My grandfather was rolling over in his grave." Ginger's family soon began receiving hate mail back in Rockford. But, as Proctor, Ginger's stepbrother, put it, "She's an adult. There's nothing we can do about it."

There was also nothing her family could do when Ginger discovered the feel-good drug of the eighties—cocaine. "When my parents found out what I was doing, when I was disowned, I had lost the acceptance from my father that I'd always had. Even though my father was gone a lot, he still loved and accepted me. My little sister couldn't talk to me. My grandmother—none of them would talk to me, and I started doing a lot of drugs." Ginger continued making hardcore films in 1984. Her income skyrocketed, but her family's rejection destroyed her. "I went on a downward spiral. When my father made that phone call, the money that I'd made, it all went up my nose."

Ginger still managed to work. The actress was honored for her 1984 movies at the first X-Rated Critics Organization Awards. She was named Starlet of the Year, Best Female Performer, and Video Vixen—the triple crown of the adult-film business. The little girl from Rockford accepted her awards in pain. "I have to get up there, and I don't know what to say, you know. I'm thanking my grandma for giving me my spunk and my energy, and I'm crying like a geek," she remembered. By the end of 1984, Ginger's career was going strong, and so was her use of cocaine. "I was the person at the party who never wanted the party to end. I never just ordered a drink or did a line. I did everything so excessively."

When Ginger Allen became a celebrated adult actress in 1984, the business was still mostly underground, but porn was about to invade America's living rooms, taking her along for the ride. By 1984, the twenty-one-year-old had more than three dozen adult movies on her résumé, from short films to full-length features. For her efforts, Ginger made up to $10,000 a picture. Producers soon realized that she guaranteed big profits. The actress knew it, too, and took advantage of the opportunity. "Whatever I asked for, they would give me, and I started thinking, 'If they are going to continuously increase my salary—pay me more, never saying no—what are these guys making?'"

In late 1984, Ginger met another rising star, Steven Hirsch. Then a brash twenty-three-year-old, Hirsch was the founder of Vivid Video. Vivid was located in the heart of L.A.'s San Fernando Valley. The company capitalized on a new technology—home videotapes. Hirsch was determined to marry home video with adult entertainment. He commented, "I think we were fortunate in coming along at a time where it was really an explosion in the video business. No longer did you have to go to an adult book-store to buy an adult film, you were able to go into your local video store. We saw that transformation happening." By combining inexpensive productions with fancy packaging, Vivid Video helped coin a new term: "Designer Porn." Said Ron Jeremy, "He wanted to take pizzazz into the market."

In 1984, Ginger signed an exclusive pact with Vivid. The agreement made her the first in a long line of contract stars in adult film—another Vivid innovation. In return, Ginger earned top dollar for each of her performances—up to $10,000 per scene, and extra money to feature her on the video box. Vivid Video teamed Ginger with the leading XXX artists of the time, including Hollywood writer Penny Antine. Antine wrote adult-film scripts under the pen name Raven Touchstone. Penny saw a rare quality in Ginger: "Ginger had something that Marilyn Monroe also had. She had a vulnerability. You wanted to take care of her." Ginger and Penny's first production, titled *Ginger*, became a XXX blockbuster. Within a month, the video sold six thousand copies, a huge number at the time. "It went right up to number one on the charts and sort of told us that our thought process was correct, which was focus on a girl, have unique sort of mainstream packaging, and a good movie, and if you put those things together, it would work," said Hirsch.

Through 1985, Ginger headlined one Vivid video after another. Most of the movies incorporated her name in the titles. While the titles were funny, the sex was hardcore. With every new movie, she became more daring. She explained, "I wanted to be able to be as completely uninhibited as I wanted to be, and as a viewer, I wanted you to watch and, rather than go, 'Oh, she didn't just do that,' I wanted you to look at it and go, 'Honey, you want to try that?' And that's what happened." Ginger also inspired a new wave of actors. Her 1985 *Poonies*—a takeoff on the 1985 film *The Goonies*—introduced future adult-film queen Bionca.

Sharon Mitchell also starred in the film. In 1985, she was an established film actress who saw "superstar" written all over Ginger. Mitchell now runs AIM, the Adult Industry Medical Healthcare Foundation. "Vivid was just on the verge of mainstreaming pornography as we know it today, and they started this formula with Ginger Lynn, and, boy, did it work. She was instantly skyrocketed to mainstream proportions." By the end of 1985, Ginger and Vivid Video were the biggest things in adult films. That year, she earned $134,000 as an adult-film star. And she appeared to love every minute.

Ginger Lynn's beautiful face and figure appeared in video stores everywhere, and each new Ginger movie flew off the shelves. Ron Jeremy offered, "It was a very nice, symbiotic, mutual relationship, because Vivid helped make her an even bigger star, and she helped Vivid get on the map, too, and become a real contender." Ginger seemed to have won the recognition she craved since childhood. "I made money, I traveled the world. I had people bringing me to Japan for two weeks to sign autographs, and putting me up at the best hotel, and doing press conferences. When I spoke, people wanted to hear what I had to say."

Yet Ginger knew something was missing from the picture. "I was living in my own soap opera, my own make-believe world that was real."

In 1985, Ginger's make-believe bubble began to burst. That year, she clashed bitterly with her adult-film rival, Traci Lords. The feud was professional *and* personal. At the time, few people knew that Lords was only sixteen—a minor—and acting in adult films illegally. Ginger described one encounter with Lords: "I met Traci Lords in a parking lot across the street from Jim's office. Traci was wearing shorts and a little T-shirt with no bra, high heels, and she looked like a slut. I just detested her." Despite her impression of Traci, Ginger worked with Lords on five adult movies. "I'm sure part of it was that she was my competition, but there was something I didn't like about Traci." The constant battle to be the biggest adult-film star wore on Ginger. Each new film usually demanded more difficult and often unpleasant scenes.

Ginger responded to the mounting professional pressure with more drugs and alcohol. In 1986, while filming *Blame It on Ginger*, the actress found she had to get high in order to perform. According to director Henri Pechard, "We were pushing the envelope on this scene, and she did it with great resentment. She was really angry at me for doing it. We finally finished for the day, and we were driving back home. We were staying on location in some hotel. I said, 'You're in a bad mood.' She said, 'Well, you'd be cranky, too, if you had your head in the toilet.'" Sharon Mitchell remarked, "To ask me if it was apparent to me that Ginger had to do drugs to do movies, no, it wasn't, because I was doing the same drugs with her. We were kept in this era of porn and drugs. One facilitates the other. I don't think one necessarily causes the other, but one facilitates the other, and it makes almost this pleasant anesthetic."

By early 1986, twenty-three-year-old Ginger Lynn reached a crossroads. The star of sixty-nine adult films announced she was burned out. Few of her friends were surprised. Reasoned Tom Byron, "A woman's career in this business cannot go on forever, specifically, having sex in front of the camera." Added Henri Pechard, "This is an industry that can put some miles on you emotionally, and sometimes the money is just not worth it." Money wasn't the only issue. Ginger was tired of being "Ginger Lynn." She said, "If I do something I don't want to do for money, I am a whore, and I never want to be a whore. I've been a slut many times, never a whore. So I went onto these movie sets, and I didn't want to be there. I didn't want to be doing it, and my attitude had changed."

Ginger wanted something more. She wanted acceptance as a real actress in Hollywood instead of the San Fernando Valley. "She wanted mainstream from the get-go," said writer Penny Antine. In February 1986, Ginger Lynn, who reached the height of XXX stardom, quietly gave it all up. She said good-bye to friends, left the adult-film world, and planned to never look back. She noted, "There was no big event that changed; I changed. I was just done."

In order to make the jump to the Hollywood mainstream, Ginger knew she had to master real acting skills. "Although I was winning awards for my sexuality and what I was doing in my performances, I thought that I had a lot that I could learn and a long way to go." Ginger's decision to leave adult films was enthusiastically supported by friends and especially her family. Said Keith Proctor, "We all thought, 'It's not a healthy environment, and we're very glad that she's getting out of the adult business.'" But escaping her past was easier said than done. Adult filmmaking was illegal in California until 1988. Before then, everyone who made these films, including Ginger, was at risk. According to Jim South, "You were allowed to watch them. You could rent them. You could buy the tapes. You could do anything you want, but you couldn't produce them or make them."

By the mid-1980s, as the porn industry expanded in Los Angeles, police turned up the heat. "There was a tremendous amount of investigations going on at that time with other heads of companies, manufacturers, distributors. They were really politically trying to crack down on the porn industry as a whole," said

Sharon Mitchell. With growing frequency, police charged adult filmmakers with violating California's antipandering law—a statute customarily used to go after prostitutes. Ron Jeremy explained, "The pandering law was, if you're paying an actress for sex, she is an escort, and you're a pimp, you're a panderer."

In 1986, the crackdown on porn turned up a shocking surprise. Someone tipped authorities that Ginger's former rival Traci Lords was a minor. The revelation ignited a firestorm in the industry. A number of stars who worked with Traci became entangled in the scandal, including Ginger. "I was asked to testify against the people that were my friends, against the people that I worked for," Ginger commented. Ginger and her costars Tom Byron and Harry Reams were all subpoenaed to appear before a grand jury, but Ginger was determined to protect her former colleagues. "I refused to testify, and I was told when I refused the first time that, if I didn't, they would make my life difficult. Those were the words. So when I did go before the grand jury, and I didn't know anything, they were pissed. They were pissed." The Traci Lords investigation eventually ended without anyone being convicted of a crime, but the adult-film business was left reeling. According to South, "It almost broke the industry's back."

The pressure of the scandal intensified Ginger's drug problem. More than ever, she relied on cocaine to get her through the day. Still, she continued to focus on a mainstream career. "I tried and tried and tried. I called every manager, every agent. Nobody would touch me," she admitted. Added Jeremy, "It is very, very difficult to transition from adult to mainstream films, but it is also very difficult to get into mainstream films, period, no matter where you come from." Ginger refused to give up. "I sent my photo and résumé to a film company that called me for the film *Wild Man*. I went in, read for the role, had a callback, and was pretty excited. I went on the call, had another one. I walk into the third meeting, and Freddie Lincoln, who has been a friend of mine and a director in the adult-film industry for years is sitting there. I said, 'I'm reading for this role. What are you doing here?' and he said, 'I'm directing the film.'"

Ginger Lynn landed a small role in *Wild Man*, but it was a big step for the actress. Although the movie went nowhere, she broke into legitimate films. "The work was very slow in the beginning," she said. "I found that I got small roles in B films. From there I went to bigger roles and leads in B films." In 1988, Ginger won the lead role in *Vice Academy*, a campy comedy about two police-women. The following year, she nabbed another sexy part in the legitimate *Cleo/Leo*. On the set, Ginger struck up a friendship with another former adult-film actress, Veronica Hart. Hart mentioned, "I was quite excited, because I'd always heard about Ginger Lynn. I might have met her before, but we really hadn't hung out, and I was so pleased when I met her on the set, because not only is she a wonderful person but a marvelous performer as well."

Ginger was thrilled to be a part of the Hollywood film world, but the actress often found her characters were limited. As Keith Proctor put it, "I don't know if mainstream Hollywood accepted her so much as they typecast her into roles of prostitutes and dumb blondes." Ginger commented, "What I found was happening is a lot of doors were being opened for me as far as casting went. I was able to get into a lot of places," but eventually realized that "not everybody had me in because they wanted to cast me in the film." In fact, Suze Randall got Ginger an audition that left her deeply hurt. The actress claimed she was hit on by the film's very famous director. "I go in, and say hello and this man asks for a nude Polaroid," she recounted. "I said, 'No, I'm here to read for this part,' and he said, 'How about a topless Polaroid?' I said, 'No, I don't think so.' I'm trying to keep my cool and not know what's going on at the time. At this point, I'm trying with everything I have to hold back the tears. I don't want to cry. I'm embarrassed, I'm humiliated, I feel degraded. I've never felt degraded on a porno set."

By 1989, twenty-six-year-old Ginger was having a tough time making ends meet. As a mainstream actress, she couldn't command the salary she once did in X-rated films. To pay the bills and support her ever-escalating cocaine habit, the actress started to dance in strip clubs. According to Sharon Mitchell, "She couldn't put one foot in front of the other. She was a horrible dancer." Laughed Ginger, "All I could think to do is to put on a lot of clothes. I'm wearing thirty items. I've got gloves on top of gloves. I've got a tutu. I've got a belt. I've got a teddy. I've got three pairs of underwear. I have so many clothes on because I don't know how to dance, and within thirty seconds I'm naked."

Ginger wasn't happy dancing, and her despair fueled her cocaine use. On one occasion, she recalled, "I decided to have a party, and I invited everybody over to my house. My boyfriend was out of town, and I had a lot to drink, and I was doing a lot of drugs, and nine days later, I'm still at the party. Nobody else is there. Everybody's gone home. I remember being on the floor, searching for a rock and shaking so bad I couldn't do anything, and I'm dry-heaving, and I was so, so sick. I called a girlfriend of mine that had been a very close friend for years, and I said, 'You know what? There's something wrong with me. I need some help.'"

During 1989, Ginger checked into a rehab center in San Diego. "I really didn't think that I was a drug addict or an alcoholic at the time. I just thought that I'd gone a little too far and done a little too much," she said, "so I stayed for my thirty days, got out, stayed sober for a couple of months, and then went back to my normal routine."

Somewhat sober and with a new lease on life, Ginger looked forward to the 1990s. Small TV and film roles came her way, and Ginger's social calendar often sparkled with celebrities. One of her favorite dates was rock star Billy Idol, whom she met when she was hosting the world's largest wet T-shirt contest. Described Ginger, "Billy's road manager came up and said, 'Billy is a big fan, and he would love to meet you,' and Billy and I just hit it off right away. We became really, really good friends."

Ginger Lynn formed another celebrity friendship in 1990, when she landed a role in the short-lived TV series *Sunset Beat*. The star was a young actor whose career was then picking up steam—George Clooney. "George Clooney was the motorcycle cop with long hair—kind of the rock-and-roll cop—and I played the stripper. I was cast as a lot of strippers. He wasn't really famous like he is now, and he was and is one of the nicest people that I have ever met," she said. After *Sunset Beat*, Ginger kept plugging away. "I wasn't taking 'no' for an answer, and I kept trying and trying and trying and eventually got to the point where I was cast in *Young Guns II*," she affirmed. *Young Guns II* was a big-budget Western that featured a troupe of Hollywood's hottest young male stars. Ginger was cast in a minor role as a prostitute, but she saw the film as a chance to shine. Offered Keith Proctor, "She thought that this was probably one of her biggest breaks into mainstream Hollywood."

On the set, star Emilio Estevez introduced Ginger to his brother Carlos, better known as Charlie Sheen. The attraction was mutual. "There was something that I had never felt before that I felt when I met Charlie," she described. "I think we laughed so hard my stomach hurt. He would start a sentence; I would finish it. We each knew what the other was thinking. There was just this click that we had." According to Proctor, "She was giddy like a little schoolgirl. She was very happy to be with him." Ginger continued, "He was sweet. He was kind, and I felt like I had met my male counterpart. I'd met the male Ginger Lynn." In 1990, twenty-four-year-old Charlie Sheen was one of Hollywood's bad boys. His womanizing was as legendary as his partying. Pals called him "The Ma-Sheen." Charlie also had two dozen films to his credit and came from a prominent Hollywood family. Ginger was impressed. "I'm sure that she had genuine feelings for him, that she loved him. She didn't view him as a stepping stone or as a tool," Proctor assessed.

Sheen, however, was engaged to model Kelly Preston. A month after his meeting Ginger, Sheen's engagement ended. As the couple's affair progressed, Ginger and her new beau learned they had much in common. "We did a lot of partying. At one point, the partying went overboard. It just got to be way too much, and Charlie's one of the first people that I met that could keep up with me, and vice versa. So we weren't exactly healthy for each other in that respect," she admitted. In August 1990, Sheen checked into a rehab clinic. He later revealed, "It was a lot of craziness, a lot of self-imposed maniacal behavior—very self-destructive, very suicidal, actually. It all came to a head, and it was time to shut it down." But rehab didn't work for Sheen. He left the clinic. The couple decided to work together to kick their addictions rather than remain in a drug-induced haze. According to Ginger, "We'd go to meetings, and we stayed sober together for fourteen months."

At the same time Ginger was seeing Charlie Sheen, she reprised her role as a campy cop in sequels to the 1988 film *Vice Academy*. Off camera, the actress battled director Rick Sloane over working conditions. Sloane commented, "Ginger just became difficult to work with by the time we were doing *Vice Academy 3*. I can't pinpoint any one reason. She would be three and a half hours late every day. She wouldn't have memorized any of her dialogue. She was demanding." Ginger countered, "We had better catering on porno sets. I think I hit my end of the *Vice Academy* series when I had said, 'I'll do this movie, but I really need a trailer if we're going to be going to ten locations in one day: I'm working for scale, and I'm making no money on these films.'"

Ginger's money problems only got worse. In 1991, the actress and a host of other adult-film stars were charged with tax evasion. The IRS claimed Ginger cheated the government out of back taxes totaling just under $2,100. Ginger was scared. "I was facing six years in federal prison." Ginger claimed she was promised a light sentence if she pleaded guilty, but she maintained her innocence, saying, "Why would I cheat for two thousand dollars?" Tom Byron was also busted in the sting. "I was looking at twelve years in federal prison for basically having sex in front of a camera and being a shoddy accountant," he quipped. The IRS charges sent shock waves through the adult-film industry. Said Mitchell, "It really hit everyone hard, and Ginger was the first of the women to go, and then all the actors were like, 'Oh my God,' because we always thought, 'Oh, they're gonna get the manufacturers and the producers first.'"

Photographers who worked with Ginger Lynn were also questioned. According to Suze Randall, "They dragged the whole industry in, had everybody come in. The prosecutor had us all in a room to testify and warned us before to testify on what Ginger had earned and this and that. And he made it quite clear if they didn't testify, he'd be chasing down their tax returns and checking on them." Ginger's trial in federal court began in May 1991. On June 3, the twenty-eight-year-old actress was convicted of one count of filing a false tax return. The ordeal left her drained, and she still faced up to three years in federal prison. "It was ridiculous what they put her through, and the money they cost her was amazing," commented Veronica Hart. Agreed an incredulous Ginger, "It cost me four hundred thousand dollars to defend myself for a crime that I didn't commit."

The blissful days of the early 1990s were soon a thing of the past. With a prison sentence looming, Ginger hired Santa Monica attorney Janet Sherman. Sherman helped the actress with the presentencing investigation. Confessed Sherman, "She was in the worst position that a defendant can be in in federal court, and that is to have gone to a jury trial and lost. Because then the government is going to seek a harsher punishment than they might have if the defendant had tried to negotiate a plea bargain and settled the case that way."

That summer Ginger met criminologist Sheila Balkan. Dr. Balkan was hired to examine Ginger's background as part of her defense. "She was quite young when I saw her, and she looked like an American apple pie, but inside was somebody trying to survive a very dysfunctional, pathological, destructive past." Balkan's investigation revealed Ginger's violent childhood, her descent into drugs, and her life in adult films. She reported her findings to the court with a request for leniency. "She had gone through an awful lot to survive, including facing a prison term, and she was really looking to change her life."

More pleas for leniency for Ginger were submitted by friends and Hollywood luminaries, including one from Charlie Sheen's father, Martin. According to Sherman, "Martin Sheen wrote a letter on Ginger's behalf that pointed out to the judge how she had faced this prosecution with great courage, but it had taken a great toll on her." Martin Sheen called Ginger "a dear friend" and said he was "proud to be able to write in her support." Charlie Sheen also petitioned the court. Sherman continued, "Charlie's letter was in a similar vein—how he had been starting at a treatment center for his own alcohol and drug problems, and that Ginger had helped him at a very difficult time of his life."

Finally, on September 23, 1991, Ginger appeared in court to hear her fate. "The day that I was sentenced was probably the most frightening day of my life," commented Ginger. "I was standing next to my attorney, and my legs, they wouldn't hold me up. My knees were shaking so badly. I'm thinking, 'I can go away for six years.'" In the end, all the adult-film stars facing charges escaped prison terms, including Ginger, but the government's efforts left Ginger with feelings of anger and resentment. "It was a joke. I received three years probation, 750 hours of community service, and mandatory drug testing," she said. On the other hand, affirmed Sherman, "It was a great victory, because Ginger was able to get on with her life and did not have to go to federal prison."

Throughout 1991, Ginger and Charlie Sheen continued to see each other and to work on their sobriety. By summer's end, however, Ginger felt Sheen had grown distant. "I think that he'd been sober for such a good amount of time that certain people in his life thought, 'Okay, it's time to move on,' and they began to pressure Charlie to leave me," she speculated. In late 1991, Ginger's love for Sheen was put to the test. The actress claimed that during a phone call with one of his assistants, she was told that he was using the services of Hollywood madam Heidi Fleiss. According to Ginger, the news of Sheen's infidelity was shattering, because "one of the things that Charlie and I had always had was honesty between us, so he wanted me to know that he was cheating on me, and I came back and I was heartbroken."

The phone call resulted in a painful confrontation. Described Ginger, "He was crying. I was crying. We couldn't—He couldn't take the pressure anymore from everybody telling him that I was going to ruin it for him." Ginger realized the relationship was over. Recalled childhood friend Patte Hamilton, "She was heartbroken, absolutely heartbroken, and I know that she started drinking again." In early 1992, Ginger failed one of her court-ordered drug tests. She said with regret, "I didn't think about it. I didn't think it through. It didn't seem to matter. It was more important to me that I get high." Police were alerted that Ginger violated her probation. "They were looking for her to arrest her, and by the time we got back to the house, she was gone. They had arrested her and taken her."

Ginger was immediately locked in a cell at the Los Angeles Metropolitan Detention Center. Her first time behind bars traumatized her. "I was there for seventeen days. It seemed like seventeen years. I saw things I never ever saw before in my life. I saw heroin for my first time. I learned how to mix and fix it, and I would shoot up in my cell," she claimed. Hamilton commented, "She was very shaken. She was very frightened." Ginger continued, "I learned how to make a knife out of a pencil and a rubber band and the razor that you shave your legs with. I was very 're-formed' while I was there."

After she broke up with the love of her life and spent time in federal prison, Ginger's luck was due for a change. On March 3, 1992, the twenty-nine-year-old was released from jail into the arms of her grandmother, but their reunion was brief. That same night, Ginger was ordered to spend the next four weeks in drug rehab. When she was released from rehab, she continued pursuing legitimate film roles. "She seemed very upbeat and sure of what she was doing. I thought she was headed in the right direction for mainstream and for what was ahead," said Hamilton. In 1992, Ginger got back in the game with the film *Mind, Body and Soul*. Ginger was cast as a young woman who is brutally beaten and raped. "It was satanic, and it really bothered me," she remarked. "I was very uncomfortable making that film. I just felt creepy. I didn't like the whole satanic vibe. I didn't like things that were going on in the film."

Ginger Lynn's outlook improved that year with the release of another dark movie, *Bound and Gagged: A Love Story*. The film featured her in the role of an abused wife who finds liberation. "No one had any fears or doubts. They were thrilled to have me in the film, and they really gave me an opportunity, and I feel that I shined," she said. In 1993, Ginger got permission from her probation officer to fly to France to promote *Bound and Gagged*. At the Cannes Film Festival, the actress and costar Elizabeth Saltarelli attracted the paparazzi. The pair weren't the only ones turning heads at Cannes. Ginger's former boyfriend Charlie Sheen was there to promote his new film, *The Three Musketeers*. She described the happy reunion: "You know that silly commercial where two people see each other, and they run in slow motion? I was doing a press junket on the beach. Charlie was doing one, and we were down the beach from each other. I saw him, and he saw me, and it was just one of those kinds of a get-together, at least it seemed like it. We hooked up." Once more, they became inseparable. She lost her heart again that spring, as well as her head. The love-struck actress flew off to Vienna with Sheen, although her probation officer had not approved her going to Austria. "When I flew back a week later, they were basically waiting for me. They drug-tested me immediately. I failed."

Ginger spent the summer of 1993 in a halfway house. During her stay, her luck seemed to improve. The actress was allowed to audition for a small part in a new ABC television series called *NYPD Blue*. At the show's production office, Ginger was asked to read for the part of a stripper. "I get the sides, and I read them, and there was a line, 'Let me lick your lollipop,'" she said. "I threw the script down, and I walked out. I called my agent, and I said, 'I'm not doing this. I am not saying that.'" Ginger then faced executive producer Steven Bochco. Recounted Ginger, "I said to Steven Bochco, 'I don't want the role,' and he said, 'Well, we'll change the line for you. We'll take it out.' So they cast me, and I would get up in the morning and leave prison and go to the lot and film." Ginger guest-starred in only one episode of *NYPD Blue*.

After her three-month confinement ended, the actress was again jobless. Ginger tried a new tack later that year, making self-improvement videos. *Ginger Lynn Allen's Superbody* was followed by *Ginger Lynn Allen's Lingerie Gallery*. Both videos were high on sex appeal. *Lingerie Gallery* rose to number six on Billboard's home-video chart. Affirmed Ginger, "I worked very hard on this, and I put a lot of time and effort and love into this piece—every little detail from the wardrobe down to everything, and so I'm very proud of it. Very proud."

During 1993 and 1994, Ginger continued her on-again, off-again relationship with Charlie Sheen. Despite their differences, she clung to the hope that their romance could be salvaged. "I'd gone out to see him, and he had asked me to marry him, and I said, 'Are you going to quit partying so much and quit sleeping with other women?' He had friends there, and he didn't like that I said that." Sheen's reaction was a wake-up call for Ginger. "It wasn't a satisfying and honest or loving relationship anymore. I had this wall that I had put up for such a long time, and Charlie was the first and only person since my grandfather that broke those walls down. He was somebody that I shared everything with." Sharon Mitchell confirmed, "He broke her heart, and I don't know if she ever recovered from that."

In September 1994, Ginger's three-year probation period ended, as did her love affair with Sheen. She celebrated by getting a tattoo—a pair of lips saying, "It is what it is." Then she found romance again with an old friend. In 1995, the former adult actress was cast in a softcore mainstream film called *The Ultimate Taboo*. Vivid Video owner Steven Hirsch was the executive producer on the film. "Steven and I became friends again. We hadn't seen each other over the last several years. I'd been off doing my thing, and we became reacquainted again." The couple's reunion soon turned into love. "There was a point where we had discussed a marriage date. He'd asked me what kind of ring I wanted, how many carats. We talked about the future." Ginger didn't wait for Hirsch to propose. She proposed to him. According to her, he accepted her proposal but then later broke off the engagement. Neither she nor he discussed the reason for the breakup.

In the summer of 1995, Ginger found out she was pregnant. Reporters hinted that the child was Charlie Sheen's. Ginger flatly denied the rumor and took a more positive outlook on the "happy accident." She offered, "Back in 1991, I had some quite serious female problems, and I was told that chances were that I probably wouldn't be able to have children. When I found I was pregnant, I was ecstatic. I was happier than I think I've ever been to know that I was going to be a mom." On March 31, 1996, Ginger gave birth to a healthy son, Sterling Wayne Robert Allen. "I had twenty-four hours of labor, and then I had this beautiful little baby that has changed my life." She withheld the name of the father from the birth certificate, claiming she signed a confidentiality agreement with the baby's father that forbade her from releasing his name.

For the next two years, Ginger Lynn devoted her life to being a mother. "I know she's done everything she can to be everything to her child, and if anything's missing, she'll make up for it in any way that she can," said Patte Hamilton. In 1999, Ginger won a promising role in *The Independent*, directed by Steve Kessler. The movie starred Janeane Garofalo and Jerry Stiller. Commented Kessler, "Ginger has what all really good actors have—she's very emotionally there. She a very natural actor. She doesn't overact, and I think that when Ginger's on camera, there's something about her that audiences connect to." Ginger complimented Kessler as well, saying, "Steven Kessler was and is a director who I hold very dear to my heart. He's somebody who doesn't care what I did. It doesn't matter to him if I did porno yesterday or a hundred years ago." Later in 1999, the actress was featured in hard rock band Metallica's video for the song "Turn the Page." "It was the first thing that my father ever saw me in, that he called up and said, 'I'm so proud of you. You're really good.'" A Hollywood filmmaker agreed, but, according to Ginger, "I went in, read for him, and then someone said, 'Do you know who that is? That's Ginger Lynn, the porn star,' and I was no longer a good actress."

Ginger still had a hard time dealing with rejection. In 1999, after thirteen years of struggling to be a legitimate actress, she faced a difficult choice. The actress considered a return to the world of XXX. She admitted, "Financially, things had become very difficult. I'm a single parent raising a child on my own. I get very little help, so it was a financial as well as an ego issue." But Ginger's friends knew that going back into adult films would also mean the end of Ginger's lifelong dream to become a mainstream Hollywood star. Antine commented, "That kind of situation involving disappointment and not having quote 'made it' is certainly not particular to Ginger. It happens to a million people who had great hopes of being movie stars, and that's the adjustment you make between your youthful dreams and the adult reality."

Ginger decided to reenter adult films. The actress approached several companies about her comeback, including Vivid Video, but former boss and lover Steven Hirsch wasn't interested. "She actually had talked to some other companies prior to talking to us, and we're not really known as the comeback company. I don't think we're really good at that," he justified. Instead, in February 1999 Ginger signed a contract with VCA Pictures for five films and a generous sum of money. At VCA, she hooked up again with friend and former adult-film star Veronica Hart. Reasoned Hart, "VCA hired her because, yes, she's a wonderful person, she's a great actress, and she's an amazing sexual performer, but best of all she's a huge draw. She sells tapes." Ginger remarked that her comeback was nerve-wracking in some ways. "I was nervous even though I wasn't competing with the new women. I really don't have any issues with eighteen- or twenty-year-olds or whatever. What I was really concerned about was competing with myself when I was twenty-one years old. Coming back at thirty-six or thirty-seven, you know, how am I to compete with myself that many years ago? But with the fabulous scripts that I had, my comeback was much more than I ever had hoped it would be, and very, very successful."

Over the next two years, Ginger Lynn continued making adult films. According to adult-film actress Kylie Ireland, "I think when Ginger came back in, she might have been a little frustrated, because, you know, the mainstream thing wasn't quite working out like she'd hoped. But, honestly, between you and me, she came back in and I asked her that same question one day, and she said, 'Oh God, it's for the sex. I miss it.'" Always busy with work, thirty-seven-year-old Ginger realized she was lacking something: male companionship. Hart took it upon herself to find Ginger a date. She summoned Los Angeles radio personality Ralph Garman, who said, "Trust me, in my wildest dreams I never thought anything was going to come from it."

In 1999, Ginger and Garman started a relationship that lasted two years. He provided support for Ginger, who was still dealing with her drug problems. "It was getting in the way of her living the life that she wanted to lead—being a mom, being a girlfriend, being an actress—all these things that she wanted to accomplish," he said. "The drugs and the alcohol started to get in the way of it, and I think she started to recognize it, much to her credit." In July 1999, Ginger confronted her long-standing battle with drugs and alcohol. "I think the night that it really hit me that this was no longer just a drinking problem or a drug problem, that I was really sick, was when I rushed through story time," she regretted. "My son's never seen me have a drink. My son's never seen me do a drug—never seen me under the influence of anything, but there was a night that I rushed through story time because I wanted to have a glass of wine." Days later, the actress entered into a twelve-step program. According to Garman, "Her perspective about her life changed in the sense that she was living a much fuller life when she got clean and sober. And she was really enjoying the program, too." Added Ginger, "The quality of my life is so improved. All of the things that I wasn't anymore, that I had lost along the way, and wanted to be again, I've become."

After finally cleaning up, the actress never expected her health would become an issue. "Back in 1991, when I was on trial, I experienced my first female problem, and over the years, I had more and more and more of them, and the last two years were very difficult for me." Ginger's friend, adult-film actress Chloe, recalled Ginger's distress: "I was with her when she was having some of her problems. We would be walking through Wal-Mart, and all of a sudden, she'd just get this stabbing pain, and she would keel over. It scared the hell out of me, and that was right before it got really bad." On September 11, 2001, the day of the terrorist attacks on New York City and Washington, D.C., Ginger underwent a complete hysterectomy. Suze Randall visited Ginger while she was in the hospital. "She was laughing and fun, and she's always upbeat. I mean, that's a really scary thing—hospitals and surgery and crap like that, but Ginger always put a great face on." The adult-film star refused to talk about the exact nature of her illness.

After the successful surgery, Ginger claimed to be healthy, said she had no regrets about her past, and looked forward to the future. Having recovered from her operation, she continued to work in the adult-film industry. In late 2001, the actress took a job as a marketing executive at the Simon Wolf Organization, an adult-film distribution company. Ginger also spent time maintaining her Web site and began writing a book about her life. "So far right now we're calling it *I Did It, I Liked It, So What?* It's about my life, my childhood, my adult-film career, and it's not so much a kiss-and-tell book as a 'how it felt' book." In addition to Ginger's work as a marketing executive, she continued to perform. In January 2002, the thirty-nine-year-old actress took home an Adult Video News Award for Best Actress in her film *Taken*.

"You know it's interesting what makes a star. With Ginger, I think it's her love of life. I think that comes through. I think that they feel a real connection, and that's what Ginger brings," Veronica Hart summed up. Ginger maintained an active lifestyle in 2002 as she approached her third year of being drug-free. Said Penny Antine, "You know the courage it takes to work through all that life style and to come out of it as sane and as straight and as loving as Ginger has come out of this." Added Sharon Mitchell, "She's come a long way. I mean, she was a little skinny girl, and now she's this wonderful voluptuous mom movie star, bigger than life, a sincere person who's clean and sober. You can't ask for better gifts in life."

In February 2002, Ginger Lynn shot her fifth film for VCA, titled *Sunset Stripped*, a spoof about aging adult-film actors. A few days after wrapping the movie, she announced that *Sunset Stripped* was her last adult film. "It's been fun," she said. "It's a lot different than it used to be. There's a certain point where it's time a girl hangs up her G-string, and I think it's about time for me to do that. I came in with a bang. I want to go out with one, too, no pun intended." Ginger still has aspirations of making a splash in Hollywood, but today her main focus remains her son, Sterling. "When she talks about her son, she'll get this smile, and it's like you're seeing that innocence that so many people—never mind adult-film industry people—just don't have anymore." Ginger affirmed, "My priorities have changed. I was so driven for so long to be something, to be somebody, to prove a point not even knowing what the point was. I love acting. I would love to grow old and always be in the entertainment industry in one way, shape, or form—doing that today is a bonus."

In the adult-film industry, Ginger Lynn is an icon. "I think that she is as popular in probably the largest part of America as any mainstream actress, even though she's in a different genre," said Veronica Hart. Bionca added, "She is a legend. Ginger Lynn is a legend and will always remain a legend in our industry. That's something that will never, ever die." In the meantime, Ginger has a few other dreams she is pursuing. She announced proudly, "I want to host *Saturday Night Live*. I want to be on *Mad TV*. I want a stamp with my face on it!" During a taped interview, she mused: "This is all about my fulfilling my fantasies. I can't believe that things like this happen. Now I know I'm dreaming. This is soap-opera land, and I'm the queen—unbelievable. So where do we go from here?" Responded costar Evan Stone, without missing a beat: "Live happily ever after."

CHAPTER 8

SISTER ACT
The Paris and Nicky Hilton Story

"They represent everything that a gossip column is about."

—*Chris Wilson, Page Six gossip columnist*

Filthy rich and hot, hot, hot. The Hilton sisters are heiresses to the Hilton hotel megafortune. From New York to L.A., they always attract attention—and lots of men. Paris and Nicky can't stay out of trouble or the tabloids. But don't hate them because they're beautiful. Rich girls have problems, too. These two sisters were made for glitz, glamour, and gossip. This is their story.

The Hilton hotel fortune is a multimillion-dollar legacy. Paris and Nicky never knew anything but luxury, thanks to their great-grandfather Conrad Hilton Sr. "He was considered the greatest hotel man in the country—in the world, probably," offered columnist James Bacon. In 1919, thirty-one-year-old Conrad Hilton left his hometown of San Antonio, New Mexico. Described Conrad's daughter, Constance Francesca Hilton, "He went to Texas to start a bank during the oil boom, and the bank was closed, but the flophouse was open. He went to the flophouse and saw there were three turnovers, because it was the oil boom, and he said, 'Wow, I could make money here.'" From that one flophouse, Conrad Hilton built an entire chain of hotels.

By 1926, thirty-eight-year-old Conrad was a self-made tycoon. He and his wife, Mary Barron Hilton, had three sons: Conrad Nicholson Jr. (better known as Nicky), William Barron, and Eric Michael. All Conrad cared about, though, was his work. In 1934, Mary and Conrad divorced. Eight years later, he married famed Hungarian party girl Zsa Zsa Gabor. The couple's daughter

Francesca said that Zsa Zsa "made a bet with some lawyer that she should get my father to marry her. My mother really fell in love with my father." According to Zsa Zsa, "I was forty-one years younger. He didn't understand me at all. I was a young girl from a very good family." Ultimately, Conrad was "more interested in buying hotels than he was in Zsa Zsa," said James Bacon, so the couple divorced.

Conrad's sons wanted to be just like Dad. In 1950, twenty-three-year-old Nicky Hilton married another famous beauty, eighteen-year-old movie star Elizabeth Taylor. "Everybody thought, God, this is going to be a great, great marriage, you know, because it was the Hilton name and the movies' most beautiful star," said Bacon. But it was not a great union. Seven months later, Taylor filed for divorce, citing "extreme mental pain, suffering and anguish." Nicky seemed to love drinking and gambling more than he loved his wife. Recalled Bacon, "Elizabeth told me that on their honeymoon cruise he spent most of his time in the casino and not with her, and he drank pretty well. Barron was a more serious brother."

Barron helped his father run the business, including New York's landmark Waldorf-Astoria. When Conrad Hilton passed away on January 3, 1979, fifty-one-year-old Barron assumed the Hilton throne. Meanwhile, Barron's son, Rick Hilton, carried on the family tradition of courting Hollywood actresses. In 1975, the nineteen-year-old met former child actress Kathy Richards, just fifteen at the time. Kathy's sister, Kyle Richards, said, "Kathy quit when she was a teenager. She was in the business, but it wasn't really for her." More than anything, Kathy wanted to be a wife and a mother. Four years later, Kathy and Rick tied the knot. According to Kyle, "Kathy and Rick have an unbelievable relationship. They've been together for a long time, since they were kids. They are truly best friends. They've never been apart from each other."

On February 17, 1981, Kathy and Rick had their first child, a daughter they named Paris. Explained publicist Catherine Saxton, "They wanted a soft, beautiful name, so they thought Paris, which is one of their favorite cities, is soft and beautiful." Kyle Richards described *l'enfant* Paris as "the most beautiful baby I've ever seen in my entire life. I was so in love with her. She had a housekeeper that nicknamed her 'Star,' because she was such a beautiful baby." Two and a half years later, on October 5, 1983, Paris got some competition. "When Nicky was born, I was in New York at the hospital, and they were like two little dolls," said Richards. Even at an early age, the girls turned heads. "I would walk the two of them down the street in the stroller, and strangers would stop me every five seconds," asking to take pictures of the beautiful tots.

But that was where the similarity ended. "Nicky was always very shy and quiet," said friend Kimberly Stewart, "Whereas me and Paris were always loud and we would be obnoxious." The sisters also had very different interests. "Paris wanted to be a veterinarian. She always had with her a stray cat, a dog, a puppy. It was nothing for her to be walking around with a rat in her hand," laughed Richards. Rescuing animals wasn't sexy enough for Nicky. Her particular talent was already apparent. "She was always into fashion, even as a kid. I have to say, she had just a flair for that," said Richards. "She was one of those kids that could throw on jeans and a T-shirt and it looked like a stylist put her together." On the outside, the sisters looked sensational. As Catherine Saxton put it, "When you are a Hilton, you are to the manor born. Paris and Nicky were born to the world of the elite and the social."

In 1989, baby brother Barron joined Paris and Nicky at the Hilton manor. Four and a half years later, Conrad was born. "Paris and Barron are the mirror images of each other, and Nicky and Conrad are the mirror images and their characters and personalities are very similar," said Sexton. "They were always the big sisters and they taught each other how to swim and how to relax and the boys always had animals around the place." According to Merle Ginsberg, the coauthor of Paris's autobiography, *Confessions of an Heiress* "Nicky and Paris and their two little baby brothers grew up in this very, sort of enchanted lifestyle in

Beverly Hills, where their parents were friends with movie stars and socialites."

Paris and Nicky also hung out with other famous kids at the elite and private Buckley School in Sherman Oaks, California. Friend Nicole Richie recalled, "Because our families were all friends and everything, we went to the same school, we had the same piano teacher." Said Kimberly Stewart, "I just remember Paris at Buckley—all the guys loved her, because we had to wear uniforms, our skirts would be a little bit shorter than everyone else's, and we always used to get in trouble for it."

School also brought the sisters the realization that their famous name made them different—sometimes even hated. Speculated Kyle Richards, "I think their peers became more aware of what they had and, you know, were jealous. I think I would definitely have to say they were picked on a bit in junior high." Paris and Nicky learned fast that being born with a silver spoon in their mouths definitely had a downside. "They're beautiful, they're rich, they have the last name Hilton, they're tall, they're skinny— they're going to get picked on. I think it definitely made them a target," Richards continued. The Hilton girls would soon find out what being a target really meant.

Growing up in the sunshine and laid-back atmosphere of Los Angeles with a last name like Hilton primed these two very special ladies for fame. In 1996, Rick and Kathy packed up and moved their family into the penthouse of the Hilton-owned Waldorf-Astoria in New York City. Nicky and Paris craved attention, and New York's social scene gave them just that. *Quest* magazine society editor David Patrick Columbia justified the girls' behavior, saying, "They were just like all the other little girls. They all wanted to go to nightclubs at night, which everybody thought they were too young to do but all of those girls did, all of them, and the Hiltons were two of them."

Nicky and Paris attended exclusive private high schools. Paris went to Dwight, and Nicky was enrolled at Sacred Heart. They mixed with the children of other power families and were soon jostling for a top spot on the social circuit. Explained gossip columnist Chris Wilson, "New York is unique in that there's sort of this culture of young girls that are from rich families . . . that like to go out to parties." Magazine editor Claus Grunitzky added with some cynicism, "You don't know what they actually do, but you see them out every night, and they're either aspiring singers, aspiring actresses, aspiring MTV VJs, or so on. They always have something really, really big that they're on the verge of making happen."

Paris reveled in the spotlight, attracting the attention of designers and the press. According to Merle Ginsberg, "Paris told me stories about designers wanting her to walk runways. She was like fifteen and I think her mother nixed that. Her mother sensed that Paris was going to be kind of outrageous and wild." Still, Kathy and Rick Hilton made sure their daughter got plenty of attention. The parents took their two daughters all over New York, to all the parties. Soon Paris and her family learned the terrifying price of a high profile. During her last year of high school, Paris was the target of a stalker. According to Catherine Saxton, "There was a stalker, and there was a stalker at the Waldorf. It's very dangerous, and for years we would say to people, 'Please don't print their address.'" Paris was taken out of school, and the Hiltons beefed up security. The stalker claim was never officially confirmed. A Dwight school representative denied any knowledge of the problem.

Regardless, the incident did little to slow down the two teenagers. Paris and Nicky managed a frantic social calendar. Typical months included art openings, charity balls, and their new personal obsession: fashion shows. But the sisters didn't just sit and watch. "I've been at shows where suddenly they pop up on the runway and they're just as good as the other girls. They know how to walk. They look good," offered *Village Voice* columnist Michael Musto. Said Saxton, "It is so amazing when you see those first pictures of the two of them coming down the runway. It was just heart-stopping, because they were so young and so beautiful." Stylist Rebecca Weinberg commented on their natural assets: "They've got the legs and the arms and the hair, and they've got the whole thing going on, so I think it was a natural evolution for them to eventually get up on the runway."

If people hadn't noticed by now, Nicky and Paris made it very clear: These two firecrackers were not your average everyday debutantes. They were hotter than hot, richer than rich, and destined to play out their lives in public. "They've kind of become the poster girls for New York young socialites," observed Chris Wilson. "I think the only way they're debutantes is really their name and their status, but other than that, it's just not who they are," qualified Kyle Richards. Musto offered that "the teenage Hiltons were of course exposed to New York social life at its finest because they had to go to very fancy, upper-class events. But they also got a taste for New York nightlife at its wildest." "They'd walk into a room, and there was a certain magnetism. People would say, 'Oh, they're here.' I always thought it was great," said family friend Donald Trump.

Unfortunately, many of the same resentments that dogged the Hilton sisters in their school days exploded in the higher-profile world of New York society. Commented Michael Musto, "The second the Hilton girls made it, you noticed a lot of backbiting on the scene." Agreed Wilson, "There's a lot of eye-rolling behind the scenes. There's a lot of whispering. There's some jealousy involved, and that's to be expected." When the backbiting took the form of mocking Web sites, Musto laughed, "Once you have a Web site that's created just to make fun of you, that means you're somebody."

"They might have developed a sense of bravado, as if to say, 'That's not going to hurt my feelings,' and maybe it's misinterpreted as arrogance," commented Kyle Richards. "I don't know, but I looked, and I know that they're just sweet girls who have feelings, and I don't think people realize that."

As the new millennium rolled around, eighteen-year-old Paris and her sixteen-year-old sister, Nicky, decided to take their fame to the next level. Musto explained, "Before the Hilton girls came around, there weren't really distinctive 'It' girls on the uptown social scene at that moment. So when they came, it was a burst of fresh air." Said Wilson, "They were showing up at all these parties, and people seemed to embrace them. From the moment they stepped into that world, they became stars." Continued Musto, "They were the new, young money. They were the people everybody wanted to be."

With their California-girl good looks, the sexy heiresses quickly became number one on nightclub comp lists all over town. "I noticed that everywhere I went, they were there. You couldn't stay away from them," remarked magazine editor Claus Grunitzky, "and it was kind of like a weird thing, posing for the paparazzi, always being at the table with a celebrity, and always seeming to have a great time." Michael Musto noticed, however, that those good times quickly became the foundation for their party-girl reputations. "They were literally dancing on tabletops. They were at everything from benefits to balls to dances, uptown, downtown, after hours, before hours. If there was a gift bag or a guest list, they were there."

The Hilton sisters attracted plenty of attention from Manhattan gossipmongers. The exploits of Nicky and Paris became mandatory reading. "They represent everything that a gossip column is about—wealth, youth, beauty, bad behavior, wild antics, and they've got it all," said Chris Wilson. "I find that they're very accessible," said Musto. "In face, the first time I met them, I just went right up to them at a party, and they weren't surrounded by any entourage at all, just the two of them together. It was almost like them against the world." For Paris and Nicky, there was no turning back. The press couldn't get enough of the wealthy party girls, and they were happy to oblige, especially Paris.

As Paris said herself, "I just don't want to be rude and yell at photographers. They're doing their job so I'm trying to make it a little easier for them by being nice."

The girls were sometimes mistaken for twins, but it was plain that Nicky had her own style. Observed Kimberly Stewart, "She's much more laid-back and conservative than Paris." Rebecca Weinberg drew the distinction that "Paris is kinetic. She's interested in everything. She's got a million things going on, and so does Nick, but Nick is a little bit more reserved." Paris, on the other hand, is always the center of attention. Stewart mused, "When I've gone out with Paris she's always the life of the party. She's out there, dancing anywhere she wants."

Paris's behavior wasn't exactly aristocratic. According to an item in the *New York Post* dated August 31, 2000, Paris Hilton allegedly went topless at a party at the Hard Rock Hotel in Las Vegas and ran laps around the pool, in full view of the guests. Paris denied the incident. Recalled Chris Wilson, "You would get these wild reports, these wild sightings of her in L.A., in Vegas, in London, in New York. It just seems like they would just come hard and heavy." For Paris and her younger sister, the constant press coverage was both distressing and strangely addictive. "There's a bit of a dichotomy whereby they complain about the publicity they get, and yet they're drawn to it. They create it themselves," said Michael Musto. Speculated Wilson, "I think they realize that at least they can use the gossip column as a stepping stone to bigger things." Whether true or highly exaggerated, the reports never let up. According to entertainment journalist Michael Lewittes, "The Hilton sisters feel good publicity or bad publicity is publicity, and the more the better. The one thing they don't like is mean-spirited publicity."

The sisters' mom worried that her girls were an easy target because of their blond hair and rich name, but countered, "They're nice girls, they're very sweet. I don't want anybody to be mean to them or pick on them." Kathy not only supported her girls, she accompanied them to nightclubs and events. "They're Hollywood people," said magazine editor David Patrick Columbia, "and I think that when this whole thing began for her daughters, she was well aware of the pitfalls that occur in the lives of very young people when they're scooped up by the media. So she stayed very close to them, and she's let it happen, but she's let it happen with a guiding hand."

The girls were proven stars in New York gossip columns, but they were about to find worldwide fame in the pages of a glossy magazine. Paris and Nicky "kind of became a brand name to themselves," said Chris Wilson. The girls were offered a spread in *Vanity Fair*, shot by world-renowned photographer David LaChappelle. However, after the issue hit stands in September 2000, Paris was nervous. According to Kyle Richards, "When the *Vanity Fair* came out, Paris called me up, and she was crying and said, 'My mom is going to kill me. I don't know what I'm going to do. She's going to kill me!'" The twelve-page spread offered a revealing look at the lives of the Hilton sisters, including one saucy photo where Paris gave the finger to the camera. The photos seemed to capture the true spirit of the two party girls, especially Paris.

The national exposure beamed the Hilton sisters out of New York City and on to the pages of major magazines around the world. They became international "It" girls. Still, they were simply famous for being famous. According to Merle Ginsberg, "They were . . . very, sort of boldly self-consciously spoiled, rich, obviously very privileged. And . . . very unapologetic." Said Rebecca Weinberg, "They are fashion. They're the girls that can afford it. They're the girls that wear it. They're the girls that are out there showing it off. They're *It*."

If Paris and Nicky's parents worried that the *Vanity Fair* photos were steamy, they soon had more to be concerned about. In May of 2002, the girls revealed their "sexier side in an *FHM* magazine spread. "When they did *FHM*, they were over eighteen. If they were to ask their mother and their father if they could do that, the answer would be no, but they don't have to ask once they're eighteen," reasoned their aunt Kyle.

Nicky and Paris's popularity was skyrocketing, and they were looking for the right guys to accessorize their lives. In August 2000, Paris began dating twenty-three-year-old Edward Furlong, costar of *Terminator 2*. Paris met Edward at a Las Vegas party.

According to a September 8 report in the *New York Post,* Paris found herself in a nasty squabble with Furlong's former girlfriend. "She took up with him right after he dated the actress Natasha Lyonne," recounted Chris Wilson. "I remember there was a party on the top of the *Playboy* headquarters on Fifth Avenue. Paris ran into Natasha Lyonne, and Natasha Lyonne kind of squared off with her. It was pretty scandalous for the party." But Paris had bigger problems. Her new beau was giving in to his own demons. Furlong's battles with drinking were well documented, and while he struggled, the press zeroed in on Paris. "She was kind of guilty by association when he'd show up at a nightclub and throw up or something," she would look bad, reported Wilson. "Ultimately, the whole relationship just fell apart," said Michael Musto.

On the rebound from Furlong, the wealthy playgirl went on a romantic rampage. E! online columnist Ted Casablanca said, "Let's talk about Paris's dating habits, because there's a lot to be revealed there—Oscar de la Hoya for a couple of months, Leonardo DiCaprio, Jared Leto," and the list went on and on. Then in late 2000, nineteen-year-old Paris fell for Internet gambling mogul Rick Salomon. Salomon was thirty-one. Musto confirmed, "Paris and Rick were deeply involved. It looked like they were whole hog." Meanwhile, the media reported that seventeen-year-old Nicky dated male models Mark Vanderloo and Marcus Scherkenberg. Kyle Richards explained, "I think that what happens to any actress or anybody well known—you're seen with somebody, and they say you're dating them."

Nobody doubted, however, that Paris was hanging out with a very rough crowd. As Michael Musto said, "Those guys are guys who, when they party, really party hard. So she was kind of brought into the vortex of some serious, heavy-duty fun." Wondered Ted Casablanca, "I don't know. It's sort of like the chicken and the egg. Is this where she picked up her party habits, or did they get worse?" Chris Wilson acknowledged, "I think there was a period where she was drinking perhaps a little too much, and she realized it, and she cut it out."

By spring 2001, Paris's relationship with party pal Rick Salomon had fizzled out. She tried to take some time off from partying and men, but the next hottie was already waiting in the wings. In April 2001, a friend introduced Paris to twenty-eight-year-old Tommy Hilfiger model Jason Shaw. It was lust at first sight. Richards described Shaw as "a really sweet, all-American, down-to-earth guy. I mean, really great guy. Our family loves him. He's reserved and kind of sits back and lets her have fun in the spotlight." Said Kimberly Stewart, "I told her she should marry him. They were a perfect match." Paris wasn't the only Hilton smitten with a handsome celebrity. Nicky also roped in a famous heartthrob in twenty-six-year-old former MTV VJ Brian McFayden. Richards admitted, "We love Brian, too. He's great. He's really funny, which works really well with our family. We're all kind of jokesters, and Nicky is really hysterically funny."

In addition to her sense of humor, Nicky Hilton also demonstrated a flare for business. In September 2001, she began studying design at the Fashion Institute of Technology and the Parsons School of Design in New York City. "She was voted [one of the] top one hundred best dressed in the world by *Vogue* at fifteen years old. That kinda says it all," said Richards. That winter, eighteen-year-old Nicky and twenty-year-old Paris signed on as spokesmodels for Samantha Thavasa, a Tokyo-based handbag company. Thavasa recognized Nicky as more than just a pretty face and invited her to create her own line of purses. Said publicist Brian Long, "Nicky really just started off designing one or two bags, and now she's doing the whole collection. They tend to be very representative of hers and Paris's sort of unique style."

For the moment, the outrageous Hilton sisters seemed ready to settle down, but fame has a funny way of pushing even the most devoted lovers to the breaking point. Though the sisters seemed to have everything money could buy—hunky boyfriends, entrée to every A-list party, and lots of publicity—too much of a good thing turned sour really fast. "Here are these two rich girls who did everything and yet they didn't seem to do much of anything except party, and it became a pitfall of their fame," said Michael Lewittes.

In 2002, the Hilton sisters were everywhere—in gossip columns, in magazines, and on news reports from coast to coast. Paris and Nicky were household names. That August, they were the subjects of a scathing satire published in a world-famous men's magazine. "*GQ* wanted to have fun at the expense of the Hilton sisters, so they created these fictitious sisters called the Marriott sisters who spent a lot of money, whose family was very rich, who went to tons of parties, and always looked fabulous— and occasionally embarrassed themselves," recalled Lewittes. However, according to Michael Musto, "Once you start spawning imitations and satires, you've really arrived."

Paris and Nicky were becoming acutely aware that they were famous for absolutely nothing except their good looks and money. But the girls wanted real careers. Nicky focused on her fashion studies while Paris took on Hollywood. Paris appeared as herself in the Ben Stiller fashion comedy *Zoolander*, but her first juicy role came in the 2002 low-budget horror film *Nine Lives*. "She prepared hard for this. She wanted to do well, I think she wanted to impress," said director Andrew Green. "She has a screen presence that I haven't seen in a long time. Whenever anybody saw the dailies, they were wild. Whenever production companies saw them, they said, 'Put more Paris in. Write something more for her.'"

Paris also landed small parts in a few more films and television shows, but the acting gigs did little to curb Paris's appetite for the party circuit. "She definitely liked to go out. She goes to parties. She goes to nightclubs. She's part of the L.A. sort of pseudo-celebrity social scene," said Chris Wilson. Somewhere between her lukewarm career and her white-hot social life, Paris lost track of the one boy who really loved her. According to Musto, "Paris really thought that Jason Shaw was Mr. Right. She thought this was it." According to Lewittes, "She loved the guy, but she realized she was very young and not ready to get married. She was also focused on her career, and she likes going out and having a good time." Concluded Musto, "It seemed a little doomed to people in the know, because she's still married to going out, and their lifestyles were so different. There was so much time apart that it seemed to combust naturally."

In February 2003, after two years together, Paris Hilton and Jason Shaw were history. Paris was determined to make it on her own. According to Michael Musto, "She really couldn't settle down with any one guy. She literally belonged to the entire world." But Paris wasn't out of the dating game for long. A few weeks after splitting with Shaw, the *New York Post* reported that she and old flame Salomon enjoyed a ten-day fling at the Beverly Hills Hotel. Rick's estranged wife, former *Beverly Hills 90210* actress Shannen Doherty, was not happy with the news. "Paris and Shannen Doherty were at Club Deluxe in Hollywood when they had words," reported Chris Wilson. "Paris says that she was attacked by Shannen Doherty. She said that she was grabbed on the face, grabbed on the arm, roughed up." Doherty said the scuffle never happened.

"It's like teenagers fighting over boyfriends," scoffed stylist Rebecca Weinberg, who continued, "It's a competitive world out there, and sometimes you have to break a nail or two." The embarrassing incident made the gossip pages of the *New York Post*.

By the spring of 2003, the public fixated on Paris's every move. Execs at the Fox Network decided to cash in. They offered the twenty-two-year-old heiress her own reality series, *The Simple Life*. Just weeks before the series premiered, Paris's life got very complicated. In November 2003, a racy video of the heiress that was made years earlier ended up on the Internet. The twenty-seven-minute tape showed Paris and former boyfriend Rick Salomon having sex. The explicit video became an underground smash. The controversy sent Paris reeling. "She felt violated. She was devastated." said Kimberly Stewart. The Hiltons and Salomon soon began a legal battle over the tape.

In the meantime, Paris's "other" reality show took off. In its first season, *The Simple Life*, starring Paris and longtime friend Nicole Richie, produced a surprise ratings bonanza for Fox. Three million viewers tuned into the first episode.

Paris soon had another new beau on her arm, Nick Carter of the Backstreet Boys. Said Michael Musto, "It was something unexpected, and the media and the American public love something that you didn't see coming. Nobody saw this kind of slightly postpeak boy group member who's embarking on a solo career hooking up with this most famous socialite celebrity in the world."

In 2004, network executives launched *The Simple Life 2*, with Paris and Nicole Richie taking a road trip across the U.S. *The Simple Life 2* became one of summer's top-rated shows.

During the trip for *The Simple Life 2*, Paris coined a new catchphrase, "That's hot!" Later that same month, Paris's first movie, *The Hillz*, opened at the Boston International Film Festival after sitting on the shelf for two years. Critics ignored the film, and it never even made it to theaters. In early July, the ambitious socialite branched out in a new direction by launching a record label, Heiress, and announced plans for an album. She even starred in a video for Haitian hip-hop artist Won-G. Soon after the video debuted, Paris and Rick Salomon ended their legal wrangling over the infamous sex tape. Paris reportedly received four hundred grand plus a percentage of the tape sales. "The next thing you know," said Musto, "Paris was in a video store, being photographed, buying a copy of the video, *One Night in Paris*, and then you really had to start to wonder what was behind this whole chain of events."

In July 2004, Paris Hilton and Nick Carter split after seven months together. Paris blamed her busy career, while Nick said their relationship was "based on distrust." One week after the split, Paris showed up in public sporting bruises and a swollen lip. Reports quickly surfaced with Carter's name attached. On August 2, 2004, he told *People* magazine that he didn't lay a hand on Paris. Nick's lawyer claimed the bruises came from a bondage-style photo shoot Hilton did for *Rolling Stone* magazine. Paris did not comment, but Musto thought, "The abuse allegations made for very scandalous tabloid headlines, and then it was just kind of diffused after Nick denied it."

And what about Nicky Hilton? Nicky and her older sister went to Las Vegas, in mid-August that same year, for a weekend of partying. Sometime during the second night of the trip, the Hilton sisters snuck off, and Nicky got hitched. The thirty-two-year-old groom, Todd Meister, worked as a money manager in New York. Members of the Hilton clan were not happy about being left out of the affair. Catherine Saxton commented, "This is a very traditional family, and I know more than anything else that Rick and Kathy want those big beautiful weddings for their big, beautiful daughters." Soon after the wedding, Nicky returned to Vegas to debut her new clothing line, Chick by Nicky Hilton.

In September 2004, stories broke about more scandalous tapes. This time footage alledgedly included pot smoking and more sex. That same month Paris launched a line of jewelry that reflected her own personal style. Soon after, Paris released her autobiography, *Confessions of an Heiress*. The book became an instant bestseller. At the same time, questions about Nicky's marriage began popping up. On October 2, the newlywed showed up at a John Kerry fund-raiser without her million-dollar diamond ring. By late October, Nicky and Todd Meister decided to have their union annulled after less than three months. The couple issued a statement saying they ended the marriage amicably and remain good friends.

Meanwhile, Paris landed the starring role in the teen comedy *National Lampoon's Pledge This!* As the holidays approached, she joined the ranks of Britney, J.Lo, and Beyoncé when she launched her own signature scent, Paris. Anything involving the Hilton sisters continued to be hot. Just one month after Nicky's annulment, the press buzzed about her latest conquest. "Nicky didn't waste a lot of time before getting on the rebound and getting a new boyfriend, actor Kevin Connelly," said Michael Musto. Meanwhile, reports linked Paris to tennis pro Andy Roddick and then bad boy Colin Farrell.

That December, Paris Hilton inked a deal to appear in television ads for T-Mobile's Sidekick, and she opened her first club, appropriately called Club Paris, in Orlando, Florida, on December 30. Three weeks later, *The Simple Life 3: Interns* debuted on Fox. Although critics bashed it, the premiere once again scored top ratings.

So what's next for the girls who have absolutely everything? Friends and family see no end to Paris's potential. Said Kimberly Stewart, "She's going to take over the universe, so, like . . . I mean, Martha Stewart, move over."

While Nicky prefers to stay under the radar, she's driven when it comes to her career. According to Stewart, "Nicky is probably going to take over the fashion world, and I'll try to keep up with her."

Famous for being famous? Not anymore. Paris and Nicky Hilton silenced many of their harshest critics while still in their twenties. There's plenty of time to keep everyone guessing about what they'll do next. Scott Gramling of *FHM* magazine summed up, "People like to watch other people having fun and nobody has more fun than the Hilton sisters."

CHAPTER 9

AMERICA'S SWEETHEART

The Katie Couric Story

"She's like Shirley Temple grown up."

—*Larry King, CNN host,* Larry King Live

Did I feel when I first met Katie she was going to be the big star she is today?" asked veteran ABC News reporter Sam Donaldson. "No. I can't say that I did. But it was clear she had a spark." In December 2001, the forty-four-year-old cohost of *The Today Show* didn't just break the glass ceiling; she shattered it. Katie renewed her contract, and the deal made her the highest-paid journalist on television. Over the years, she weathered many storms, personal and professional. She survived them all. Katie is persuasive and packs a punch. She is fearless, she has made TV history, and has become America's sweetheart. However, NBC's spunky golden girl wasn't always at the head of her class. In fact, Katie nearly flunked out during her jerky first days on air, but she quickly won over audiences with her personality and intelligence. She's been dealt devastating blows, but she's roared back all the way to the top. As America has learned, there's a lot more to Katie Couric than meets the eye, and this is her story.

Katherine Anne Couric, the youngest of four children, was born on January 7, 1957, in Arlington, Virginia, a suburb of Washington, D.C. Early on, Katie learned how to hold an audience captive. Described *TV Guide* senior writer Mary Murphy, "Katie is musical, and, as a kid, she was always dressing up in her neighborhood, singing 'Let Me Entertain You.'" Katie's parents were full of loving support for their young daughter. "She comes from a wonderful family, and she was always encouraged to be talkative to the point of giving her opinions and listening to others," explained Don Farmer, former congressional correspondent for ABC News. In 1972, Katie enrolled at Yorktown High School. She was active in track and field, gymnastics, and cheerleading. Katie was a wholesome kid, but she did have a mischievous side. On one occasion, said Murphy, "Katie was caught in a bathroom with a cigarette, and she was suspended for a while, but the truth is, she said to her mother, 'No, I wasn't smoking it, I was just holding it for a friend,' and she convinced her mother." It was a minor indiscretion by an otherwise stellar student. In 1975, eighteen-year-old Katie graduated with honors.

That fall, she enrolled at the University of Virginia, one of the top schools in the country. Katie majored in American Studies and served as associate editor of the campus newspaper, *The Cavalier Daily*. She also interned at local radio stations. "Katie learned how to do interviews from being on the radio. She learned how to be to the point, and she learned how to listen," said Mary Murphy. Katie graduated in 1979 with one goal in mind—to be a journalist. Next stop: Washington, D.C. When she got there, according to Murphy, Katie "marched into ABC" and scored a job as a desk assistant. "No one could say she started at the top," said Sam Donaldson. "Katie started at the bottom, right here." Still, Katie was determined to make the most of the entry-level position. Donaldson, who was renowned for terrorizing grunt-level recruits, took a liking to Katie, because she "was always tough. I think from the very beginning, it was clear that Katie was one who had some steel there." It was also clear that Katie's enthusiasm and charisma were infectious. A week after she arrived, Donaldson serenaded her, singing, "K-k-katie, K-k-katie, you're the only one that I adore when the moon shines over the cow shed, I'll be waiting at the k-k-kitchen door."

In 1980, several members of the news team left ABC to launch the Washington bureau of cable start-up CNN. According to Don Farmer, "The network was only in about 1.7 million homes. Few people had cable at that time, so it was a good time to make our mistakes." Katie got the chance to hone her skills in front of the camera and behind the scenes. She joined her colleagues as an assignment editor, a position that allowed for some intermittent on-air reporting. Recalled Katie's friend Wendy Walker Whitworth, "There was so much need for material, nobody cared if Katie went out and put it on the air." However, the cofounder of CNN, Reese Schonfeld did care. Schonfeld knew exactly what he wanted, and a rookie reporter named Katie Couric wasn't it. "One morning, I wake up, and there's Katie on the air," recounted Schonfeld. "She looks twenty years old. She's shivering with fear. Her voice is trembling, and I immediately call Washington and ask, 'Why is she on the air?,' and he says, 'The anchor didn't show up, and I had to put her on. I had nobody else!' And I said, 'Never do that again! I don't ever want to see her again!'"

"Katie could have just said, 'Okay, I'm done, I'll just be a producer,' but she didn't," commented Mary Murphy. Katie's drive and competitive nature kept her afloat when many people in her position would have sunk. Nevertheless, Katie did have to regroup. She left CNN's Washington bureau and moved to network headquarters in Atlanta. There, she accepted a position as associate producer on *Take Two*, a daily news and information program hosted by Don Farmer and Chris Curle. Said Curle, "Katie would run the camera, she would write, she would produce. She would do anything and everything." In the trenches, the versatility and natural skills that now underscore Katie's on-air persona began to flourish. Larry King, host of CNN's popular *Larry King Live*, said frankly, "CNN misjudged her, didn't think she had the talent to be a broadcaster." These days, Schonfeld himself even kids, "You know what is going to be on my tombstone? 'Here lies Reese Schonfeld. He didn't recognize Katie's talent.'"

According to Farmer, Katie "seemed to really put a hundred percent into every task no matter how menial," during her first months at CNN. The hard work paid off when Couric was promoted to producer. In April 1982, twenty-five-year-old Katie and the rest of the *Take Two* team traveled to Havana, Cuba, for two weeks of live broadcasts. "Katie was able to cut through all the tension between the Cubans and the Americans, and do this monumental program. She had the ability to keep everybody at an even keel," said Farmer. For the next couple of years, Katie worked hard on her career behind the scenes. But the young producer longed to be in front of the lens. In the summer of 1984, she got her wish. Katie returned to the capital as a temporary on-air correspondent for CNN during the presidential campaign. Farmer recalled that her greatest talent was "talking to politicians and getting serious answers" without ever coming "across as a bulldog."

That fall, the election season drew to a close, and so did Katie's short on-air stint at CNN. She began a period of personal and professional change. Katie was determined to pursue her dreams in spite of discouraging reviews of her onscreen talent. "She was very depressed," said Chris Curle, "and she said, 'I want to be a reporter,' and we said, 'Well, then, quit and go be a reporter.'" So Katie left CNN. For the next four years, she tackled local news as a street reporter at NBC affiliates in Miami and Washington, D.C.

In her personal life, Katie Couric dated occasionally, but focused mostly on getting her career on track. That all changed in 1988 at a Washington, D.C., cocktail party. "Katie was talking to these guys and they said they were lawyers, and she said, 'Yuck.' Then this other guy said, 'Well, I'm not a lawyer, I'm an artist,'" described Mary Murphy. His name was Jay Monahan, and it turned out that he was a lawyer. Jay and Katie shared an instant connection. Ten months later, they were engaged. The couple married on January 24, 1989, when Katie was thirty-two and Jay was thirty-four. "Katie and Jay were really devoted to each other," commented Sam Donaldson. "I think they were truly in love, and you couldn't see them together without understanding that."

But Katie's career wasn't so together, and she was determined to turn it around. In July 1989, Katie left local news for a job as deputy Pentagon reporter for NBC. David Martin, a CBS

Pentagon correspondent, recognized from the start that Katie "was trouble . . . I wanted to hang a sign outside her door: BEWARE, SHE MAY LOOK SWEET AND INNOCENT, BUT SHE'LL STEAL YOUR LUNCH." Donaldson agreed, "When she was over at the Pentagon for a while, quite clearly she made a mark for herself." Five months into the gig, the U.S. military invaded Panama. NBC sent chief Pentagon correspondent Fred Francis to cover the invasion, leaving Katie in the hot seat at home. During this pivotal trial period, Katie earned her stripes as "credible, reliable, and willing to work," said Farmer.

Meanwhile, over on *The Today Show*, an invasion of another kind was underway. Cohost Jane Pauley left after thirteen years on the air. Pauley was replaced by news anchor Deborah Norville, which caused quite a few waves. Pauley had been a beloved anchor, and, according to Robert Thompson, director of the Center for the Study of Popular Television, a lot of people viewed the change as "the young, pretty person who was knocking Queen Jane off of her throne." Explained Michael Gartner, former president of NBC News, "Deborah was very smart. She was beautiful, she was very capable and talented, but as an anchor with Bryant it just didn't work very well." The lack of chemistry between Norville and veteran anchor Bryant Gumbel was apparent, and ratings began to slip. Meanwhile, Katie joined *The Today Show* as a national correspondent. In January 1991, American forces were deployed to the Middle East for the Gulf War. Katie was assigned to cover the conflict. Her reports resonated with viewers back home. "Katie's secret is that she has no secret. She is that person you see on television. She's not faking it," said David Martin. Agreed Gartner, "She had what my 101-year-old father calls an 'affidavit face.' She's believable."

Back at NBC headquarters in New York, the new cohost of *The Today Show* was really feeling the heat. In late February 1991, Norville went on maternity leave. On February 25, 1991, Bryant Gumbel greeted *The Today Show* audience with his trademark style, but one aspect of the broadcast was different: with Gumbel's embattled coanchor on leave, Katie filled in for Norville and made the most of the opportunity. "I think America instantly fell in love with her," said Michael Gartner. According to Robert Thompson, "Back then people were following *The Today Show* cast changes like a soap opera. Some people saw Katie Couric was the one that was going to knock that evil Deborah Norville down a few pegs." While being on during the early morning hours is "the most difficult job in all of television," said Andrew Tyndall, publisher of *The Tyndall Report,* Katie pulled it off because "she can go from one segment to the next, change her mood entirely, and look perfectly credible in doing so."

Though *The Today Show* had lost ground in the morning–talk show battle after Jane Pauley's departure, with Katie Couric on board, viewers came back and stayed. Mary Murphy commented, "As soon as Katie arrived, the ratings started to climb, and NBC executives realized immediately that they had to keep Katie." Willard Scott, *Today*'s beloved weatherman, had an insider's perspective. Scott noticed that "she became so popular so fast because people really did hone in on her. The fact is she was really a breath of fresh air and sort of cleared the air." It was a delicate situation, and it soon became evident that Norville wasn't going to come back. On April 4, 1991, Katie Couric officially became cohost of *The Today Show*. Ironically, she was also pregnant at the time. Bryant Gumbel and Couric connected instantly, but there was more. She injected a special brand of energy into every aspect of the show. "Katie is now a permanent fixture up here," said Gumbel, "a member of our family, and an especially welcome one."

Katie came into her own in her new slot as *Today Show* coanchor. Much of Katie's success could be attributed to her quick wit and her always effervescent personality. "She's probably the first woman on network television in a serious job to not take herself too seriously," offered Murphy. Jeff Zucker, then executive producer of *The Today Show*, recalled, "I immediately liked her, because, you know, here she was, just a normal, regular person."

Normal, but tough. From the beginning, Katie insisted on

being treated as Gumbel's equal. According to Andrew Tyndall, Katie insisted on actively participating in, even leading, interviews. "She held her own. She was not intimidated. She carved out her own place as cohost," said Chris Curle. *Today Show* viewers also embraced Katie's impending motherhood, and on July 23, 1991, Katie gave birth to a daughter she named Ellie. The new mom couldn't help but share her joy with America. "She has really incorporated being a mother into being an anchor," remarked Murphy, "which is something that also was not done in the generation before her, because they thought it was taboo."

While Katie was receiving praise, her popularity reportedly began to unsettle her cohost. Robert Thompson commented, "I actually loved watching Bryant Gumbel and Katie Couric, because there was a tension there that was kind of palpable." Still, the brass at NBC knew they were onto a good thing. Katie was offered a huge deal to stay on *The Today Show*: $1 million a year for five years. Katie didn't hesitate, but balancing her personal and professional lives wasn't easy. Katie's husband Jay still practiced law in the nation's capital, and the couple commuted on weekends to be together.

On October 13, 1992, a *Today Show* assignment brought Katie back to Washington, D.C., for a White House tour with First Lady Barbara Bush when the live segment took an unexpected turn. Recounted Jeff Zucker, "President Bush happened to wander by, Katie grabbed him and did an impromptu, spontaneous, twelve-minute interview." Katie seized the moment with some hard-hitting questions about the Iran-Contra controversy and other major national issues. "That shows what a good journalist she is, because she didn't miss an opportunity," said Mary Murphy. And the incident didn't go without notice. Katie Couric was the stuff of front-page headlines the next day for her approach with the president. "Katie is deceptive as a journalist," explained her friend and fellow TV journalist Geraldo Rivera, "because you think, 'Oh, look at this charming young lady. Look at that dazzling smile,' but she's really a top-notch, tough-as-nails journalist."

By late 1992, Katie was thirty-five years old and one of NBC's fastest-rising stars. Ratings on *The Today Show* continued to climb, and Katie inked a multimillion-dollar contract. Life at home with daughter Ellie and husband Jay was also good. In 1993, Katie's husband left his Washington practice to take a job with a New York City law firm. Weekend commutes were over, and there was another bonus—NBC executives tapped him to be an on-air legal analyst. Said Geraldo Rivera, "He was the sharpest lawyer on television, period. To see him master that challenge in the shadow of Katie's amazing success was remarkable." Over at *Today*, Katie's popularity was surging. As a result, her bosses gave her a chance to test the prime-time waters as a cohost of the news magazine *Now with Tom Brokaw and Katie Couric*. Brokaw himself had been a *Today* anchor before transitioning to the *NBC Nightly News*. Professionally, Katie's life seemed to be falling into place.

Despite her hectic schedule heading up two major network shows, thirty-nine-year-old Katie Couric still made time for family. In January 1996, she gave birth to a second daughter, Carrie. But that October some sobering news hit the set of *The Today Show*. Executive producer Zucker, who was only thirty-one years old, was diagnosed with colon cancer. Katie not only stood by her friend, she made things happen. "Katie found my doctors," said Zucker, "and without her persistence and vigilance, I might not have gotten the great care that I did." Meanwhile, Katie's husband Jay began flying back and forth between New York and Los Angeles to cover the O. J. Simpson trial for NBC. The routine was grueling.

Over at *The Today Show*, cohost Bryant Gumbel made a surprise announcement. Gumbel was moving on after an unprecedented fifteen-year run. On January 6, 1997, former NBC news desk reporter and pinch-hit cohost Matt Lauer filled Gumbel's seat. Katie and Matt clicked from day one, and the transition was smooth. In fact, ratings went up a remarkable 13 percent. "Matt Lauer seemed to have been the final important block in this new structure. Matt was the male equivalent of Katie. He could do a lot of the same kinds of things that she could do."

The Couric-Lauer team was clearly a hit, but Katie's world came crashing down in April 1997. Her husband Jay was diagnosed with colon cancer. Unlike Jeff Zucker's cancer, which was diagnosed early, Jay's cancer had advanced and spread because he had ignored symptoms for months while covering the O.J. trial. "I think, in a way, she was just in shock that all of a sudden, this wonderful life was falling apart," said Wendy Walker Whitworth. Katie struggled to maintain her "perky" on-air image.

"It was the perfect successful life that everybody dreams about. 'I'm a star. I'm a success. I love my husband, and I have two adorable children.' And then that whole world, in her personal life, fell apart," summed up Mary Murphy. Katie used her proactive nature to "keep Jay alive by doing her own research about what drugs were out there," said Whitworth. Offered Sam Donaldson, "Katie fought very hard, and Jay fought very hard, too. And sometimes, if you fight hard it makes a difference, but so often in cancer it doesn't." Over the next ten months, Jay battled the cancer that laid siege to his body. Katie was at Jay's side for multiple radiation and chemotherapy treatments. Meanwhile, Monica Lewinsky threatened to bring down President Bill Clinton. In late January, Katie was scheduled to interview First Lady Hillary Clinton in New York about her husband's alleged affair, but Katie never made it. On January 24, 1998, Jay Monahan lost his battle with colon cancer. He was only forty-two.

Thousands of fans offered support to Katie following the heart-wrenching loss of her husband. "She let us grieve for her, but she never, ever let us feel pity for her," remarked Murphy. On February 24, 1998, Katie returned to *The Today Show* exactly one month after her husband's death. She thanked her loyal viewers, saying, "The heartfelt and compassionate letters and cards that so many of you sent to me were enormously comforting, and I'm so grateful." After her touching "thank you," Katie got back to business. It wasn't easy. "After her husband died, Katie went back on television wearing a chain with his ring on it, and that ring and that chain said so much more about what she was going through than anything that she really said on television," said Murphy. Even the first lady shared Katie's pain, saying, "We held our breath for Katie, we held our breath for her daughters and her family."

In June 1998, Katie's *Today Show* contract was up, and negotiations began. NBC's programming lineup took some heavy hits with the loss of NFL football and *Seinfeld*. The network was not about to lose its morning star. Despite her devastation, Katie was, as Geraldo Rivera put it, "the hottest talent in television" at the time. The peacock network came through with a sweet four-year deal worth $28 million, putting Katie into an elite league. Katie was set financially, but she longed to turn the tragic loss of her husband into something positive. At this point, "Katie became absolutely devoted to the cause of cancer and to helping people," said Mary Murphy.

In March 1999, Katie cofounded the National Colorectal Cancer Research Alliance. With the name of Katie Couric attached, the organization was an instant success. Millions of dollars were raised, and Congress declared March "Colon Cancer Awareness Month." Jeff Zucker, who understands the toll of colon cancer and the necessity of health awareness, applauded Katie's efforts: "Katie has turned that terrible tragedy into a great cause, and she has saved thousands upon thousands of lives in the great work that she's done." In the spring of 1999, Katie Couric brought that same compassion to a national tragedy in Colorado. On April 20, two students went on a rampage at Columbine High School, killing thirteen people before taking their own lives. She took the first plane to Denver and landed an exclusive first interview with the father of one of the victims. "This was an unbelievably emotional interview where the father was on with Katie, and he started crying, and Katie reached over and grabbed his hand and held it through the whole interview," remembered Zucker. Mary Murphy, too, remembered Katie "sitting there with the snow falling in the background, doing this incredibly poignant interview, and it was riveting."

Six months later, in October 1999, Katie's own resolve was tested once again when Jeff Zucker suffered a relapse of colon cancer. "They have a very special bond. No matter what you do, you cannot break a bond like that, because they both suffered and have gone through this together," explained Murphy. Said Zucker, "She's incredibly giving and warm and caring, and she's somebody who you just would want to call your friend." Zucker survived his second cancer scare, but his close call led Katie to launch an even more aggressive assault on the silent killer. Recalled Lisa Paulsen, president and CEO of the Entertainment Industry Foundation, "Katie said, 'I think that the best way for me to try to really demystify colon cancer screening is to have a colonoscopy of my own and broadcast for all of America to watch.'" The decision was bold and brave, because "a colonoscopy is a procedure that is about as invasive and personal and unpleasant as you're going to get," explained Robert Thompson.

On March 6, 2000, forty-three-year-old Katie Couric underwent a colonoscopy live on *The Today Show*. It was a television first, and millions of viewers were riveted. For years, audiences embraced Katie's quick wit and friendly smile, but that day, she forged an indelible bond. Jeff Zucker agreed. "Everybody feels that they know Katie, because they watch her in such an intimate way."

"I'll never forget when she saw her 'pretty little colon,' as she put it. I think it was just one of the great moments of live television," remembered Zucker. Katie herself justified this bold on-air experiment by saying, "Because of what happened to Jay and what he went through, it just made it so important for me to get the message out and to educate and inform people about colon cancer." Her can-do, will-do, must-do attitude was picked up on by Lisa Paulsen, who recalled, "I've never heard Katie say, 'Why does this happen to me?' I've heard Katie say, 'How can I help prevent this from happening to other people?'" Ultimately, Katie's televised feat served to benefit scores of people when "the Couric Effect" took over and thousands of people made appointments for colonoscopies.

In 2000, Katie received the prestigious Peabody Award, journalism's highest honor, but her greatest gratification came in the mail. "This is the proudest moment of my career," she said, "but it's because of people like Karen Mann, who sent me a letter last April. Karen had the courage to call her doctor and make an appointment, and her doctor found fourteen polyps in her colon. Karen ended her note by writing, 'Thank you, thank you, thank you. You saved my life.'" After forging triumph from tragedy, Katie added a new title to her résumé in the spring of 2000: activist. "She started to use this tragedy in her life to help other people, and she did it most provocatively and to the great benefit of millions of Americans," offered Mary Murphy.

That same season, Katie decided to indulge herself with a whole new look. The transformation included a stylish haircut, workouts with a $7,500-per-week personal trainer, and a playful new wardrobe. "Katie was able to move into a sexier, more feminine look, and it has not in any way detracted from our respect for her," said Murphy. Donning sexy slingbacks and showing off her legs, Katie began to exude "confidence, exuberance, and a real lust for life," remarked Teri Agins, author of *The End of Fashion*. With Katie's more fashionable wardrobe, people began to speculate about her personal life. In 2000, Katie met Tom Werner, owner of the Boston Red Sox and former producer of shows like *Roseanne* and *The Cosby Show*. She gained "a certain lift in her voice, sparkle in her eyes, and an exuberance that she hadn't had for quite a while," said Agins.

But Katie's joy was soon tempered by yet another cancer diagnosis. This time, it was her sister, Virginia state senator Emily Couric. "Katie was devastated when she found out about Emily's pancreatic cancer and moved mountains as she had done with Jay to try and make sure that Emily was receiving the best possible care," remembered Lisa Paulsen. While Emily underwent cancer treatment, Katie traveled to Sydney, Australia, to broadcast *The Today Show* live from the Summer Olympics. The Olympic torch was extinguished on October 1, 2000, and *The Today Show* team returned to New York, but change was in the wind. The show expanded its time slot from two to three hours, which pitted them against more competition. "It was a risk," commented Murphy, "it demanded so much more work for Katie and Matt."

With its new format, *The Today Show* pulled even bigger numbers. Then, in the fall of 2000, Al Gore and George W. Bush squared off in one of the closest presidential elections in history. Katie and Matt reported as the drama unfolded, and ratings doubled. Twelve and a half million viewers tuned in to *The Today Show* on November 7, 2000. Mary Murphy attributed the show's increased share to "the way that news was beginning to shift and the increasing power of the morning news shows." Over the next year, *The Today Show* solidified its spot as the number one morning show on TV. Katie was enjoying time with her two daughters, Ellie and Carrie, and spending more time with Tom Werner.

In the wake of the tragedy of September 11, 2001, Katie Couric once again proved her professional character by staying on the air all day. All networks turned into twenty-four-hour newscasts as the nation was gripped with confusion and fear. "Katie wanted to stay on-air," mentioned Sam Donaldson. "As a professional, that was her job. As an American, she was as shocked and outraged as the rest of us." Katie was the rock for a grieving nation, but once again she endured personal sorrow. On October 18, 2001, Katie's sister Emily lost her courageous fight with cancer. Commented Michael Gartner, "People deal with grief in different ways. Katie is a public person, and she dealt with the grief publicly."

As 2001 drew to a close, Katie's NBC contract came up for renewal. There was no shortage of offers for a woman ranked as number 11 on *Entertainment Weekly*'s list of the "101 Most Powerful People in Showbiz." Katie was approached by several major networks and Hollywood production companies about doing everything from her own syndicated talk show to a spot on *60 Minutes*. "Everybody wanted Katie," said Don Farmer. But only Katie knew what she wanted. Though many suitors came calling, Katie remained at the place where she grew up, her home at NBC. She signed another four-year deal, this time for a reported $65 million. The eight-figure payday was the biggest ever for a network newscaster. "When she signed her most recent contract, she broke barriers—sound barriers, atmospheric barriers," said Farmer. Willard Scott reasoned, "They give you money because you're making money. She is the franchise, as we say in show business, on that program."

"You can't replace Katie," Michael Gartner noted. "When you find someone that good, you just say, 'What do you want?' and make the deal." The big contract ruffled some feathers at the peacock network. NBC was in the middle of staff cutbacks caused by the nation's economic downturn. "I think Katie Couric deserves everything she's gotten," asserted Sam Donaldson. "She not only paid her dues, she showed that she could compete and surpass the competitors. So, if you say to me, 'Look at her. Look at all the fame that has come to her. Look at all the material wealth,' I say, 'Hooray! The good guys win in the end.' She's one of them." Some speculate that Katie's decision to stay with the job was largely influenced by her comfortable schedule. "I think she will stay at NBC as long as it suits her family life. She's a great mom, and I think that will play more on her decision than almost anything else," said Don Farmer. While Katie's career was flying high, her love life bottomed out. In July 2002, Katie and Tom Werner split. Though the bicoastal couple teamed up again one month later and stayed together for two more years, they finally ended their romance in late 2004. Shortly afterward, in October, Katie publicly acknowledged that she was on the receiving end of some sweet serenades from forty-seven-year-old jazz trumpeter Chris Botti, whose star was rising because of his chart-topping album—appropriately titled *When I Fall in Love*.

On November 12, 2002, Katie Couric hosted a cancer awareness benefit called "42nd & Vine." The star-studded event raised more than $5 million for the Jay Monahan Center for Gastrointestinal Health. Six months later, Katie took on a different challenge. On May 12, 2003, *The Today Show* host and *The Tonight Show* host, Jay Leno, swapped places. It was the first time Leno had let anyone sit behind his desk. Wendy Walker Whitworth said that the experience "gave Katie a lot of confidence," and Don Farmer called it "a slam dunk. It was a killer performance." *Tonight Show* ratings went through the roof. Jay Leno scored a nice number for *The Today Show*, too. Then, in October 2003, Katie was chosen for induction into the Academy of Television Arts and Sciences Hall of Fame. Assessed Robert Thompson, "I think there's no question about it. Katie Couric has become an American icon."

"Would I say that Katie Couric is just like the girl next door?" asked Michael Gartner. "If the girl next door is really smart and really nice-looking and makes several million dollars a year, she's just like the girl next door." Said Mary Murphy, "Katie has the stamina, the drive, the ambition, the compassion, and the humor to have an incredibly successful life whether it's in front of the camera or behind." But Katie's measure of her own success has little to do with fortune or fame. "I always thought that on my tombstone I'd like to have written, 'She was a damned good reporter,'" Katie mused. Katie's close friend Jeff Zucker summed up, "Whether she's interviewing President Bush or Kermit the Frog, she's brought an intelligence and wit and compassion to a medium in a way that probably no one before her had, and I think she's become the single most important female journalist in this country, and a role model for everyone." For the *Today* star, tomorrow has no limits.

CHAPTER 10

EIGHT DAYS A WEEK

The Heather Mills McCartney Story

"She has great strength of character and a real inner belief that what she's doing is important."

—*Marcus Stapleton, former fiancé*

On June 11, 2002, the small town of Glaslough, Ireland, prepared for a big-time event. "This had all the earmarks to be a Princess Di/Prince Charles kind of wedding," described *US Weekly*'s senior editor Jeremy Helligar. In fact, the aura of royalty was everywhere. Former Beatle Sir Paul McCartney took social activist Heather Mills to be his bride. It was a match made in media heaven with a story that rivaled any fairy tale. Flashback twenty years: Paul was a fabulously rich rock star. Heather was a homeless teenager living on the streets of London. She survived, only to face another, more harrowing ordeal—a near-fatal car wreck that cost her a leg. Heather fought back by becoming a human rights activist in a region torn by war. Heather was nominated for the Nobel Peace Prize, but when she captured the heart of a British icon she was vilified as a conniving gold digger. Said CNN personality Larry King, "She's her own person. She is Heather Mills. She is not Mrs. McCartney." Heather Mills is a courageous woman who refused to give up, and this is her story.

Heather was born to Mark and Beatrice Mills in the English town of Aldershot on January 12, 1968. A year later, Heather and her older brother, Shane, were joined by a sister, Fiona. Life in the Mills home was far from stable. The family kept moving from town to town while Mark Mills launched one unsuccessful business scheme after another. By 1977, Beatrice had had enough. She left Mark and her children. The children returned home from school to the traumatizing news. Just nine years old, Heather was put in charge. "It became Heather's role to buy the food, to cook the food, and to generally take over the running of the household," noted Pamela Cockerill, coauthor of Heather's autobiography, *A Single Step*.

In 1981, Mark Mills failed at another business venture, and his past finally caught up with him. Mills was found guilty of fraud and spent six months in prison. "This was a dramatic intervention in their lives," said Pamela Cockerill, "and her mother was forced to step in because they were too young to look after themselves." Heather and her siblings moved in with her mother Beatrice and Beatrice's new boyfriend. It was a disaster. After a year, something had to give. "My mother was given an ultimatum from her boyfriend," remembered Heather. "He said, 'Either she goes or I go.'" According to Susan Rozsnyai, editor-at-large of London tabloid *Hello!*, "Heather knew that her mother wouldn't choose her, so, she pretty much went off on her own."

Heather, only fourteen years old at that point, was soon homeless, sleeping under the bridge at a train station in London. "I lived in the sort of Waterloo Arch area—as it was called in the U.K.—and I stole food, and I stole clothes just to survive," she said. "I didn't want to sit begging." The conditions were truly down and dirty, and in 1983, after living on the streets for four months, Heather had a moment of realization that this was not for her. As Susan Rozsnyai described, "She woke up one morning to find her hair quite damp, and in fact, a tramp had urinated on her hair, and she thought, 'Okay, enough. Now is the time to change my life.'" Heather may have grown up fast, but she was nobody's victim. She moved in with friends and found work in the city.

One day, she saw an advertisement in the *Evening Standard* looking for a catwalk model. "She went along, knocked on the door, and got the job. It was just working in a small showroom, but it gave her a taste," Pamela Cockerill said. By 1986, eighteen-year-old Heather set her sights on becoming a model. With her long legs and curvy figure, she seemed to fit the part, but doors were slammed in her face everywhere she went. As Mills recalled, "I went to every agency in London, and they all said, 'Forget it. You're too tall. You're too short. You're too fat. You're too thin. Your boobs are too big.'" In fact, her 32E bust size was her biggest liability. Heather then decided to use those assets to her advantage. "She got a lot of the so-called glamour-type modeling jobs," offered Susan Rozsnyai. The jobs weren't exactly top shelf or haute couture, but they were Heather's ticket into the industry. As Jeremy Helligar put it, "Some of the pictures are pretty racy. Some of them are pretty cheesy. Some of them were not fully clothed. Some of them were more clothed." Heather to this day insists that she was "never ashamed" of her foray into glamour-shot modeling.

Meanwhile, in the summer of 1986, Heather began dating Alfie Karmal, a divorced businessman. "He was a very sophisticated man. I think in some ways he swept Heather off her feet, because he represented the sort of thing she was looking for. And he took charge of things," said Pamela Cockerill. Twenty-five-year-old Karmal said he wanted to help Heather succeed as a model. He read about a British newspaper sponsoring a beauty contest and secretly submitted Heather's photo. Recounted Piers Morgan, editor-in-chief of England's *Daily Mirror,* "She entered a Dream Girl competition in the *Daily Mirror,* and the judges rather liked the look of her from her picture and rang her up, and she got in the paper." The exposure landed Heather some fashion jobs, but she craved more. "I think she realized that although she could earn a good living with modeling, it wasn't going to be the ultimate goal in her life," said Rozsnyai.

Heather was never shy about what she wanted, and, in December 1988, she wanted to get engaged. Revealed Cockerill, "She bought a wedding ring, walked into his office, opened the box, and said, 'Alfie, will you marry me?'" Alfie accepted Heather's proposal. Meanwhile, Heather hoped to reconnect with her mother Beatrice before the wedding. The two had been estranged since Heather left home. "Heather began to see much more of her

mother, and I think Heather felt she understood her mother better and probably forgave her," said Cockerill. Then, in February
1989, forty-seven-year-old Beatrice was hospitalized for minor
surgery, but something went horribly wrong. "She got a blood
clot that went in her heart and lungs, and she died. It was really
sad, because I'd only got close to her three weeks [earlier],"
Heather said.

Heather Mills and Alfie Karmal went ahead with their wedding
plans, but the absence of Heather's mother hung like a dark cloud
over everything. Still, the couple married on May 6, 1989. At
twenty-one, Heather was not only a wife; she was a mother to two
stepsons. "Here was a woman who always had to look out for others and pretty much struggled to look after herself. And then suddenly here was a man who wanted to look after her," described
Susan Rozsnyai. Eighteen months after her wedding, Heather
discovered she was pregnant, but she developed a dangerous condition known as an ectopic pregnancy. Her baby was growing inside her fallopian tube and could not survive. Heather was
devastated by the loss. Her relationship with Alfie suffered. Said
Heather, "My husband wasn't there for me at all. He would just
sleep on the couch every weekend." Speculated Rozsnyai, "I think
that obviously made a mark on their marriage, but it wasn't just
that. Although she wanted security, I don't think she actually
wanted to settle down and become a suburban housewife."

In fact, Heather still had her sights set on becoming a fashion
model. In January 1991, she underwent breast-reduction surgery
to refine her appearance. The painful procedure left Heather exhausted and in need of a break. She decided to take a ski trip to
the mountains of Yugoslavia. The trip took a pleasant yet unexpected and complicated turn. "This is when she met Milos, who
was the ski instructor, and [she] pretty much fell head over heels
in love with him," said Rozsnyai. The breakup with Alfie Karmal
was hard, but it was even more traumatic when Heather discovered she was pregnant. Once again, Heather suffered an ectopic
pregnancy and lost the baby. Heather, having lived through only

twenty-three years on the planet and more than her share of tragedy, again pushed past her grief and left England. She moved to Yugoslavia in February to start a new life with Milos, and trained to be a ski instructor to earn her living.

Four months after Heather Mills ran off to the Balkans, civil war broke out. Yugoslavia and its fiercely independent ethnic groups were torn apart. "She found herself in this extraordinary situation where there were friends of hers who were actually being killed and injured," said friend Anya Noakes, "and she brought them back to the U.K. She also thought, 'I've got to do something.'" Heather spent the next two years helping with the war effort. She traveled back and forth from London to Croatia with food, clothing, and medical supplies. "She really threw herself into the thick of it. She was driving across the country with supplies, herself in danger of being blown up," said Rozsnyai. Heather's courage saved countless lives.

By January 1993, twenty-five-year-old Heather ended her relationship with Milos, and her divorce from Alfie Karmal became final. That summer, Heather began dating Italian banker Raffaele Mincione. The romance was troubled from the start.

On August 8, 1998, Heather and Mincione went for a walk to talk things over. At the corner of De Vere Gardens and Kensington Road, Heather stepped into the intersection. Suddenly, all hell broke loose. "I heard two police cars go flying by, and there was a red double-decker bus. So I sort of took a step back, and another step very cautiously, after these police cars had gone by, and a motorbike came out and chopped my leg," she described. "She was thrown to one side of the road and she could see her leg at the other side," said Susan Rozsnyai. Heather continued, "And I was conscious, lying down, and my head was split, and my pelvis was completely crushed." Moments later, medics arrived at the scene. Heather was airlifted to Mount Vernon Hospital outside London. Doctors worked frantically to save her life. "I got to the hospital, and they announced to my sister about four times that I was going to die."

In addition to her crushed pelvis and severed leg, Heather also suffered a punctured lung and broken ribs. "I woke up, and my sister came in. All I remember is this horrible feeling in my pelvis. That was the most painful area, because my entire pelvis was crushed. My sister came in and was crying and she said, 'You're not going to believe this. You've lost your leg.'" Doctors were unable to reattach Heather's severed left limb. In fact, the damage was so severe they had to amputate even more of her leg. After the initial shock, Heather Mills bounced back. Heather remembered, "A woman did come in the hospital once, a counselor, and said, 'Heather, you're being far too positive about this.'" Heather's spirit was surprisingly unbreakable. She had, said Piers Morgan, "no self-pity, no sense of 'This is going to ruin my life,' but a real sense of 'Get up and get on with it.' Life has dealt her another very bad blow, but she won't be beaten by it."

Still, Heather's financial situation was desperate. She had no income, and it seemed her modeling career was over. "I was paying for my brother in college, and I was funding my sister at the time, and all I kept thinking about was, 'How am I going to pay all the bills?'" The ravenous British press provided the answer. Reporters from several publications competed for Heather's story. "She personally negotiated selling her story to one of the papers and turning a tragedy into an opportunity," assessed Morgan. Heather's harrowing ordeal hit the front page of the *Sunday People*. Over the next month, Mills earned nearly $250,000 selling her tale to various newspapers, magazines, and television shows. Heather became a media darling. "They put me on this pedestal because I overcame it very quickly," she noted.

On September 10, 1993, Heather was released from the hospital. Less than a month later, a serious infection sent her back to the operating room. "My leg kept getting more and more infected, and they chopped more and more off. And I didn't want to lose my knee." The second operation was a failure. Desperate, Heather turned to alternative medicine at the Hippocrates Institute in Florida, healing herself "with grass and carrot juice."

Heather was treated for five days. The infection disappeared, and her knee was saved. Then, the reality of her condition began to sink in. "You don't like looking at your leg and having that reminder every day that you can't wear a skirt, that you can't feel feminine, that you can't feel normal, because everyone is looking at you every two minutes."

Heather teamed up with medical adviser Bob Watts to design her prosthetic leg. Heather's personal experience with prosthetics gave her an idea. "She noticed that when you were actually having your artificial limb fitted, you would have to get several, because obviously it would change size as your leg healed," said Susan Rozsnyai. When Heather asked Watts what happened to the artificial limbs after their owners no longer needed them, he told her they were thrown away, and she couldn't believe it. In Yugoslavia, Heather saw firsthand the devastating effect of land mines. Thousands of innocent victims lost limbs in the brutal conflict, and Heather now knew how to help.

On October 29, Heather Mills flew to Zagreb, Croatia. Two trucks hauling nearly five thousand artificial limbs arrived the next day. "The first child we fitted, Martina, moved me the most," said Heather, "because here was a young girl who had lost her leg from a land mine and some of her fingers. And her parents were very poor, so they could never afford to pay anyone to make a limb. I was just very gentle with her, and when I showed her my leg, she just felt that it wasn't such a bad thing." Offered Piers Morgan, "Heather ended up shipping tens of thousands of these limbs to places like Sarajevo, Bosnia, Kosovo—places like these, where lots of people had suffered from land-mine injuries. She saved these people's lives and gave them the quality of life they would never have dreamt of." Reasoned Heather, "I definitely lost my leg for a reason, without a doubt. There is no way. I mean, now people are walking that wouldn't be walking had I not lost my leg."

In February 1996, for her work as a champion of amputees around the globe, twenty-eight-year-old Heather Mills was honored by one of the most prestigious organizations in the world. "Heather was nominated for the Nobel Peace Prize. That came out of her work in Cambodia and Croatia, providing limbs to people or providing assistance to amputees," said Nahela Hadi, executive director of Adopt-a-Minefield. Heather didn't win the Nobel, but simply being nominated was reward enough for a kid who once lived on the streets. Over the next few years, Heather kept up her frantic pace raising money and awareness for land-mine victims and fellow amputees. "She will be anywhere at any time, and someone will ring her up on a mobile, and she'll be counseling them—other amputees," remarked Bob Watts.

Meanwhile, another passionate social activist was fighting for her life. In April 1998, Linda McCartney lost her battle with breast cancer. She was only fifty-six. Linda left behind four adult children and her husband of twenty-nine years, Paul McCartney. While Paul dealt with the loss of his beloved wife, he disappeared from the public eye. On May 20, 1999, McCartney resurfaced. He attended the Pride of Britain awards to honor Linda, an animal rights activist, by presenting an award in her memory. Heather was also a presenter at the event. According to Piers Morgan, "It was all sort of very fortuitous, and he came in late, just in time to hear Heather speak." He continued, "She made a very dynamic speech on stage, and it was about her charity work, and we had a young girl who'd lost her legs to meningitis, and Heather was very powerful about her and very inspiring to everybody in the audience."

But Paul had to wait. A few days after the ceremony, Heather flew to Cambodia to film a documentary on land-mine victims. During the trip, she fell in love with BBC director Chris Terrill. Ten days after they met, the couple was engaged. "It was another whirlwind romance, which Heather seemed prone to, probably before they knew each other terribly well," said Pamela Cockerill. Heather returned to London two weeks later. There was a message waiting for her from Paul McCartney. "I thought it was a joke, so I didn't return the call. And then I found out that he was

interested in the charity," she recalled. Susan Rozsnyai speculated, "He was very keen on meeting her and I think probably
used the charity as a slight excuse although, obviously, he was
very interested in helping her charity." Piers Morgan added, "He
rang up and gave $150,000 to her charity, which was an extraor-
dinary thing to do."

Heather was thrilled with the generous donation, but Paul had
more than charity on his mind. "Clearly, he was very, very interested in her in other ways as well, but playing it very slowly and
carefully, and she had absolutely no idea at all," laughed Anya
Noakes. On one occasion, said Cockerill, "She'd gone to the lift,
and she just had a sense that somebody's eyes were on her. She
turned around, and she saw Paul, and she thought, 'He's looking at
my bum!'" Following that incident, "it became clear that they
were very, very attracted to each other," said Rozsnyai. While her
attraction to Paul grew, Heather was having second thoughts
about her relationship with Chris Terrill. In July, she called off the
engagement. "It broke up fairly acrimoniously," said Cockerill,
"when they discovered differences that they hadn't been aware of."

Single again, Heather couldn't deny her growing attraction to
Paul McCartney. "They hit it off, and they've never looked back,"
said friend Sir Richard Branson, the founder of Virgin Records
and Virgin Airlines. Paul and Heather kept quiet about the romance at first. They insisted the relationship was strictly business. "So Paul McCartney suddenly released a statement, saying,
'We're just friends,' and of course that's the classic phrase that to
any tabloid newspaper means, 'Okay, we're secretly having sex,'"
commented Morgan. Still, Heather and Paul stuck with their
story. "I'm sure they knew that once people knew about it, their
life would never be quite the same again," commented Branson.

Finally, on March 15, 2000, fifty-seven-year-old Paul McCartney and thirty-two-year-old Heather Mills made the big announcement: They were in love. "I am very lucky I found Heather.
She's a beautiful, impressive woman," Paul glowed. But Heather

quickly learned there was a flip side to dating a legend. "Heather went from this rather heroic figure who we all admired and were inspired by to Public Enemy Number One because she'd nicked Paul McCartney from the country," said Piers Morgan. Heather was always savvy with the press, as was McCartney, but this story wasn't easy to spin. Morgan continued, "The trouble with getting involved with a Beatle in this country is that they're a national institution. It would be like the Queen Mother taking a last-minute lover. It really would grate with the country."

"I was always open and honest about everything all the time, and when I met Paul, he was very private, so I just put on my answering machine 'I have no comment,' which was the biggest mistake," Heather recalled. Undaunted, tabloid reporters began digging for dirt. They tried everything from interviewing Heather's ex-husband and lovers and dredging up intimate details to paying people a mint to defame her name and call her crazy. Friends defended Heather. Former fiancé Marcus Stapleton dismissed the bad press as merely a way to sell newspapers. Reasoned Stapleton, "Everybody's entitled to an opinion, and unfortunately the public perception is generated through the public form of media. Having worked in the media, I know that media sells very well when the press has a negative bias."

The media scrutiny was stressful for both Heather and Paul, but it was even more taxing on McCartney's four children: Heather, Mary, Stella, and James. The media salivated over the idea of a McCartney family feud. "I think they found it difficult when this new, young woman came into their lives," said Morgan. "Some of the kids aren't that much younger than Heather, so there's friction." Commented Heather, "As far as I'm concerned, it's a myth. Paul has never mentioned it." Regardless, she was wounded by the exaggerations and half-truths. "I think it's very difficult for her," said Stapleton. "I think it's tough for her to be perceived negatively—as it would be for anybody. If you're a good person, and you're trying to live your life in the right way, you would hope people would look at you as a person and think of you as a good person. I think with so much negative press being written about her, I do think that's very difficult for her."

Heather decided to ignore the negative stories. Instead, she focused on her charity work. By the time she was thirty-two, Heather had joined forces with Adopt-a-Minefield, an organization dedicated to ridding the world of land mines. "We knew when she joined us that this was going to be a great partnership. Heather's extremely committed to this issue," affirmed Nahela Hadi, the program's executive director. Added Stapleton, "She's very strong, has great strength of character and a real inner belief that what she's doing is important. And she'll work very hard to achieve that." Heather worked relentlessly to raise awareness for Adopt-a-Minefield. "It's no good that we keep fitting people up with artificial limbs, if these mines keep going off," she argued.

Paul supported her efforts, and with his powerful connections Heather's message was heard by diplomats and presidents. "It's all fate," Heather remarked, "We truly think that we were meant to be put together not just for ourselves but for a greater cause. Had I not met Paul and fallen madly in love, I wouldn't have met some of these heads of state that have helped make a huge difference to the charity." Said Susan Rozsnyai, "She has directly addressed President Bush and President Putin, and is really trying to effect changes in the actual laws that govern land mines."

In January 2001, Paul surprised Heather with a special present for her thirty-third birthday—a trip to India. Heather fell in love with the country, but, two days after they returned to London a massive earthquake rocked northwestern India. Heather immediately took action. "I went back three weeks later and set up amputee clinics there," she said. Nahela Hadi described, "A lot of these people feel very alone and helpless. So she goes with that message of goodwill." In March 2001, Heather returned from her trip and launched the British branch of Adopt-a-Minefield.

By July, she needed a break. Paul swept his lady away to a romantic hotel in the Lake District, a scenic area north of Liverpool.

Paul surprised Heather with a diamond-and-sapphire ring he had secretly purchased in India. "Paul sort of bowed to his knees and presented this amazing ring and proposed," recounted Rozsnyai, "and she immediately said 'yes.' He was in absolute tears over this, and she says that at that point, 'I really realized this man really, really loves me.' And obviously she had met her match as well."

The happy couple returned to London to plan their future. In Britain, their marriage ceremony was hailed as the most anticipated wedding since Lady Diana and Prince Charles in 1981. "There was a frenzied interest in when it was going to be and where it was going to be and who was going to be invited," recalled Anya Noakes. But not everyone shared their joy. In the months before the wedding, the papers churned out one negative story after another about the bride-to-be. In May—one month before the wedding—rumors surfaced that the engagement was in trouble. Press reports accused Heather of being unwilling to sign a prenup. Without the prenup, Heather would become an heir to the McCartney fortune. "He's worth almost a billion. He's worth so much money. There was no prenuptial agreement although Paul was encouraged to get Heather to sign one," said Jeremy Helligar. Heather defended herself, "I said, 'I want to sign a prenuptial. I want to say that I don't want anything, so that you feel really comfortable about it.' He said, 'It's not romantic to sign a prenuptial. I'd never want to do that.'"

Heather brushed aside the drama. She was determined not to let anything ruin her dream wedding. Paul and Heather kept the details a closely guarded secret. Ironically, said Piers Morgan, "Nobody was going to know about this at all. Then this quaint old guy just came out and told everybody by mistake." The quaint gentleman was Sir John Leslie, and it was on his property—the Castle Leslie Estate in Glaslough, Ireland—that the wedding was scheduled to take place. The news was out about the location, but Heather and Paul still hoped to keep the date a mystery. Eventually, they realized their chance of keeping it quiet was pretty zero anyway," said Morgan.

Glaslough locals welcomed the couple like old friends, while journalists camped outside the castle walls. "It was all of the excitement, all of the details that emerged beforehand that people found so tantalizing. I think that made it even a bigger thing," commented Rozsnyai. On June 11, 2002, three hundred guests, including Paul's four children, arrived at Saint Salvatore's, a seventeenth-century Protestant church. The lavish celebration was the stuff of dreams . . . and deep pockets. "It was a wedding that came with a $3 million price tag—very glamorous, very extravagant, bold-faced guests like Eric Clapton, Sting, and Paul's fellow former Beatle Ringo Starr," noted Helligar. Added Noakes, "Heather walked down the aisle to the song he'd written for her, which is called 'Heather.' It was very moving, and Heather got completely choked up." The newlyweds emerged from the church through a shower of rose petals. A pair of rainbows arched overhead. Despite all the media criticism, no one could deny Sir Paul and Lady Heather's happiness. "They were meant for each other, so it's going to be very hard tearing them apart," said Paul's brother, Mike McCartney. Added Morgan, "Paul McCartney doesn't do splitting up. It's for life with him."

In October 2002, thirty-four-year-old Heather Mills McCartney released the book that she cowrote with Pamela Cockerill—her autobiography, *A Single Step*. Heather donated all her proceeds to Adopt-a-Minefield. When Heather appeared on *Larry King Live* to promote the book, she shook up the unshakable Larry King. King asked her what an artificial leg looks like. "She surprised us all by taking off her leg and putting it on the desk," recalled Wendy Walker Whitworth, the show's senior executive producer. "When she takes off her leg on Larry King, you have to sit back and go, 'She's some broad,'" said Morgan with admiration. King himself commented, "It happened to be, I think, a wonderful moment in television when she took it off and described it. She was gutsy to do it."

Heather's days of bad press seemed to be behind her, but on May 7, 2003, a scathing tell-all documentary called *The Real Mrs.*

McCartney aired on British television. The show attacked Heather's character and opened old wounds. "She wasn't even present on the documentary. It was all people who she'd known in her earlier life who were upset with her for whatever reason," commented Susan Rozsnyai. They claimed that Heather fabricated parts of her rags-to-riches story. Continued Rozsnyai, "It's a high-drama story. But I think that's what makes her such a good speaker, such an inspiring speaker, because she actually knows how to tell a story, if you'd like." Heather fought back. Said Anya Noakes, "She decided to take part in Piers Morgan's *Tabloid Tales* series. What he wanted to do was to give people a fair hearing." Recalled Morgan, "She looked me straight in the eye and defied you to prove she had lied about any aspect of her life. Funny enough, it's very hard to prove she ever had. The public, I think, really got a new insight into what she was like and rather liked her, too."

Heather had something more important to focus on—she was pregnant. No one was more surprised than Heather herself. "I've had two ectopic pregnancies." The chances of me getting pregnant are not much." Anya Noakes agreed, "The chances had seemed so slim of her becoming pregnant that when she found out she was pregnant—completely unexpectedly—it was the most wonderful surprise for her and for Paul as well." On May 28, 2003, the McCartneys announced they were expecting their first child. Three months later, on August 30, Stella McCartney married magazine publisher Alasdhair Willis. If there were differences between Stella and Heather, they weren't evident that day. "I think they've really pulled together even more since Heather became pregnant and Stella herself got married," said Noakes, "and I think they've got better things to do than to get caught up in any silly rivalries."

Heather, unceasingly concerned with her work, didn't let pregnancy slow her down. With Paul's help, she continued to raise money for her cause. Praised Nahela Hadi, "Heather's truly a tireless goodwill ambassador for Adopt-a-Minefield. Every opportunity she gets, her first thing is not 'What's in it for me?' but 'What's in it for Adopt-a-Minefield?'" In September 2003, a very pregnant Heather attended a high-profile fund-raiser in the United States. Paul was always at her side. "But he's always careful to step back. He knows that his presence could overshadow all the work that she's done, and really that's her thing," said Susan Rozsnyai. On October 28, 2003, Beatrice Milly McCartney was born. "I think the baby is going to be a wonderful new challenge," smiled Noakes.

Heather Mills McCartney persevered through tough times and personal tragedy to bring hope to countless, helpless victims of war and violence. "She's totally speaking from the heart, and that's when people listen," affirmed Hadi. And through her life's work, Heather found love and the family she always wanted. "This is a woman who's run really all her time to find somebody to love and be loved by," commented Piers Morgan, "and I think she gets that from her charity work. I think she gets that from Paul McCartney. Finally she's arrived at a place she's probably been seeking for a long time—somewhere to find a bit of love."

CHAPTER 11

THE GIRL NEXT DOOR
The Doris Day Story

"If you didn't fall in love with Doris Day, something was wrong with your heart."

—*Jamie Farr, silver screen costar*

THE GIRL NEXT DOOR

The Doris Day Story

All I ever wanted was to get married, have a nice husband, and have maybe two or three children and live happily ever after," she once said. Doris Day was dubbed "the Girl Next Door," but few really knew the woman behind the image. The star's private life was filled with anguish, drama, and pain. Prince Charming eluded her, and instead she found a manager who betrayed her trust, spied on her, and tried to rape her. Doris faced financial ruin but survived a near-fatal car crash, abusive lovers, and overwhelming personal loss. Then she vanished from the public eye. Mysterious, wholesome, tortured, beloved, she is the woman who sang "*Que sera, sera*—whatever will be, will be," and she proved she could roll with the punches. Her name is Doris Day, and this is her story.

For five decades, Doris Day captivated audiences with her sunny charm and upbeat optimism. Through the 1950s, women identified with her sassy spirit, and men appreciated her physical virtues. "She had this beautiful sweet face and dressed in good-girl clothes, except for the fact that the good-girl clothes were hiding a knockout body underneath," revealed biographer James Gavin. Something else was hidden underneath that good-girl image—a lifetime of sorrow and struggle. Film critic Rex Reed commented, "The girl-next-door image was really false. Doris had a tragic life, and she had three really very destructive marriages. And still she had this wholesomeness. I mean, you can't disguise that." A. E. Hotchner, another of Doris's biographers, summed up,

"Whenever you get the masks of tragedy and comedy in one person, you certainly have the elements of drama, and it was a dramatic life."

Doris Day was born Doris Kappelhoff on April 3, 1924. Her parents, Alma and William, gave their young daughter a middle-class upbringing in Cincinnati. "Her mother was a lovely woman, full of good cheer, as Doris is," said A. E. Hotchner. "Her father was very dramatic. He was a choirmaster in the church and a music teacher. He was very dictatorial around the house and very strict with Doris." William wanted little to do with Doris and her older brother, Paul. Alma didn't get much love from her husband, either. William's affection was reserved for another woman. Reported Hotchner, "He, unbeknownst to his family, was having an affair with the mother of [Doris's] best friend."

When she was just ten, Doris discovered her father's infidelity. She overheard William having sex with his mistress. The memory haunted Doris for the rest of her life. Doris kept her father's dirty secret, but her mother eventually learned of his betrayal. The couple separated in 1935, and forty-year-old Alma became a single mother of two. Despite her own problems, Alma tried to provide Doris with a normal childhood and a well-rounded education. Doris described, "I went to dancing school almost every day of the week. My poor little grandmother would trundle me off and take me. And I studied acrobatics, ballet and toe, tap dancing, personality class, and I thought maybe one day I might be a ballerina."

Then, fate intervened. "She met up with [a] boy, Jerry, and the two of them began to dance together at recitals and local affairs," said Hotchner. In the fall of 1937, thirteen-year-old Doris and her partner, Jerry Doherty, entered a dance contest in Cincinnati. The duo won top prize—a check for $500. Alma and Jerry's mother came up with a radical plan—pack up and head to Hollywood! Their reasoning, according to Hotchner, was to "enroll in the famous dance studio where some of the choreographers who worked in film would sometimes go to see the talent." After four weeks at the Fanchon & Marco Dance Studio, Doris and Jerry were encouraged to stay in Hollywood indefinitely. Doris was thrilled. Even at age thirteen, she felt that dancing was her calling.

Before moving to Hollywood, Doris and Alma returned to Ohio to tie up some loose ends. On Friday, October 13, 1937, Doris's friend threw her a small going-away party. The celebration ended in tragedy. Some friends decided that they should take a trip to a drive-in movie. On the way back to the party, the four friends, including Doris, crossed an unprotected train track, and, the car was demolished by a train. The driver and the girl in the front passenger seat were thrown headfirst into the windshield, and the boy sitting next to Doris was miraculously unharmed. Doris, however, was not so lucky. She sustained extensive leg injuries and was hospitalized for a year.

With a shattered leg, no one knew "whether she would walk again much less dance," said Hotchner. Doris was fitted with a cast from her thigh to her toes. Devastated and depressed, Doris looked for a new creative outlet. The teenager discovered an untapped talent that would be her ticket out of Ohio. "My leg was broken in many places, and I didn't walk for a long time, much less dance. That's when I started singing—so every break is a good one," she recalled. Remembered Doris's friend composer Frank Comstock, "She started listening to Ella Fitzgerald records or somebody on the radio, and she started to sing along with them. When she found out she couldn't dance professionally anymore, she started singing."

Alma did everything she could to keep her daughter's spirits up. She introduced Doris to Grace Raine, a vocal coach with connections at all the local radio stations. Laughed Doris, "She couldn't sing a note, but she was a great coach. She was the best. We'd go over to her place, [I'd be] on crutches, and I would have to scoot up this long flight of stairs to the second floor. We didn't have much money at the time, and voice lessons are expensive, but she thought that I had some talent, and she said to my mother, 'I'm going to give her three lessons for the price of one.'"

According to A. E. Hotchner, "This woman became Doris's long-time guru and really helped her formulate her style of singing. Although she was still on crutches . . . Doris got an engagement to sing with a band."

Doris made her debut in 1939 at the Shanghai Inn in downtown Cincinnati. The fifteen-year-old vocalist earned $5 a night, a fair salary in the 1930s. Doris regained the confidence she lost as a result of her accident, but the young singer's setbacks were far from over. Doris formed a lifelong attachment to dogs while she was bedridden. She had a little dog that Hotchner called a "constant companion who became a symbol of hope that she was going to get better." Then, when Doris was on the upswing, recovering and beginning to walk, the dog was run over, which "had a terrible depressive effect on her."

After eighteen months on crutches, Doris graduated to a cane. The timing was perfect. A local bandleader, Barney Rapp, heard Doris sing on an amateur radio show. Rapp auditioned Doris and offered her a job, but there was one hitch. When he asked Doris her name, recalled Doris, "He made this terrible face, and he said, 'That has to go. I hope you don't mind.' And he said, 'You know, I loved the way you sang that song "Day After Day." I think maybe your name should be Day.'" Doris thought the stage name was more appropriate for a stripper, but she went along with the suggestion. Her decisions wouldn't always be so smart.

Doris Day began performing six nights a week with the Barney Rapp Band at Rapp's club, The Sign of the Drum. She was struggling to make it, but she was back on her feet. Her golden voice and good looks did not go unnoticed. The following year, 1940, the sixteen-year-old started dating the band's twenty-two-year-old trombone player, Al Jorden. Jorden was tall, dark, and dangerous. Actress and friend Kaye Ballard called Jorden "good-looking, very good-looking, but I hear he was a little nutsy, you know, temperamental and jealous." In fact, Doris nearly lost her life on a date with Jorden. The musician liked to tempt fate. During an outing on his speedboat, Jorden's daredevil antics flipped the boat, sending the couple overboard and perilously close to a nearby steamboat. They were rescued by a local reporter, and the next day the incident made front-page news. The romance continued even after Al took another job in New York. Doris was also ready to move on.

The singer attracted the attention of one of the top musical groups in the country. "The Les Brown Band was a very good swing band, but it was not revolutionary," commented Gavin. "They had hit records, and I think Doris's presence in the band is what really made it important." Said Doris herself, "Les Brown was just the greatest guy in the whole world, as were all the boys in the band. They were all like brothers to me." Brown admitted, "I think every man in the band was in love with her in a sisterly way, and she was a pal to everybody in the band." Doris was also a welcome distraction. "Doris Day wore very sexy clothes. She was renowned for having a great butt and great boobs," said James Gavin.

From all reports, Doris got along famously with the guys in the band. They joked and gave each other nicknames. But life on the road wasn't always happy for Doris. Touring with the band for months on end was grueling. "It's like being in the circus, without the elephant dung," said Frank Comstock. "You just get on the train or plane or car or whatever it is and drag your horn and your suitcase, and you don't know what town it is even." Conditions on the road were brutal, but the real torture for Doris was being apart from her bad-boy beau. In the spring of 1941, Al Jorden proposed.

"It was the happiest time that I could even imagine," said Doris, "but that's when I stopped my career right at a fabulous time in my life and said to Les, 'I'm going to go home to Cincinnati and get married.' And he said, 'You're going to do what? You're just starting.' And I said, 'Well, I'm in love, I think.'" According to Hotchner, "Les was putting pressure on her not to leave the band and marry Jorden, but despite Les Brown's advice and [that of] other members of the band who became very fond of her but were not fond of Al Jorden, she did marry him—with terrible results." A few weeks before her seventeenth birthday, Doris married twenty-three-year-old Jorden. But the honeymoon didn't last long. "He was very abusive," characterized Comstock, "and I guess he was very jealous from what I understand. Les used to comment about how he had to protect her almost."

Doris became pregnant shortly after the wedding. She hoped a baby would somehow calm her husband's jealousy and rage. The reality was not what she expected. "Not only was he psychologically jealous, but when Doris discovered she was pregnant, he demanded that she get an immediate abortion, which she said she would not do, because it was against everything that she believed in," said Hotchner. Al did more than suggest an abortion. He tried to handle the situation himself. "He got a big pan of boiling water, and he said, 'Put your feet in this pan.' It nearly scalded her feet. Then he gave her some large tablets that he had picked up, and made her swallow those. It made her deathly ill." Al's plan didn't end the pregnancy, but he continued to plead with Doris, because he thought that the child would take away her attention. "She had to really persevere and fight him off."

Jorden's rage eventually subsided, and on February 8, 1942, Doris gave birth to an eight-pound, one-ounce baby boy. Doris later summed up, "One beautiful thing came out of that marriage, and that was my son. If I hadn't married . . . I wouldn't have my terrific son, Terry. So you see, out of these awful experiences comes something wonderful." The last part of this statement was fast becoming Doris's mantra. Something important also came out in her giving birth—Doris's recognition that her marriage was a no-win situation. "Once Terry was born, she realized that she could not have any further relationship with Al Jorden, and she showed the other side of Doris Day, which is very firm, very committed," said Hotchner, who continued: "So she did push Al Jorden out of her life and went back to live with her mother in Cincinnati."

When she returned to her hometown, Doris admitted, she

"didn't have a penny, and the funny part of it is, is that I never thought that I couldn't get a job whenever I wanted it. I've always been very positive." A single mother, eighteen-year-old Doris found work singing on a local radio station. Once again, her voice caught the attention of an old friend. Les Brown happened to be traveling through town and heard his old singer on the radio. He thought she'd never take him up on an offer to rejoin the tour, but he asked her anyway, and then, as he put it, "all the good things happened." Doris signed on for the tour, and the musical road trip became a family affair as Doris's mother and her little boy often joined the band on the road.

Les Brown was constantly finding new material for the band. In 1942, at a late-night rehearsal, Brown asked Doris to try out a new number. "'Sentimental Journey' was just incredible," recalled Doris. "This was right after the war. I remember when, at rehearsal, after the dance job that night, he passed out this music. He gave me the sheet music. I said, 'That's a lovely title,' and he said, 'Wait'll you hear it.'" "Sentimental Journey" was released in January 1945. The single was an immediate hit and made Doris an overnight sensation, largely because of the emotional resonance it had with World War II servicemen.

"It came just in time for all the guys overseas to fall for it, and the song and her, you know—nice timing," said Frank Comstock. Doris herself felt touched by the song: "It makes me cry almost," she said, "because all the servicemen were overseas and they were about to come home. The letters started coming in and that song said so much." James Gavin also noted that much of the song's appeal had to do with Doris's "bedroom voice," as well. "When she sang 'Sentimental Journey' during the war, she had a way of making the servicemen feel that she was snuggling up next to them and she was cooing in their ear. She had a lot of sex appeal, seemingly without knowing it," he offered. It was that combination of sex and sincerity, wholesomeness and hotness that "made Doris. It brought her to the attention of the moguls out there in Hollywood," said Les Brown.

With the success of her wartime ballad in 1945, Doris began a love affair with the American public. Doris was the fantasy and muse of U.S. servicemen. As the war was winding down, Doris and the Les Brown Band traveled abroad with Bob Hope to entertain the troops. Upon her return, twenty-one-year-old Doris fell in love with another musician, nineteen-year-old saxophonist George Weidler. The physical attraction between George and Doris was intense. Without much else in common, the couple tied the knot on March 30, 1946. Described Doris, "We were married in Mount Vernon, New York, and on the way I was looking out the window and, I remember, I thought to myself, 'I really shouldn't do this.' Something told me not to—it was wrong. And I did it."

Doris and George left the Les Brown Band and moved to Los Angeles. She landed a gig singing on a local radio station, but the pay was low, and Doris needed to find more work. She accepted a monthlong engagement in New York City. Soon after opening night, Doris received a devastating call from her new husband. "I was singing at the little club in New York," she said, "and that's when we broke up on the phone. I mean, you just don't do that. So I wanted to go to California to talk with him and see if we could maybe work things out." Ted Baker, a friend of Doris, remarked that George Weilder "was a real nice guy, and they complemented each other and enjoyed being with each other. But her career started to take off, and he just couldn't handle being Mr. Doris Day." Doris returned to Los Angeles and begged her husband not to leave her. Doris told him she didn't care about being a star. Weidler insisted that stardom wasn't Doris's choice—it was her destiny.

After only eight months, the marriage was over. Doris was depressed and ready to leave Hollywood for good. The singer's agent at the time was Al Levy. Levy was very fond of his young client and, to cheer her up, took Doris to a party in the Hollywood Hills. "She went with him reluctantly to Jule Styne's house and everybody was getting up and singing, and Jule Styne and Sammy Kahn asked her to sing," described Rex Reed. Doris admitted that she hated this Hollywood tradition, but she obliged. "Doris is very shy. One can't imagine how an actress who exposes herself in singing and movies can be shy, but she was shy," said A. E. Hotchner. After she hid behind a palm tree, Doris eventually got up and sang "Embraceable You," and the crowd was blown away.

Doris Day was presented with a golden opportunity when she was offered a part in the Michael Curtiz musical *Romance on the High Seas*. Executives at Warner Bros. needed a leading lady, and fast. The studio's first choice, Judy Garland, was unavailable, and her replacement, Betty Hutton, became pregnant and dropped out. Curtiz, the Oscar-winning director of *Casablanca*, was more than happy to meet Doris. As Doris went toe-to-toe with the man that Reed called "the most important director in Hollywood," she was distracted. Upset about her impending divorce, she didn't fully appreciate the offer at hand. Her agent, Al Levy, persuaded Doris to audition for Curtiz the next day. "She was in tears the whole time," said Reed.

"I went in there. They were rolling my hair, and I was thinking of George," said Doris. "They were putting makeup on, I was thinking of George. I knew my lines, so I tested, and I didn't think about it anymore." Doris also doubted her ability to perform, because she had never studied acting. But that was actually her power, decided Reed: "Her impact was immediate. She didn't come up through the rank and file, she actually became a movie star in one picture."

Romance on the High Seas was a musical comedy set aboard a cruise ship. Doris played a young singer and was cast opposite leading man Jack Carson. Janice Paige, who also starred in the film, speculated, "I think Mike Curtiz saw something in her and guided her beautifully in that first movie. Any actor or actress who can have a Michael Curtiz as their first director is damned lucky." The relationship between the director and starlet had a great dynamic. He gave great direction, and she took it, eager to learn. "She was offbeat, kind of kooky. She had a different kind of speaking voice, and she could sing, and she was wonderful talent."

Despite her rave reviews and a big take at the box office, Doris didn't consider herself a star. "Doris remained confused—'What did I do?' she says. 'I never had an acting lesson. Everything I do is completely by instinct and what you see on the screen is what you get,'" recapped Rex Reed. Regardless of Doris's feelings, audiences and Hollywood executives also liked what they saw on the screen. In 1948, Warner Bros. offered her a lucrative seven-year contract. "I was so thrilled to not be on the road, to have a permanent place, to bring my baby and have a home, and bring my mama and go to work in the morning, and not to work at night," smiled Doris.

But life became complicated once again for the twenty-four-year-old optimist. Doris's agent became interested in more than the singer's career. Said A. E. Hotchner, "Unfortunately, Al Levy had a not-too-concealed passion for Doris. He spied on her under all kind of conditions. He would spy on her locations on a movie set and whatnot. And finally he attempted to rape her in one of her hotel rooms, and she regretfully had to part with Al Levy." Agent Marty Melcher took over, but Doris and Marty's partnership sent the movie star down a disastrous path.

After the success of *Romance on the High Seas* in 1948, Doris led a glorious, glamorous life on screen and a tumultuous, traumatic off-screen existence. She tried to achieve her dream of establishing a home by buying a house in the quiet neighborhood of Toluca Lake. To keep her head above water following the success of her first film, Doris worked nonstop. She starred in ten movies over the next three years, including *Tea for Two* with Gordon McCrae and *Young Man with a Horn* opposite Kirk Douglas, who, according to Hotchner, had "negative chemistry" with the upbeat blonde. The chemistry was positive, however, between Doris and actor Ronald Reagan. The two spent time together off-screen while making the film *Storm Warning*. "He was a marvelous man. We had a few dates. We liked dancing together, and we danced well together," reminisced Doris.

Doris soon fell for the man behind the scenes, though. She began an affair with Melcher. Described Hotchner, "Marty Melcher was one of those suave, sweet-talking Hollywood agents who bounced from client to client. In this case, he bounced into a really good one, because, with Doris, he was able to make a career." At the time, Melcher was married to Patty Andrews of the singing group the Andrews Sisters. But Patty's schedule kept her on the road much of the time. At weekend get-togethers, Marty and Doris's friends thought something was up between the two of them. Song publisher Mickey Goldsen remembered one occasion when his wife said, "I've just got a feeling that Marty and Doris have a closer relationship than just manager-client." Day insists she didn't get involved with Melcher until Marty and Patty broke up in 1950. Once Marty was unattached, however, he started spending many evenings with Doris and her son, Terry.

On her twenty-seventh birthday, in 1951, Doris Day married thirty-five-year-old Marty Melcher at Burbank City Hall. After a quick honeymoon trip to the Grand Canyon, Doris, Terry, and Melcher moved into a new home. Doris set up her mother in a nearby apartment. "In the beginning, [Melcher] got along great with Terry, and Doris felt, 'Well, now I've got a real father for him.' In fact, he adopted Terry," offered Hotchner. Marty also adopted Doris's religion. The actress's second husband had turned Doris on to Christian Science. Doris lived by the code, and Marty embraced her beliefs. "They became much more involved in Christian Science, and they got involved with a guru, kind of a confidant, and they started to develop a new group of acquaintances through the church," said Mickey Goldsen.

Doris seemed to have found everything she wanted: a lucrative career, a family, and a man she could trust. While the actress concentrated on making movies, her husband Marty invested her money. According to Hotchner, he was "buying oil wells, buying hotels, putting her into all sorts of purchases that she really didn't know much about. And Marty would just come and say, 'Just sign this,' and she signed all these things." Doris also let Marty handle her film and music career. Her friends questioned Marty's taste, but audiences wanted Doris—any way they could have her. "Doris Day's persona in the fifties was a big turn-on to young men, because, despite her virginal image, Doris Day was a tease in a lot of those films," commented James Gavin.

"She just has magnetism. She was like the girl next door. If you didn't fall in love with Doris Day, something was wrong with your heart," offered Jamie Farr, her costar in *With Six You Get Eggroll*. In 1953, Doris shed her girly image to play a butch cowgirl in the musical *Calamity Jane*. As she put it, "*Calamity Jane* is probably my favorite, because that's the real me. When I was a little girl, I was a tomboy. I loved climbing trees and skating and doing all the things that the boys did. Yet I loved dolls. So I'm a half-and-half mixture."

But making the movie was an ordeal. The twenty-nine-year-old star was exhausted. "She began to have trouble breathing. She tried to keep it from Marty, but it became more and more pronounced. And, at some point, it got so bad that she sort of had a little breakdown," recounted A. E. Hotchner. A doctor identified the problem immediately—Doris was having panic attacks; she was unable to cope with her overextended schedule. *Calamity Jane* was a hit, but Doris was in no shape to enjoy her success. For once, Doris put her health first and pulled out of a publicity tour for the movie. The unforgiving critics responded. "The Hollywood Press Club gave her what was called its Sour Apple Award for the least cooperative star," said Gavin. Doris offered a sweet-as-sugar response. Described Hotchner, "She made a big effort to gather the press together again and give them as much time as they wanted and get back in their good graces." Critics couldn't stay angry with Doris for long.

Rested and ready to return to work, Doris Day looked for some new challenges. In 1954, she was offered the lead in a lavish MGM biopic, *Love Me or Leave Me*. The role was the hard-boiled, hard-drinking torch singer Ruth Etting. Thirty-year-old Doris knew the movie was a great opportunity, but she wasn't sure she had the acting chops. "I had made many musicals at Warner

Bros.," said Doris, "but this was an extravaganza. This was going to be a biggie. It was thrilling to me, but I wondered if I would be right for that particular part, because I was always considered the girl next door." She asked leading man James Cagney for some advice. The response from "Jimmy"? "You're going to be better than any woman I've performed with." And she was.

"She's approaching it as a musician, a singer, as opposed to approaching it as an actress. So the acting took care of itself," said friend and *Romance on the High Seas* costar Page Cavanaugh. The sight of the wholesome singer boozing it up and wearing sexy costumes offended some fans. Nevertheless, Doris won rave reviews. Cagney was nominated for an Academy Award for Best Actor in 1956. Despite her performance, Doris was overlooked at Oscar time. With the success of *Love Me or Leave Me*, she wanted to tackle much more complicated roles. But Melcher, the actress's husband and manager, didn't want Doris Day to tarnish her pristine image. She began to realize that love and business should be separate affairs, saying, "The romance goes out the window when you suddenly feel that you're married to your father." Doris had no idea she was losing a lot more than romance.

By 1955, Doris's performance in *Love Me or Leave Me* had landed her in the company of the most sought-after leading ladies of Hollywood. It didn't take long before acclaimed director Alfred Hitchcock wanted to add Doris Day to his pantheon of beautiful blondes. That same year, Hitchcock cast Doris in his film *The Man Who Knew Too Much* about an American couple whose son is kidnapped during an exotic vacation. That summer, the cast and crew packed their bags for a grueling shoot in Morocco. The thirty-one-year-old leading lady embarked on the adventure with great hesitation.

Upon her arrival in Marrakech, Doris saw her fears realized when she witnessed the cruel treatment of animals. Commented Hotchner, "She wanted to rescue all of them, which of course was not a project that the filmmakers were about to undertake." Doris refused to work until all the animals in the film were properly fed, and, as she put it, "they were all fat as toads by the time we left." Doris also had a problem with Hitchcock. According to Hotchner, "She said, 'We've done half the movie. You haven't said one word of direction to me.'" But Doris's fears in this instance were unfounded, Hotchner continued. "He said, 'There's nothing to tell you. Just do what you're doing. It's exactly what I want you to do.'" Despite the challenges on the set, Doris managed to get through the production. She was surprised when the movie's theme song *"Que Sera, Sera"* became a smash hit and won an Oscar for Best Song in 1956.

Back in the States, Doris's third husband and agent Marty Melcher parlayed his wife's success into a new business opportunity for himself. He produced her next film, the dramatic thriller *Julie*. "Marty Melcher was a businessman and quasi-producer without a great deal of taste. And Doris did not fight for better scripts," assessed Rex Reed. The story about a flight attendant and her obsessed husband didn't interest Doris at all. Nevertheless, she went along with her husband's wishes. Production began in the spring of 1956 in Carmel, California. Two weeks into the shoot, Doris fell ill and wanted to return to Los Angeles to see a doctor, but Marty insisted that she follow her Christian Science beliefs and refuse medical treatment. "I couldn't tell you why he did it, but I would just say, a guy has a good thing going, he's going to milk it as far as he can, I guess," said Frank Comstock.

Doris started hemorrhaging and was suffering intense pain. Her producer husband refused to let her have any time off. Mickey Goldsen remarked, "Doris Day was not the kind of a person that you could make do what she didn't want to do. She was not a patsy. She was a strong person, and I don't believe that there was any evil intent." The film finally wrapped on May 15, 1956. Doris, then thirty-two years old, immediately returned to L.A. to seek medical attention. Tests showed she had a tumor the size of a grapefruit growing in her abdomen. Surgeons performed a hysterectomy and rebuilt part of her damaged intestine. The realization that she could never have another child sent Doris into deep depression. "All I ever wanted was to get married, have a nice husband, and have maybe two or three children and live happily ever after," she once said. But that dream had seemingly been destroyed, and she was devastated.

Always a fighter, Doris Day accepted her fate. In 1956, executives at Warner Bros. decided to bring the hit Broadway musical *The Pajama Game* to the big screen. She was cast as star opposite leading man John Raitt. Rehearsals got off to a rocky start. Director Stanley Donen put Doris and her leading man through some difficult dance moves. John had to catch her from a running leap. He caught her all right, but he also broke one of her ribs. Never a quitter, Doris recovered quickly and immediately returned to the set. "She gave one hundred fifty percent no matter what. Anything that they put in front of Doris Day, she found a way to make it completely convincing," said James Gavin.

For the moment, Doris could do no wrong, but professionally and personally things were about to change. In 1958, a respected Hollywood trade paper rated Doris one of the top-ten box-office favorites. Regardless, she was still depressed after her hysterectomy. She was about to face yet another blow. After Doris wrapped production on *The Pajama Game,* she received devastating news. Her brother, Paul, died of heart failure. As always, Doris turned to her work for solace. She began filming a comedy with Clark Gable called *Teacher's Pet.* Mamie Van Doren costarred and was "ecstatic" to work with Doris, but she soon realized Doris wasn't as excited to work with her. Van Doren commented, "She was very aloof . . . And she had that face that smiled, and she could sing, and she could act, and you'd think that she'd be kind of like she was on the screen, but she wasn't like that." Van Doren wasn't shy about letting the press in on her feelings about Doris.

Teacher's Pet was a success, but Doris's next two films, *Tunnel of Love* and *It Happened to Jane,* didn't strike a chord with moviegoers. Audiences seemed bored with Doris's girl-next-door image, and, frankly, so was Doris. Marty Melcher was very concerned. Doris's earning power was tied to her popularity, and he always had his eye on the bottom line. His preoccupation with Doris's income put a strain on their marriage. Doris also wondered about some of Marty's investment schemes, developed by attorney and financial advisor Jerry Rosenthal. Marty pitched every venture with enthusiasm all the while keeping Doris in the dark. One such plan involved building a hotel near San Francisco. "Marty had told her that he wanted her to come to the opening of a hotel, and she said, 'I don't go to openings of anything.' He forced her," said A. E. Hotchner. "They drove up the driveway and there before her was the most garish, awful, unacceptable piece of architecture she'd ever seen. So she just went out of there weeping, thinking that she had put her money into that place."

In 1959, after a string of disappointing movies, thirty-five-year-old Doris was ready for a change. Recounted Hotchner, "Along came a man named Ross Hunter, and he had a script that he wanted to do with Rock Hudson. *Pillow Talk* was a light romantic comedy in which you have a suggestion of sex, but not really a sexual comedy. Nevertheless, it was sexy, and it's got to do with two people getting together and the way that they go together." Doris loved the script and knew the movie would be special, but not many people shared her enthusiasm. Westerns and war movies were in vogue. Romantic comedies were considered old-fashioned.

In 1959, Universal Studios released *Pillow Talk*. The film was an instant hit. Doris's portrayal of a savvy interior decorator led to her first—and only—Academy Award nomination. The movie's success put her back on top. *Pillow Talk* also sparked an enduring friendship between Doris and her leading man. "They had to add a week on to the shooting schedule because we could not stop laughing," Rock Hudson once said. "I used to think about terrible things, to try not to laugh, but I think that's the wonderful part about when you see two people on the screen—if you like them, if they like each other, and you sense that they like each other," said Doris, asking, "Isn't that good? Don't you feel that?"

"He was her favorite costar because he made her laugh and she made him laugh. They were inseparable during the time she lived in Hollywood," commented Rex Reed. Hudson once described their friendship, saying, "You know when you find a friend, you can see right through and into a friend because a friend allows you to. And you allow a friend to see into you. I think that's part of it. Other people have a facade, which is fine, too, by the way, but they have to choose to let you in. And that's very flattering when you are let in. It is." Doris chipped in without a beat, "That's the way we are together."

Doris followed *Pillow Talk* with another romantic comedy, the 1960 movie *Please Don't Eat the Daisies*. Then, in 1961, she re–teamed with Hudson in *Lover Come Back*. The next year, Doris shared the screen with actor Cary Grant in another fluffy romantic comedy, *That Touch of Mink*. The actress's on-screen image became decidedly sexier, and the gossip columns were filled with unsubstantiated rumors of scandalous affairs between Doris and some famous African-American sports figures. "There was a rumor of an affair she had with Maury Wills, who was a shortstop for the Dodgers. Another with Elgin Baylor, who was a basketball player. It got a lot of attention in the press, especially Maury Wills. Everybody thought it was a foregone conclusion. All of which she denied," said Hotchner. In his biography, Wills claimed the rumors were true.

In reality, Doris's personal life was far more complicated. She and her husband drifted apart. According to Doris, their sex life dried up. Then, in 1962, Marty hit their son Terry during an argument. For Doris, it was the last straw. She kicked Marty out, but he was back within a few weeks. He convinced her that a divorce would create a financial nightmare. She still loved him, though she wasn't "in love" with him. The two agreed to remain married and live together under the same roof but to lead separate lives.

While her marriage crumbled, Doris's career took a hit. Though she was a number one box-office draw four years in a row and had substantial Hollywood clout, the actress was signing on to substandard projects, following Melcher's advice. "Doris

Day, within a couple of years, went from being the number one box-office draw to making terrible movies like *Caprice* and *Where Were You When the Lights Went Out?*, which she found herself having to do because her husband, in desperation for money, had made the deal," said James Gavin. "She became associated with lousy material and, unfortunately, in some people's eyes she became kind of a joke."

In 1967, Marty Melcher signed Doris Day to make the film *The Ballad of Josie*. Even though she had no interest in the picture, she gave it her all. Costar Peter Graves remembered one scene that required Doris's character to drink a large glass of brandy. "Before the scene, the prop guys came through, and they said, 'Doris, what would you like in there? You want some iced tea or Coke or something?' She said, 'No, put brandy in there,'" he recounted. All in all, "she must have tossed off about six brandies, and this is a girl who doesn't drink and doesn't smoke—is the most healthy thing. And her eyes were crossed, and she was stoned," he laughed. Despite the talented cast, *The Ballad of Josie* was not a hit. In 1967, Marty produced *With Six You Get Eggroll*, a family comedy about a couple of divorced people who have to blend their two families. Jackie Joseph, who made a brief appearance in the film, offered, "The atmosphere was like you were at the home of the character Doris played. You were suddenly a friend. You were just another actor, and she was another actor. She's just a basically happy, upside woman."

For Doris, true happiness didn't come from her work or from her marriage. Instead, it was her love of animals that helped Doris survive each day. Her concern for their welfare became a number one priority on screen and off. Jamie Farr, her costar in *With Six You Get Eggroll*, offered, "There's a scene in the movie where one of the vehicles runs into a [chicken] truck driven by Vic Tayback. After the scene was over, she'd go in it and examine the chickens to make sure that the chickens were all right. That's the way she was—a very kind lady." Director Howard Morris also saw Doris's love for animals. "She always brought the dogs with her," he said, "and she had a chauffeur fired because the dogs had their heads out the window. It was parked and the windows were wide enough for the dog to stick its head out, and the driver hit the electric button that sent the window up."

As shooting progressed, Doris had other concerns. Her husband became ill during the film's production. He began losing weight and complained that he was cold all the time. A staunch Christian Scientist, Melcher refused medical attention, and his condition worsened. The day the movie wrapped, he went to bed. He stayed there for the next three months. Finally, at Doris's urging, a doctor examined Marty and sent him straight to the hospital. Explained A. E. Hotchner, "The doctor discovered that he had an enlarged heart and had for some time. There is also a condition that has gone to his brain that had been neglected for so long that there was really nothing they could do for him." Doris was stunned by the diagnosis.

On April 20, 1968, Marty Melcher died. The unexpected loss of her companion of seventeen years left Doris devastated. For weeks, she stayed home with the curtains drawn and rarely spoke on the phone. Ironically, the last film produced by Marty, *With Six You Get Eggroll*, was a surprise success. But Doris found no comfort in her work, her usual escape in times of crisis. Doris's son Terry offered this about his adoptive father, "He was a really big factor in my life and my mom's life, and we both really loved him, but some of his actions did cause us a lot of problems." That was an understatement. Melcher's tangled legacy caused huge stress when twenty-six-year-old Terry tried to sort out Marty's estate. What he found was shocking.

According to Hotchner, "It was all fantasy." Marty's claim that the investments were booming was not true. Doris Day was nearly penniless. Terry immediately fired Marty's lawyer and investment adviser, Jerry Rosenthal. Then he gave his mother the bad news. All of her lucrative investments were fiction, all of the money-losing ventures were fact, and she owed the government $500,000 in back taxes. After forty-two films, Doris had nothing to show for her hard work. Tens of millions of dollars were gone. She felt betrayed by her late husband, the man she shared her life with for so many years. "There was a peculiar transference at Marty's death—since Terry now becomes the executor, he becomes in charge of Doris's affairs," said Hotchner, "and also he has to take charge of her life virtually with all the finances gone and her belief in Marty shattered." Summed up actress and friend Rose Marie, "Marty had loused it up. I don't know what they did with it. I mean, what do you do with $26 million?"

"I think Doris Day, like a lot of busy women of her generation in Hollywood, trusted too much in a man. She had a seemingly strong man by her side who was making all the business decisions, and because evidently she wanted so much to believe in his sincerity, she just let him handle that," observed biographer James Gavin. The final straw occurred while Doris was going through Marty's things. She found out that he had signed her to one last project. Hotchner explained, "Doris had discovered in Marty's desk after his death that he had signed a contract and had taken an advance of half a million dollars from a television network for Doris to star in *The Doris Day Show* and there were two scripts already done. This really destroyed her."

Rather than file for bankruptcy, Doris was determined to pay her debts. Though she hated the idea of the television series, she realized the work would help her get back on her feet. The series premiered on September 24, 1968. "The first season was very, very dreary, and she didn't like it at all," described Gavin. Determined to make the best of a bad situation, Doris took control of her TV series. Unlike the down-home, farm-based family show from the first season, said Gavin, "She insisted on becoming a San Francisco businesswoman, as opposed to a boring woman on the farm trying to raise a brood of kids, which she wasn't happy with at all." Doris hired her own director and producers.

The revised storyline helped *The Doris Day Show* gain popularity. The show became a ratings winner for CBS. The steady paycheck also helped Doris pay off some of her debts, but the forty-five-year-old actress still felt suckered into doing the series. "She was very unhappy," said Kaye Ballard, "but she never let anybody see that side of her. She is a very private person and yet she's accessible in public. She's very happy to give anybody an autograph or to talk to them, and she's very courteous and warm, but yet she's a very private person." Doris's love of animals helped her survive the daily grind of the series. "There were all these dogs on the set. They were in her dressing room, and near the end of the day, she would pick a couple of them to come out, and they would sit up on directors' chairs like friends visiting the set. When you're doing your job and there's a dachshund going *Hmmmm*, you know, it's just fun," mused costar Jackie Joseph.

In 1971, Doris was becoming more and more preoccupied with animal rights. She cocreated a new organization, Actors and Others for Animals. When *The Doris Day Show* ended production in 1973, Doris made animal activism her full-time job. Offered Joseph, "Her feeling was, if people read about actors being kind to animals, then maybe they'll think they want to emulate an actor. Listening to someone like James Garner advising him to spay and neuter a dog, some guy who would think 'Never my dog' would think, 'Maybe James has something.'" Described Rex Reed, "She was on a crusade. She was the Joan of Arc of the animal world, of the four-legged set in Los Angeles."

Doris was also on a crusade for herself. In 1974, she took control of her life and took Marty Melcher's attorney Jerry Rosenthal to court. At stake were millions of dollars that Doris told the judge she believed Rosenthal had squandered. Doris desperately wanted to learn if her late husband was the real culprit. On March 31, 1975, Doris got her day in court. Judge Lester E. Olson found Rosenthal liable for legal malpractice and fraud. The court awarded Doris a whopping sum close to $23 million. Doris made a statement later that day: "I just knew that justice would prevail. I've known it all along, and I was assured of that this morning." Rosenthal appealed the verdict. In the meantime, his insurance companies offered Doris a settlement totaling almost $10 million.

Doris accepted, but no amount could help her come to terms wi
her husband's culpability. "I don't think Marty meant to do it.
think that he just trusted the wrong person completely and found
himself really in trouble," she said. Mickey Goldsen agreed, saying, "Marty got hurt along with Doris Day, so I just feel that Marty
was an honest guy but happened to pick an advisor who put them
in the wrong deals."

With Marty gone, Doris would never have all the answers. So
the fifty-one-year-old focused on the future and on her greatest
passion. "All of her life, Doris had an ongoing concern for the
dog. The dog was, to her, an embodiment of all the best things
that should be in human beings," reasoned A. E. Hotchner. Kaye
Ballard recalled Doris opening her heart to stray dogs on multiple
occasions. Rex Reed, too, remembered an incident where Doris
entered a bank to chastise a dog owner for tying his dog to a me-
ter post outside. According to Reed, "She said, 'Give me the
check. I'll take your place in line and cash the check, and you go
and take care of the dog,' and he did—while the whole bank applauded." After that stirring incident, Doris had a new role: savior
of defenseless animals. "She was constantly picketing animal
shelters, and she gave away all of her clothes to raise money to
pay for the animals," recalled Reed. Doris described her calling,
saying, "If we can just get the animals out of the laboratories, I'll
be very happy about that. We're trying to change the laws and
make it a better world for the animals."

But Doris wasn't through with show business yet. In 1975, a
producer convinced her to return to television for a one-time variety special called *Doris Day Today*. The show scored big ratings
and fifty-two-year-old Doris seemed right at home, hamming it up
on-screen. Off-screen, Doris was also ready to take some chances.
"We went to have lunch one day in a health food restaurant in
Beverly Hills, and a tall, rather handsome man came over and
gushed all over her, saying that he was just dreaming of the day
that she would come in. That he was a fan, that he had seen
everything and, you know, practically threw himself in her lap at

that point," said Hotchner. The man was forty-one-year-old restaurant manager Barry Comden. Laughed Reed, "She thought he was related to Betty Comden, the songwriter, and she also thought he owned a restaurant. It turned out he was really I think the maître d' of a restaurant." Hotchner continued, "The next day, she said, 'Well, why don't we go to that health food restaurant again,' and I couldn't believe my eyes, but this guy was making the move on Doris."

Forever the optimist, Doris started dating Barry Comden. Their courtship included a publicity tour for her autobiography, *Doris Day: Her Own Story*, which A. E. Hotchner cowrote. When they promoted the book in New York, "he came, and he was Mr. Doris Day. I, of course, knew that this was ill-fated, but she married," Hotchner said. On April 14, 1976, the couple tied the knot in a quiet ceremony at the home of a friend in Carmel, California. It was Comden's second and Doris's fourth walk down the aisle. "He was very handsome, and they probably had a very sexy time of it for a little while until she decided that she was getting more unconditional love from her pets than she was from her husband," commented Rex Reed. Doris preferred to share her bed with countless canines more than with Comden. "That's when she really made the decision to devote all of her time to animals and not people." In the summer of 1979, after only three years of marriage, the couple separated.

"It's not surprising that having made all of the terrible choices in men that Doris would then turn to the warm, embracing bosom of her animal family," said James Gavin. At age fifty-five, Doris Day gave up the glamour of Hollywood for a dog's life, or at least a life revolving around her four-legged friends. But Doris continued to use her show business notoriety and contacts to improve the lives of the creatures she loved so dearly. In 1980, Doris's former costar Ronald Reagan became president of the United States. Though her fear of flying kept Doris from visiting the Reagans, she took advantage of having a friend in the White House. When Reagan wasn't as receptive to her suggestions for animal rights legislation as Doris might have liked, mentioned Reed, "She told the lady on the phone, 'Listen, you tell him this is his costar calling. I was married to him when he was just Grover Cleveland Alexander the baseball player. He better call me back if he knows what's good for him.' He was back on the phone in about four minutes." Doris always had an easier time with her leading men than her husbands.

"I don't know if I was looking for my father by getting married so often," said Doris, "because I lost my father at a very young age. Perhaps I missed that in my life. It could be that I wanted to have a man with me all the time sort of telling me what to do." On January 5, 1981, fifty-six-year-old Doris Day filed for divorce from forty-five-year-old Barry Comden, husband number four. Friends wondered if she'd ever take another risk on romance. "I think if she met the right person she would, but how many times can you try? And how many times can you be disappointed? You have animals, and they're always there," assessed Kaye Ballard. Doris settled in Carmel, a picturesque town on the coast of central California where she filmed the thriller *Julie* in 1956. The location was a perfect setting to raise and care for animals. "There's where she found a peaceful place. It just spoke to her soul, and she's made a life there," remarked Jackie Joseph.

By 1981, fifty-seven-year-old Doris may have forgotten Hollywood, but she didn't lose her sense of humor, and she was content to stay out of the public eye. She concentrated on animal rights. In 1985, she returned to the small screen to champion animal welfare with a cable TV series shot in Carmel called *Doris Day's Best Friends*. The show featured more than just dogs. Doris also invited some Hollywood pals to make appearances. In July 1985, she welcomed her most special guest, *Pillow Talk* costar and longtime friend Rock Hudson. Doris hadn't seen Rock for years, but their reunion was bittersweet. Hudson was suffering from AIDS. His gaunt appearance shocked his former costar. "It was a real awakening for Doris," said Reed, "and then she became more aware of AIDS, more aware of human problems." Added Mamie

Van Doren, "Of course nobody knew what AIDS was at that time." Commented Joseph, "It was very brave of Rock, because he was very protective of his illness and, God bless him, he doesn't know what he's done to help others. Doris adored Rock Hudson." On October 5, 1985, three months after his appearance on *Doris Day's Best Friends*, Hudson died of AIDS at age fifty-nine. Doris cried for weeks, but the sixty-one-year-old actress found comfort with her family and her animals.

In the spring of 1986, Doris finally got closure on the biggest legal battle of her life. After more than a decade, Doris's former finance adviser finally exhausted the last of his appeals. With no distractions, Doris dedicated herself to the protection and well-being of animals. The actress's home became a virtual wildlife sanctuary. As Rex Reed described it, "You walk in the door of Doris's house and you are bombarded by a screaming menagerie of animals. They have a whole section of the house with their own kitchen, and they have wonderful meals. They eat better than I do." In 1987, the actress founded the Doris Day Animal League, a national organization that lobbies for animal rights legislation. "I just hope that I can really make it better for the animals. I know I have so far with my pet foundation. We've placed so many doggies and cats in wonderful homes with terrific people, and that is just thrilling to me," she said. With the help of her son, Terry, Doris also ran the pet-friendly Cypress Inn in Carmel, where four-legged guests were treated just as well as their owners.

In 1989, Doris Day accepted a Golden Globe Award for her lifetime achievements. It was the last time the beloved star made a public appearance. After a career that spanned nearly five decades full of success and heartbreak, Doris walked away from Hollywood and never looked back. "Like an actress who becomes a nun, Doris is a huge star who has walked down from the mountain after finding it lacking and has found peace in a very nice green valley," said Reed. Janis Paige, her costar, commented, "I think she's happy up there. You know, that's something that people just don't understand—that you can be happy without this job. There's life after show business." Concluded James Gavin, "She's not interested in revisiting her singing career or her acting career. She may have loved them while they were happening, but she seems to be equally fulfilled in her life with her animals in Carmel and doesn't want to live in the past."

Still, the paparazzi lurked. In 1991, the supermarket tabloid *The Globe* printed a misleading article that claimed Doris lived like a bag lady, rummaging through garbage cans, searching for food for her dogs. Doris insisted the story was false and sued the tabloid for $25 million. Six months later, *The Globe* printed an apology and the lawsuit was dropped. Doris didn't let the controversy change her way of life. Nor did she miss the spotlight. When President George W. Bush awarded Doris Day a Presidential Medal of Freedom in June 2004, she did not attend the ceremony because of her fear of flying. She was honored, though, for the recognition. "I am deeply grateful to the president and to my country," said Doris, who was eighty. "But I won't fly." This moment would soon be followed by another tragedy, when, in November 2004, Doris's beloved son Terry Melcher died at the age of sixty-two.

Today, audiences have to be content with the gold mine of songs and films the actress leaves behind. Considered Rex Reed, "It would be a terrible tragedy if Hollywood has seen the last of Doris. I keep hoping there will be some sensational role for an eighty-year-old glamour girl." Added Peter Graves, "I don't know anybody who was bigger or sustained it over a longer time than Doris, and she was absolutely wonderful at it."

CHAPTER 12

KEY TO CAMELOT

The John F. Kennedy Jr. Story

"He gave you that feeling that time was short and put as much into a day as possible."

—Jamie Auchincloss, uncle

At eight o'clock on the night of Friday, July 16, 1999, John Kennedy Jr., along with his wife, Carolyn, and sister-in-law, Lauren Bessette, arrived at Essex County Airport in Fairfield, New Jersey. Moments later, they climbed aboard John's Piper Saratoga airplane. He was flying his sister-in-law to Martha's Vineyard, a one-hour-and-fifteen-minute flight. After dropping Lauren off, John and Carolyn were to continue on to nearby Hyannisport, Massachusetts. They hoped to arrive no later than 10:00 P.M. The couple planned to attend a family wedding the following day. Thirty-eight-year-old John, a novice pilot, was at the controls of the single-engine aircraft. At 8:38 P.M., as the plane took off, clear summer weather gave way to hazy skies—less than ideal flying conditions.

An hour earlier, experienced private pilot Kyle Bailey canceled plans to fly to Martha's Vineyard because of the weather. "That particular night was such an eerie night," said Bailey. "I mean, the visibility was terrible. It was kind of like the calm before a thunderstorm. I assumed, based on these conditions, that there was an instructor on the airplane with him." John, who had had a cast removed from his left ankle only the day before, decided to fly solo. At 9:33 P.M., fifty-five minutes after takeoff, a thickening haze shrouded the aircraft as John headed out over the Atlantic Ocean toward the Vineyard. The horizon that guided his way was no longer in sight. The plane failed to arrive at Martha's Vineyard Airport. Friends of Lauren Bessette, who were waiting to meet the flight, alerted an airport maintenance worker at 10:05 and went home. No one was overly concerned, at least not yet.

At 1:55 the following morning, the Coast Guard station in Woods Hole, Massachusetts, received a worried phone call from Kennedy family friend Carol Radziwill. Radziwill told the Coast Guard that John's plane never arrived at Hyannisport. Coast Guard officials swung into action, sending several cutters out to sea. Shortly after sunrise, as word began to spread, the world watched and waited for news of the missing aircraft. According to Byron Scott, a local TV reporter, everyone watching was "Hoping against odds, hoping against the evidence that searchers would find some sign of life; of course, at this point that had not yet happened."

The outpouring of emotion was widespread just as it had been thirty-six years earlier, following the assassination of John's father, President John F. Kennedy. The tiny boy who saluted his father's flag-draped coffin captured the hearts of stunned, bereaved Americans. He became their son as well. Howard Chua-Eoan, who chronicled John's amazing life story for the readers of *Time* magazine, commented, "They were hoping that one day this would be the next great Kennedy. And, of course, that's part of the entire tragedy that there was all this hope that the prince and the heir of Camelot would one day come and take his rightful place. That did not happen. It will never happen." If the Kennedys are America's royal family, then John F. Kennedy Jr. was its crowned prince, a legacy sealed by his untimely death.

In November 1960, three years before the assassination, Jack Kennedy and his very pregnant wife, Jackie, were basking in victory. Two weeks after he was elected president, Jack planned to fly to the family compound in Palm Beach, Florida, to finalize his cabinet choices. Jackie's stepbrother, Jamie Auchincloss, warned Kennedy not to leave Washington. "I said, 'You shouldn't go to Palm Beach after dinner tonight.' He was planning to fly down and have Thanksgiving Day with his parents," said Auchincloss, "and he said, 'Why not?' And I said, 'Because Jackie's going to have a baby boy,' and he laughed, and he said, 'Well, she's not expecting until December 11." Jamie's prediction was right. Shortly after Kennedy arrived in Palm Beach, Jackie was rushed to Georgetown University Hospital. A frantic Jack was flying back when his wife underwent an emergency cesarian section. John F. Kennedy Jr. was born at 12:22 A.M. on November 25. He was the only son ever born to a president elect.

John Jr. weighed a healthy six pounds three ounces, but he spent his first six days in an incubator because of respiratory problems. When his condition improved, he was baptized in the hospital in the same christening dress that his father had worn in his time. The press turned out en masse for the ceremony. Noted biographer Christopher Andersen has written three books on the Kennedy family, including *The Day John Died*. Anderson commented, "I can't think of a single American in this century who lived out his entire life in the spotlight. All thirty-eight years this guy was center stage, and I think that's why people in this country came to view him as sort of a member of the family."

Jack Kennedy, a forty-three-year-old two-term senator from Massachusetts, was the youngest president ever elected. His wife, thirty-one-year-old Jacqueline Bouvier Kennedy, a former New York debutante, was the youngest first lady. The dashingly handsome couple represented a golden period in America, later referred to as "Camelot." Susan Toepfer, executive editor of *People* magazine, noted, "The Kennedys are the closest we've come to royalty. I don't think any other family has had [such] an impact in this century, certainly on Americans." John Jr. and his three-year-old sister, Caroline, were conspicuously absent when their father was sworn in as the thirty-fifth president of the United States on January 21, 1961. They stayed at home with their nanny. Jackie, who grew up with an alcoholic father, was determined to give her kids as normal a childhood as possible, even in the White House. Commented Jamie Auchincloss, "Her most famous quote is, 'If you blow raising your children, no matter how much you succeed in everything else, you've blown everything.' So she put that as priority number one."

Inside 1600 Pennsylvania Avenue, Jackie had Caroline's bedroom painted pink and white, and she created a special nursery for John Jr. Boxes of toys were brought in. A menagerie of animals including guinea pigs, ducks, and rabbits were also kept on the grounds. Outsiders were warned to keep a proper distance from John and Caroline. "Jackie, even when they were in the White House, made certain that the Secret Service knew, for example, that they were not to pamper these kids," said Christopher Andersen, "She didn't want grown men picking up after her children. There was one memo that I thought was fascinating. In it, Jackie says, 'When we're at the beach, drowning is my responsibility. Don't worry. I'll take care of them.'"

Jackie was adamant about protecting her children and their privacy, but she also recognized the public's immense interest in her family. On a few special occasions, the first lady allowed pictures and home movies to be taken. Americans saw John Jr. ride his first pony and spend time with his father on the beach in Hyannisport. He, like his dad, craved adventure. "He didn't have any real sense of danger. He would run off the high diving board when he was a year and a half old and two and a half old. In the summers he would hurl himself into the air and plummet to the water," said Auchincloss, "and Jack would delight at that." John's sense of adventure wasn't limited to the diving board. Andersen mentioned, "When he was a little kid, he used to run out to see Dad land on the White House lawn on the helicopter. As a matter of fact, Dad would kneel down and embrace his son, and little John would run right past Dad toward the helicopter. He always had this love of flying."

Jack Kennedy may have been the president of the United States and one of the most powerful men in the world, but the forty-five-year-old leader was also a doting father. He routinely started his day by sharing breakfast alone with John Jr. and Caroline. John often followed his dad into high-level meetings. On one memorable occasion, he disrupted his father's weekly radio address. Jack was so charmed by his outgoing son that, unlike his wife, he wanted to share him with everyone. In December 1962, while Jackie was visiting Greece, Kennedy summoned a photographer friend to the White House. Stanley Tretick from *Look* magazine was asked to take pictures of John playing in the Oval Office. The result was a series of priceless photographs, including a famous shot of John crawling inside his father's desk. Laughed Jamie Auchincloss, "There are wonderful pictures of John in the Oval Office, and those are moments when she was out of town, and they were snuck in. Then Jack would have to probably give her some pretty nice gifts to calm her down."

Even though Jack and Jackie didn't always agree on the amount of publicity their children received, they were overjoyed when Jackie found out that she was pregnant again in the spring of 1963. Two-year-old John and sister Caroline excitedly awaited the arrival of their new sibling. That August, Jackie was rushed to the hospital and underwent her second emergency cesarian. As one reporter recapped, "The dramatic miracle of birth and a fight for life takes place at the Otis Air Force Base Hospital on Cape Cod as Mrs. Jacqueline Kennedy bears a premature son who has been baptized Patrick Bouvier. The president rushed from Washington to be with his wife. As is often the case with premature babies, Patrick had difficulty breathing, and he was whisked to Children's Hospital and placed in an isolet, an oxygen-fed incubator. The baby, the first to be born in a White House family in sixty-eight years, was the object of worldwide attention during his dramatic fight for life."

Patrick Bouvier Kennedy died on August 9, 1963, two days after he was born. Physically weak and depressed, Jackie did not attend the funeral. Auchincloss described, "The casket looks tiny, and that's a very poignant sight. It was a white casket, and Jack was really, really emotionally crushed by that. He so looked forward to actually having a son born in the White House years."

When the first lady emerged from seclusion three months later, in November 1963, she joined her husband in Dallas for a parade in his honor. Texas was a Republican outpost, and the liberal Kennedy braced for protests. In fact, the Secret Service was on high alert.

At approximately 12:30 P.M. on November 22, 1963, the presidential motorcade drove past Dealy Plaza, greeted by cheers and waving flags. President Kennedy and his wife sat together in the back seat of a convertible limousine. Suddenly, shots rang out. A frantic reporter stated, "Something has happened in the motorcade route. Something, I repeat, has happened in the motorcade route. Park Land Hospital has been advised to stand by for a severe gunshot wound. It appears someone in the limousine might have been hit by the gunfire." President Kennedy was shot in the back of the neck and in the right side of his head. Doctors at Park Land Memorial Hospital worked feverishly to save him, but the damage was too extensive. Walter Cronkite informed a mourning nation, "From Dallas, Texas, the flash apparently official, President Kennedy died at 1:00 P.M. Central Standard Time, two o'clock Eastern Standard Time—some thirty-eight minutes ago."

Jackie accompanied her husband's body back to Washington, D.C., aboard Air Force One. Still wearing her bloodstained suit, she stood beside Lyndon B. Johnson as he was sworn in as the thirty-sixth president of the United States. In his impromptu inaugural address, Johnson declared, "This is a sad time for all people. We have suffered a loss that cannot be weighed." John Jr. and Caroline were unaware of their father's assassination when they were taken to their grandparents' home that afternoon. Jackie arrived at the White House too distraught to break the tragic news to her children. She left that task to their nanny, Maud Shaw. The following morning, the president's body lay in state at the Capitol Building. John and Caroline were given a moment alone with their father. Explained Jamie Auchincloss, "Jackie asked Caroline to write a letter saying good-bye to her daddy and for John to draw a picture, and they opened the casket, and they put them in the casket so the children saw their father, and then they closed it."

For the first time, Jackie contemplated life without Jack. She shared her feelings with President Kennedy's press secretary, Pierre Salinger. "This is something that I think is maybe one of the most important things that I have ever heard," he said, "because she said to me, 'Look, Pierre, I've only got one thing to do now in life. I've got to take care of these kids. I've got to make sure that they get up well. I've got to make sure that they become intelligent, that they move forward in life, that they get good jobs, because if I don't do that for them, they'll spend their whole life looking back at their father's death. I want them to have a real future.'"

On November 25, three days after his assassination, President Kennedy was laid to rest. As his father's coffin was being wheeled to Arlington National Cemetery, John Jr. made a simple gesture— a gesture that was forever sealed in the hearts and minds of fellow Americans. Auchincloss described, "He stepped forward and put his feet together, and he came up with his right hand, which, for those of us who knew of John's left-handedness, really broke us up. It was a truly poignant moment of 'I'm going to get it right this time, because this is when it counts. This is that one take.'" Affirmed Christopher Andersen, "One of the great symbols of that period—maybe the greatest—is the moment when John gave his salute to his father's coffin. He delivered what is, I think, the most famous salute in history, and it's part of the iconography of this country and the twentieth century."

President Kennedy's funeral fell on the same day as John's third birthday party. That evening, still wearing her black dress, Jackie threw her son a party. Jackie's cousin John Davis never forgot the brave facade the guests displayed. "The somber mood of the day and the somber mood of the reception at the White House was dissipated entirely into a children's party with people tooting horns and singing 'Happy birthday to you, John Jr.' It was an amazing thing to watch," Davis commented. Jackie and her children took up temporary residence in a two-story brick house on N Street in Washington. Curiosity seekers camped outside the house day and night. Police were forced to erect barricades and put up roadblocks. Edward Klein, who later formed a friendship with Jackie and authored the book *Just Jackie: Her Private Years,* noted, "It became apparent to her that as long as she stayed in Washington she would be treated solely as the widow of the slain president, and she would be a captive of the public imagination, so she decided to move to New York where there's a lot more chance for anonymity."

In 1964, Jackie bought a fifteen-room apartment at 1040 Fifth Avenue on Manhattan's tony Upper East Side. Soon after Jackie and the kids settled in their new home, four-year-old John started kindergarten at Saint David's, a Catholic school two blocks away. On his first day, John was accompanied by Secret Service agents who would protect him until he turned sixteen. One of John's classmates, Mark Rafael, recalled, "I actually was in grade school with John, and we were always aware of his presence. But I think there was also a respect of allowing him distance—so there was something very guarded about him at that age."

For the most part, John was a popular and well-liked student, but on occasion he was treated like an outsider. Jackie witnessed some of the other kids' acts of unkindness. "As they left school, this gang of classmates came up and said, 'Your daddy's dead. Your father's dead,' over and over again, chanting this," recounted Andersen, "and Jackie was horrified. John reaches up, takes her hand, and kind of leads her down the street. She later on said, 'You know, here's this boy who had the presence of mind to think what my feelings were like, trying to protect me.' So I think he was always in that special position. Ultimately, of course, he won everybody over even as a child."

Jackie was proud of John, but she felt that he needed a strong male influence in his life. She turned to Jack's younger brother Bobby for help. "Bobby, who was the next oldest Kennedy brother and therefore assumed immediately the role of the head of the family, felt an obligation to take care of Jackie and her children, which he did," said Edward Klein. In 1968, when John was seven years old, Bobby decided to run for president. That June, moments after he won the California primary, Bobby was brutally gunned down following his victory speech at a Los Angeles hotel. Bobby Kennedy died the following day, June 6, 1968, at the age of forty-two. According to Klein, "When Jackie heard that her brother-in-law had been assassinated only five years after her husband had been assassinated, she was absolutely certain that there was no safety for any Kennedy, including especially herself and her children. And she said, as has been well reported, 'If they're killing Kennedys, they're going to kill my children, and I want to get out of this country.'"

At an age when most young boys stressed over their baseball card collection and arithmetic homework, John F. Kennedy Jr. suffered through the horrific deaths of his father and beloved Uncle Bobby. Although John was just three years old when his father was assassinated, he was seven and well aware of the grim circumstances when Bobby Kennedy was killed in 1968. "It was a wonderful, close relationship" between John and Bobby, declared Jamie Auchincloss. Added John Davis, "Bobby was a devoted substitute father to those two children, and he was a great source of strength to Jacqueline. When he went, everything that sustained her was sort of knocked out from under her. She was in a terribly, terribly profound depression."

For John Jr. the trauma didn't end with Bobby's death. His mother, desperate for financial and emotional stability, made a startling decision. In October 1968, thirty-nine-year-old Jackie married Greek shipping tycoon Aristotle Onassis. The ceremony was held on his private island of Skorpios in the Mediterranean Sea. At sixty-two, Onassis was regarded as the richest man in the world. "She married a man who had so much money and so much power—and a seventy-five-man security force, I might add. That was part of it. He could provide the kind of security that she didn't really feel the Secret Service could provide for her children," said Christopher Andersen. Onassis met Jackie in the early 1960s when he briefly dated her sister, Lee Radziwill. The two maintained a friendship and saw each other on numerous occasions. Nevertheless, their wedding took everyone by surprise, particularly Jackie's family. Said Auchincloss, "Onassis was older than my mother, and so my mother's looking at a daughter marrying somebody older than the mother—it just didn't look right—and all that money and all those business dealings. It just looked like terrible PR."

John, still only seven years old, was especially upset. He barely knew Onassis, who was old enough to be his grandfather. Onassis had a grown son and daughter, Alexander and Christina, from a previous marriage, but Aristotle made a concerted effort to win the affection of his new stepchildren. "He basically tried to buy them off," said Andersen. "He'd take them to FAO Schwarz, the big toy store on Fifth Avenue in New York, and just buy out the store. He did spend time with them, but they never got past that. John never got past calling him Mr. Onassis." Auchincloss, pointing out the family's constant awareness of their celebrity status, added, "If John was going to say anything, it would be that he liked him and that he was a very generous man—whether he was or not—because John knew that anything other than that would make headlines. There are some nice pictures of John with Ari. If one believes pictures, it seemed all right."

Onassis's money provided John with a lifestyle of supreme privilege. He spent his summers and holidays on Skorpios as well as sailing around the world on his stepfather's elegant yacht, the *Christina*. Jackie had the protection she craved for her children, but she also understood their need for some normalcy, so John and his sister continued to attend school in New York City. For the immensely private Jackie, living in New York City during the school year presented many dangers, including the prying eyes of the paparazzi. Photographers routinely camped outside John's school, and they followed him in Central Park where he played with his friends. In one 1969 incident, photographer Ron Galella startled John when Galella jumped out from behind a bush to take his picture. When Jackie found out about the incident, she ordered Secret Service agents to smash Galella's camera and arrest him for harassment. Galella shot back, suing for false arrest and harassment. Jackie filed a countersuit, and a judge eventually ordered Galella not to come within thirty feet of John.

The ruling was a victory, but Jackie knew that a court order alone wasn't going to protect her son. "What really bothered her the most, I think, is that he would not be resilient enough to survive the kind of fame, the relentless glare of publicity that he was going to be subjected to," offered Christopher Andersen. To make sure John was resilient, Jackie arranged for a series of summer excursions designed to build character. In 1971, ten-year-old John sailed, canoed, and rock-climbed on an island off the coast of Wales. In subsequent summers, he rebuilt earthquake-ravaged homes in Guatemala and participated in a twenty-six-day survival course in Maine. "It was a good way to bring somebody up to not teach them fear, to let them do as much as possible. Usually, they're safer that way rather than less safe," said Jamie Auchincloss.

The challenging summer adventures prepared John to deal with yet another family crisis. In May 1975, sixty-nine-year-old Onassis died in Paris from bronchial pneumonia. At the time of his death, the tycoon was estranged from Jackie and her children. Onassis left very little of his vast estate to Jackie, so she contested the will. The bitter battle played out in newspapers around the world. Christina, Onassis's daughter and the executor of the will, eventually settled with her stepmother for $26 million. When the legal wrangling ended, John was fifteen years old. He had been through more turmoil than most adults. Not surprisingly, John became rebellious. "John was a handful. Jackie had a lot of trouble controlling him from a very early age," said Edward Klein. "He also hated authority and was always getting into trouble. She would say that Caroline was very focused, and John was very scattered. She would say, 'Oh, John, he's always getting into a jam.'"

In 1976, John was sent to boarding school at Phillips Exeter Academy in Andover, Massachusetts. John took advantage of his newfound freedom by openly experimenting with alcohol and drugs. He was caught several times by the Secret Service agents and school officials, but he was never suspended or expelled from school. Academically, John also had problems. Auchincloss explained, "John had a difficult time reading and learning how to read and things like that, so there were remedial courses. I don't think he was ever a particularly good student." Andersen made the point more forcefully: "John was a lousy student. There's no question about it. I think today he would have been diagnosed with Attention Deficit Disorder, to be honest with you, because he had all the classic symptoms: He couldn't sit still, he couldn't concentrate. He apparently had a touch of dyslexia, as well. He hated the fact that people thought he was dumb."

At boarding school, John flunked math and was forced to repeat the eleventh grade. In the summer of 1978, before his senior year, John was sent to work on a ranch in Wyoming. Owner John Perry Barlow was instructed to instill "lots of discipline" in his new ranch hand. Described Barlow, "John had a general problem with authority. He didn't particularly care about being told what to do. As a consequence, I think people came to the conclusion that he wasn't as bright as he was, but he had a more free-roaming kind of intelligence than was likely to be well suited for any kind of less-structured environment." Barlow took seventeen-year-old John under his wing, and the two formed a lasting friendship. Barlow continued, "We had him doing all the stuff that people do on ranches: digging postholes, putting up fences, driving cows, irrigating. He had boundless energy and needed to have something to focus it on. John was always tough enough for anything. He had kind of Kennedy testosterone and Bouvier sensitivity, which was a nice combination."

John settled down for his senior year and graduated from Phillips Exeter in May 1979. Despite his less-than-stellar academic record, John was accepted to Harvard University, where both his father and sister had graduated, but he chose to go to Brown. "John wanted to avoid having to go to school in the shadow of his father at Harvard," said Christopher Andersen. "Of course, it was expected that he would enter Harvard, but at Brown he could escape that to some degree and be his own man." Added Barlow, "It was a golden time at Brown. It was just right for him, because it was kind of bohemian but also intellectual and fairly wild and experimental but not insane." John joined the 1,300-member freshman class at Brown University in Providence, Rhode Island, in the fall of 1979.

When he finally arrived at Brown, eighteen-year-old John had more to do on his first day than select his courses. He answered questions from dozens of reporters assigned to cover the historic event. Mark Rafael, John's childhood classmate, was also a freshman at Brown that year. "People knew that he would be there, and you wonder, 'Gosh, I wonder if our paths will cross,' because you can't help but know you'll be in his class," Rafael said. As he had done in previous schools, John worked hard to blend in. He drove a beat-up Honda Civic, played rugby in the quad, and wasn't afraid to show his sense of humor. John even joined a fraternity and had to swallow goldfish and streak across the campus naked as part of the initiation. Recalled Rafael, "We joined this fraternity, and we all rushed together and all lived there in our sophomore year. We'd all go out, play football, whatever. There was a bar in the basement, and we'd have big parties on the weekend. John's door was pretty much open all the time, so you could wander in."

John was accepted as one of the guys, but he couldn't completely shield his identity. America's famous son developed into a strikingly handsome adult, and a large flock of female admirers took notice. "Strange women would just sort of turn up on the doorstep of the frat, who had traveled several days and several thousand miles to meet him," laughed Rafael. John Perry Barlow also remembered John's sudden transformation into a heartthrob: "As much time as I spent around him, I would turn to him, see him at close range, and it would just take my breath away, because he was perfect physically. But he knew that, and he dealt with his vanity as he dealt with most things, by turning it into something ironic. I mean, his vanity became a joke."

The freewheeling lifestyle John had adopted at boarding school continued in college, and the attention from girls was flattering, but at times it was also overwhelming. John soon found a far more consuming passion than partying, in Brown's theater department. One of Brown's popular professors, James Barnhill, described, "I didn't know him until his sophomore year, and he came and said he wanted to take the basic acting course, and it was all right with me." As Mark Rafael put it, "He enjoyed the notion of being in another pair of shoes. He loved that aspect of acting—the whole transformation, getting into the head and mocking around and seeing what the character's about. He really had that kind of curiosity."

"He really wanted to go off and be an actor," said Barlow, "and I think that he continued to entertain those thoughts all along. He never really got over the idea." John made his college stage debut in the fall of 1980. He portrayed a professional soldier in the drama *Volpone*. Opening night drew widespread media interest, but the initial reviews were less than kind. "It was difficult when he did theater, because he'd get national press to review him in a show, you know, that would be just a show that we'd do at Brown. He was conscious that he was always under a microscope," remarked Rafael. John was undaunted. Over the remaining two years, he poured himself into acting and appeared in four more productions. Jackie attended several of her son's performances, but she discouraged John from pursuing acting beyond college. Speculated Barlow, "She had a very fine-tuned sense of what was appropriate, and she didn't feel that being an actor was appropriate for him, and I think there was some strife between them on this."

"I don't think anyone had to sit him down and say, 'You know, this probably wouldn't work out.' I think he was aware of that.

Logistically, it would have been a nightmare," said Rafael. There was no talk of an acting career when Jackie attended John's college graduation in June 1983. They were joined by hundreds of members of the press as John received his bachelor of arts degree in history. Following graduation, twenty-three-year-old John returned to New York City to sort things out. His mother suggested law school, but John wanted to give acting another shot. He called theater director Robin Saex, a former classmate from Brown, and begged her for a part. "He still had the yen for the stage, and he asked me what I was doing," she said, "and I was just about to go into rehearsals with a new play that I was directing—a one-act at a theater called Manhattan Punchline. He wanted to come in and audition, so he did, and it was wonderful. He did a wonderful job, but in the end we went with a different actor, because he really was too young for the part."

Robin Saex was impressed with John's talent, and she eventually found him the perfect role. In 1984, Saex cast John in a two-person play titled *Winners*. The story featured a pair of Irish teenagers involved in a tragic love affair. Christina Haag, another Brown alumnus, was cast as the girl. "When you see an actor who's a real actor, you know it," she said. "They have this ability to almost channel characters through them. And John—John had that talent. He loved to get inside a character and figure out what made it tick, especially somebody who was really removed from his life and his life experience." The ninety-minute play debuted in August 1985 at the Irish Art Center in Manhattan. There were six performances at the seventy-five-seat theater, and all were by invitation only—no critics allowed.

"We had packed houses every night, but it was controlled. All of our friends, and everybody who came from Brown, of course," remembered Saex, "and it was a magical time, it really was. There were people who thought they were coming to see John Kennedy and forgot that it was John and became involved in the performance. I really think that his work as an actor transcended the celebrity." She received multiple offers to do *Winners* off-

Broadway, but she declined, and the play closed as scheduled. John never appeared onstage again. Decided Saex, "He had so many interests in his life, and, in a sense, I think that acting was too limited for him. It was a part of him, but it couldn't encompass all of him."

Winners marked the end of John's acting career, but it was just the beginning of his romantic relationship with Christina Haag. Explained Saex, "John and Christina had known each other since they were fifteen and were very good friends in college, so when they became romantically involved, there was a lot of history there and a lot of depth that had already been established." John was regarded as one of the country's most eligible bachelors, but he preferred steady dating to the swinging-singles life. Offered Andersen, "During his lifetime, this guy never had one of his girlfriends say anything bad about him—not a single one— and these were people who could have been paid vast sums of money to write a tell-all for a tabloid or a book. None of them would do it, because, I think, he treated them all so well even after they broke up."

In July 1986, Christina Haag accompanied John to his sister's wedding, where he served as best man. Caroline Kennedy, then twenty-eight years old, married forty-one-year-old Edwin Schlossberg, a freelance writer and artist. Two months later, John made a drastic change in his own life—he began law school at New York University. "It wasn't so easy for him to just focus exclusively on being in law school, because there were other demands of his name, real and important demands," said Robin Saex. John's grade point average did not rank among the top of his class, but his high profile earned him some of the most coveted internships in the country. In the summer of 1988, John received a salary of $1,100 a week to clerk at the prestigious law firm of Manatt, Phelps, and Phillips in Los Angeles. Chief executive Paul Irving, who supervised the internship program, commented, "I can't tell you that John Kennedy walking around the office was not a special event for us, because it was. He was striking. He had a big personality. He evoked secondary meaning for an awful lot of people in the firm, so it was a special thing for all of us."

During his internship, John was given several days off to make his first major public appearance. Christopher Andersen explained, "There had been a period where he had been sort of off the screen. People hadn't seen him for a while, and then in 1988 he suddenly appeared at the Democratic National Convention to introduce his uncle Ted." During his introduction, John Jr. declared, "Over a quarter century ago, my father stood before you to accept the nomination for the presidency of the United States. So many of you came into public service because of him. In a very real sense because of you, he is with us still." Commented Andersen, "People were stunned. I mean, here was this person who had grown up, who was articulate. And a lot of people hadn't heard him speak as an adult, and they were surprised at how far he'd come." John received some of the loudest cheers at the convention.

The reception fueled speculation that he was about to follow in his father's footsteps and run for office. "Everybody was assuming that this was the debut of his political career, but John was not particularly interested in being a politician in the usual sense of the word," offered John Perry Barlow. John himself said, "For the future I've just tried to do the things that interest me and do it in my own way, and I've managed to consume myself with things other than politics at the moment." Added Robin Saex, "He lived with people's expectations of him, and he really fought to live his own life—to be true to his own path as opposed to ideas that people imposed upon him." On an almost daily basis, for the rest of his life, John was asked if he had political aspirations. John explained his reticence by saying, "A public career is a lot to bite off, and you better be ready for it, and you better have your life set up for it, and you better be prepared to do it for the long haul. That's the nature of the thing—that you stay in it—whether it's seniority in the House or the Senate, and I had some other interests and other sort of things that I was eager to do."

Had John ever run for political office, he certainly had the appeal to get elected. In September 1988, two months after his rousing speech at the Democratic convention, twenty-seven-year-old John F. Kennedy Jr., crowned *People* magazine's "Sexiest Man Alive," was at a crossroads. He was caught between the public pressure of fulfilling his father's legacy and his own ambitions. The young man who desperately wanted to forge his own identity had plenty more surprises. "He suddenly emerged as this mature adult to be reckoned with," said Andersen, "and I think then being the 'Sexiest Man Alive' put him into this whole new category of sex symbol where he hadn't been there before. So it did change America's perception of him, and from that point on, I think people paid a lot more attention."

John graced the cover of countless magazines, and he was also a favorite subject of the gossip columnists and the tabloids. Much of the media coverage John received concerned his love life. In 1988, the "Sexiest Man Alive" was still dating Christina Haag, but, in the press, he was regarded as an eligible bachelor and was linked to several famous women, including actress Sarah Jessica Parker and the Material Girl herself, Madonna. Said Saex, "He tried not to take the media attention too seriously, and most importantly, he didn't want that attention to inhibit his ability to live his life, and it was amazing. He was amazing in that way."

The media distraction didn't stop John from his goal of finishing law school, either. He graduated on schedule in May 1989. His mother was by his side when he received his degree. John accepted a position with the Manhattan District Attorney's Office. He earned an unprincely sum of $30,000 a year. Former assistant district attorney Beth Karas witnessed the hysteria surrounding John's hiring: "Well, as you can imagine, when word spread that JFK Jr. was going to join the D.A.'s office, people were very excited—a lot of anticipation—and when he finally arrived, the television cameras were crowded around, camped out on One Hogan Place, the entrance to the D.A.'s office, and not just for his first day but for the first weeks. We all were entering the D.A.'s office, having to part with the cameras so we could get in ourselves."

John was assigned to the Special Prosecutions Bureau. He received no extra security and shared a small office with several other first-year assistant district attorneys. Coworkers were offered thousands of dollars to get a single photograph of their famous new colleague. "When your name is John Kennedy, and you've got a face like that, it's hard to just blend in," said Beth Karas, who continued, "but let me tell you, his mother did a great job raising him, because I thought he was a humble individual, at least in my observations of him. In my conversations with him, he was humble, and he never said a thing that couldn't have been repeated."

John's first year on the job was full of challenges. In November 1989, he found out that he flunked the New York Bar exam. When he took the test a second time in February 1990, the result was the same. The press had a field day. Two New York daily newspapers ran the headline "The Hunk Flunks." "It's terrible enough to flunk, but then to have everyone reading about it—and they think it's a reflection of your intelligence, and it's really not. It's what kind of a test-taker you are," commented Karas. "Obviously I'm very disappointed again, but, God willing, I'll be back there in July, and I'll pass it then. Or I'll pass it the next time. Or I'll pass it when I'm ninety-five," John joked.

With his job and reputation on the line, John finally passed the bar examination on his third try. Manhattan's most talked about assistant district attorney was promptly assigned his first court case, prosecuting the notorious Sleeping Burglar. On November 1, 1990, David Ramos allegedly broke into the apartment of schoolteacher Sonia Schwartz and stuffed her jewelry in his pockets and then, inexplicably, Ramos took a nap on her bed. Ramos was still asleep when a startled Schwartz came home later that afternoon. Beth Karas asserted, "Well, they gave him a rock-solid case. You're talking about a burglar who goes in, steals someone's possessions, puts them in his pockets, and then falls asleep on her bed. If you can't win that one, I mean, you shouldn't be a trial lawyer." In August 1991, before a packed courthouse, John was visibly relieved when the jury delivered a guilty verdict. "It was the beginning of some horror story in my life that ended up with this unusual event of meeting this grandiose individual," Sonia Schwartz concluded.

John's legal victory drew widespread attention, but his social life still dominated the headlines. In 1991, John ended his six-year relationship with Haag and was now romantically linked to actress Daryl Hannah. The thirty-year-old blond starlet was in the 1984 hit movie *Splash* and later appeared in such popular films as *Wall Street* and *Steel Magnolias*. The Kennedy men had long been associated with famous actresses. Jackie tried to steer her son away from that family tradition. "She had opinions about all of his girlfriends. From what I understand, Jackie liked Daryl Hannah very much, but I don't think she felt that was the woman for him, and she let him know it," observed Christopher Andersen. Despite his mother's objections, John moved into Hannah's New York City apartment in 1993. They were the hottest couple in town, and the press stalked their every move. The nonstop attention often created friction between the two. Noted John Perry Barlow, "When I first met her and spent time around them, I told them both that I liked both of them better when they weren't in one another's company. I don't think they brought out the best in each other."

In the fall of 1993, John's attention shifted from his volatile relationship with Hannah to his mother. That October, Jackie was taken to the hospital after a horseback riding accident left her unconscious for a half hour. Doctors discovered a more serious problem, however—Jackie had swollen lymph nodes. Her condition soon worsened. "She went to see a doctor, and they did biopsies, and they discovered that she had non-Hodgkin's lymphoma, a very dangerous form of cancer," explained Edward Klein. Jackie underwent an aggressive regimen of radiation and chemotherapy. The treatments didn't work though, and by the spring of 1994,

Jackie's cancer had spread. Determined to fight until the end, she allowed her doctor to perform an experimental surgery. As Klein described, "The only way that the disease could be counteracted would be if he drilled a shunt in her scull and fed the chemotherapy directly to the brain and combined that with radiation. She did that, but it didn't work."

On May 19, 1994, sixty-four-year-old Jacqueline Kennedy Onassis lost her battle with cancer. John was at his mother's side when she passed away. "John Kennedy Jr. went downstairs in front of her apartment building at 1040 Fifth Avenue, and there were thousands of people outside and cameras from the television studios, and it was a huge scene," said Klein. To sum up the life of his powerful mother, John said, "My mother passed on. She was surrounded by her friends and her family and her books and the people and the things that she loved. And she did it in her own way and on her own terms." Three days later, Jackie was laid to rest beside her first husband at Arlington National Cemetery.

Even though they often disagreed with each other, Jackie had always been the driving force in John Jr.'s life. His mother's death was an undeniable call for growth, change, and self-reflection in John's life. Recalled Barlow, "I talked to him right after she died, and he said that he felt like nobody became a grown-up until both of their parents were dead." John was so devastated by the memory of his mother that, in the months following her death, he dramatically changed his life. He sold the New York City apartment where Jackie raised him, ended his relationship with Hannah, and resigned from the New York City District Attorney's Office. At the age of thirty-three, John was determined to begin yet another chapter.

He soon found comfort in the arms of another woman who allowed John's memories to transition into his hopes for the future. "I don't think it's any accident that Carolyn Bessette was very much like Jackie in some ways," observed Andersen. "She had this aloof quality. I think that's what appealed to John about her in that she was the first woman he had ever met that really played hard to get, and he had to pursue her." John met twenty-seven-year-old Carolyn Bessette in October 1993. The captivating blonde worked in public relations for fashion designer Calvin Klein. Among her many job responsibilities, she shopped for Klein's celebrity clients. After she sold John three business suits, the two exchanged phone numbers and were soon spotted together around town. Their relationship heated up when John broke up with Hannah in the summer of 1994.

"If you extracted all of the qualities of the women that I saw John with, and created some kind of essence of what they had in common, I would say that Carolyn was that essence," Barlow assessed. Carolyn was born in 1966 and grew up in Greenwich, Connecticut. In her 1983 high school yearbook, she was voted "The Ultimate Beautiful Person" of her senior class. Five years later, she graduated from Boston University with a degree in elementary education. But Carolyn had her sights set on a far more glamorous career. In 1990, she tried her hand at modeling, posing for a series of jeans ads. The following year, she was hired as a salesclerk at the Calvin Klein store in Boston. A corporate executive, impressed by Carolyn's sophisticated looks, recruited her to New York City. John was equally charmed by the young beauty. In April 1995, after less than a year of dating, John asked Carolyn to move in with him. Offered Barlow, "She could rivet somebody's attention more completely than anybody I'd ever met, with the exception of John's mother. She just had that gift of being endlessly interesting."

During this period, John's professional life also went through changes. After he left the District Attorney's Office, he secured a job in front of a television camera as the host of a new PBS series *Heart of the City*. John's participation in the show triggered a flood of TV offers, but John had a different and unexpected career choice in mind. In the fall of 1994, John approached Robin Saex with his idea. "We had dinner one night, pretty close to the time that he came up with the concept of *George*, and he told me of this idea and his plan and then what the name would be. I thought it was wonderful. I thought it was really the right direction for him to go," she described.

John secured $20 million from French publishing company Hachette Filipacchi to start *George*. Although he had no journalistic experience, John took on the title of editor in chief. The idea, as John saw it, was simple: "*George* doesn't just cover politics. It celebrates it. We will celebrate it." *George* hit newsstands in October 1995. To promote his venture, the usually private John went on a publicity tour. Predictably, most of the interview questions were of a personal nature. When asked about the challenges of life in the spotlight, he said, "I have a pretty normal life, surprisingly. I mean, every now and then sort of strange things happen, but up until the cavalcade of publicity for *George*, I was a private citizen."

Inside the New York offices of *George*, John was adamant that his personal life remain private. Employees were required to sign confidentiality agreements forbidding them from talking to the press about their boss. Richard Blow was a senior editor at *George*, and his office was next to John's. "John at the beginning was anxious about the idea of being a celebrity and going to the office every day with a bunch of journalists," Blow said. "I mean, John Kennedy did not hang out with journalists before starting *George* magazine, and I think he was understandably concerned about going to work with all these people he'd never met before."

While John demanded privacy, he was also a hands-on editor who often worked late into the night. He approved story ideas, edited copy, wrote a column, and interviewed a wide range of notable politicians. One of John's interviews was with former Colorado senator and ex–presidential candidate Gary Hart. The former senator recalled, "He showed up in our office here in Denver all by himself with a little tape recorder. I think people who saw him in the elevators were stunned, because it was clear who he was. There is something about American people who think that if you're famous or a celebrity you're constantly surrounded by a group, and here was John Kennedy Jr., on an elevator going up in an office building nearby here in Denver, being polite and smiling. I think we heard about it for weeks thereafter."

John's celebrated status drew interest and made *George* an initial success. The first few issues sold more than a half million copies and contained more than one hundred pages of advertising—impressive numbers for a new magazine. "Clearly, the magazine is going to get attention because of John," said Richard Blow. "How do you redirect that to get people to pay attention to the magazine rather than just saying, 'Hey, *George*, that's where John F. Kennedy works. Who's he going out with now?'" As hard as John tried to be taken seriously as a journalist, his personal life continued to dominate headlines.

Everywhere John went with Carolyn, they were hounded by questions about their future plans. John and Carolyn kept mum on the subject publicly, but privately they agreed to marry. By the summer of 1994, the two had concocted a plan for a completely private wedding. Only forty guests were invited to the secret ceremony, and none of them knew the exact location until they arrived. "It was a great practical joke, if nothing else, that he was able to get forty of us onto this island off the coast of Georgia," said John Perry Barlow. "That was a burning secret. It was really hard not to tell somebody." On September 21, 1996, inside the tiny First African Baptist Church on the remote Cumberland Island, thirty-year-old Carolyn Bessette and thirty-five-year-old John Fitzgerald Kennedy Jr. were married. The newlyweds immediately left on a honeymoon to Turkey. When they returned home two weeks later, the press had staked out their apartment building.

"She was this vibrant, lively, beautiful girl. After she married John, the publicity changed her completely. She was completely altered by this business of being in the spotlight. She wasn't prepared to have people camping on their doorstep and leaping out from behind bushes to take her picture," Christopher Andersen remarked. Carolyn's aversion to the press is graphically shown in a video in 1996. While Carolyn, John, and two friends waited for their car, photographers surrounded them. As was often the case,

Carolyn couldn't bear to show her face. Richard Blow observed, "The difference is that Carolyn wasn't born into this. Carolyn made a choice to join it because she loved John, but at the same time, she wasn't used to it."

"I think the greatest weakness of their marriage was external. She just had a really difficult time being turned into a thing by the press, and she had to turn into a thing—and not a particularly likable thing, either," assessed John Perry Barlow. The intrusive press put John and Carolyn's young marriage to the test. Months after returning from their honeymoon, the couple reportedly began having problems. Observed Barlow, "Like a lot of intense relationships, I think they could barely stand to be together at times, and yet they knew that they couldn't stand to be apart. It was a great love story, but most great loves stories have a tragic undercurrent, and this one did, too."

The complete lack of privacy wasn't the only thing Carolyn was unhappy about. In the weeks leading up to his wedding, John began to pursue his longtime interest in flying. Jackie had always discouraged her son from flying, for fear of his safety. Carolyn told friends that she was equally terrified. In August 1996, John purchased his first Ultra Light, an odd-looking contraption called a Buckeye Powered Parachute. "I just could not believe that he was up there, just a speck against the sky in what amounted to a snowmobile with a propeller and a parachute for a wing," said Barlow, adding, "it seemed like an insane thing." Insane or not, John was hooked. In December 1997, he enrolled in flight school, and earned his pilot's license in just four months.

In April 1998, John purchased his first airplane, a four-seat Cessna 182. Barlow recalled prophetically, "I was a little nervous about it, because John could be distracted. He also had a kind of raw determination to go on no matter what, which can be a dangerous quality in a pilot." John soon became a regular fixture at Essex Country Airport in Fairfield, New Jersey, where he stored his plane. During the summer of 1998, John flew to Martha's Vineyard nearly every weekend. He eventually started using his plane for business travel as well. By 1999, thirty-eight-year-old John logged about two hundred hours of flight time, but he was still considered a novice pilot. That didn't stop him from eyeing his next, bigger, faster airplane.

John faced many challenges as 1999 got underway. His two-and-a-half-year marriage was strained as a result of nonstop media coverage, and the luster surrounding *George* had also worn off. In its third year of publication, the magazine was losing an estimated million dollars a month. There was one place John could escape his problems: in the air. In April 1999, he purchased a new plane, a Piper Saratoga II, from New Jersey businessman Munir Hussain. Hussain explained, "The Saratoga is a high-performance and complex plane, because the gears go up, the speed is a little faster, and it was more powerful than his old plane, and there were a lot more instruments in there."

John's wife, Carolyn, was concerned about the sophisticated new aircraft. John was still a relatively inexperienced pilot. He wasn't instrument-trained, and often flew with an instructor at night and in bad weather. Carolyn's fears were further realized on the Memorial Day weekend. John crashed his other aircraft, the Ultra Light, on the beach in Martha's Vineyard and broke his left ankle. Recalled Barlow, "I saw him take a couple of landings in that, and it was a wonder to me that he survived those. He had kind of the ability to get on the edge with it." John returned to New York City hobbling on crutches, his ankle in a cast. The accident didn't discourage him from flying, though. On Monday, July 12, John flew with an instructor to Toronto to meet with potential new investors for *George*. "Those of us who saw him knew that flying was something he took very seriously and was quite diligent about studying and training for," said Richard Blow, "and it was disturbing to see or hear any suggestion that John was not a serious pilot, that he was not safety-conscious, or cautious. He was."

On Wednesday, July 14, two days after he returned from Toronto, John met his wife and sister-in-law, Lauren Bessette, for lunch at the posh Stanhope Hotel. The three finalized plans for the upcoming weekend. Lauren wanted to visit friends on Martha's Vineyard. John and Carolyn were committed to attend the wedding of John's younger cousin Rory Kennedy. The wedding was to be held at the Kennedy compound in Hyannisport. John volunteered to fly. His cast was being removed the next day, and the flight would be his first without an instructor since he broke his ankle. Carolyn, who often had been reluctant to fly with John in the past, agreed to the plan.

On Friday, July 16, John's cast was off, but he was still limping when he met Richard Blow for lunch. "We had a really nice, casual, terrific lunch. It was a Friday, so we were both feeling kind of relaxed," offered Blow. Following lunch, John returned to work to tie up loose ends before leaving for the weekend. He made sure to respond to an e-mail from John Perry Barlow, whose mother had passed away a couple of days earlier. Barlow commented, "The last thing he did before leaving the office the day that he went down was to write me a message back saying that he was sorry to hear about my mother's death. He had been with his mother when she went, and he was glad that I had that experience. And that was the last I ever heard from him."

Lauren arrived at John's office at approximately 6:30 P.M. The two agreed to carpool to Essex County Airport in New Jersey, where John parked his plane. Carolyn was going to take a limousine service and meet them there. Traffic out of Manhattan was unusually heavy, and John and Lauren didn't pull into the airport parking lot until almost eight o'clock—forty-five minutes later than they anticipated. Carolyn had arrived a few minutes earlier. Pilot Kyle Bailey was also at the airport and had canceled plans to fly to Martha's Vineyard just minutes before he saw John warming up his plane. "Every time I've seen him in that airplane, he had an instructor with him," reported Bailey. "He had an airplane prior to that, a Cessna 182, and I would often see him flying that solo or with his wife and also with his dog, but that particular airplane, the Piper Saratoga, was the first time I ever saw him get into the airplane by himself." Munir Hussain, who landed at Essex Airport shortly before John took off, commented that, because of the weather, "My friend and I both, just automatically, thought he must be flying with an instructor."

Though an instructor had offered John assistance in navigation that night, John declined in favor of flying solo. By 8:38 P.M., the sun had set, and the sky was hazy when John taxied his Piper Saratoga out to the runway. Carolyn and Lauren sat in the back, their seats directly behind John. "I saw the plane take off from Runway 22," said Kyle Bailey, "and the airplane made about three right turns, exited the airport traffic pattern and proceeded towards the northeast direction towards Long Island Sound." John took his usual route up the Connecticut coast, using the city lights along the way to guide him. When he reached the town of Westerly, Rhode Island, John opted to break from the coastline and take the fastest shot to the Vineyard. He veered the plane right over the Atlantic Ocean toward Martha's Vineyard Airport, only thirty-eight miles away.

Over the ocean, the haze turned into a heavy fog. Since John was not instrument-trained, he depended on the horizon to guide his way. "Visibility was poor, and especially when you're going over the ocean, top and bottom are almost the same, and visibility is less. You have no landmark, and once you're in that window, and you're not instrument-rated, you're really going to get disoriented, because you have nothing to follow now," Hussain explained. At 9:33, fifty-five minutes after takeoff, John's small aircraft began to lose altitude. "Doing the right thing under those conditions runs directly counter to your intuition. You want to look for the horizon if you can't see it, and when you look at the instrument under those conditions, they don't make any sense to you at all, because your body's telling you something different," reasoned Barlow. Bailey added, "Your first instinct would be to pull back on the control column, to raise the nose and climb, but in the graveyard spiral, since you're actually in a turn, when you pull back the controls, it would actually tighten the spiral and make it worse."

At 9:41, eight minutes after John first experienced altitude trouble, his plane disappeared from radar. Speculated Barlow, "It was probably completely out of control fifteen seconds before they hit the water. If he tried at that point to really regain control of the aircraft, it would have torn itself apart. He didn't have a lot of time to figure it out." When the plane failed to arrive at Martha's Vineyard, family and friends began to worry. At 1:55 A.M. Saturday morning, the Coast Guard station in nearby Woods Hole, Massachusetts, received an urgent call from Kennedy family friend Carol Radziwill, who was at the Kennedy compound. Captain Russell Webster immediately organized an extensive search. "The initial focus was a one-hundred-mile stretch from the eastern shore of Long Island Sound up to Martha's Vineyard. Planes were launched nearly immediately and began searching by air," Webster stated.

As the rescue attempt got underway, President Bill Clinton was awakened by aides and informed of the situation. At 4:00 A.M., Richard and Anne Freeman, the stepfather and mother of Carolyn and Lauren, were alerted that their daughters were missing. John's sister, Caroline, was on vacation in Idaho to celebrate her thirteenth wedding anniversary when she was told the news. As daylight broke, the Coast Guard deployed a small armada of boats and planes in a massive search effort. "By nine o'clock in the morning, the area was virtually saturated with search rescue units with the sole purpose of finding survivors," Capital Webster said.

At the Kennedy compound, Rory Kennedy's wedding was put on hold. The family held a vigil while they waited for updates. By now, news of John's missing plane was all over the television airwaves. Bill Clinton addressed the nation: "I think we should keep our thoughts with the families as events unfold, and my thoughts and prayers are with them." Recalled John Perry Barlow, "There was a fleeting moment where I thought that he had actually decided to make good on his occasional threat to simply disappear, get some plastic surgery, and lead a normal life." Munir Hussain held the same hope that maybe, just maybe, John had "landed somewhere else. Maybe he saw the weather was bad there and went somewhere else and didn't report." In front of John and Carolyn's Manhattan apartment building, well-wishers constructed a makeshift shrine of flowers, candles, and cards.

By Saturday afternoon, hope began to fade. "There was a headrest that came ashore. There was personal luggage. There were materials from the inside of the plane. Unfortunately, all of the materials, including the earliest discovered materials were accordant with a result of a crash," explained Captain Webster. By Sunday afternoon, one day after John's plane was first reported missing, the Coast Guard switched its operation from search and rescue to search and recovery. The flags at the Kennedy compound were lowered to half-staff. Ted Kennedy, John's uncle, issued a short press release addressing the family's unspeakable grief. Barlow described, "I tried to figure out a scenario that would result in John and Carolyn and Lauren being alive, and, as hard as I tried, I couldn't come up with one—at least not one that made any sense."

As the world watched and waited, the search for John, Carolyn, and Lauren continued on Wednesday, July 21, 1999. Five days after the three disappeared, their aircraft was found seven miles off the coast of Martha's Vineyard, 120 feet below the ocean surface. The victims were still strapped into their seats. John's uncle Ted was immediately taken to the crash site. Several hours later, at the request of both families, all three bodies were cremated. John, Carolyn, and Lauren's ashes were scattered at sea in a private ceremony attended by close family members. The following day, on Friday, July 23, more than three hundred mourners, including First Lady Hillary Clinton and President Bill Clinton, attended a memorial service for John and Carolyn in New York City. Ted Kennedy gave a touching eulogy, saying about John, "Like his father, he had every gift but length of years."

"The time that we spent with John and the time that we were all together was just one of the most joyous times in all our lives," said Mark Rafael, "and it's sad that he's not around. It really is. He'll never have so many things that he should have, so many experiences that he should have had." In the months following the accident, an autopsy revealed that John had no alcohol or drugs in his system the night his plane went down. The National Transportation Safety Board concluded that the crash was caused by John's failure to maintain control of the airplane during a descent over water at night, which was a result of spatial disorientation. "I think that, had he been using an auto pilot, he might have been all right. Had he had more time in the aircraft, he might have been all right. Had he started a little earlier, he might have been all right," offered John Perry Barlow. "There are so many things that you can say like that, but the fact is all those negatives added up to one great big negative."

At the time of his death, thirty-eight-year-old John was worth an estimated $100 million. In his will, most of John's money went to his sister Caroline and her three children. Grief-stricken over the loss of her two daughters, Anne Freeman filed a court motion in the year 2000 that left the door open for a wrongful death suit. A year later, the Freeman family reportedly reached an out-of-court settlement with the Kennedys for $15 million. In January 2001, *George* magazine ceased publication. The final issue that March was the only one to ever feature John on the cover. "My office was next to John's. I wouldn't leave without saying good-bye to him every day, and for some reason that day I didn't. I don't know why. He might have been on the phone. I will always regret that," said Richard Blow.

"I keep trying to tell myself that I shouldn't be so bereft, because I was incredibly fortunate to have him as long as I did, and sometimes that works. But I sure do miss him," concluded Blow. In the years after John's death, Blow and others wrote books about their friend. In 2003, Klein's *Kennedy Curse* shocked many by saying Carolyn used cocaine. A year later, model-turned-actor

Michael Bergin claimed in his tell-all, *The Other Man*, that he was intimate with Carolyn before and after she married John. John's friends refuted the allegations. For the family and loved ones of John F. Kennedy Jr., his death meant the loss of their prince—the prince of Camelot. "He gave you that feeling that time was short and fleeting, and put as much into a day as possible," said Jamie Auchincloss, "and if it meant going a little faster and a little bit higher into that dark night, you'd do it."

CHAPTER 13

TRIPLE THREAT
The Naomi, Wynonna, and Ashley Judd Story

"The truth is that nothing comes between the three of them. Nothing."

—*Angelique L'Amour, family friend*

I think Wy, Ashley, and I are a family sitcom that can't be canceled," laughed multitalented matriarch Naomi Judd. Three extraordinary women, one famous name. From Nashville to Hollywood, the Judds live by their own rules. But in reality, the Judds are all too human. Naomi and Wynonna have conquered country music while Ashley has brought beauty and brains to the big screen. But fate dealt the girls some nasty blows. Naomi faced a deadly disease. Wynonna struggled with her appetite. Ashley dealt with an obsessed fan. This is the bigger-than-life tale of the ultimate all-female showbiz clan. They are a tried-and-true trio of endless talents. They are the Judds, and this is their story.

On May 10, 2004, Naomi, Ashley, and Wynonna Judd appeared on the *Oprah Winfrey Show*. During an emotional hour, Wynonna spoke candidly about her life, including the often-stormy relationship with her mother, Naomi. Wynonna's younger sister, Ashley, also opened up about some of her issues that remained mostly in the shadows. "We are pretty dramatic women," admitted Naomi. "You put all three of us in a room . . . Man, oh, man, we can suck up the oxygen in that room pretty darn quick." The epic saga of the Judds began in the small, northeastern Kentucky town of Ashland. Glen Judd ran a local filling station. His wife, Polly, took care of their home. On January 11, 1946, the couple welcomed their first child, Diana Ellen Judd, who later became known to the world as Naomi. According to Bob Millard, author

of *The Judds: A Biography,* "They called her the China doll, because she had such a porcelainlike face."

During the next six years, the Judds had three more kids, but
Naomi remained the center of attention. "She would dominate the
conversation," said Naomi's mother, Polly, "and many times telling
all these stories I'd have to say, 'Now you be quiet and let someone
else talk.'" Naomi's love of the spotlight went beyond family and
friends. In 1954, the eight-year-old aspiring entertainer upstaged
some local kids at an area tap-dance show. Recounted Polly, "The
music hadn't ended, but the others started trooping offstage, and
she stayed and continued to dance as the curtain came down. She
liked being out there by herself, and the audience is applauding
and she's all alone, so that was interesting."

Naomi blossomed into a pretty teenager. She attended Paul
Blazer High School in Ashland and, at age fourteen, caught the
eye of sixteen-year-old Michael Ciminella, a student at a nearby
military academy. Bob Millard described, "Michael was the son of
one of the wealthiest people in Ashland. They had an aluminum
manufacturing company; they were country club people." Added
Polly, "He was a smart, nice-looking young man, very polite. They
just started this romance. It wasn't pleasing to me, because I
thought she was limiting herself." The relationship faded after
Ciminella went away to college, but Naomi and Michael continued to see each other from time to time.

Then, in 1963, Naomi's fifteen-year-old brother, Brian, was diagnosed with Hodgkin's disease, an illness that eventually took
his life. "Polly was just emotionally crushed," said Millard. Naomi
was often left in charge of the younger children. One night, the
seventeen-year-old had the house to herself. She spent the evening with Charlie Jordan, who played on the high school football
team. In a television interview with Larry King, Naomi said she
lost her virginity that night. The teenager soon discovered she
was pregnant. According to Naomi, Jordan skipped town after
hearing the news. She turned to Ciminella. They had also been in-

timate. As Kenneth Hart, reporter for Ashland's *Independent*, related, "She came to him, informing him that she was pregnant, and he assumed that it was his child. She did not present any other alternative. They decided to wed because he thought it was his baby, and he married her out of a sense of responsibility." Hart added, "She felt his family would be better able to care for her financially, that his family, in fact, had more money than Mr. Jordan's family."

The couple married in early January 1964. Five months later, on May 30, Naomi gave birth to Christina Claire Ciminella. Later in life, Christina took the name "Wynonna." "She was a delightful child. She was very energetic and wanted everything full-speed. She was just always adventurous, laughing a lot and just a joy," said Polly. But for Naomi, the "joys" of motherhood collided with reality. "I was married at eighteen, and I had a kid and was scrubbing floors and cooking and cleaning when I was eighteen and other kids are just graduating from high school," she explained. Ciminella finished college in 1967 with a degree in business. The family moved to Sylmar, California, where he worked as a marketing rep for an aerospace company.

On April 10, 1968, Ashley Tyler Ciminella was born. Four-year-old Wynonna was thrilled to have a younger sister. According to Polly, "She just figured she was going to have a doll around to play with, and she was interested in her. They were totally different personalities." Added Naomi, "Ashley was reserved, quiet, and had a marvelous grace about her." In an interview with newspaper reporter Hart, Ciminella said he noticed other differences as the girls got older: "What he told me was that he just looked at [Wynonna], and he knew that she was not, in fact, his biological child." Agreed Bob Millard, "It was just obvious that the children didn't have the same father. They had different sizes, different facial features." Michael says he didn't confront Naomi, but the girls were still small when she told him the truth—Wynonna's biological father was really Charles Jordan. They decided to keep the secret from Wynonna.

According to Ciminella, the couple still tried to make their marriage work. However, Naomi wrote in her autobiography, she felt stifled and bored. Naomi also grew suspicious of her husband's late nights at work. "There was no love there anymore," observed Polly. In September 1971, Michael moved out. The couple soon filed for divorce to end their seven-year marriage. Said Hart, "He told me that it was a very mutual decision. That they had both arrived at the point where they realized that it wasn't working." Noted Naomi of that period, "I'm all of a sudden divorced, you know, and I'm on my own with two kids trying to work and find my way in life."

Early in 1972, now a divorcée and a single mom, twenty-six-year-old Naomi rented a house just off Hollywood's Sunset Strip and started a new life. Naomi dreamed of "making it" in showbiz, but all she got was a cold dose of reality. As she recalled, "I was living in Holly-weird just doing minimum-wage, unskilled jobs." She worked as a clerk in a health food store, a girl Friday for a millionaire, and a secretary for a rock band, among other thankless jobs. Still, she kept her dream alive. "Naomi did want to get into show business some way or other, and she meant for it to be in front of a camera. She did do some modeling," said Millard. The modeling gigs helped pay the bills. So did being a contestant on game shows like *Hollywood Squares* and *Password*.

Meanwhile, eight-year-old Wynonna trudged off to class at West Hollywood Elementary. Explained Wynonna's friend Angelique L'Amour, "The big shocker was that Wynonna walked to school by herself, which meant she had to come down the block to Sunset Strip and definitely walked past two strip joints on the way to school. She had to be very sure of herself." Four-year-old Ashley stayed close to home. Neighbors looked after the youngster, but she entertained herself. "I did things that were bizarre and imaginative—talking to myself for hours on end," she laughed. Despite the tough times, Naomi was determined to give her girls a normal childhood. "She was still very present in her daughters' life," remarked L'Amour, "and she was a Brownie troop leader. Naomi must have had tons of energy to be able to take care of two kids and work several jobs and not have anybody helping her really at home." Naomi also found time to date. The pretty single mom from Kentucky was lonely and vulnerable—the perfect target for Hollywood playboys. "They prey on these young women that want somebody to love them, and they want to love somebody. I think she made some bad mistakes, but she also learned from her mistakes," Polly acknowledged.

In the summer of 1974, twenty-eight-year-old Naomi gave up on Hollywood. She packed up the girls and headed back to Kentucky. They moved into a house rented by Naomi's ex-husband. Naomi enrolled in the nursing program at Eastern Kentucky University. Wynonna and Ashley attended school. Michael dropped by the house often, and on one visit he brought a special gift for ten-year-old Wynonna. Recounted Kenneth Hart, "He bought her very first guitar when she was a very young child, and she cut her teeth playing Joni Mitchell songs, which Michael said that he had to leave the house after a while because he got so tired of hearing them."

In her autobiography, Naomi said Michael spent more and more time at the house. Soon, the two began to argue. Naomi and the girls eventually moved to a rented home in nearby Morrill, Kentucky. Naomi continued her nursing studies. She also helped Wynonna develop her musical talent. "They started singing, and Wynonna knew this is what she wanted to do. She just became so completely engrossed in the music and expression," noted Polly. While mother and daughter belted out tunes, seven-year-old Ashley fell in love with reading. Naomi especially liked her girls' burgeoning hobbies because they "took away the TV set. The girls had to develop their own imaginations."

In 1976, Naomi decided to move again. That summer, the three Judds hit the road for northern California and the hip enclave of Marin County. Naomi continued her nursing studies and waited tables. Wynonna, then twelve years old, and her eight-year-old sister were forced to adjust to new schools. Wynonna soon began to act out. Still, she seemed destined for greatness.

Mary Anne Kolanoski, Wynonna's eighth-grade teacher, recalled, "There was something very haunting about Wynonna's voice. She entered the talent contest and won it. Everybody recognized the fact that here was a girl who had something special, but I don't think Wynonna really quite understood that yet. However, her mother recognized it, and her mother tried really hard to get her to do that."

Naomi toyed with the idea of forming an act with her two girls. She enrolled them in music lessons, but there were problems because Wynonna was constantly at odds with her instructor. Observed John Pederson, owner of Amazing Grace Music, "She wouldn't always play exactly what Pete [her instructor] was showing her, because he had very distinct views on how bluegrass mandolin should be played, and I don't think she really cared about his views that much." As for Ashley, music just wasn't her thing. "Ashley played fiddle, and they soon found out Ashley really wasn't that good on the fiddle. And she really couldn't sing that well, so it became a two-member group," explained James L. Dickerson, author of *Ashley Judd: Crying on the Inside*.

Naomi graduated from nursing school in December 1977, but working in a hospital seemed a lot less appealing than performing on stage. She and Wynonna landed gigs at some area clubs. Mom passed off the fourteen-year-old as her kid sister. Recording studio owner Robin Yeager said, "[Wynonna] definitely looked older than her years. When her mom and she would play as the Judd Sisters, that was able to get her into venues that might otherwise have not allowed her to be in there." In July 1978, Naomi convinced the owner of a local recording studio to make a demo tape. Some of the arrangements called for Wynonna to sing solo, which at first seemed easier said than done because "she was kind of fidgety and kind of uncomfortable," characterized Yeager, "and she just said, 'Can I have my mom out here?' So I just killed the mic so Naomi could go out. I waited for the thumbs-up to open the mic, and Naomi was still there. Wynonna was a lot more comfortable having her mom at her side."

Meanwhile, Ashley stayed on the sidelines. "She appeared to be kind of sad to me, but with good reason," Yeager mentioned. "Her mom and Wynonna were out doing all kinds of stuff, and Ashley desperately wanted to be a part of it." But there was no part for the youngest Judd. In late 1978, Naomi sent ten-year-old Ashley back to Kentucky to stay with her dad.

There were more changes to come. Naomi, who still went by Diana, and Wynonna, who was born Christina, officially transformed into Naomi and Wynonna Judd. Reasoned Polly, "'Diana Ciminella' didn't sound country, and so she decided on 'Naomi' from the Bible, and Wynonna got her name from the song 'Route 66.'" Naomi drove a 1957 Chevy with license plates stamped RED HOT. With Wynonna in the passenger seat, the Judds careened from Austin, Texas, to Hollywood, California, to the Las Vegas Strip, but success was elusive. Described Yeager, "She saw where she wanted to be, but she didn't know quite how she was going to get there, and every day was another step closer."

As they crisscrossed the country chasing stardom in the late 1970s, Naomi and Wynonna set their sights on the mecca of country music—Nashville, Tennessee. In May 1979, thirty-three-year-old Naomi and fifteen-year-old Wynonna arrived. They went to the Country Music Hall of Fame, and Wynonna remembered feeling "an overwhelming sense of 'look at all of the people who have come before me.'" Naomi waited for her Tennessee nursing license to come through. In the meantime, she took a secretarial job on Music Row, the heart of Nashville's music scene. Naomi didn't wait to push her singing career. She showed up at the Country Music Hall of Fame and detailed her life story to anyone who would listen. Robert K. Oermann, former librarian at the Hall of Fame, recounted, "She told me about making lye soap and living in this farmhouse . . . just having a tremendous barrage of ambition, that's the only way to put it. The other staffers were frightened of her. They kind of ran away when she came."

Mother and daughter made the rounds in their flashy 1957 Chevy. Naomi always dressed to impress. "She was flirtatious and met a lot of people, but she knew what she was doing. She knew that this was an asset," offered Bob Millard. Added Oermann, "She was desperate. I mean, she wanted to get in, and she was just trying to figure out any way she could do it." While Naomi strutted her stuff, Wynonna kept a low profile. Oermann continued, "Wy was very much the sort of gifted, moody teen. She didn't say much early on. Momma did most of the early talking." That summer, eleven-year-old Ashley rejoined her mom and sister in Nashville.

In July 1979, Naomi met thirty-three-year-old Larry Strickland, a former backup singer for The King. "She loved Elvis and that whole Elvis thing of the gospel quarter and always being there kind of thing," said Oermann, "and I think that was Larry's appeal to her. Larry was her Elvis." However, the relationship was stormy at best. "They were on-again, off-again. She would find a note or a phone number from some girl in a wallet. It always seemed to be a pretty big, major deal," said Woody Bowles, the Judds' former comanager and publicist. Then Naomi's nursing papers arrived. She began working at some local hospitals while the hunt continued to score a record deal.

In late 1979, the Judds landed on the doorstep of Nashville's Soundshop Studios. Explained music producer Jon Shulenberger, "It wasn't until we heard Wynonna sing that our interest was piqued. This kid was fourteen years old, and she sang like a pro." Shulenberger and his partner agreed to a one-year development deal. "Our vision was always Wynonna as the star," he said, "but as time went on in the recording process, we realized that Naomi was driving this engine. She was going to be the person that made them into a duet—like it or not." Naomi's blind ambition often turned studio sessions into a battleground. As Shulenberger put it, "There were clashes between Naomi and Wynonna, because Naomi was driven, as we say, and Wynonna was being driven pretty hard by her mom at that time. We didn't know where that was all going to end." To get her way, Naomi sometimes resorted to bribery. For example, he recalled, "Wynonna had a tendency to want candy bars and things, and Naomi would give her those as rewards."

In February 1980, Naomi and Wynonna landed a gig on a local TV show. "She and Wynonna would get up early, four o'clock in the morning, and go be on the Ralph Emery morning television show at six o'clock in the morning as the Soap Sisters. This was a name that she had created because she made her own homemade soap out of lye, and these were great hooks," said Woody Bowles. The sudden notoriety made the junior Soap Sister a little cocky at high school. When Wynonna consistently came late to his home-room, teacher Eugene Howard Wade remembered Wynonna saying unrepentantly, "Mr. Wade, when I strike it rich and make it good, you can keep the books for me."

Meanwhile, twelve-year-old Ashley found her own creative outlets. Described Jon Shulenberger, "Ashley had a little cassette recorder and Ashley played this little game of recording commercials, and she would make up commercials. She introduced my daughter to that, and they would spend two hours in the other room doing these little commercials and things with the cassette tape." But there was nothing make-believe about the music business. Naomi and Wynonna shopped their brand-new demo tape all over town. According to Shulenberger, "The response was 'I just don't get it. I just don't hear it.' We were dumbfounded, because we heard it. We just weren't sure at this point whether we could separate the daughter, or whether this was a duet."

Still, record executives were drawn to Naomi's beauty, charm, and enthusiasm. "I think there was a tendency to be confused as to whether Wynonna was the object of this talent search here or was it Naomi," said Shulenberger, "because Naomi came on so strong that she pretty much smothered the audition, and men would look at Naomi—she's a very attractive woman." He and his associates finally threw in the towel. "I realized we had taken them as far as we could take them. Naomi's vision and our vision were completely different. If we followed Naomi's path, they would be pretty country singers. If they followed our path, it would be Wynonna, and she would be more pop than country. I said, 'I don't want to hold you back. Let's tear up our agreement and you guys move on.'"

Meanwhile, Naomi continued to work as a nurse to pay the bills. One of her patients at Williamson County was Dianna Maher, the daughter of noted record producer Brent Maher. When Brent Maher was leaving the hospital with his daughter, Naomi made the pitch of her life, handing him a demo tape. He was blown away and agreed to work with the Judds. They spent the next few months picking songs they could record in his studio. That spring, Wynonna graduated from Franklin High School class of 1982. Naomi skipped the ceremony after she and Wynonna found themselves in yet another dustup. Despite the battles, the Judds managed to begin recording some songs, but Naomi realized they needed representation.

In June 1982, the women arrived unannounced on the doorstep of talent manager Woody Bowles. They claimed, despite evidence to the contrary, that they had an appointment that afternoon. When Bowles arrived, they performed on the spot. Said Bowles, "I was sitting there going, 'I can't believe that nobody else has jumped in and has seen the potential here.' I saw these girls being able to be every man's fantasy and every woman's role model. This was a gold mine." He worked to line up a recording company while the Judds rehearsed with Brent Maher. Mother and daughter continued to snipe, but the duo managed to pull their act together. A short time later, Bowles delivered some exciting news: the Judds were up for the audition of their lives.

In 1983, stardom seemed within reach for Naomi and Wynonna Judd, but frequent blowups between mother and daughter threatened to derail the dream. Woody Bowles characterized, "It was like tying two cats' tails together and hanging them over a clothesline." On March 2, 1982, the Judds arrived at RCA headquarters in Nashville. Their management team had arranged an audition with RCA vice president Joe Galante. Brent Maher said, "They were gonna have to stand up and be counted for that evening, 'cause you're not gonna get that sit-down twice." Galante said, "When Wy opened her mouth and sang, it was just—the room rocked. It was just awesome."

The women were asked to step out. Forty-five minutes later, the deal was done. When the Soap Sisters got their deal, Bowles was "so excited I could have threaded a sewing machine with it running." Joe Galante ordered a mini-album of eight songs, but Bowles feared the Judds would never survive the recording sessions. He explained, "At the time when most mothers and daughters are cutting those apron strings, and the daughter is going off to college or getting married, moving out, getting an apartment, here they were being thrust together." Bowles played referee while he pushed RCA executives to change the name of the album. While RCA wanted to feature Naomi's name first, he pushed to shine the spotlight on Wynonna so that she could still pursue a solo career if the duet gimmick didn't work. In the end, his foresight won out.

"Wynonna and Naomi" went to work on the album, but it was a struggle. Meanwhile, fifteen-year-old Ashley came into her own. She joined the Franklin High School cheerleading squad. Unlike Wynonna, "Ashley was more bubbly, more outgoing, more self-confident," said Robert K. Oermann. "She had so much presence," said Brent Maher. In fact, Ashley was smart enough to "work the system" at school, making friends with her high school counselor to bypass attendance monitors when she was late to class. In the spring of 1983, Ashley decided to branch out. She recalled, "I had won a little modeling contest in Nashville, Tennessee, and I ended up being signed by Elite and somehow or another I persuaded my mother to let me go to Japan by myself." Naomi made sure everyone in town heard the news.

While slender, beautiful Ashley was spreading her wings, Wynonna was still land-bound with Naomi. "Naomi seemed very proud of Ashley and her modeling and her photographs," said Woody Bowles, "and with Wynonna, it seemed like she continually put Wynonna down. You know there were times when I felt

Wynonna was having to work her way up to low self-esteem." Wynonna earned money as a temp, doing secretarial jobs. She also continued to live at home until yet another flare-up with Naomi sent her packing. Wynonna sought refuge with Bowles and his wife while the Judds continued to work on their album.

Distance did not make the heart grow fonder. The mother-daughter battles turned downright nasty. "I remember one day they locked themselves in a bathroom at my house for about three hours, screaming and yelling at each other, throwing shampoo bottles," he described, "and Naomi would come over and say things to Wynonna that I never heard a mother say to a daughter—she would tell her what a slob she was and how worthless she was and that if she couldn't sing she would never amount to anything." On the contrary, Naomi's publicist Kathy Allmand defended, "You are always going to have things that are 'Oh, I shouldn't have done that' or 'Maybe I should have said this or that.' You're always going to second-guess yourself as a mother, but she always had the best interest of her daughters in mind."

Bowles did his best to understand the tempestuous relationship. "I wondered if maybe having Wynonna at such an early age didn't get in the way of some of her dreams, and therefore maybe she resented Wynonna on some level. At the same time, she knew that Wynonna was her ticket to celebrity. It was very complicated, their love/hate relationship. It was almost like, 'I hate you, don't leave me,'" he observed. Brent Maher, who was less understanding, told both women to get their act together or else. He delivered an ultimatum and told them to shift their thinking about each other, saying, "You've got to get that relationship on a business level, or we're going to have some real struggles here."

In the fall of 1983, the Judds embarked on a nationwide publicity tour to promote their upcoming debut album. Naomi entertained reporters with colorful tales of her struggles to raise two girls in rural Kentucky. According to Woody Bowles, she may have spruced up the tales a little to play into the image of the family's rags-to-riches ascent. "A lot of the things she told me turned out not to be exactly the way she told them to me," he admitted. Said Bob Millard, "Naomi didn't tell any outright lies. She would, you know . . . it's the angle you put on, the twist you put on, the things you leave out." The Judds pushed hard to sell themselves.

On November 16, 1983, RCA released the Judds' first single, "Had a Dream." Recounted Bowles, "I remember taking them out to WSM radio in my car, the first night they heard their record on the radio, and the tears were just flowing." The record hit number seventeen on the country charts. In February 1984, Naomi quit her nursing job for good. A month later, the Judds geared up for their first concert appearance, opening for the Statler Brothers in Omaha, Nebraska. The scene was unlike anything the pair ever experienced. Maher himself was even a little amazed—"I saw ten thousand bodies. It looked like a sea of humanity. I said to myself, 'They have no idea of how many people are out here. When they do they're gonna check out and faint or they're gonna do great.' Man, I said every prayer, any vices I had I swore off, and I said, 'Just let this happen.' And they just did great."

By 1984, thirty-eight-year-old Naomi and twenty-year-old Wynonna were the hottest up-and-coming act in country music. "Mama He's Crazy," their follow-up single after "Had a Dream," came out in July 1984 and blasted to number one on the country charts. Entertainment reporter Jimmy Carter attributed the Judds' success to their "timing, talent, and material." The mother-daughter dynamic duo was on its way. In the summer of 1984, the Judds began a tour of North America to promote their self-titled debut album. Naomi adored life on the road, taking on the nickname "Mama Judd." Wynonna was more impressed with the money. The sexy mother-daughter act rocked audiences, and record sales continued to climb. According to Joe Galante, while Naomi played the sweet, adoring mother, Wynonna was the smart-ass kid, "putting a little zinger in there every once in a while."

In October 1984, the Country Music Association named the Judds Most Promising New Act. "Suddenly they went from nurse and high school student to superstars. That's an amazing adjustment to make," said Robert K. Oermann. Ashley was making adjustments and igniting a few sparks, too. "She was extremely good-looking. She acted more like an adult than the other kids did," said Ashley's high school counselor, Bill Siefert. She attended a private school in Lexington while her mother and sister rolled from town to town to town on the concert trail. Angelique L'Amour offered, "It would be very difficult to be fourteen, fifteen years old and have your mother take off with your older sister. I think she really threw herself into her schoolwork and threw herself into her life in Kentucky." Woody Bowles mentioned, "Naomi tried to continue to give Ashley as much attention as she possibly could, but because of travel schedules, interviews, the industry events, and everything, she was pretty busy."

In 1985, seventeen-year-old Ashley moved again, this time to her grandmother's house back in Ashland. She enrolled at Paul Blazer High School, Naomi's alma mater. "She was an excellent student, and the teachers really enjoyed her, but she was lonesome," Polly said. However, Ashley soon found a friend. "His name was Bill, and the teachers described him as a Huck Finn type: red hair, freckles. He was not the football hero. No one could ever figure out why she dated him, but she did. She tended to pick people not because of their status but because she liked something about them," said Jamas L. Dickerson.

On the road, Naomi and Wynonna were up to their old tricks. One night, tensions reached a boiling point when Wynonna stayed out late with the boys in the band. Remembered Wynonna, "Here comes Mother into the bar with her coat on, underneath her coat in her flannel pajamas, no shoes on, and says, 'Wynonna, it's time to get on the bus!' I was so embarrassed." Jim Yockey, a family friend, said, "Wynonna looked and wanted to be an equal, and that's something that no parent and sibling can ever be." While Wynonna was sowing her wild oats, Oermann said that Naomi was "really the grounded one during this period. She was the one who understood you have to treat this as a business." And personally, said Bowles, Naomi didn't pull any punches when it came to Wynonna. "Naomi did pick on her a lot about the weight. 'Why can't you lose weight? You're just a slob.'" Wynonna said, "For me it was trying to live up to the expectations. I was constantly reacting."

For the Judds, life on the road became a free-for-all. "We had a number of show cancellations that would occur because they'd get back in the back of the bus and scream and yell at each other, and Wynonna would strip her vocal cords," Bowles explained. Wynonna joked, "My theme was, 'Throw Momma From the Bus.'" Bowles went on to observe, "You'd bring them together and there were tears and hugs, and then within another two days, they'd be back at it again. They both realized that they needed each other, and I believe in my heart that they both resented each other because of it." Despite the catfights, the Judds continued to rack up record sales, pack in audiences, and win awards. "They both were smart enough and desired this to continue in their life—that they were going to resolve it," Polly concluded.

That spring, eighteen-year-old Ashley graduated from high school. In the fall of 1986, she enrolled at the University of Kentucky in Lexington. Ashley joined a sorority, took a mixture of acting, anthropology, and French classes, and became a big fan of the Wildcats powerhouse basketball team. While Ashley adjusted to college life, her famous sister searched for a love life. In 1988, Wynonna met thirty-year-old Nashville musician Tony King at a church service. "I really liked Tony. I thought he was a real easygoing, low-maintenance kind of guy," Brent Maher said. Wynonna and Tony began going out, often double-dating with Naomi and her longtime boyfriend, Larry Strickland.

On May 6, 1989, Naomi and Larry made their ten-year relationship official. They married in a lavish ceremony in Nashville. Offered Robert K. Oermann, "By the time Larry married Naomi, the Judds were as big as it gets in country music. We're talking multiple, bazillion awards, millions of sales, the adoration of millions of crazed fans, I mean, the whole thing. It was a production." Offered Polly, "Larry Strickland has been possibly the best choice that Naomi ever made. He's just a gentleman. He is conscientious, and he's very level-headed." Naomi would need a calming, supportive person to steer her through the troublesome times to come.

On January 11, 1990, Naomi turned forty-four. She felt tired. The next day, she saw her doctor for a routine checkup. Blood tests revealed that she was infected with hepatitis C virus, which causes inflammation of the liver. It's unclear how she contracted the virus, but during her days as a nurse she was often exposed to risk. According to Naomi's physician, Dr. Bruce Bacon, "Like many healthcare workers, before we knew about HIV and hepatitis C, it's not that we were careless with things that we did, but we weren't as compulsive in handling needles." The prognosis was grim. Said Naomi, "Another doctor in a starched white lab coat told me I was going to be taking a six-foot dirt nap. That is, in about three years, I was going to make the old celestial transfer."

In light of the tragedy, Wynonna turned to boyfriend Tony King for support. The couple were soon engaged. Ashley, twenty-two years old, also made an announcement: She wanted to be an actress. "Finally my own spirit rebelled and said, 'I have to go do this. I'm not going to be a happy human being if I don't give it a try,'" she explained. Naomi feared the news of her condition would derail Ashley's dream. She decided not to tell her youngest daughter. In the summer of 1990, Ashley left the hills of Kentucky for the hills of Hollywood. "I can remember very well the day that she packed up her little U-Haul and hooked it up to her car and said good-bye and drove off to California. From the beginning, she was fearless," said family friend Jim Yockey.

Ashley stayed with a college friend and quickly landed a job as a hostess at the trendy Ivy restaurant. She also enrolled in an acting workshop. Ashley's acting coach, Robert Carnegie, described his young pupil as "nondescript, wore very inexpensive and not flattering clothing." He continued, "Her hair wasn't particularly well done, and she was suffering from what looked to be kind of an inferiority complex. She was actually the worst in the class. She took so much criticism from me that the class and myself had kind of a joke. It was going to be a lottery pool, and everybody would guess when she would quit." But Ashley refused to quit. Carnegie continued, "She took every bit of criticism in the most positive and upbeat manner that one could imagine and just took it in and then tried to correct herself."

Ashley worked hard and studied hard. She had no idea her mother was critically ill. Ashley was devastated when Naomi finally gave her the news. Then, on October 17, 1990, Naomi let the world know about her illness, saying, "Today is pretty much the most difficult day of my life." Wynonna, still only twenty-six years old, sat by her mother's side. Naomi made a tearful announcement: "I prayed about it for several weeks and then realized just how bad the situation was becoming for me. I have to resign. I have to retire from the music industry that I love so much." During the time, "people were weeping. Hardened news reporters were weeping," said Oermann.

Naomi decided to participate in a farewell tour to support the album, but Bob Millard was more cynical about her generosity to her fans. "She was being real dramatic. Then it was, like, 'Oh, God. Mama's gonna die. So she can only tour one more year,'" he sniped. "Anybody noticed that this woman who's on her deathbed is doing a farewell tour for a year?" Dr. Bruce Bacon explained Naomi's decision, saying, "Going on the road gave her energy from fans that supported her and also if you're doing something, you're not necessarily thinking about the fact that you've got this problem, and you can deny it a little bit or avoid it a little bit."

Naomi's life-threatening illness forced all of the Judds to reevaluate their lives. At twenty-two, Ashley continued to chase her dream of being an actress. Despite Wynonna's combative relationship with Naomi, the twenty-six-year-old singer couldn't imagine life on the road without her. "I don't know what the future will hold," she said, "but the word 'solo' just isn't in my mind right now." Eventually, the reality that Naomi was not going to come back settled in with Wynonna, and she began recording a solo album as she prepared for one last road trip with Mom. "We are both having the heaviest time of our lives and the most emotional," she admitted at the time.

In February 1991, the Judds' ten-month farewell tour kicked off. In city after city, forty-five-year-old Naomi fought fatigue and pain. She often struggled to get through a performance. "Naomi would be onstage, and afterwards she was in bed. I think she was reserving her energy all the rest of the time she was offstage," said Angelique L'Amour. The tour eventually stopped in Los Angeles. Ashley brought Robert Carnegie to meet her famous mom. "Backstage, she was in a wheelchair, and it was like I had to have a special audience with her because she understood, I'm the person that's in charge now of her daughter's light. She grilled me. I realized something, that this woman thought that she might be dying, and she was very concerned what would happen to Ashley," he said.

Naomi had reason for concern—Ashley's career was going nowhere. In the spring of 1991, Ashley auditioned for the part of "Tool Time Girl" on a new sitcom called *Home Improvement*. She lost out to Pamela Anderson. Then came the chance to play a lead role opposite Christian Slater in the film *Kuffs*. According to Carnegie, "She was saying 'They want me to do it, but I have to take my top off,' and she said, 'I'm not going to have my mother see me in my first movie without my top on.'" Ashley opted for a nonspeaking role, and continued to work hard to impress her coach and her mom. On one occasion, Carnegie remembered that Naomi came to watch Ashley in acting class and began to realize what her daughter was trying to do. At that point, he said, "She gave her complete blessing and encouragement to Ashley."

In the fall of 1991, Ashley got a break. She scored a small role on two episodes of *Star Trek: The Next Generation*. Ashley also became a regular on the TV drama *Sisters*, playing the socialite daughter of Swoozie Kurtz. Kurtz marveled at her young costar's maturity and poise. Ashley was focused on her craft, but she did make time to play the Hollywood dating game. "She's sort of an intellectual pinup. She called last night and she said, 'I'm going out to dinner with a bunch of people and Jack Nicholson.' I went, 'Oh my God!' I thought I had problems with Wynonna," laughed Naomi.

After years of fighting, mother and daughter fought hard to let go. "We sleep together on the bus, you know, the dressing rooms, the adjoining motel rooms, we share a stage. So just the fact of not being together physically every waking, every sleeping moment" was devastating, according to Naomi. Added Wynonna, "I'm going through some things right now where I wonder if I'll be strong without her. I'm twenty-seven years old, and I'm still living at home, and I'm trying to leave. And it's the hardest thing I've ever done." The Judds "Farewell Tour" sold out in city after city. More dates were added. "It's a hard break," said Angelique L'Amour. "I'd hear people say, 'Oh well, it's a never-ending final tour, right?' It didn't surprise me, because I thought, 'When you love being on stage, you're talented, you have this tremendous thing you've built from this seed with your child, you just want to do it.'"

Then, after 125 concerts in 155 cities, the tour rolled to the finish line for one final show. The setting was an arena just outside Nashville. True to form, Naomi and Wynonna turned the sold-out, pay-per-view event into high drama. Recounted Brent Maher, "We did a sound check, and [Wynonna] couldn't sing, could not sing. We actually talked about maybe having to cancel it, but the reality of that was impossible, because it was being filmed." Robert K. Oermann explained that "a lot was riding on Wynonna's shoulders. She had to make a record that was going to take her to the next step. And deal with the fact that her mom is so sick. And by the time they go to the last concert, Wynonna's voice was gone." A doctor treated Wynonna right up to show time. On December 4, 1991, the Judds took the stage for one of the most anticipated concerts in music history. "It was one of the best shows they've ever done. It's almost as if the energy from the people that were in the venue—crew, audience, band members—was feeding Wynonna and Naomi that night." He continued, "When it was over, it wasn't just a concert ending. It was an era ending. The Judds were no more."

In 1991, forty-five-year-old Naomi said a tearful good-bye to the music business to battle a deadly virus. At twenty-seven, Wynonna prepared to launch a solo career while her younger sister, Ashley, took on Hollywood. "I'm gonna do just what it takes to keep this smile on my face. I'm gonna drive my car," said Wynonna. The question of whether Naomi's oldest daughter and partner in song could make it on her own was quickly answered. In March 1992, her debut solo album, *Wynonna*, hit number one on the country music charts. The album went platinum in just five days. "All of that fire that she always had in her voice was allowed to blaze," noted Oermann. "That record was met with both critical and popular success to probably everyone's relief."

To promote the album, Wynonna launched a nine-month, 110-city concert tour. However, before leaving Nashville, Wynonna decided to break off her engagement to Tony King. Reasoned Angelique L'Amour, "I think it's very hard to travel three hundred days a year and have a relationship." Art McCloud, a family friend, added, "It was real sad. Like she lost her best friend." Even though she put on a happy face about it, Wynonna wasn't okay with taking the stage alone. For eight years, Naomi was there at her side. "I've never done anything on my own," Wynonna confessed. "I feel like I'm twenty-eight and leaving home for the first time. Mom did everything but cut up my meat for me." In one phone conversation, Wynonna mentioned her uncertainties to L'Amour, who countered with a positive spin, affirming, "This is when you get to earn your voice."

Audiences, too, quickly answered Wynonna's self-doubt when they flocked to her concerts. "Places were packed. Everybody wanted to see her," said L'Amour. Commented Wynonna, "People ask me, 'What's it like being solo?' It's give and take. On one hand, I get to stay up as late as I want and no one can tell me what to do.

I can drink from the milk carton on the bus. After the show, the lights have dimmed, and I am by myself. I am learning a lot about grace, about how to be alone and not feel alone." But in a 2004 interview on the *Oprah Winfrey Show*, Wynonna said she did feel lonely at times. The singer turned to food for comfort. She began putting on weight. In 1993, Wynonna met forty-one-year-old Arch Kelley on a cross-country flight. The singer and the Nashville yacht salesman began dating and soon moved in together. "He was a nice guy, very charming. He was a sharp-dressed guy, good-looking, blond hair," said Jimmy Carter, "and you could see why he might be able to turn the head of Wynonna or many other girls."

In the meantime, Wynonna's twenty-five-year-old sister, still out in Hollywood, was turning a few heads herself. Ashley completed her first lead role in a coming-of-age film that hit very close to home. As James L. Dickerson described, *"Ruby in Paradise* was an excellent movie about a girl from Tennessee who loads up her car and goes to Florida to find her dream. The parallels to her own life are obvious." Ashley said of the script, "This movie is why I am an actress. I have never read anything that touched me so much in my life." In January 1993, Ashley flew to the Cannes Film Festival to promote the movie. On October 8, 1993, *Ruby in Paradise* opened in the United States. The film scored with critics, and so did Ashley. She won an Independent Spirit Award for Best Actress in a Leading Role. "From that point on," noted Robert Carnegie, "Ashley started getting all these offers, and her career just really took off."

"Ashley is every bit as special and as talented as Wynonna," Naomi commented, "and it is very gratifying to me as her mom to see that people finally know about Ashley." Yet Ashley wasn't completely ready for high-powered fame. "Amazing as it may sound, I don't really want a spotlight still. What I want to do is act. I wake up every day, and that's when I want to act. I am like an alcoholic. Instead of booze, I want a scene," she once stated. Just as Ashley's star began to rise—in fact, while she was still out of town promoting *Ruby in Paradise*—she received some terrible news: her small house in Malibu burned down in a raging wildfire. But the bonds of family were strong, and Wynonna stepped in to buy Ashley a new home not far from her own place in Franklin. Ashley happily moved back to Tennessee, where Naomi lived just a few miles away. Affirmed Carnegie, "I would have expected that, because Ashley's just not a Hollywood kind of creature. She has other values, which I think she got from her mother."

Around the time Ashley was returning to her roots, Naomi completed her autobiography, *Love Can Build a Bridge*. The book was published in November 1993 and quickly landed on the *New York Times* bestseller list. The book was filled with sensational stories as only Naomi could tell them. "Mama Judd" defended: "This is my perception. This is my reality, and I take responsibility for it." Wynonna joked with reporters that she wanted to write a book of her own and call it *The Truth*. One thing was undeniable—Naomi seemed to be winning her battle with hepatitis.

Once again successful in her professional ventures, Naomi Judd returned to the personal, focusing on improving her relationship with her daughters. "We went into therapy—our family did—and one day our therapist told me that I should become a practicing psychologist. That night, I just casually mentioned it at supper. Wynonna and Ashley bolted up out of their seats at the dinner table and ran screaming outside," she laughed. Naomi's ex-husband, Michael Ciminella, also took part in the therapy sessions. Michael and the therapist planned to tell Wynonna the long-kept secret that her biological father was Charles Jordan.

However, according to Ciminella, Naomi rushed in and broke the news to Wynonna herself. Wynonna then had a heart-to-heart talk with the man she thought was her father. "There was a very tearful meeting between the two of them," said Kenneth Hart, "and he told me afterward she wrote him a note that was very sweet and kind and tender, saying that she still loved him. And he, in fact, told me that he still loved her very much as well." Naomi kept a low profile. According to Hart, "Her publicist said, 'We kind of feel this is a nonstory. We have no comment about it.'" Ashley had known the truth for years. Michael had told her. In fact, many members of the Judds' camp were in on the secret. Naomi revealed the news to Bowles in the '80s. "I don't know why she chose to share that little bit of information with me, but she did, and I just didn't feel it was my place to get into that with Wynonna," he remarked.

Within weeks of learning the shocking news, Wynonna discovered that she herself was pregnant with boyfriend Arch Kelley's baby. Executives with Curb Records feared the worst—a backlash from the media and fans. Recalled Angelique L'Amour, "Years before, some tabloid had said she was pregnant, and because some sponsor got concerned about this, out of wedlock, she had to go have a pregnancy test when she wasn't pregnant. I don't think she even had a boyfriend at the time." This time, Wynonna came out swinging. "I think the way she handled it was the right way, which is that you throw your life open to the public and say, 'Good, bad, or indifferent, this is who I am. I hope you can accept me,' and I think it worked," assessed Robert K. Oermann. On December 23, 1994, Wynonna gave birth to a son, Elijah Judd Kelley.

Even though the Judds were riding on a wave of success in the mid-1990s, they remained a family where drama ruled and trouble followed. In September 1995, twenty-seven-year-old Ashley began work on the courtroom thriller *A Time to Kill*. Ashley played the wife of an attorney played by Texan Matthew McConaughey. During the shoot, the line between reality and make-believe blurred. "The entire time that she was playing his wife, she would often call him and leave sexy love messages on his machine," said James L. Dickerson. The film wrapped, and so did the relationship. However, the split was amicable and the couple remained friends.

Back in Tennessee, Ashley's older sister was pregnant again. Wynonna and Kelley decided the time was right to tie the knot. The relationship was anything but boring. "When Arch asked Wynonna to marry him, he was living in this big luxury teepee out in the backyard," offered Bob Millard. Wynonna explained, "We have a teepee that we go and sit in and pretend that we are Indians. It's like a movie thing." Millard continued, "He wrote his most romantic thoughts, so he went in and read it to her and proposed, and she accepted." Gushed Wynonna, "It is very touching, because he actually got on his knees, and it got very mushy." The wedding took place on January 21, 1996. Wynonna was thirty-one, Kelley forty-three. Then, on June 21, 1996, just five months later, the newlyweds became the proud parents of Pauline Grace. Wynonna relished her role as mother. "You have to change," she affirmed. "You have to become selfless, which for a working woman like me, in my life, every day starts out with 'What am I going to wear? What am I going to do? What am I going to say? What am I going to sing?' And now I wake up saying, 'What can I do for my kid today?'"

Wynonna's life was on track while Ashley struggled. She finished shooting the thriller *Kiss the Girls* in July 1996. According to published interviews, Ashley soon began suffering from depression. Once again Wynonna jumped in to help her troubled sister. She thought of a fellow singer who might complement her sister: "I knew that Michael Bolton was an awesome singer. It's nice to know that someone on his level of success is a warm and caring being." Explained Dickerson, "So bells went off in Wynonna's mind, and she decided that Michael was the perfect match for Ashley. They started going out and very quickly became a couple."

Still, Ashley's depression didn't go away. She decided to seek help. In an interview, Ashley said she was told by her therapist that her condition stemmed from unresolved childhood grief. According to Ashley, she then sat down with her mother and sister to talk things out. The actress kept details of the conversation private. "Family to her is not something that she puts out in every article or in every television interview," commented Jimmy Carter, "and if you try to go there, she'll shut you down pretty quick." Michael Bolton continued to support Ashley during their ten-month romance. The relationship settled into a close friendship. The 1997 premiere of *Kiss the Girls* gave twenty-nine-year-old Ashley a much-needed lift. The movie opened strong at the box office and went on to gross more than $60 million. The thriller proved Ashley was no damsel in distress. "*Kiss the Girls* was the first of the famous Ashley Judd 'independent, strong female in jeopardy and danger who wins the day at the end' roles, and it was a huge success," observed Robert Carnegie.

The same could not be said for sister Wynonna. Sales of her new albums *Collection* and *The Other Side* barely made a blip on the billboard charts. Old insecurities resurfaced, and Wynonna's weight began climbing higher. Reasoned Wynonna's grandmother Polly, "I think she felt unsure of her career. We substitute food for love and for satisfaction from our lives, and she was doing that." Meanwhile, Wynonna's marriage also went south fast. The marriage lasted nearly three years, but on November 6, 1998, Wynonna filed for divorce, citing "irreconcilable differences." Despite failed marriages, surfacing secrets, and a saga that often played out like a sad country song, in good times and bad, the three Judd women knew they could depend on one thing: each other. In 1998, Wynonna brought Naomi and a very nervous Ashley onstage during a charity concert. The Judds performed as a trio for the very first time.

In the spring of 1999, thirty-one-year-old Ashley's romantic life looked up. She attended the wedding reception of a friend, where one of the guests really got her engine revving—race-car driver Dario Franchitti. According to Dickerson, Ashley and Franchitti "hit it off immediately, and they started going out the next day." Carnegie added that "being a risk-taker herself, she would naturally be attracted to another risk-taker." But, as Naomi asserted, "This guy, he's a ten on the boyfriend scale. We love Dario. We always have and we didn't even know he was a famous race-car driver. I just knew him as this smart gentleman who obviously adored my daughter and loved to show up for my tuna casserole."

That September, Ashley solidified her status as an A-list actress with the release of *Double Jeopardy,* which costarred Tommy Lee Jones. The thriller quickly blasted through the hundred-million-dollar mark in ticket sales. Hollywood was impressed, and so were Mom and Sis. "She was as proud as she could be of her daughter, and Wynonna was as proud as she could be of her sister. There was no sense of any kind of internal jealousy," Carnegie remarked. But fame put Ashley in real-life jeopardy. On September 27, 1999, Ashley and Franchitti were relaxing at her Tennessee home when an unwanted guest arrived. According to Dickerson, "A man walked into the kitchen, showed her a badge and said he was the police, and asked how she was doing."

It wasn't the first time Ashley encountered the intruder. In fact, she already had a restraining order issued against him. She was so afraid that she called 911 to get outside assistance, but Franchitti took charge of a potentially explosive situation. "Dario escorted him out the door, walked him out to his car, wrote down his license tag, and got in his car when the stalker drove away and chased after him," Dickerson recounted. The police confirmed the man's identity and arrested thirty-two-year-old Guy Paul Dukes on the spot, charging him with stalking and criminal impersonation of a police officer. Dukes pleaded guilty. He was put on probation and ordered to stay away from Ashley.

Three months later, Ashley and her beau were engaged, and Naomi and Wynonna made plans of their own for a reunion concert tour. The Power to Change tour kicked off New Year's Eve 2000, but this time things were different. As Angelique L'Amour put it, "Before, her mother had been the one in charge of everything and running the show, and then her mother was coming to her party. It redefined their relationship, definitely. It tilted the scales in another direction." The successful twenty-city tour ended in March 2000. That August, Naomi's relationship with Larry Strickland hit a road bump. Naomi filed for divorce, but the couple reconciled soon after.

That same month, Wynonna learned her biological father had

passed away. Charles Jordan, fifty-five when he died, never met his famous daughter. "He chose to stay silent. He could have shown up at a concert and said, 'Hi, I'm actually your father,' at any point. Then time ran out," said L'Amour. "I know it affected her deeply. I know she was at a loss as to how to deal with it." Wynonna was saddened by the news. She turned to her body-guard, Dan Roach, for comfort and support. Roach had been a steady and steadying influence for ten years, and the professional relationship soon turned personal. In August 2001, he proposed marriage, and Wynonna accepted. "Oh yeah," she laughed, "I'm definitely stepping into the circle once again."

Wedding plans were also in the works for Ashley and her race-car-driving fiancé. The bride-to-be swore her family to secrecy. On December 12, 2001, Ashley Judd and Dario Franchitti married. Ashley was thirty-three, and her new husband was twenty-eight. The elaborate ceremony was held inside a Scottish castle, but the real action happened outside. Described Dickerson, "While the wedding was actually taking place, a golf cart caught on fire out-side the hotel. Firefighters rushed in, but because they knew there was a wedding going on, they turned their sirens off. It was like a silent movie of them putting out this fire in the golf cart." After facing lots of fiery ups and downs in their relationship, the couple soon settled into a low-key lifestyle. "Dario doesn't seem to want the spotlight, and when Ashley's with Dario, she doesn't seem to want the spotlight either," said Dickerson.

Naomi, at age fifty-five, was constantly promoting her new projects, among them a children's book, a skin-care line, a radio show. "I'm little but I have big ideas," she plugged. The media were also in hot pursuit of Wynonna, but for very different and less pleasant reasons.

One of the worst nights in Wynonna's life began on the evening of November 13, 2003. The thirty-nine-year-old singer was driv-ing her SUV through the streets of Nashville. According to police reports, around 1:00 A.M. cops pulled Wynonna over for speeding, and an officer smelled alcohol on her breath. "Wy had been out partying with her girlfriends prior to her marriage to Dan Roach—a bachelorette party, if you will. She made a bad judgment call and got behind the wheel," concluded Robert K. Oermann. Police said Wynonna failed a field sobriety test. She then took a Breathalyzer, and the results indicated levels twice the legal limit. The country superstar was arrested and charged with driving under the influence.

Wynonna Judd quickly issued a public apology, in which she stated, "I am always thinking about the safety of others and that of my family, and have learned a very serious lesson." Angelique L'Amour affirmed, "I think she did exactly the right thing." Added Jimmy Carter, "And she felt very bad, even extra bad that her mother had been embarrassed, because her mother is a spokesman for the Mothers Against Drunk Driving." Wynonna pleaded guilty to a DUI, paid a $350 fine, and received one year's probation. However, happier times were ahead. On November 22, 2003, Wynonna wed bodyguard Dan Roach. "It's like Mr. Right was right there all along," said Oermann. "I think it's a wonderful relationship. He is a wonderful guy." Added Polly, "Roach is a good, solid man with insight, and he's very steadfast. He's just a rock."

Still, the new bride wanted to deal with some unfinished business. "Wynonna has battled weight problems from day one— from being a teenager. It's not something she hides, it's something she's proud of," explained Oermann. L'Amour mentioned, "Her weight has gone up as her career has gone on. She has two children. It's not easy for anybody to get weight off." Wynonna appealed to friend Oprah Winfrey for help. In February and again in May 2004, the singer bared her soul on Oprah's talk show. Wynonna described her struggle with low self-esteem and loneliness and the comfort she found in food. "It's great therapy if you got the whole world rooting for you," said Carter. "She says now that when she goes to a restaurant, she's getting paranoid because people are looking at her to see whether or not she's eating four desserts."

Meanwhile, thirty-five-year-old Ashley Judd made some tough decisions, too. She stunned Hollywood insiders by turning down $10 million to star in the film *Catwoman*. Instead, she took on Broadway as Maggie in *Cat on a Hot Tin Roof*. "Tennessee Williams and one of his greatest plays on Broadway—it doesn't get any better than that, or more challenging. She's a risk-taker," said Carnegie. Ashley's run was cut short in February 2004, when she sprained an ankle. However, the injury didn't prevent Ashley from rooting for her beloved Kentucky Wildcats or from mulling over new movie roles. During her break from the performance, Ashley kicked back with her husband.

Naomi Judd and her husband also enjoyed quality time together. Said Jimmy Carter, "You know, Naomi's a wild card, and Larry is probably there to support her, but maybe to be a sounding board for calm sometimes, because Naomi is a tornado." As for Naomi's health, she's holding her own. "I have tested negative to the hepatitis C virus for a year now. They cannot find the virus," she stated proudly. Carter added, "She said, 'I don't have time for hepatitis.' She wills it away. It adds to the lore and gossip about the Judds—she's so powerful she can get rid of disease!" Naomi, booming along at fifty-eight, also remained front and center, making TV appearances, writing books, and telling it like she says it is. "She certainly has an opinion about everything and certainly doesn't mind sharing that opinion," laughed Brent Maher. Robert K. Oermann added, "She will always be in the public eye, because she needs to be."

"All three of the Judds, each in their own way, is a drama queen," assessed Oermann. Wynonna, however, justified that regal air: "The Judd women were incredibly challenged in life. We shouldn't have made it, and yet we did." Added Ashley, "I'm so proud of my family, and no one can ever live the way that we lived, and no one can ever understand everything that we've been through together." From the hills of Kentucky, Naomi, Wynonna, and Ashley Judd escaped a life of poverty to become major players on the entertainment scene. The three continue to live a few miles apart in Franklin, Tennessee. They are known the world over, yet they remain first and foremost a family. As Angelique L'Amour summed up, "The truth is that nothing comes between the three of them. Nothing. And nothing will."

CHAPTER 14

BLOND AMBITION

The Goldie Hawn and Kate Hudson Story

"It's really quite amazing . . . mother and daughter—best friends."

—*Mary Murphy,* TV Guide *senior writer*

They're blond, beautiful, and ambition is in their blood. They're the hottest mother-daughter act in Hollywood. Goldie Hawn's costar Steve Martin once said "When we watch Goldie on the screen with her beautiful timing, her intelligence, her spirit, you just think *Yeah, baby*." The same holds true for her radiant, talented daughter, Kate Hudson. Leslie Bennetts, contributing editor of *Vanity Fair*, commented, "There are times when Kate flashes this dazzling smile, and you suddenly see Goldie in her." Goldie was a go-go dancer who gyrated her way to stardom. Kate was a pampered princess who wanted to be just like Mom. Together, their romances drew international attention. But one man—Goldie's ex-husband and Kate's father, Bill Hudson—fell out of the spotlight. For these golden blondes, it's a family affair. Goldie Hawn and Kate Hudson are a force to be reckoned with, and this is their story.

On March 25, 2001, Kate Hudson walked down Oscar's red carpet with her new husband, Chris Robinson, lead singer for the Black Crowes. Kate was favored to take home the Academy Award for Best Supporting Actress after winning the Golden Globe for her breakout performance in *Almost Famous*. It was a coincidence that turned a new page in Hollywood history. Thirty-two years earlier, Kate's mother, Goldie Hawn, won both awards for her first major film role, in *Cactus Flower*. Goldie was twenty-four. Kate was only twenty-one. "It is interesting how synchronized our lives are, and I think it's also a blessing," said Kate.

Catch them at the right angle, Goldie and Kate look like twins. But beneath the surface are two very different women.

Kate Hudson grew up a movie star's kid on the beaches of Malibu. She wanted for nothing, except an acting career of her own. Goldie's childhood was far different—and so were her aspirations. Goldie Jeanne Hawn was born in Washington, D.C., on November 21, 1945. Her father, Edward Hawn, was a successful musician who often played at the White House. Edward gave Goldie the "perspective on people" that made her understand that she had to set achievable goals for herself. "I was completely a realist," said Goldie. "I think it was my father's gift to me—to be real, to live a real life, was what was important."

Goldie's mother, Laura Hawn, ran two businesses in Takoma Park, Maryland—a watch-repair shop and a dance school. Goldie and her older sister, Patti, became students as soon as they could walk. According to Mark Shapiro, who wrote the biography *Pure Goldie*, "Her mother did, at an early age, push her into dancing. She said, 'This is going to open doors for you.' Goldie didn't quite understand at the time." In 1956, Goldie got her first taste of showbiz. The touring Ballet Russe de Monte Carlo paid her $1.50 to perform in *The Nutcracker*. But one year later, she traded an arabesque for a pelvic thrust when she discovered Elvis, and it was "Bye-bye ballet, hello rock 'n' roll!" Lawrence Grobel, contributing editor at *Playboy*, has tracked Goldie's career. "It gave her the kind of stirrings that it gave tens of thousands if not millions of other young girls that age. All of a sudden she's putting on lipstick, and she's trying to wear tight skirts, and her father's yelling at her for it."

Because of her own insecurities, Goldie quickly learned how to make up in moxie what she lacked in confidence. "I never thought I was pretty. I tried everything I could," said Goldie. "I wore falsies, and I wore skirts with lots of padding so I looked like I had a better figure than I did. And I did all those things that men seem to respond to." Goldie also relied on humor. Childhood pal Sylvia Berman has fond memories of Goldie's robust personality.

"She would just make us laugh all the time. By tripping over something on purpose or starting her giggling while we were watching TV and then we would all start giggling." Goldie's comedic talent, coupled with her dancing ability, made her a natural for the theater department at Montgomery Blair High School. In 1962, she landed a small part in the school's production of *Bye Bye Birdie*. Berman recalls that Goldie's hair was always tousled from her enthusiastic dancing. She was a hit on stage, but her grades were "just so," said Lawrence Grobel: "She didn't do that well in school, but she had a tremendous sense of optimism. She had great ambition, too."

In the fall of 1963, Goldie Hawn enrolled at the American University in Washington, D.C., to study acting. She soon tired of academic life, and in 1964 she dropped out of college and headed for Broadway. "She had it in her mind to be a dancer. Goldie actually did hitchhike to New York. She was dropped off, literally, in downtown New York . . . and she was looking all around. I mean, she knew she was going to take New York by storm, and it was all great," recounted Mark Shapiro. Goldie scored her first job in a matter of weeks. According to Grobel, though, it wasn't her dream quite yet. "She danced the can-can in the Texas Pavilion at the New York World's Fair in 1964. She was making $180 a week, and I think it was quite a lot of money for her, but she wasn't landing the big Broadway dance parts, either." Said Shapiro, "Then she started the real rough-and-tumble life of a struggling dancer. When jobs were really slim, she was doing dancing in some really questionable clubs." Goldie said in an interview, "I worked in terrible places. I danced on tables, I danced in cages, I had those men pressing their noses up to the cage, and they just looked absolutely grotesque. It was frightening, really."

And then there was the infamous casting couch. Al Capp, creator of the *L'il Abner* comic strip, "claimed" to be looking for an actress to play Daisy Mae in an upcoming film. Goldie was called in to read for the part. The fifty-five-year-old cartoonist had a surprise for her. And it wasn't his artificial limb. "He took the wooden leg, and lifted it up on the couch . . . it was so awful," re-called Goldie, "and he had this, like, robe on, which was already suspect, you know, and he leaned back, and I gasped. I swear to God it was, like, 'Mr. Capp!' I said, 'I will never get a job like this!' He said, 'Well, you'll never go anywhere in this business.'" Goldie was determined to prove him wrong. According to Judy Bach-rach, a contributing editor to *Vanity Fair*, "She took all the insults the men dished out, and all the humiliations, and she basically buried them."

Twenty-one-year-old Goldie Hawn had no intention of staying on the go-go circuit for the rest of her life, so she packed up her car and drove west in 1966. "Mentally, she gave herself a six-month self-imposed deadline: 'If I don't find work or become some kind of success in six months, I'm going to go back to Takoma Park and marry the dentist and live happily ever after,'" said Mark Shapiro. But, in truth, she never looked back. Once she got to the West Coast, she landed several shows in Southern California, and she met choreographer Gus Trikonis. Trikonis was twenty-eight years old and classically Greek—tall, dark, and handsome. Goldie couldn't resist his charm. As Shapiro described it, "It was literally love at first sight. They hit it off immediately. Not too long after that, they moved in together. They were struggling occasionally. Shows would take him out of town, so there was a whole strain on their relationship." Broke and often lonely, Goldie needed a break, and in 1967 she got it. While Goldie danced and sang in an Andy Griffith television special, there was a high-powered agent sitting in the audience.

In an ultimately auspicious deal, superagent Art Simon imme-diately added Goldie Hawn to his client list at the powerful William Morris Agency. A short time later, Goldie was cast in an ABC pilot, *Good Morning World*. It premiered on September 5, 1967, but was canceled after only thirteen episodes. However, viewers remembered Goldie. The fans, according to Lawrence Grobel, were very different from the customers who had ogled her at the go-go clubs. "People are asking for her autograph, and she's getting to stay in good hotels, and they're giving her champagne as gifts." That same year, Goldie landed a small role in her first film, playing the "Giggly Girl" in Disney's *The One and Only, Genuine, Original Family Band*. The film's costar was a cute fifteen-year-old actor named Kurt Russell, who later played a key role in Goldie's life.

Although *Good Morning World* was canceled, Goldie had caught the eye of George Schlatter, executive producer of *Rowan & Martin's Laugh-In*, a frenetic sketch comedy that turned the rebellious sixties upside down. According to Schlatter, "She came in, and we had an interview, and she sat down, and I said, 'I think you're just wonderful. You're going to do.' But I was still wondering, What am I going to do with her? She was a go-go dancer."

Despite his reservations, George Schlatter gave Goldie Hawn a trial run on *Laugh-In*. Of course, she was the most outrageous member of the cast. Schlatter decided to take advantage of Goldie's go-go experience rather than avoid it, so every week she donned a teeny bikini. One lucky crew member painted far-out messages on her body. *"That,"* quipped Schlatter, "was the most sought-after job at NBC." Goldie's role contributed to the ditzy stereotype that fans worldwide grew to know and love. "I had to pretend to sing badly and dance badly, because I wanted to be like everybody else. I couldn't be this vacant, bubbleheaded, fun person and know how to do a triple pirouette," she explained with some resignation. But perhaps Goldie's ditzy persona wasn't completely a ruse. Dick Martin himself recalled that "she was a terrible sight-reader, and it was hysterical, because she'd miss something and just giggle." Goldie herself admitted, "I'd get all mixed up, and, of course, I have a sense of humor about myself, thank God."

The show debuted on January 22 to astronomically high ratings. "Sock it to me," Goldie's go-go catchphrase, became a national craze. As George Schlatter recalled, those were heady times that were all about fun and craziness that "opened up a whole new kind of television." But Goldie wasn't a hit with everyone.

Feminists, for one, took issue with her belly-baring, hip-gyrating, airhead persona. "They would say to me, 'Don't you feel that it's irresponsible to be doing what you're doing in this time of history when women are actually declaring their independence, and it's women's liberation?'" said Goldie. "And I remember at the age of twenty-one, I looked up at them and I said, 'You know, I don't understand that, because I already feel liberated.'"

Goldie smiled through the criticism and enjoyed the fame, but she also craved a normal family life with her live-in lover, Gus Trikonis. Mark Shapiro speculated that the friction at home started to become more intense because of her sudden success. "Gus, again, being the traditional Greek, wants to be the bread-winner. He wants to make the money. He wants the love of his life to stay home and have babies, and as clichéd and conservative and traditional as that sounds, Goldie was thinking the same way." Goldie and Gus married in Honolulu on May 16, 1968. She was twenty-three, he was thirty. Said Lawrence Grobel, "Goldie wanted to keep relationship first, career second, but when you have a career that's just bursting into the sky and agents and managers telling you 'Hey, this is your time, kid, you better start taking advantage of it,' the marriage itself went by the wayside."

In the summer of 1969, Goldie Hawn was asked to read for a role in *Cactus Flower*, the film version of a popular Broadway play, but she refused to audition. "Goldie felt that she knew the role so well that they should either give it to her or not give it to her, because she had that part down. I think it took the producers aback a little," summed up Shapiro. Producer Mike Frankovich and executives at Columbia Pictures eventually caved in. They offered Goldie the part, a $50,000 salary, and a four-picture deal. Mary Murphy, senior writer for *TV Guide*, thinks Goldie's brash demands were a bid for autonomy in a male-dominated, controlling industry. "She was always going to be more in charge of what she did than just be an actress for hire, and that was really smart. She's really smart."

In late summer 1969, Goldie returned to the *Laugh-In* set for season two. A few months later, *Cactus Flower* opened in theaters nationwide. The film received mixed reviews, but Goldie's heartfelt performance was widely praised. Then, in January 1970, Goldie turned down a huge salary increase from the producers of *Laugh-In* and walked away from the popular series. She was off to London, to shoot the comic romp *There's a Girl in My Soup* with Peter Sellers. Meanwhile, back in L.A., nominations for the Forty-second Annual Academy Awards were announced. "She's in England and gets a phone call saying it's the Academy Awards and she had been nominated for Best Supporting Actress," offered Grobel, who said that the nomination was a total surprise. "She had no feeling that she could win the thing." Goldie made no plans to attend the ceremony. Instead, she stayed in England, certain the Oscar would go to Dyan Cannon for *Bob & Carol & Ted & Alice*. "I forgot about the Academy Awards the night they were on. I went to sleep. I was in London," recalled Goldie, laughing. "I was awakened by a phone call, and he said, 'You got it! You won!' And I went, 'I got what? I won what?' He said, 'You won the Academy Award!' and I went, 'Oh, my God, it was on last night?'" Goldie was surprised: "I felt that the role really didn't warrant an Academy Award. I felt that I had so much more inside me, and I thought that probably that would be the last award that I would get for a long time."

The self-doubt followed Goldie back into her marriage. Her star and salary continued to rise, but her relationship with her husband was crumbling. "It was a time when she should have been at her happiest, and she wasn't," said Mark Shapiro. "I mean, she was losing weight. She was going to therapy. She wanted everything to be perfect. She wanted everybody to be happy around her, and it just wasn't happening. She could go to work on a film, and everything is great. She comes home, and Gus is sitting there, not working." Goldie desperately wanted to be a mother. Gus wanted to wait until he was more financially secure. With plans for children on hold, twenty-six-year-old Goldie returned to her roots. "During this period, Goldie would occasionally do forays back into television. She did a song-and-dance show. She did a *Laugh-In* reunion," offered Shapiro.

Later that year, the Oscar winner who refused to audition for *Cactus Flower* campaigned hard to play Jill in *Butterflies Are Free*, but director Milton Katselas preferred the actress who originated the role on Broadway. "I wanted Blythe Danner to do it, because she had done it in New York and she won the Tony. Mike Frankovich had a deal with Goldie, so he kept suggesting Goldie, and I kept thinking about Goldie. Then we met. I found her to be extremely sensitive and very intelligent, and I went back to Frankovich and said, 'If you want it, I'd like to see her do it.'" Goldie Hawn and Milton Katselas got along famously, and he taught her not to make faces at the camera, a bad habit she picked up on the set of *Laugh-In*. When *Butterflies Are Free* opened to rave reviews and box-office success in 1972, critics agreed that Goldie's Oscar was no fluke. The girl could act.

By 1972, the Kid from Takoma Park was making $300,000 a picture and had an Oscar on her mantel, but the golden girl was restless. Despite critical acclaim for her roles in *Cactus Flower* and *Butterflies Are Free*, Goldie had a tough time shaking her TV image as a ditzy blonde. As Judy Bachrach pointed out, "Goldie Hawn recognizes that what she did in *Laugh-In* was not her most perfect product and that she was selling a commodity that's easily erasable—namely, her good looks." Her next opportunity to move beyond hip-shaking, face-making, and giggles was a serious project called *Sugarland Express*. Based on the true story of Lou-Jean Poplin, the film was about a woman who breaks her husband out of prison and kidnaps a police officer, all in the name of motherhood.

"*Sugarland Express* would be Steven Spielberg's first movie," said Mark Shapiro. "Goldie thought enough of the script that she basically said, 'You know, I'll do this for less than what I normally get,' and by this time she was making decent money already." But Shapiro added, "This would ultimately be a turning point for Goldie, for good and bad." Universal executives took the gamble, but the rookie director had his doubts about Goldie's acting chops. Said Lawrence Grobel, "Let's face it, Spielberg was also young at the time. He wasn't Spielberg yet—he hadn't done *E.T.*, he hadn't done any of those films. Goldie, who was trying to make the leap, saw immediately what it would be." On the plus side, according to Bachrach, the film "allowed all of us to see her in a new light. She's not just some wriggling bimbo with blond hair." Shapiro also commented that the role was, in many ways, a sort of initiation for Goldie. "This was her first dramatic role. There's some black humor running through *Sugarland Express*, but this was essentially a straight, hard-edged acting role for her."

Her career was thriving, but, Goldie Hawn's relationship with her husband Gus Trikonis continued to unravel. By December 1973, the disparity in income and celebrity pushed the couple to the breaking point. "Neither of them wanted to get a divorce," said Shapiro, "so they just filed for a legal separation." Goldie spoke of the disillusionment of marriage, saying, "Basically, the big fantasy of cooking dinner every night and wearing an apron and bringing up your children and making wonderful talk with hubby when he comes home . . . I mean, it's an enormous responsibility, and you can't mix that with work, God knows." While Goldie adjusted to single life, *Sugarland Express* opened in the spring of 1974. The movie failed to generate much heat at the box office, but critics agreed it was her finest performance to date.

As Goldie approached her thirtieth birthday, she was ready to take control of her life and her career. In a bold move, she left the William Morris Agency and Art Simon. Despite attempts on both sides to be cordial, Goldie eventually ended up in court. Simon sued her for six and a half million dollars, charging breach of contract. Goldie settled the case out of court, but the setback was only temporary. Soon enough, according to Shapiro, "Warren

Beatty came along with the offer of *Shampoo*. *Shampoo* was considered a risky project. It was basically taking the seventies and putting them into . . . not necessarily the most positive perspective." Beatty was set to direct and star in the film. He convinced Goldie to sign on for the project, but it cost him a bundle. Goldie's new agent negotiated a deal that included 7 percent of the profits. "She was talented, and she was very clever. This is rare in Hollywood among women of that generation, in a business sense," commented Judy Bachrach.

Shampoo was released in early 1975, and the racy sex romp scored big at the box office, but what Goldie wanted most—a family—was still a dream. Then fate intervened in an unlikely place: the first-class cabin of a jetliner where Goldie met a new man, musician Bill Hudson. Of that first meeting, Hudson remembered, "A guy in the band comes up and says, 'Look, that's Goldie Hawn over there,' and I remember looking over there and it was just like this golden light coming from the heavens." Goldie and Hudson, then twenty-five years old, clicked right away. His group, the Hudson Brothers, had a hit variety show on CBS and an album climbing the charts. Somewhere between New York and L.A., the two set their first date, which was "very romantic," according to Hudson. "There was something in the air." Mark Shapiro found that, in addition to Hudson's loving nature and humorous personality, "he was doing better than she was at that point. That was the beginning of a big part of the attraction."

Bill Hudson was also a family man. Abandoned by their father at a young age, he and his two brothers remained extremely close to their mother and to each other. Within a matter of weeks, Bill and Goldie were living together in the Bel Air home she once shared with her estranged husband. "We were enjoying one another. We were in what I thought was love," he summed up. Four months later, Goldie was pregnant. There was just one problem: Goldie was still married. Said Shapiro, "Goldie and Gus went back to court to legally file for divorce so Goldie could marry Bill Hudson. In the meantime, Goldie is pregnant and getting more pregnant by the minute." In June 1976, Trikonis agreed to a $75,000 divorce settlement: half the original purchase price of their Bel Air home. A month later, Goldie and Bill said their vows in the backyard of her parents' home in Maryland. The bride was eight months pregnant, and the ceremony was a disaster. During the event, officiated by both a priest and a rabbi, the priest's sleeve caught on fire while he was uniting the bride and the groom; then, Goldie couldn't complete the Jewish tradition of breaking a glass until the second try. All of this did not bode well for the young couple, but they were too in love to notice.

Goldie and Bill settled into a new home in Malibu and anxiously awaited the birth of their baby. They waited . . . and waited . . . and waited. Finally, on what should have been a joyous occasion, Goldie went into labor in her tenth month of pregnancy on September 7, 1976. But there were complications. "She had a cesarean section, and he was so big. He was in there too long, and he had breathed the fluid in and suffered from what they told me was called meconium aspiration, which has all this bacteria," remembered Hudson. Oliver Rutledge Hudson came into the world weighing a hearty eleven pounds, but he was extremely ill. "He was on a respirator and had IVs in his head. There were two times where they called me from the room in the middle of the night, saying he wasn't going to make it through to the morning," said Hudson. Thirty-year-old Goldie was also in bad shape. She suffered with a high fever and couldn't get out of bed. Hudson was worried and afraid. But the new parents refused to give up on baby Oliver. Hudson remembered, thinking, "I love this boy and so does she. He's not dying, and we are going to have our son." A week later, the baby's fever broke, and his condition rapidly improved. Oliver was allowed to leave intensive care and return home.

After the trauma of nearly losing her child, Goldie Hawn was more than happy to put her career on hold to care for Oliver. She took a year off and even declined the coveted role of Lois Lane in *Superman*. Meanwhile, *The Hudson Brothers* show was canceled by CBS, but the group still drew big crowds on tour. "For a time, the family life was good. The marriage was good, and it was like Oliver coming into the picture cemented it," said Mark Shapiro. In late 1977, Goldie grew restless with life as a stay-at-home mom. Then, an ideal project came along: the movie *Foul Play*, a comedy-thriller costarring Chevy Chase. "They wanted Farrah Fawcett, who was hot at the time on *Charlie's Angels*," recalled Bill Hudson. But, he maintained, "Goldie was the right one for *Foul Play*, there's no question about it." The chemistry between Goldie and Chevy was pure screen magic. *Foul Play* hit theaters in July 1978 and was a huge hit.

While Goldie was back on top, Hudson's career was bottoming out. Album sales hit the skids, and concert dates dried up. "We had started doing Vegas and Atlantic City," said Hudson with some regret. "For the Hudson Brothers, it was more on the downside of our career." In the summer of 1978, the group took another shot at television. They filmed a syndicated variety show in London. Meanwhile, thirty-two-year-old Goldie starred in *Lovers and Liars*, a small, art-house film produced in Rome. The globe-trotting couple began to drift apart. Hudson attributed their dissolving marriage to a mounting emotional and geographical distance between the pair as well as the craziness surrounding the success of *Foul Play*. Still, sometime during a rendezvous in London, Goldie conceived a second child. This pregnancy was different. Goldie planned to work straight through to the end.

Goldie Hawn formed a production company and learned on the job how to be a producer. Lawrence Grobel praised her drive and determination. "Goldie could easily be a studio mogul if she wanted to. When she gets passionate about something, she goes ahead and does it." He continued, "And that's just what happened with *Private Benjamin*." *Private Benjamin* told the story of one Judy Benjamin, a naïve rich girl who gives up her pampered lifestyle for the U.S. Army. Goldie began to shop around her pet project to studio executives when she was already six months pregnant. In April 1979, the go-go-getter cut a deal with Warner

Bros. to produce and star in the film. Her contract included back-end points if the film was a success. "It was a smart thing, one of the smartest things she's ever done. She found a vehicle that was good for her, and she went ahead and did it," commented Grobel.

A few days later, on April 19, 1979, Goldie delivered her second child, Kate Gerry Hudson. Laughed Goldie, "Katie came out, I mean . . . you *know* with your children. She didn't come out saying 'I want to read Proust.' She came out saying, 'Da-da-daaaaa! Mommy, I'm here!'" Despite his happiness over the birth of a beautiful, healthy baby girl, the blessed event was bittersweet for Bill Hudson. "There was just one moment, one glimmer, when Kate was born, of 'Maybe this could still work out,' you know? Kate brought joy into an otherwise sad situation." Just weeks after Kate's birth, thirty-four-year-old Goldie went into production on her other labor of love, *Private Benjamin*, which Judy Bachrach described as "a nice Jewish girl in an unlikely situation but showing some of Goldie's determination and strength in the character itself." Baby Kate and Oliver watched their mom in action.

"She was so into the idea of playing a woman in basic training and in a combat situation that she actually went through six or eight weeks of real boot camp. It was at moments like this where you saw the real, strong-willed Goldie Hawn," said Mark Shapiro. Armand Assante, who costarred in the movie with Goldie, applauded her positive portrayal of women. "She made women feel good about themselves. It wasn't just about a character saying, 'I'm in the army now. I want to break from the routine.' It was about proclaiming 'I'm a person, and I want to break from the routine and all the angst that women have.'" Goldie also soldiered through the casting process, signing top-notch actors Eileen Brennan and Harry Dean Stanton. There was also a lesser-known actor Hawn took a liking to, Frenchman Yves Renier, who auditioned for the role of Henri, Judy Benjamin's French love interest. Ultimately, Renier did not get the part. Goldie gave the role to Assante instead.

Private Benjamin started shooting in early 1980. Goldie Hawn juggled the dual roles of producer and star. According to Assante, as a producer she "really was at the helm. Goldie really held the reins of the project. She had a tremendous understanding of what she wanted as a producer and as an actress." When *Private Benjamin* moved to Paris for its final scenes that summer, Goldie reportedly ran into a friendly face, Yves Renier. By the time production wrapped, she was spending a lot of time with him. Though Goldie has never to this day divulged any details of an affair with Renier, rumors of a romance floated across the ocean. According to Shapiro, for Bill Hudson the thought of Goldie being unfaithful "was the last straw."

On August 15, 1980, he filed for divorce. The cold reality of a second failed marriage left Goldie shell-shocked. In public, said Shapiro, "She was dismissing the marriage and the divorce, saying that sometimes these things don't work. But in private moments there was a lot more going on."

Rarely one to let personal turmoil put a damper on her professional ambition, Goldie Hawn went back to work on the film version of Neil Simon's *Seems Like Old Times*. The slapstick comedy reunited her with *Foul Play* costar Chevy Chase. Goldie, however, was stretched thin. She was starring in a film, editing *Private Benjamin*, and being mom to Oliver and Kate. Armand Assante, who witnessed Goldie's hectic lifestyle, still credited her with "very much balancing her life as an actress and a producer and a mom. Her kids were around all the time, and it was a very lovely feeling, and I have the feeling that probably in all her films she creates automatically a sense of familiarity. It's quite wonderful to be around."

The long hours and grueling schedule paid off. On October 10, 1980, *Private Benjamin* opened to rave reviews and huge box-office returns. In addition, for the first time in her life, Goldie was popular with feminists. The role had also gained her the admiration of the Academy, and she was nominated for a Best Actress Oscar. "I was just jumping up and down like a little girl," squealed

Goldie at the time. She also felt validated by the acknowledgment of her colleagues: "The best of it is that Nancy Meyers, Charles Shyer, and Harvey Miller were also nominated for Best Screenplay, and Eileen Brennan was also nominated for Best Supporting Actress. We are going to have a big party." On March 31, 1981, Sissy Spacek took home the coveted Oscar for her role in *Coal Miner's Daughter*. Still, Goldie's work on *Private Benjamin* marched her into some elite company. "She is probably one of the few actresses who emerged from a show like *Laugh-In* to being a major international film star. It was a big plus for her career," commented Assante. Goldie also received a boost of confidence from the film's success, commenting in hindsight that "suddenly everything changed. I became a movie mogul. Suddenly I became a person who can carry a movie by herself."

Goldie Hawn was riding high. She had two beautiful, healthy children, critical and public acclaim, and an asking price of a half million dollars per film. Unfortunately for Goldie, her happiness was tempered by sorrow. All during this time, she was finalizing her divorce from Bill Hudson, and her soon-to-be ex-husband was anxious to settle. He was engaged to *Laverne & Shirley* star Cindy Williams and set to marry in three months. On March 9, 1982, the divorce was official. Goldie was awarded full custody of the children and given two homes. She was philosophical about the end of her marriage. "I'm not going to lie and say I'm the most perfect person in the world to live with, because I'm not," she admitted, "and I think we all come with our bag of problems, but the outside, extenuating circumstances are much bigger than both of us."

While Goldie's husband left her life, her father was slowly wasting away. In January 1982, he fell ill with emphysema. Edward Hawn, who had been living in L.A. for ten years, was admitted to Cedars-Sinai Medical Center while Goldie was on the set of another romantic comedy, *Best Friends*, costarring Burt Reynolds. "She was very much her father's daughter. This hit her very hard. She was obligated to do *Best Friends*, but it was emotionally probably one of the worst times for anybody to be working, let alone working a high-pressure motion picture," summed up Mark Shapiro. Goldie began to realize that it would be better if "God would take him, [her father] because he was so unhappy and so ill." On July 7, 1982, Edward Rutledge Hawn died at the age of seventy-three. Goldie characterized the loss as "a big emptiness that has never been filled up," adding, "I want to have just one more day, five more minutes."

On top of this trauma, a sudden and unexpected calamity occurred. On October 28, 1982, three months after the death of her father, Goldie dined out with her *Private Benjamin* costar Eileen Brennan. As they were leaving the restaurant, Lawrence Grobel said, "Eileen started to cross the street, and a car came and hit her and crushed her legs, and Goldie thought she might have died. Goldie was right there. She was on top of it. She was screaming and trying to calm Eileen down." Brennan, then forty-eight years old, was rushed to the hospital with life-threatening injuries. Goldie blamed herself for the accident and fell into a deep depression. "It was a tremendously emotional time for Goldie," according to Grobel. Brennan herself characterized the experience by saying, "I don't believe in accidents, but I do believe in angels, and I do believe that Goldie has been mine."

After an extremely painful and taxing year in 1982, the newly single Goldie threw herself back into work. The first project of 1983 came in the form of a World War II–era film called *Swing Shift*. The story considered war from another angle, explained Goldie, from the perspective of people at home. She quickly discovered that studio executives weren't interested in a war movie with no war in it. Assessed Mark Shapiro, "This was another script she's championed. She really wanted to do this. She went through the same situation trying to convince studios to do it." Offered Goldie, "I must say, when you do build your own empire—and God knows I have, and everybody else knows it, too—they don't knock on your door as readily as they would if you were just an actor or actress for hire." Goldie Hawn finally convinced the brass at Warner Bros. to green-light her movie. *Swing Shift* went into preproduction in late February 1983. Goldie had no idea her life was about to take a dramatic turn.

"One day, while she was casting the male lead in the film, who walks in but Kurt Russell? They kind of remembered each other from *One and Only, Genuine, Original Family Band,* and he gets up to leave at the end of the audition and says, 'Even if I don't get the part, I'd like to take you out some time.' Needless to say, Kurt got the part," said Shapiro. Russell, at thirty-two, had been acting in film and television for twenty-six years. He, like Hawn, was riding high on the success of his latest film, *Escape from New York.* Kurt's role as Goldie's love interest in *Swing Shift* soon led to romance off the set. "They both realized that they had to play it a little bit coy, because you don't want anybody on the film to know what's going on. People on the set during the making of *Swing Shift* would see them look in each other's eyes and hold hands and sneak off to the trailer every once in a while, so it was not a very well-kept secret," said Shapiro.

Goldie got along with her costar, but she was constantly butting heads with the director of *Swing Shift*. "Jonathan Demme was exerting control and influence on the film that Goldie was not happy about," said Shapiro. Hawn explained, "We had problems in the story with that film, and who our characters really were. So there were so many things that were undefined about who we were playing that it was very hard to get into those scenes where they just clicked and felt great." By the time *Swing Shift* wrapped in June 1983, Goldie was deeply in love with her Kurt. Goldie, Kate, and Oliver soon welcomed Russell and his two-year-old son, Boston, into the fold. "The kids really took to Kurt as Poppy, you know, and they called him that and he really became their father. They just wanted to be good parents to their kids," said Lawrence Grobel. Bill Hudson, on the other hand, already began to feel discontent with the way Goldie made "a conscious decision to say 'I'm going to make it my family, my way.'"

On April 13, 1984, *Swing Shift* opened to terrible reviews and dismal box office. Goldie Hawn realized that the role of producer seemed to hurt her acting career and experienced what she called "a backlash." People saw her as "a person who wanted to control everything I did," but, she clarified, "this was the perception, this was not the truth. Suddenly, I became kind of a one-man band. I mean, even directors would try to get out of my contract some things that I had won over the years, of approvals and things like that." Goldie and her new beau decided it was time to escape from the Hollywood scene. The couple bought a seventy-acre ranch in Colorado, where they intented to build their dream home. Offered Goldie, "Aspen, Colorado, for us is an answer to a lot of these things. Our children don't have time to watch MTV and this kind of assault on their purity. So that's why we love it there."

In the fall of 1984, Goldie went into production on another comedy, *Wildcats*. Six-year-old Kate Hudson watched her mother from the sidelines, green with envy. "Kate wanted to be in *Wildcats*, and I think her mom said the right thing—'If you want to be a stand-in, that's one thing, but you're not ready,'" described film critic Richard Roeper, adding, "Obviously, there are going to be charges of nepotism if she did, but probably it was a smart thing, a protective thing, of her not to thrust her daughter into the spotlight so quickly." Professionally, Goldie was frustrated by the old perception that she was little more than a ditzy blonde. "I think that people like to see me be funny, and I think that in a way it's difficult for me, because it doesn't allow me to branch out successfully, and all of the time I'm thinking, 'When is that moment going to come in my career that I find the absolute right script to do that will give me the canvas to be able to paint it with some neurotic, interesting woman that isn't necessarily a laugh a minute?'"

While Goldie waited for that special screenplay to come along, she found just the right vehicle to change her image—*Playboy* magazine. In November 1984, she shocked Hollywood by posing for the cover. Grobel, who interviewed Goldie for the magazine, described the cover as "very popular," and remarked on the fact that she was a standout among celebrity playmates. With this particular addition to her résumé, Goldie gave gossip hounds who questioned the legitimacy of her live-in relationship with Kurt Russell plenty to talk about. Proclaiming that they didn't need the Hollywood lifestyle, the couple and their kids commuted regularly between their homes in and around L.A. and their deluxe ranch in Aspen. The familial joys increased in November 1985, when Hawn got a big surprise for her fortieth birthday— she was pregnant with Russell's baby. Even though it was a dream come true, Goldie's age and her previous mishap with Oliver did cause some worry, but on July 10, 1986, she gave birth to son Wyatt Russell. "Our life is full. It's wonderful. It's as good as anything could ever get," beamed Goldie.

Despite a stable and happy partnership, with three divorces between them the new parents had no plans to marry. This decision was and continues to be a cause for much discussion among those who see the pair at events and write about them regularly. Lawrence Grobel attributed their choice to bypass marriage to the fact that "they felt secure in the relationship they had, and that's all that really matters for the kids. What's a piece of paper? And who would get more between Kurt and Goldie if they had to split up?" Mark Shapiro again brought up the fact that Goldie's previous marriages had been hurt by her success. "I think Goldie had it in her by this time that anybody she had a relationship with at this point had to meet a certain criterion. If it's an actor, he's going to have to be doing at least as well as she is."

In early 1987, Kurt and Goldie found a project that would make them acting partners for the first time since *Swing Shift* as well as enrich their bank accounts. *Overboard* was a screwball comedy about a rich amnesiac (Goldie) who gets conned by a conniving widower (Kurt) and his four sons. With Oliver, Kate, Boston, and baby Wyatt in tow, shooting became a family affair. Eight-year-old Kate—whose "entrance in the room was always a main event," according to Goldie—didn't have a part in the movie, but she was already showing signs of stardom. *Overboard* sunk with audiences and critics when it opened on December 16, 1987. The couple was hit hard by the failure of their second on-screen venture. "It stopped the two of them from doing another film together," speculated Grobel.

Goldie Hawn's personal life was also troubled. Her ex-husband Bill Hudson wasn't happy with the amount of time Oliver and Kate spent in Aspen. According to him, Goldie repeatedly ignored his visitation rights, and he lashed out in the press, calling her a "cold-eyed shark." Goldie didn't hold back either, and in a *Vanity Fair* article she compared Hudson to a "baby" and a "scorned woman." Defending himself, he remarked, "I'm in this position where I don't want to be the guy who says, 'It's my weekend, and my kids are coming with me,' and Goldie says, 'Your father wants you. You can't have fun on the slopes of Aspen.' I was set up to fail. If it was Thanksgiving, and they were in New York, what am I going to do?"

While Hawn and Hudson battled, their daughter threw herself into acting classes. In the fall of 1989, eleven-year-old Kate was accepted into the children's division of the esteemed Santa Monica Playhouse Conservatory. Of her training, she noted, "I took voice lessons. I played the piano. I think it was really important for my mom, because she knew I always wanted to act." Offered Evelyn Rudie, co-artistic director of the Santa Monica Playhouse, "Kate was very talented, but more than that she was very serious. She was extremely serious for a girl of her age, and the other kids liked her a lot. She was very focused. She had a lot of energy and a lot of enthusiasm." Kate studied hard for four months. By the spring of 1990, she was anxious to put her talent to the test by auditioning for *The Howie Mandel Show*. "She auditioned, she actually got the part, and, believe it or not, Goldie Hawn just didn't want her to get it, and didn't tell her," said Ken Baker, West Coast executive editor of *US Weekly*. As far as Goldie was concerned, her daughter was still not ready for showbiz. An entire year passed before Goldie revealed the truth to Kate. Said Baker, "It actually turned out to be one of the best bits of parenting she could have done, because she really preserved Kate to find her own acting skills and to blossom without the public eye on her."

By 1991, Goldie had dodged the slings and arrows of Hollywood for more than two decades. She also had survived two marriages and one nasty battle over child visitation rights. Meanwhile, she was still hounded by questions about whether she would marry Kurt Russell. "People ask me all of the time, will you and Goldie ever get married?" commented Russell. "It's a fascinating question to me. Why do you care? I could never figure it out. I still can't figure it out. What business is it of yours? I don't respond to it, nor does it mean anything."

Goldie Hawn had other things on her mind, namely, her career. She needed a hit after a string of movie flops. Her salvation came with the outrageous 1992 comedy *Death Becomes Her*, costarring Bruce Willis and Meryl Streep. "I loved being able to play this crazed, maniacal character—someone who is just hate-driven. Who is able to be fat and plain and deprived and depraved," Goldie summed up. "There were just a whole mess of reasons why I wanted to do this movie." But the fun was cut short when Goldie's mother, Laura Hawn, suffered a severe heart attack. Goldie tried to maintain her production company while caring for her ailing mother, but found that her "heart really wasn't in it. It was time to take off. It was time to leave something that I've been doing a long time and be with my family." In the summer of 1992, *Death Becomes Her* was released. The film eventually earned $150 million worldwide and became Goldie's biggest hit to date. At forty-six, the golden girl proved she was still fun, sexy, and hot.

Goldie's success didn't go unnoticed by her thirteen-year-old daughter. *Vanity Fair*'s Leslie Bennetts paraphrased something Kate once said to her, remarking, "You know, there's your mother, and she's gorgeous. She's a movie star, and she's on magazine covers. And you get to be a teenager and you say to yourself, 'Well, what about me? Am I beautiful, too?' And you compare yourself to her. She's a hard act to follow." But on November 27, 1993, mother and daughter were both heartbroken when eighty-year-old Laura Hawn passed away. Goldie realized that she needed to take some time to "understand what life was really all about and know how to live without her." She focused on being a better mom to Oliver, Kate, Wyatt, and Russell's son Boston. When Kate celebrated her sixteenth birthday, Goldie adopted a different view of her daughter's dream of being an actress.

When Goldie Hawn finally warmed up to Kate Hudson's acting as a potential career, the opportunities seemed to pour in. First, under Goldie's advice, Kate worked summer stock to see what the acting life was really like. In 1996, she landed her first small role on the popular television series *Party of Five*. That same year, Goldie turned fifty, and her light continued to shine. As Kate's career was getting started, Goldie flaunted her talent in an all-star cast for the film *The First Wives Club*. Along with Bette Midler and Diane Keaton, she completed a trio of women who wreak havoc on their cheating exes. According to Judy Bachrach, some of the implicitly biographical elements in the film cut a little close— "Here was a beautiful blond actress playing a beautiful blond actress. Here was an aging woman playing an aging woman. Here was a woman playing a lady who had gotten a lot of plastic surgery. A lot of liposuction. Maybe Goldie didn't like that so very much." Still, she didn't pass it up.

Seeing three legendary actresses work had a profound effect on sixteen-year-old Kate Hudson. "At the end of *The First Wives Club*, there is this huge dance number, so we had a lot of rehearsals," said director Hugh Wilson, "and that was the first time Goldie introduced me to this lovely high school student, Kate, who was sitting politely by, watching the rehearsal." On September 20, 1996, *The First Wives Club* became a box office smash, eventually making more than $100 million. Goldie was back on top again. After years of fighting for autonomy in her career and for an image beyond that of the "ditzy blonde," Goldie Hawn figured out that, as Mark Shapiro put it, "People want to see her as the funny, comedic actress. That's what she's given them. You don't want to say that she's given up, but in that sense, she's given up. She's basically saying, 'Okay, if this is the only thing that people are going to want to see me in, this is what I am going to give them.'"

In May 1997, eighteen-year-old Kate graduated from Crossroads High School in Los Angeles. The aspiring actress was accepted into New York University's prestigious Tisch School of the Arts, but she had other plans. Said Goldie's former director and head of the Beverly Hills Playhouse Milton Katselas, "Goldie had an idea that she would send Kate to university after studying with me for a while, and I said, 'You must be nuts. You can't do this.' She asked why, and I said, 'Well, within a year she's going to be a star.'" Katselas knew of Kate's talent and her drive. She had set her sights on professional acting and struck a deal with Goldie and Russell to defer her enrollment at NYU for a year and try her luck as a real actress. It took Kate only a month to land her first job, a supporting role in the indie drama *Ricochet River*. Her lifelong dream was finally coming true. In the movie, she played a naïve, small-town girl with big-city dreams. In reality, Kate Hudson was anything but naïve.

Kate followed *Ricochet River* with two more independent projects, *Desert Blue* and *200 Cigarettes*. "They were both films about rebellious youth and people finding their way," said Richard Roeper, adding: "But guess what? Nobody saw them. I mean, hardly anybody saw those movies when they came out, so she had a chance to develop a little bit of an on-screen persona." Kate, at nineteen, was getting an education no college could provide. Despite steady work, she remained in the shadow of her famous mother, but Kate said without hesitation, "If people want to associate me with my mother, that's fine, because I'm proud of my mother. I really have no problem with that." At the same time, mentioned Ken Baker, "She got tired of journalists asking her how much her mom was involved. In fact, it got to the point where, I know in one particular instance, her publicist went and told a journalist, 'Don't ask about Goldie Hawn.'"

Ironically, it looked like fifty-three-year-old Goldie Hawn's career was hitting a dry spell. In November 1998, she was dropped from the film version of *Chicago*. The part of Roxie Hart eventually went to a much younger actress, thrity-three-year-old Renée Zellweger. "I think that Goldie's star was fading as a big-time, money-making commercial actress," said Lawrence Grobel.

As soon as Kate's career began to soar, the gossip magazines started focusing on her personal life. She began to date Eli Craig, the son of another Oscar-winning actress, Sally Field. Speculated Baker, "Eli Craig was a lot older than Kate and had been at the acting game a long, long time, and Kate immediately was having this success, and I have to imagine that it did have some sort of strain on their relationship. Unfortunately, they broke up right when her career started taking off." Kate didn't stay single for long. "She always hung out with famous guys from a young age," said Baker. "She always sort of grew up in those celebrity circles. I remember learning that she was dating Matt LeBlanc from *Friends* and that she'd gone out with Lenny Kravitz. So we all started paying attention to 'Goldie Hawn's daughter.'"

Then, in early 1999, everything changed for Kate Hudson, who was still just nineteen. A script called *Almost Famous* was generating a lot of buzz, and she fell in love with the role of groupie Penny Lane. Cameron Crowe, the director of *Jerry McGuire*, had already cast Sarah Polley in the part. Then fate stepped in when Polley dropped out, and Kate got the gig. "It was so wonderful to go into that world and then to go there with Cameron. I wanted to make his story something special for him. So, working with him was very, very humbling and such a wonderful growing experience personally," summed up Kate. *Almost Famous* wrapped filming in the spring of 2000.

A few days later, Kate moved into her mother's apartment in New York City. She quickly went from playing the girlfriend of a rock star to being the girlfriend of a rock star when she fell hard for thirty-three-year-old Chris Robinson, lead singer of the Black Crowes. From the beginning, journalists questioned the relationship, suggested Leslie Bennetts, who cited the age difference and Robinson's divorced status. Added Baker, "When Kate hooked up with Chris Robinson, there she is, all cute and pretty and blond, and there's Chris Robinson . . . the scraggly look and the long hair. All the armchair psychologists in Hollywood came out and did their own little armchair analysis. Chris Robinson, the rock star, this is very much like Bill Hudson, and she must be in some way getting close to her father." Kate admitted that "all the rules went out the window when we met," but most people assumed that the relationship would be nothing more than a fling.

While Kate Hudson's personal life was creating buzz, so was her performance in Cameron Crowe's labor of love *Almost Famous*. Job offers poured in. Kate passed on *Spider-Man*, choosing *The Four Feathers* instead. She thought the period drama, which boasted two other up-and-coming leads in Heath Ledger and *American Beauty*'s Wes Bentley, would be "a real breakout role for her," according to Ken Baker. As Kate began to prepare for *The Four Feathers*, *Almost Famous* premiered at the Toronto Film Festival on September 8, 2000. Critics were blown away by her performance. "It's one of the most spectacular debuts that any actress or young actor has made," offered Richard Roeper, adding, "it's a great part, it's really well written, it's a complicated character, and she nailed the role. She owned that part. It was a blend of comedy and romance and drama, and we saw right off the bat her range." That same week, Kate graced the cover of *Vanity Fair* magazine.

However, as her mother had found out before her, with success there will always be doubters and speculators. Despite the great reviews for *Almost Famous*, many celebrity watchers thought the attention was premature. Remembered Baker, "I can't tell you how many people looked at that *Vanity Fair* cover and said, 'Who is that girl? Oh, Goldie Hawn's daughter. That's why she's on there. She doesn't deserve it.'" The press also focused on Kate's relationship with her father. Bill Hudson felt attacked, saying, "Kate has this huge press machine behind her and kind of started perpetuating that myth about me abandoning her." But, according to the *Vanity Fair* article, Kate Hudson did feel abandoned. She said, "I know what went on with the divorce, but the bottom line is you call your kids on their f-ing birthday." Bill Hudson countered, "Even though there was a period where we were, uh, estranged, um, I was there for most of it." Leslie Bennetts explained that, in the end, Kate felt disappointed by Bill's lack of attention, but concluded that "she did get really good fathering, it just wasn't from her birth father."

Despite her personal troubles, by September 2000, Kate was becoming a bona fide movie star. She was also making plans for her future with Chris Robinson. The September 13 premiere of *Almost Famous* in New York City was a star-studded affair. Critics began using the words "Oscar" and "Kate Hudson" in the same sentence. The media played up another big story that night, too, when reporters spotted a huge diamond on the twenty-one-year-old's left hand, but Kate denied she was engaged. On December 21, she received a Golden Globe nomination for Best Supporting Actress. Ten days later, on December 31, Kate shocked Hollywood by marrying thirty-four-year-old Chris at the family ranch in Aspen. One person was specifically left off the guest list—Bill Hudson.

On January 21, newlywed Kate sparkled on her husband's arm as she walked down the red carpet at the Golden Globes to vie for the same award her mother had won thirty-one years earlier for *Cactus Flower*. Like Goldie Hawn, Kate Hudson came away a winner. "It was the most exciting thing ever. I was totally overwhelmed," she said of the experience. Then, on February 13, she received an Academy Award nomination for Best Supporting Actress—just like her mom did three decades before. And, as her mother had been, she was also in England when she got the news. "I'll be honest," confided Kate, "my mom's and my life have been very synchronized. It is quite bizarre. You know, she found out when she was nominated while working in London. Same thing happened to me. We both got married at the same age. So, yeah, it's pretty amazing, actually. I feel blessed to have her as a mother and a mentor." Finally, the big night of the Seventy-third Academy Awards arrived, and all bets were on Kate. Goldie expressed mixed feelings about her daughter's instant success, "It was very exciting. It was incredibly interconnected. You know, she's my child. I wish that she would win. I wish that she wouldn't win. There are many conflicting things because she is so young."

However, on March 25, 2001, history failed to repeat itself. Unlike her mother, Kate didn't take home the Oscar. According to film critic Richard Roeper, some believed Kate lost because "she was so young. It may have worked against her." Roeper added, "This kid has already had a lot of breaks in her life." But Kate's youth did not protect her from one of the darker sides of fame. In a shocking blow, she found out that "her personal assistant had embezzled over $60,000 from her and was using it to buy gifts and things like that," said Ken Baker. On August 15, 2001, Kate Hudson filed a lawsuit against Margaret Miller in Los Angeles County Superior Court. Miller was ordered to pay off a promissory note of $35,000 to her former employer. "I think it really upset her. I know that Kate isn't the type to want to sue people, but she had to, and she was proved right," decided Baker.

Kate and Goldie continued to make Hollywood history. On September 17, 2002, the pair became the first mother and daughter to have films released on the same day. Kate starred in *The Four Feathers*. Goldie offered up *The Banger Sisters*, a comedy costarring Susan Sarandon. Hawn and Sarandon played aging groupies who reunite after their lives take different paths. Exactly two years after Kate made her mark as a "band aid" in her breakout role, Goldie's turn as a groupie trumped *Four Feathers*. Audiences didn't connect with the overblown epic style of Kate's picture. Kate's relationship also hit a sour note with Black

Crowes' fans when Chris Robinson decided to pursue a solo career away from the band. "Crowe-heads" made a new Yoko Ono of Kate, vilifying her for allegedly causing the split.

Kate went back to work in the fall of 2002. She starred opposite Matthew McConaughey in the romantic comedy *How to Lose a Guy in 10 Days*. Director Donald Petrie was pleased because Hudson and McConaughey "had such an easygoing chemistry that allowed me to let them experiment." *How to Lose a Guy in 10 Days* opened on February 7, 2003, and was a box-office smash. Suddenly, Kate was bankable again. Her asking price jumped from $4.5 million to $7 million per picture. The good news kept on coming. A month after the premiere of her movie, she discovered she was pregnant. The golden, beaming twenty-three-year-old was adding "mother" to her résumé. Richard Roeper claimed, "I think the fact that she got married at such a young age and that she is now starting a family at such a young age might actually help her as an actress in the long run."

Ready to make her mother a grandma (or "Glam-Ma," as Kurt Russell would describe Goldie in later interviews), a pregnant Kate attended two premieres for her new movies in the spring of 2003. Though *Alex & Emma* and *Le Divorce* were both box-office disappointments, Hudson's family rallied behind her. "I call them 'Goldie's Tribe,'" appraised George Schlatter. "It's interesting how much that family loves one another. They are totally, tightly knit and in love with one another. They care about one another." As Kate's twenty-seven-year-old brother Oliver pursued an acting career of his own, Goldie and Kurt saw a different kind of star power in their seventeen-year-old son, Wyatt. As a talented goal tender in hockey, Wyatt inspired Goldie and Kurt to buy a house in Vancouver, British Columbia, splitting their time between the ice rink and the sound stage. The decision to move north wasn't made on a whim. Wyatt started playing hockey as a young kid. Ironically, Kurt became even more familiar with the sport when he won the part of coach Herb Brooks in the Disney film *Miracle*, which told the incredible story of the 1980 Olympic hockey team. As Kurt Russell poured his heart and soul into that part, Goldie Hawn was preparing for her new role as a grandmother.

One thing that prepared her to become a mentor for Kate's first child was a "sense of spirituality," commented Lawrence Grobel, as well as an "understanding of joy like few people I know, and she wanted to do a book about it." That dream came true in February 2003, when Goldie put her feelings on paper and signed a deal to write a memoir about her life, her career, and her spiritual journey. Asked Goldie, "How was I to know that not only can I achieve my lifelong dream of happiness but, in the midst of this insane and crazy business, that my joy would grow with every passing year?" As for Goldie's marital plans, she and her life partner have no plans to "fix what ain't broke." Agreed Kate, "They've been together for twenty years. They're already married. They're not planning on getting married. I'm sure everybody would love to see them tie the knot eventually, but I don't think that will happen. They're happy people. Twenty years later—still going."

On January 7, 2004, Goldie and Kate celebrated another milestone as Kate's baby boy, Ryder Russell Robinson, was welcomed into the world. Said Kurt Russell, "I was thrilled that they included my name in his. It was really an amazing surprise to me. It meant a great deal to me, obviously." The addition of Ryder seemed to fuel even more mother-daughter comparisons. Said George Schlatter, "Everything that Goldie was and is has been handed down to Kate. Kate is not Goldie, but there's no way that she is not Goldie's daughter." Offered Mary Murphy, "It's really quite amazing to me that these two women, obviously, from everything I know about them, are best friends. Really, mother and daughter—best friends. I am amazed that Kate has been able to carve out such an independent career for herself." As for the family matriarch, Goldie Hawn continues to make her own rules and live life on her own terms. "When you look at Goldie's life, she's a giggly girl from *Laugh-In* . . . she's had two failed marriages, she's lost both of her parents, one of her best friends got run over in front of her eyes. It hasn't been the easiest life in the world, but it has been a very rich life," said Grobel. And who better to have the final say on Goldie but the dynamo herself? "All the time I wouldn't change for anything in the world," she affirmed. "I mean, it's been a gift. I've enjoyed it. I've made the most of it."

CHAPTER 15

UNLIKELY ROMANCE

The Arnold Schwarzenegger and Maria Shriver Story

"The most unlikely two people to get together that I could imagine."

—Douglas Kent Hall, *Schwarzenegger biographer*

His world is synonymous with muscles and mayhem. Her world revolves around the Kennedys and Camelot. Born eight years apart and more than 7,500 miles away from each other, the odds against Arnold Schwarzenegger and Maria Shriver ever meeting, let alone marrying, were staggering. He is known as Mr. Universe, the Terminator, and governor. She is known as an award-winning journalist, devoted mother, and first lady. He's a Republican. She's a Democrat. Arnold and Maria, an unlikely tale with more twists and turns that any big-screen blockbuster. Said Arnold's on-screen costar Sandahl Bergman, "I mean, really, you're talking about a Kennedy and a bodybuilder." This is their story.

Arnold Alois Schwarzenegger was born in Thal, Austria, on July 30, 1947. He was the second son of Gustav and Aurelia Schwarzenegger. Gustav was the town's police chief. Aurelia was a homemaker. Described Arnold's former girlfriend Barbara Outland Baker, "This was a family recovering in Austria postwar. No one had much wealth in the community. The school system was rigorous." School was challenging, but Arnold's father was even more demanding. Gustav was a former member of the Nazi Party. Professor Michael Blitz clarified, "If you were an adult male in Austria or Germany, and you weren't Jewish, you were going to be in the Nazi party. He was not involved in any particular atrocities." As Arnold described his childhood, discipline ruled the Schwarzenegger household. "We had a very strict upbringing because of him being on the police force," he said. "We had to be the perfect example—couldn't do anything bad. And it was kind of uptight feeling at home because of it."

"Gustav Schwarzenegger was a big guy. He behaved like he was a strong man, like this serious 'Arnold, don't do that, do that,' and nothing was funny," characterized Arnold's friend and former Mr. Olympia Franco Columbu. Barbara Baker agreed, "It wasn't from Arnold's father that he became so warm and loving." Arnold and his brother, Meinhard, turned to their mother for comfort and understanding. It was survival of the fittest. One year younger than Meinhard, Arnold had a tough time measuring up. "Meinhard was the firstborn, and so, I think, whether rightly true or not, Arnold felt as if Meinhard was the preferred son," said Baker. Added Wayne DeMilia, former vice president of the International Federation of Bodybuilders, "He was always being pushed down, and he was always pushed to try harder, try harder."

Meanwhile, a world away, in Chicago, Illinois, Maria Shriver was born on November 6, 1955. Maria was the second child of Eunice and Sargent Shriver. Eunice's brother was John F. Kennedy. "If Arnold's father was a great disciplinarian, Sargent Shriver was a generous, loving parent. He is a true aristocrat," described J. D. Heyman, associate editor of *People* magazine. Television journalist Mary Alice Williams offered, "Eunice is a matriarch. She's a force to be reckoned with. She's lovely and embracing and inclusive with everyone—and very powerful." Laurence Leamer, author of *Sons of Camelot*, added about Eunice, "She's also one of the most impossible women of the twentieth century. She's a perfectionist. Nothing is ever good enough. But in terms of doing great work in the world, she's done that."

The Shriver family eventually grew to five kids while the Kennedy mystique soared to new heights. In January 1961, Maria's uncle Jack was sworn in as the thirty-fifth president of the United States, urging his citizens to "ask not what America can do for you, but what together we can do for the freedom of man."

The following year, Maria's dad was appointed director of the Peace Corps. The Shrivers relocated to Rockville, Maryland. "What sets the Shrivers apart from the other Kennedy families is how normal their lives were," observed Lawrence Leamer. Maria got along famously with her older brother, Robert.

On the other hand, Arnold and his older brother were fierce rivals. "Meinhard was so good-looking. He was the guy that could find more girls than Arnold," said Franco Columbu. According to Wayne DeMilia, "His father favored his older brother, and his father ridiculed him. The father pitted one brother against the other." The two Schwarzenegger brothers competed at everything. Arnold was a solid player on the high school soccer team, but he wanted to be the best. Douglas Kent Hall, author of *Arnold: The Education of a Bodybuilder*, remarked, "He started doing lifts and things to get his legs built up. He loved the fact that his arms were starting to grow. He was a tall kid, weighed 150 pounds, but I think he enjoyed the pain. No pain, no gain."

Then, in 1962, fifteen-year-old Arnold Schwarzenegger had an epiphany. As he described himself, "Way back when I started training, I visualized what my body should look like to be the best in the world." He began pumping iron. He devoured protein meals and read muscle magazines. "All of a sudden he did get a lot of attention from the female set," recounted Barbara Baker. "He was really successful with girls on the lake." The young bodybuilder idolized the reigning Mr. Universe, Reg Park. Chuckled Park, "His mother apparently said she thought he was gay, because all his friends had photographs of pinups around the wall, and he had photographs of me, but nothing could be further from the truth."

"He just saw this massive muscular physique with the lats hanging and the pecs really full and shoulders shining," detailed Reg's son, trainer Jon Jon Park. To Arnold, Reg Park was much more than a bodybuilder. He was pure inspiration. Reg Park starred in several Hercules movies, which motivated Arnold to continue striving for physical perfection. Arnold recalled, "I went through this trip of 'Did you want to be strong like you see in the Hercules movies?' You get impressed by all that. You can't wait for the time to be a man. Kids grow out of that and go on. I never grew out of it. I wanted to be a strong man all the time." Arnold began molding himself after Park, who had everything Arnold wanted—plenty of cash and a successful movie career. "Arnold was always on his way to the United States. He must have always felt that Austria, the little town that he grew up in, even other big towns in Europe were still too small for him," speculated director Paul Verhoeven, who worked with Arnold on 1990's *Total Recall*.

While sixteen-year-old Arnold dreamed of living in America, America's dream of Camelot shattered. On November 22, 1963, John F. Kennedy was assassinated in Dallas. For eight-year-old Maria, her uncle Jack's death was a crushing blow. "Can you imagine how it defined the Kennedy family?" asked Mary Alice Williams. "It had to do with Maria's sense of her place in the world and her responsibility to the world." Offered Laurence Leamer, "They knew that the world was not a safe place. They knew that maybe their father was not safe." Many people believed the American dream died with forty-six-year-old John F. Kennedy.

Arnold Schwarzenegger wasn't one of them. "He always said he wanted to be a champion bodybuilder, become the biggest movie star in the world, and he said he wanted to go into politics," acknowledged Wayne DeMilia. But Hollywood and public service had to wait. On October 1, 1965, Arnold was drafted into the Austrian military. Yet all the eighteen-year-old could think about was bodybuilding. "There was a point during Arnold's year in the Austrian army when he heard of a contest for Mr. Junior Europe, and it was in Germany," said Douglas Kent Hall. Arnold pleaded with his commanding officers to allow him to compete. When they turned him down, the new recruit went AWOL.

As Hall told it, "He had only enough money for a third-class train ticket. He had to borrow posing trunks. He had to borrow the oil to oil up his body. He got there late, he went on stage, and he won the contest. It was the first time that he really knew what it felt like to be a winner." The thrill of victory didn't last long. Arnold was thrown into the brig for a week. Soon everyone on the base was buzzing about the young private's adventure. "He had won this trophy, and the majors in the army were impressed by this," said Hall. "They thought, 'Wow, this'll bring us some good publicity.'" Before he knew it, Arnold went into real basic training, working out up to six hours a day with army-bought equipment, and crafted his own routines and workouts.

In 1965, eighteen-year-old Arnold Schwarzenegger was serving in the Austrian army. He competed his one-year military obligation in the fall of 1966. He had pumped himself up to 225 pounds, and he wanted to get even bigger. He left Austria and moved to Munich, the mecca of European weight training. Franco Columbu became Arnold's workout buddy and friend. The two musclemen worked hard and played harder. Recalled Columbu, "I said, 'Beer is really good for working out. You sweat and get muscles.'"

Soon Arnold became the manager of a small gym on Schillerstrasse. He not only found a job, in fact, he also found a place to sleep—in a corner of the gym. Columbu laughed, "It was a tiny little room, and the bed was five feet long. I said, 'Arnold, if you lie down, what do you put outside the bed? The ankles or the head?'" Arnold continued to pump iron, and in late September 1966 he entered the Mr. Europe contest. He won, which qualified him for the Mr. Universe contest in London, where he came in second to a young American bodybuilder, Chet Yorton.

Then, in January 1967, Arnold finally met his childhood idol, Reg Park. Said Park, "I instinctively knew that I had an effect on him. I had an influence on him. I think he was once quoted as saying I was a fantasy father." Lou Ferrigno, a two-time Mr. Universe, offered, "When Arnold met Reg Park, he couldn't take his eyes off him, because he watched every move he made." According to Douglas Kent Hall, "Reg Park was somebody who could see in Arnold something his father couldn't see." Arnold studied Park, determined to follow in his footsteps and become Mr. Universe. Arnold religiously adhered to Park's rigorous weight-training program. "He would always want me to lead in the workout, pick the exercises, the sets, the reps," said Park, "and that was clever, because all he was doing was picking my brain."

The hard work paid off. In October 1967, Arnold Schwarzenegger won the Mr. Universe Amateur Division. He was only twenty years old, the youngest winner in history. But there was a catch. "When Arnold won his Mr. Universe title, he thought to himself, 'I'm King Kong. I'm the king of the world,'" said Hall, but "somebody mentioned to him that there was another Mr. Universe and another Mr. Universe. He said, 'Well, how can this be?'" Hall then explained, "There are different federations in bodybuilding, and each one of these federations has its contest." Arnold, however, wanted to be king of all bodybuilders. He returned to Munich more obsessed than ever.

"The way he chose to shock the muscles was to get a bunch of guys together, and they would carry out into the forest 250 pounds of weights and a keg of beer. They would eat food. They'd make love to women. It was a total orgy!" said Hall. Barbara Baker commented, "They were just so driven—their testosterone. This was the sixties now, it was very easy to find women and men who liked to engage in wild activities." Arnold's muscles were bulging, and, according to his autobiography, so was his ego. "He had been around in the bars having fights, generally making himself a nuisance because of being a celebrity, being arrogant. He had kicked people around just because he could," reported Hall.

Far from the macho world of bodybuilders, twelve-year-old Maria Shriver enjoyed a much different life in Rockville, Maryland. She was an "A" student at Stone Ridge of the Sacred Heart, a private Catholic girls school. She loved spending time with her parents, brothers, and famous cousins. According to good friend Theo Hayes, "Ethel and Bobby's kids were coming over to their house to play football or go swimming or whatever. Her mother and father really liked it when kids came to their house, and my parents were okay with that, so I was there a lot. We had sleepovers all the time." Sister Anne Dyer, headmistress of Stone Ridge, recalled, "Maria was an active, generous, happy, smiling, carefree kid. Her mother was active in parent activities and drove the carpool—did all the things that moms do."

"She loves her mother and father. Her mother is her best friend and vice versa," said Theo Hayes, who continued, "Mrs. Shriver was forming and molding into this person that was just aware of everything that was going on around her." In April 1968, Sargent Shriver was named ambassador to France. The Shrivers moved to Paris. "That was an important time," said Hayes. "Again, that made their family tighter, because it was just them, and they had to depend on each other. I know Maria really loved that experience living in the embassy. She learned to speak fluent French."

Not yet a teenager, Maria was fast becoming a woman of the world. Then, on June 5, 1968, tragedy struck the Kennedy family again. Democratic presidential candidate Robert F. Kennedy was shot to death in Los Angeles. In less than five years, Maria had lost two famous uncles. "The dual assassination had a profound impact on all of them—that these two healthy, vital men could be shot down in the prime of their lives," summed up Laurence Leamer. The death of Robert Kennedy was devastating, but the Kennedys soldiered on. On July 23, 1968, Maria's mother, Eunice, founded the Special Olympics in honor of her disabled sister, Rosemary.

Meanwhile, in September 1968, twenty-one-year-old Arnold Schwarzenegger won his second Mr. Universe title in the professional division. The competition was sponsored by the National Bodybuilders Association in London. There was no prize money, but Arnold walked away with an invaluable contact. Joe Weider, a publisher of bodybuilding magazines, made Arnold's dreams come true when he invited the young champion to America to train with the world's top bodybuilders. A few days later, Arnold hopped a plane for Miami. As he himself has said on many occasions, "America is still the land of opportunity."

"He had a dream of coming to America and being a sensation right away," said Douglas Kent Hall. On September 25, 1968, Arnold stepped on stage for another Mr. Universe contest. This one was sponsored by the International Federation of Bodybuilders. Arnold made an impact, but he still came in second to American Frank Zane. "He cried all night," said Hall, "that was his big dream. That was the point where the big dream had let him down." However, Arnold didn't hang his head for long. "He moved to California after that, and he learned how to refine his physique," recalled Lou Ferrigno.

In early 1969, Arnold's friend and workout buddy Franco Columbu arrived from Germany. They shared a small apartment in Santa Monica, near the legendary "Muscle Beach" in Venice, and the birthplace of weight training in the United States—Gold's Gym. "We would work out and then eat, then we would go to Venice Beach and work out in the sun just in shorts. This way we got a tan working out again," recalled Columbu. At the time, most serious bodybuilders took steroids to help build muscles. According to Arnold, he was one of them. He stopped using the drug in the early eighties when testing proved there were damaging side effects, but, back in 1969, he was concerned with only one thing—staying on top.

"Let's say, before a contest, if I get emotionally involved with a girl, that can have a negative effect on my mind and destroy my workout, so therefore I have to cut my emotions off and be kind of cold," Arnold admitted in a video interview. Hall agreed, "He didn't want to get romantically involved with them. His dreams just didn't have room for that." But in the summer of 1969, something unexpected happened: Arnold fell in love. The bodybuilding world took a sudden detour when he met Barbara Outland, a twenty-year-old hostess at Zuckie's, a popular deli.

"When I saw him sitting at the counter, of course eating french fries, he said, 'You are so sexy, I must ask you out,' and it was like, 'Okay, I think I'll say yes,'" mused Arnold's old girlfriend, now known as Barbara Baker. Arnold soon fell hard for Baker, who was at the time an English and history major at San Diego State University. "She was sophisticated," said Franco Columbu. "Arnold loved to converse with her." Hall agreed, "She was substantial. She was blond. Barbara was a person with a mind." Baker herself remembered, "I came from this academic world, and now I'm immersed into a world of pecs and biceps, and I didn't know there was such a thing as leg biceps."

In September 1969, Baker returned to school while Arnold landed his first film role in *Hercules in New York*. The salary for the lead role was anything but Herculean at a mere $12,000 for three months' work. Director Allan Seidelman chuckled, "I think I spent the first three days of dealing with Arnold talking to his right arm, because it was larger than most people." Still, Arnold had the time of his life in the Big Apple. "When you're a bodybuilder, and you're supposedly the best-built man in the world, women want to come after you. They think you're the best built in every single body part," remarked Wayne Demilia.

Arnold loved the attention, but he missed California and his girlfriend. "It was a real revelation for him to actually find that he cared," said Baker. *Hercules* wrapped in late 1969, and Arnold returned to Santa Monica. He didn't see Baker often, and when they did connect there were plenty of distractions. "I would have to kind of fend off women and men. Because gay men love muscular bodies by and large, they would make their advances known, and it's like, 'Come on, he's mine,'" grumbled Baker. Despite the lack of focus he showed to her at times, Baker loved Arnold for both his body and his mind. "I have never met anyone who has the ability to focus in the moment of now like he can. It's uncanny. It's surreal. It's almost metaphysical. I think that comes from his gym experience."

But Arnold Schwarzenegger's optimism couldn't save *Hercules in New York*. The low-budget film hit theaters in February 1970.

Critics trashed the movie and its star. J. D. Heyman called it "a classic 'B' movie. It's laughable." Esteemed critic Richard Roeper agreed, saying, "Based on his early work, I would not have guessed that he would have gone on to do anything other than probably get a job in the food service industry very quickly." Arnold licked his wounds and went back to the gym. On September 19, 1970, he was crowned Mr. Universe, beating his childhood idol, Reg Park.

Meanwhile, Maria Shriver and her family returned from Paris to their home in Rockville, Maryland. Maria, then fourteen years old, instantly made a name for herself at school. "She was on the newspaper here. She was headed in that direction. She certainly was a leader and involved in a lot of activities," commented Sister Anne Dyer. Laurence Leamer reasoned, "Maria had this incredible pressure from her mother. She wanted her kids to be perfect. She wanted them to go out in the world and to do great things. That was the mandate." But Maria also knew how to have fun. Laughed Theo Hayes, "It would never occur to me to tell a nun a joke. Whereas Maria would do that, or she would say something funny to get there." Eunice also brought Maria up "not to live through her beauty," said Leamer.

While Maria was funny, beautiful, and driven, Arnold was equally serious. On September 20, 1970, he won Mr. World just one day after winning the Mr. Universe contest. Four weeks later, he nailed the Triple Crown. He became Mr. Olympia, bodybuilding's ultimate prize. "Arnold is glamour and personality and energy that projects to whoever is in front of him. That is Arnold's way of doing things, to intimidate others and be better," characterized Franco Columbu. Over the next few months, Arnold toured the world in posing exhibitions, sometimes earning $10,000 for a competition. Ten grand was a sizable payment. Still, he was always thinking about clever ways to make money. In February 1971, Arnold and Columbu launched a new construction company, which struck gold in the wake of a particularly damaging earthquake.

Arnold also had success selling his image. "That was the first bulk of his money saved, which he then eventually applied to the down payment on not just a home but an apartment building," Barbara Baker mentioned. Douglas Kent Hall expanded, "Having possessions, having money, having power were important things for Arnold. Real estate was a way that he felt that he could get bigger." Unfortunately, in May 1971 Arnold's winning streak ended during a posing exhibition in South Africa. When a board collapsed, his knee was dislocated. Nevertheless, he pulled his leg out of the hole in the stage and continued to pose.

Still, the pain was excruciating. Doctors told Arnold he needed surgery right away. He refused and immediately made reservations to return to the States. According to Columbu, "He arrives in New York. He's changing planes. Arnold picks up a pay phone and says to me, 'Franco, I dislocated my knee. I'm coming back early, and I'm coming home. Pick me up from the airport.'" In the meantime, Columbu received a disturbing call from Arnold's parents, saying that Meinhard had died in a car accident. Franco broke the news to Arnold when Arnold arrived in Los Angeles. "He was shaken up more for his parents' sake," said Columbu. "Meinhard was as much a stranger as if, you know, he were a kid down the block. There was just not an incredible love between the two boys."

Arnold was rushed to a hospital in Inglewood for emergency surgery. Cringed Columbu, "They put a cast up to the knee, and it was so tight it almost exploded. It was so painful when I got there; he was, like, digging the cast out with his hand. He was opening it with his hands. That's the only time I saw him crying." Arnold made a speedy recovery. Five months later, in October 1971, the twenty-four-year-old won his second Mr. Olympia title. In February 1972, Barbara Baker graduated from San Diego State and returned to Santa Monica. The couple moved in together. "I was pretty sure that this would be the stepping stone to marriage," she said, "so why aren't we getting married? And he just couldn't say why not." Instead, Arnold kept busy with other engagements.

That same year, sixteen-year-old Maria Shriver discovered her passion for television. She recalled in an interview, "My senior year in high school, when my dad ran for vice president, I spent a lot of time in the back of the plane with the reporters. I thought to myself, 'This is what I want to do, because these people are energized about their job. It changes every day. They're almost in school, because they're learning all the time, they're writing, they're creating.' And I thought, 'This is what I want to do.'" Said Theo Hayes, "She loved every second of it. She loved campaigning, she loved being on the plane. She loved listening to her father." Sargent Shriver teamed up with presidential candidate George McGovern on the Democratic ticket. Voters went to the polls on November 7, 1972. The pair was trounced by Richard Nixon and his running mate, Spiro Agnew.

Ironically, Nixon was one of Arnold's heroes. As Maria's family was suffering political setbacks, tragedy struck the Schwarzenegger household again. This time, it was Arnold's father. At the age of sixty-five, Gustav suffered a fatal stroke on December 11, 1972. "Toward the end of Gustav's life, Arnold was able to go over there about six months before, and there was a completion. That's very nice. He did get some degree of acknowledgment from his father," said Baker. Arnold ultimately chose not to go to the funeral. "He was getting ready for a contest, and he couldn't pull himself away from his routine," explained Hall.

By late 1972, twenty-five-year-old Arnold had muscled his way to the top of the bodybuilding heap. He wanted desperately to succeed as an actor, like his idol Reg Park, but Hollywood producers weren't exactly busting down his door. "They said, 'Look, forget it. Your body looks strange. Your accent is strange. Your name cannot be pronounced. Beat it,'" Arnold recalled. He had no choice but to concentrate on his bodybuilding career. Then, in November 1974, *Pumping Iron* was published. The book focused on the art of the muscle business. George Butler took more than 7,500 photographs of Arnold. "You supposedly got a window into this world people didn't understand and thought was bizarre and relegated to the back pages of comic books, Charles Atlas–type ads," explained J. D. Heyman. The book became a surprise best-seller.

Arnold Schwarzenegger's relationship with his live-in girl-friend, however, wasn't doing so well. "I really wanted to get married," said Barbara Baker. "He thought that his father's marrying at the age of forty was a really good age to get married." In April 1975, the couple broke up after six years together. Douglas Kent Hall commented, "She had different desires from Arnold. She wanted a quiet life—this was not Arnold." Said Baker, "He's such a jokester, and there's that level at which you can joke and there's an edge. There's just that little edge where it's like, 'No, that goes to hurt. I don't want to be the brunt of your jokes. I want to be the love of your life.' This is not a man who understood intimacy."

As Arnold ended his first serious relationship, Maria was be-ginning to explore her love life and her ambitions as a student at Georgetown University. "It's a natural thing for Maria, having four brothers. She understands boys, men. She gets it, and she had lots of boyfriends that were obviously very romantically in-terested in her," said Theo Hayes. In spring 1975, nineteen-year-old Maria took a part-time job off campus. "She worked at this seafood bar at this restaurant in Georgetown. I think she did it just for the fun of it."

Maria Shriver wanted to blend in. Arnold Schwarzenegger wanted to stand out. Later that spring, he landed a small role as a personal trainer in *Stay Hungry*, a drama about an ambitious real estate developer who attempts to buy a seedy gym. "He wasn't just a grunt or a weight lifter," said Arnold's acting coach, Eric Morris. "He had a sensitivity. He had a romantic aspect of his per-formance, and he had a depth and people obviously saw it. *Stay Hungry* opened in April 1976 to weak box office, but Arnold re-ceived strong reviews. In December 1976, the Hollywood Foreign

Press Association shocked the showbiz community by honoring twenty-nine-year-old Arnold with the Golden Globe Award for Most Promising Newcomer. He was the talk of the town.

The glory-bound muscleman scored again with critics on his next film project, released in January 1977. Offered film critic Richard Roeper, "*Pumping Iron* is the key early moment in our appreciation of Arnold Schwarzenegger as somebody a lot smarter than people might think at first glance." The film documented the Mr. Olympia contest in Pretoria, South Africa. Arnold was exposed as a powerful bodybuilder and master manipulator. He patted his own back on film, saying, "I don't have any weak points. It's perfect already. Oh yeah. It's down to a point. Wait when you see it."

Suddenly, Arnold Schwarzenegger was everywhere, and his ambitions were boundless. "I heard that Arnold wanted to marry into American royalty. Arnold wanted to marry into an influential political family, you heard these rumors," said Wayne Demilia. Press agent Bobby Zarem added, "The one thing that Arnold wanted most in the world was to meet Jacqueline Kennedy Onassis. It was a luncheon at Elaine's to promote the movie. They met, and the picture of them together appeared all over the world the next day." Arnold was thrilled to hobnob with Jackie O. In August 1977, Arnold met another member of the Kennedy clan, Eunice Shriver. The event was the Robert F. Kennedy Charity Tennis Tournament in Forest Hills, New York. But Arnold was more interested in Eunice's daughter than in watching tennis.

Twenty-two-year-old Maria noticed Arnold, too. He was tough to miss. "She approached her friend, Tom Brokaw," recounted J. D. Heyman, "and said, 'I want to meet that guy.' Tom Brokaw felt like if he didn't introduce her right away, she would have run over him." Arnold and Maria made an instant connection and took a plane straight to Hyannisport that day. "She knew what she wanted," said Heyman. Arnold's friends were stunned, because, according to Douglas Kent Hall, "They were the most unlikely two people to get together that I could imagine." Maria's

friends couldn't believe it, either. Theo Hayes expressed the sentiments of Maria's family, saying, "Maria, listen, you're going to
marry a lawyer. You're going to marry someone like your dad.
You know, this guy is just a phase."

"No mother would want Arnold Schwarzenegger knocking on
the door and going out with her daughter. Because here's this
muscle-bound guy who was assumed to be kind of stupid and
narrow. And guess what? He wasn't any of those things," commented Laurence Leamer. Over the next few months, Maria went
wild for her thirty-one-year-old Austrian paramour. "It was when
they first started calling each other 'baby'" that Hayes realized the
two lovebirds were the real deal. The couple was off to a great
start.

Maria Shriver's career was heating up, too. In the fall, she
nabbed her first TV news job at KYW in Philadelphia. According
to Heyman, "Maria was working hideously long hours. She really
did pay her dues. She ran errands, she brought people coffee. She
wasn't someone who traded on her Kennedy name." Maria belonged in television, and a year later, she accepted a job as a field
producer on *Evening Magazine* in Baltimore. Oprah Winfrey, then
twenty-two years old, also worked on the show. Said Hayes,
"When she saw Oprah on-camera is probably when she started
thinking about going on-camera herself." By 1979, Maria's television star was rising.

In early 1980, in her third year of seeing Arnold, Maria took
some time off to work for her uncle, Senator Edward Kennedy.
Uncle Ted was a long shot to win the Democratic presidential
nomination, and in August 1980, he dropped out of the race.
Maria wanted back in TV news, but this time on-camera. In the
summer of 1981, the twenty-five-year-old journalist landed a job
as an on-air correspondent for *PM Magazine,* a syndicated news
and entertainment show.

Arnold, on the other hand, was in a slump. His fifth film, *The
Villain,* was a clunker and flopped at the box office. He was furious. He hated to fail at anything. That fall, thirty-three-year-old

Arnold secured the title role in the fantasy adventure *Conan the Barbarian*. A few months later, he flew to Spain to start shooting the film. "It was invented for him, that story. Conan is the kind of guy, you can look at the comic books, it's like this enormous guy, and he had not much to say," commented *RoboCop* director Paul Verhoeven. "He looks like a man of steel, but he is a human being, so we all got banged up a lot," said Sandahl Bergman, his costar on the film.

Conan the Barbarian hit theaters in March 1982. Audiences flocked to see Conan take vengeance on his enemies. The film was Arnold's breakthrough. "Saying that Arnold was not good in that is almost missing the point. I mean, it's not requiring much. It's not like he beat out Olivier for the role," said Richard Roeper. "You can't really hurt his feelings. You cannot embarrass him. He will not show emotion, and this is from being a competitor," described Rae Dawn Chong, another of Arnold's costars, in a later film. But on September 17, 1983, Arnold showed plenty of emotion when he became a U.S. citizen. At thirty-six, he realized a life-long dream. "Today I'm finally an American citizen, and I feel just wonderful," he said.

That same month, twenty-seven-year-old Maria Shriver left *PM Magazine* for a junior on-air reporter position with *CBS Morning News* in Los Angeles. At the same time, rookie director James Cameron was prepping a low-budget film about a futuristic killing machine called *The Terminator*. O. J. Simpson was considered for the title role as the villain. Arnold Schwarzenegger auditioned to play the hero, Kyle Reece, but Cameron doubted the beefcake's ability to deliver the goods. "I had huge reservations, because the other character had twenty-five pages of expository dialogue," said Cameron, "and Arnold hadn't done that sort of work yet. He had only played Conan, and that's all I knew. So I suggested the Terminator, kind of cringing, thinking that he would get upset, and he loved the idea."

O.J. was out, and Arnold signed on to play an unstoppable killing machine bent on destroying mankind. However, actress

Linda Hamilton was not impressed with her costar. "I think I was inclined not to take it as seriously when I found out it was Arnold. Up to then, he hadn't done any significant acting work," she remembered. In March 1984, *The Terminator* began shooting in downtown Los Angeles. Arnold had only seventeen lines, one of which became an instant classic—"I'll be back." During the shoot, Cameron pushed cast and crew to the limit and beyond. *The Terminator* wrapped in June 1984.

Arnold immediately shed his black leather jacket and picked up a machine gun. In *Commando*, Arnold played a retired soldier hunting the kidnappers of his young daughter. Rae Dawn Chong was smitten with Arnold. "My first visceral experience of him was that he glowed. I remember coming home and saying, 'He's like the sun.' I really enjoyed looking at him every day," she gushed. The part called for Arnold to gun down hundreds of bad guys to save the life of his little girl. However, off the set, Arnold was a pussycat. "He had every opportunity to squeegee my bits, but I just didn't get that, so I'm feeling gypped. I just want to go on record and say, 'I wish you had done those things to me, because I have a huge crush on you. I would have loved it,'" she deadpanned.

Meanwhile, on October 24, 1984, *The Terminator* hit theaters nationwide with a bang. Audiences and critics loved the film and its badass villain. *The Terminator* became a landmark in the sci-fi genre and launched Arnold's career into the stratosphere. He was anxious to have Maria join him on the ride. In the summer of 1985, the couple disappeared for a few weeks. Recalled Theo Hayes, "He proposed to her in Austria, and I just remember saying, 'Finally.'" The wedding date was set for April 1986. The couple agreed on many things. Politics wasn't one of them. "I asked her a long time ago, 'How do you deal with this?'" described Hayes, "and she said, 'You know what? He's an immigrant, and I understand where he's an immigrant, and I understand why he's a Republican.' But that's also a little bit of a spark in their relationship."

In the fall of 1985, Maria Shriver had much more than a dream wedding to plan. Her career was also taking off. After two years as an on-air reporter on the *CBS Morning News*, Maria became the anchor. Television journalist Boyd Matson commented, "She is natural and comfortable on-camera, and she is articulate. If you have that going in, you're ahead of the game." Maria joined an elite group of female anchors, but critics took shots at her from day one. According to J. D. Heyman, "Maria had tough going. I mean, Maria still gets a lot of ribbing. She gets ribbed about her hair. She gets ribbed about how she looks. This is not a woman who gives up easily." Ratings for *CBS Morning News* were low, and Maria continued to battle the critics.

In October 1985, *Commando* premiered and became another big hit, grossing more than $100 million worldwide. Five months later, capitalizing on his big-time action-star status, Arnold went to Mexico to fight a murderous alien in *Predator*. He immediately bonded with costars Carl Weathers and pro-wrestler-turned-actor Jesse Ventura. Joked Ventura, "Arnold has problems understanding American customs. He was going to marry Maria, so I schooled him every day down in Mexico to learn the term and I said, 'Arnold, you have to say it from the diaphragm, *I do.*'"

Arnold took that advice to heart and on April 26, 1986, Arnold and Maria tied the knot after nine years together. The lavish ceremony took place at a historic site, St. Francis Xavier Roman Catholic Church near the Kennedy family estate in Hyannisport, where the couple had spent their first moments together. Arnold was thirty-eight, and Maria was thirty. Franco Columbu was Arnold's best man in what Heyman called "a classic Kennedy ceremony." Guests included Jackie Onassis, John F. Kennedy Jr., Andy Warhol, and Grace Jones. The pope and President Ronald Reagan sent their blessings. Mr. World was on top of the world. "He kind of presented Maria, so the people would just see her for herself. And the way he held up her hand, it was like, 'Look at this beautiful woman. Look at this amazing lady,'" described

Hayes. A few days later, Arnold and Maria left for their honeymoon in Antigua.

The couple returned to Los Angeles for the premiere of Arnold's new film *Raw Deal*. A month later, Maria got a raw deal herself from the executives at *CBS Morning News*. "Everything was great about it except for the ratings. The ratings were a disaster, and that's what television is all about," explained Leamer, who continued, "she's a good investigative journalist. She's a good questioner, but do you want to wake up with her every morning for a couple hours? I mean, Arnold does, but America didn't want to." Maria was devastated. She walked out of CBS and never looked back, saying, "People who are successes do fail. It's not the end of the road. It's not like 'Oh my God, I'll never amount to anything.' It's okay."

In September 1986, NBC hired Maria Shriver as a general assignment reporter. She was asked to take a hefty 70 percent cut in pay for the new gig. Laurence Leamer offered, "She was a journalist, and she worked very hard. She was an absolutely compulsive woman, a perfectionist. She started there and worked her way up." In June, NBC added a weekend edition of the *Today Show*, called *Sunday Today*. Network brass offered Maria the coanchor position with Boyd Matson. She began commuting from L.A. to New York. At the time, she expressed her feelings, saying, "It's exciting to be back doing morning television. I'm excited about the prospects of having a home, so to speak, and a place to be able to do good work."

Initial ratings were low, but Maria kept her focus. After six months on the job, *Sunday Today* began building an audience. As the show got better, the commute only continued to get worse. Sid Feders, her producer, recalled, "The problem was she was flying back and forth. She didn't have any children at the time, so it was wearing on her." Maria was away from Los Angeles three nights a week. The schedule put a strain on her young marriage. "The best thing they had going for them in those years were their frequent flyer miles. They had plenty of those," joked Leamer, "but beyond that, they didn't have very much time with each other, and it was difficult—as it would be in any kind of relationship."

Even if his marriage was struggling, Arnold was enjoying a string of hits, including *The Running Man* and *Predator*. Then, in April 1988, Arnold made a surprise move: he signed on to costar with Danny DeVito in the comedy *Twins*, about two brothers—hardly identical—who are separated at birth. While Arnold credited the movie's humor to the intersection of a comedic culture clash, Richard Roeper insisted, "*Twins* was a hit based on the poster. You see Danny DeVito and Arnold Schwarzenegger in the flowery shirts and the same pants and these identical outfits, and they're playing twins—that's a funny idea." Still, executives at Universal had their doubts about Arnold's comedic chops. They insisted on an unusual deal. Arnold would only make money if the film made money. He took the deal because, as Roeper put it, "He has such supreme self-confidence in his own abilities."

Maria all the while was anchoring not one but two national newscasts on the East Coast, the Saturday edition of *NBC Nightly News* in New York and *Sunday Today* in Washington, D.C. While Maria continued to cover the newsmakers, Arnold was making political news when he campaigned for presidential candidate George Bush, Ronald Reagan's vice president and heir apparent. On November 8, 1988, Bush won in a landslide, beating his Democratic opponent, Michael Dukakis. That December, Maria and Arnold joined the president and Mrs. Bush at the premiere of *Twins*. Arnold and his shorter, saucier costar were hilarious as the bumbling siblings. The film went on to gross more than $100 million at the box office. Arnold took home a reported $30 million.

In April 1989, while Arnold was basking in his successes, NBC asked thirty-four-year-old Maria to anchor yet another show, a new program called *Yesterday, Today, and Tomorrow*. Mary Alice Williams was Maria's coanchor, and the two ladies got a pleasant surprise when early into the program they both found out they were pregnant. The pregnancy didn't slow Maria down or alter her schedule. She continued hopscotching between L.A., New York, and Washington, D.C. Meanwhile, forty-one-year-old Arnold was off to film the futuristic sci-fi thriller *Total Recall*. The Mexico-based shoot was plagued with difficulties. The script went through some forty drafts.

On December 13, 1989, the forty-two-year-old action hero took on a much more significant role—proud papa. Maria gave birth to a baby girl, Katherine Eunice Schwarzenegger. "He called me in the middle of the night to tell me that the baby was born," remembered public relations adviser Charlotte Parker. Arnold loved being a father, but his friend President Bush needed a high-profile commando. On January 21, 1990, Arnold reported for duty. In a public announcement, he decreed, "President Bush has asked me to be the chairman of the President's Council on Physical Fitness and Sports and help him in getting the country back in shape. He wants to declare war on the couch potatoes, and I'm the five-star general in this war." In the job description were meetings with all fifty governors in the United States—a challenge that Arnold gladly undertook.

While Arnold traveled America as the superman of fitness, Maria discovered she couldn't be both supermom and working mom. Her bicoastal commute became too much. "I had this child, Katherine," she said, "my life was in Los Angeles, and I realized this wasn't working. I tried it for four or five months, and it didn't work." She went to the network and asked to relocate on at least one job. When the executives wouldn't budge, Maria chose family over fame. Said Hayes, "It wasn't like anybody had to sit Maria down or that she had to spend a lot of time thinking about it. She just knew." On July 4, 1990, Arnold escorted both Maria and his mother Aurelia to the star-studded premiere of *Total Recall*. The film eventually earned $261 million worldwide, Arnold's biggest box-office haul to date.

As for Maria, she relished being a mother, but the former network anchor wasn't ready to give up on television, and NBC wasn't about to give up on Maria. In August 1990, network executives offered her a plum job in L.A. hosting her own series of specials titled *First Person with Maria Shriver*. "That's when she really sort of broke out into what I call stardom," assessed Sid Feders. Juggling work and motherhood was about to get twice as tough, however. In October 1990, Maria learned she was pregnant with her second child. That same month, Arnold reunited with James Cameron and Linda Hamilton on *Terminator 2: Judgment Day*. Arnold made $750,000 for the first *Terminator*, and this time commanded an unprecedented $15 million for the sequel.

There were some changes involving Arnold's character this go-around. "It was really nice to take an additional challenge not only to play this one-dimensional character but to make the characters evolve and add all these extra dimensions and play a Terminator with a heart," he said at the time. The National Coalition Against Televised Violence was not impressed by the kinder, gentler *Terminator*. Some members of the group staged a protest at the film's premiere in July 1991. Arnold took a diplomatic approach, responding, "I think it's great when people go out. It's their point of view, and they should express their point of view. It's a great movie about peace." *T-2* annihilated the competition when it hit theaters Fourth of July weekend. The movie went on to make a half billion dollars worldwide. At age forty-four, Arnold Schwarzenegger was one of the biggest movie stars in the world. He and Maria capped off a stellar month with the birth of their second child, Christina Maria Aurelia Schwarzenegger, on July 23, 1991.

Arnold then joined forces with rival action stars Bruce Willis and Sylvester Stallone in a restaurant venture called Planet Hollywood. "It's just a very entertaining place where you can hang out and at the same time have great food," characterized Arnold. The Southern California opening-night gala was star-studded. Arnold, it seemed, could do no wrong. Neither could his wife, who was racking up awards for her news series, placing herself in the company of the top female journalists on television. "She was another one of those at NBC like Jane Pauley. These were few and far between, these kind of people that can pick up a telephone and call and get celebrities," said Sid Feders. Maria and Arnold had become Hollywood's ultimate power couple.

That summer, Maria Shriver returned to the familiar territory of politics, serving as NBC's correspondent for the Republican and Democratic conventions. Reasoned J. D. Heyman, "Her political work is well regarded by everyone in the business." Following the conventions, NBC started production on a two-hour special about the 1962 Cuban Missile Crisis. Network brass sent one of their own big guns, Maria Shriver, to interview Fidel Castro. Maria proved herself a formidable force when Castro tried to delay their interview, and Maria stuck to her originally scheduled slot so that she could return to America and her family on time. "Castro always admired her for that," said Feders.

While Maria continued on as a successful working mom, forty-five-year-old Arnold began filming *The Last Action Hero*. "People were falling all over themselves to throw money at this project, saying this is so brilliant, because this movie was a take-off on action movies," said Richard Roeper. Expectations were indeed high. Arnold hawked the film at the Cannes Film Festival in May 1993, but it didn't help. The movie opened a month later and bombed. Roeper continued, "Audiences hated it, and critics were trying to top each other saying how much they hated it." *The Last Action Hero* was Arnold's first flop in five years, but he was undaunted. Just a few weeks later, he began shooting his next movie, *True Lies*, with Jamie Lee Curtis.

Back on the West Coast, Maria was in labor. Patrick Arnold Schwarzenegger was born on September 18, 1993. "Arnold and Maria were very inspiring. What they did is they put family first, as I have always seen them do, and they worked everything else around that," commented Charlotte Parker. On July 14, 1994, Arnold experienced another proud achievement when he merited

Hollywood immortality. He was enshrined at Grauman's Chinese Theater in Hollywood. *True Lies* opened a day later, and it opened big, raking in more than $25 million its first weekend. The film eventually grossed $354 million worldwide.

Riding high on the success of *True Lies,* Arnold then returned to comedy in the gender-bending spoof *Junior,* teaming up again with costar Danny DeVito. The far-out plot featured Arnold as a wacky scientist who becomes pregnant after taking an experimental drug. Emma Thompson, who costarred in the film, remarked, "He was absolutely enchanting in makeup, actually. I think the whole experience of pregnancy really brought out the gentle side of him." Arnold drew from his experience with his three-times pregnant wife, explaining, "I don't think I could have done the role without having to have gone through this three times at home myself." This time, however, the magic from *Twins* didn't last. *Junior* hit theaters in November 1994 with a resounding thud. Reasoned Richard Roeper, "They weren't ready to see Arnold Schwarzenegger giving birth. It was embarrassing for him. It's just awful."

After *Junior* tanked, Arnold decided to take a break from making movies. In early May 1995, Arnold established the Inner City Games Foundation for Disadvantaged Youths in the state of California. Arnold spoke out against drugs, including the use of steroids. "So for us," he offered, "the challenge was to create the Inner City Games so those kids are not hanging out on the street and don't get involved in drugs and violence and in gangs and in crimes and all of those things, but rather join our family of the Inner City Games and participate in sports."

While Arnold continued his volunteer work, Maria landed a job promotion. That August, thirty-nine-year-old Shriver was named on-air correspondent for the network's flagship prime-time news magazine, *Dateline NBC*. Meanwhile, Arnold worked tirelessly over the next eighteen months to promote the Inner City Games. Then, just a few months shy of his fiftieth birthday, America's action hero was stopped cold. In April 1997, he checked himself into USC University Hospital in L.A. to replace a congenitally defective aortic valve in his heart.

The intricate procedure took several hours. Maria and their three children waited anxiously for the results. "He almost died from that. That's a serious operation. They literally take your heart out of your chest to do this," said journalist John Connolly. The surgery was a success. One week later, Arnold was released from the hospital with a new outlook on life. During an interview, Maria offered, "He has a great new working heart. He's not going to show the scars, so don't ask. Do you want to say something, honey?" Arnold replied jokingly, "Right now, I am very speechless because at home I'm not allowed to talk. For the first time probably my wife says, 'Do you want to talk, too?' This is really a big shock for me, so thank you very much. I think after my operation, she did get nicer."

Despite his teasing, Arnold enjoyed spending time with his wife and three kids while recuperating from the surgery. Then, on September 27, 1997, Arnold and Maria welcomed a new addition to the family, a second son named Christopher Sargent Shriver Schwarzenegger. But less than a year after Christopher's birth, Arnold was dealt a shattering blow. His mother Aurelia collapsed and died at age seventy-six while visiting her husband's grave in Austria.

The tragedy didn't stop there. In the summer of 1999, Arnold and Maria joined the Kennedy clan in Hyannisport for the July 17 wedding of Maria's cousin Rory Kennedy. Meanwhile, another cousin, John F. Kennedy Jr., chose to pilot his own plane to the ceremony. John's wife, Carolyn, and her sister, Lauren Bessette, were also on board. Somewhere off the coast of Martha's Vineyard, something went horribly wrong. JFK Jr. lost control of the plane and crashed into the sea. There were no survivors.

Once again, the Kennedy family rebounded from a devastating tragedy. Maria went back to work. So did Arnold. On December 6, 1999, he began shooting his thirty-first film, *The Sixth Day*, playing a helicopter pilot who meets his clone. In November 2000, the film opened and barely made a ripple, but Arnold's appearance on the British morning show *The Big Screen* did create some huge waves. After the interview, the show's hostess, Anna Richardson, alleged that Arnold groped her on the set. Arnold's camp fired back, saying it was nothing more than a flirtatious exchange initiated by Richardson. "One of Arnold's difficulties is that he's such a playful guy. That's him. How would Maria handle that? She just shrugs and goes on. How would anybody handle that?" commented Laurence Leamer, author of *Sons of Camelot*.

Meanwhile, Maria Shriver's star continued to shine bright. On December 24, 1999, she received thrilling news. She was honored with the prestigious Peabody Award for Outstanding Achievement in Television Broadcasting. While her career soared, Arnold Schwarzenegger's career sank to a new low. On March 24, 2001, the fifty-three-year-old was nominated for three Golden Raspberry ("Razzie") Awards for *The Sixth Day*—Worst Actor, Worst Supporting Actor, and Worst Screen Couple. "We seemed to be in the middle of an Arnold Schwarzenegger backlash at that point. We were seeing several bombs in a row," said Richard Roeper.

In his next project, *Collateral Damage,* Arnold portrayed a Los Angeles fireman seeking revenge against terrorists. Then on September 11, 2001, just three weeks before the scheduled premiere of the film, the nation was stunned by a series of real terrorist attacks. Executives at Warner Bros. postponed the release of *Collateral Damage* indefinitely. On September 28, 2001, Arnold and Maria donated one million dollars to aid victims of 9/11. *Collateral Damage* was finally released in February 2002, but filmgoers stayed home. The picture grossed only $68 million worldwide, a bust for a big-budget action movie. Commented Roeper, "You get to a certain point in your life if you're fifty years old beating up a bunch of twenty-two-year-old guys, there's just a certain point where it starts looking silly."

Like America, Arnold was up for a change of pace. On September 18, 2002, the bodybuilder-turned-actor became the lead spokesman for Proposition 49, a California law designed to help inner-city schoolchildren. Journalist Margaret Talev commented, "What Proposition 49 did for him was give him a successful campaign. He seemed to say, 'I'm putting my money behind this, I'm putting my name behind this, and I want you to support me and to join me.' And people did." On November 4, 2002, Proposition 49 passed. Arnold was a hero again, but in a new arena—politics.

By the summer of 2003, forty-seven-year-old Maria was also maintaining her success as a correspondent for *Dateline NBC* and the backbone of the Schwarzenegger household. Then, as Arnold's film success was flickering, the screen icon reprised the role that made him an international sensation. In *Terminator 3: Rise of the Machines*, fifty-five-year-old Arnold once again became America's favorite killing machine. "To me, it was an incredible feeling to put back on this leather jacket, to put on the leather gloves, to put on the sunglasses. I mean, you slip right back into that character of Terminator," he said. On July 3, 2003, *Terminator 3* opened big, raking in $44 million its first weekend. The worldwide gross eventually soared to more than $430 million. Arnold stayed true to his promise from the first film. He was back! "The Terminator is part of our cultural vocabulary now—*"Hasta la vista, baby,"* all these kinds of things that have become part of American life," commented J. D. Heyman.

Meanwhile, California voters began a movement to recall Governor Gray Davis. "When Gray Davis's mother named him, she did a great job because no man could be grayer than this man," griped Laurence Leamer. The state was bleeding red ink, and the governor tripled license fees for all car owners. That decision outraged almost everyone. Also, according to Leamer, "The energy crisis was mishandled as well, in terms of the regulation of it. It cost California a fortune." On July 23, 2003, supporters of the "Dump Davis" petition submitted 1.6 million names—700,000 more than were needed to trigger a recall. The next day, the election date was set for October 7, 2003.

Arnold Schwarzenegger began flexing his political muscles. "A lot of people were saying to him because of the horrible state of affairs, 'Don't run. Why do you want to take over a state that has this many problems? This is terrible,'" recalled Arnold's chief of staff, Bonnie Reiss, "and, frankly, because Arnold is a man that really welcomes a challenge—and that almost motivates him more—he wanted to step in and take on this challenge." While Arnold was ready to step into the game, Maria "understood the cost of politics at every level. She understood what it meant, losing her two uncles, and she didn't want that in her own life," said Leamer.

"They really were able to weigh the pros and cons, because there's no doubt about it, running for high elected public office in this day and age particularly, when you're as famous as someone like Arnold is, there's a lot of sacrifices that go along with that," said Bonnie Reiss. Despite her misgivings, Maria warmed up to Arnold's political ambition. "Once she saw his heart was so into it, he wanted it so badly, he really wants to make a difference, how could she not say yes?" questioned Theo Hayes. On August 6, 2003, Arnold announced his candidacy to a stunned audience on *The Tonight Show with Jay Leno*. After the taping of the show, he followed up with a public declaration outside of NBC studios, saying, "My wife told me that she will support me no matter what the decision is, and I therefore decided to run for governor of this great state, because I feel very strongly that we have some serious problems. I will go to Sacramento, and I will clean house."

An unprecedented 138 competitors lined up to deliver a knock-out punch to Gray Davis, the doomed governor of California. Fifty-six-year-old Arnold quickly emerged from the pack as Davis's most formidable foe. Soon after Arnold announced his candidacy, the gloves came off. "Arnold Schwarzenegger attacked him on all his fronts and also sort of implicitly attacked him for not being able to connect with the people," recapped Margaret Talev. The harsh realities of life on the campaign trail were foreign to Arnold but not to his politically savvy wife. In early August

2003, forty-seven-year-old Maria took a leave of absence from *Dateline NBC* to support her husband full-time.

"If you've got the money, anybody can run for governor. That's democracy," affirmed Leamer. The field of gubernatorial challengers included political rivals like State Senator Tom McClintock, Lieutenant Governor Cruz Bustamante, and activist Ariana Huffington. Among the other hopefuls were former *Diff'rent Strokes* star Gary Coleman and porn princess Mary Carey. "It's such a fun bunch, but they all paled in comparison with Schwarzenegger in the end," commented Talev. Leamer continued, "The rest of the country saw the recall, and they thought of California as being just a bunch of loonies." With his charisma, enormous media appeal, and tough-talking approach to solving the state's financial woes, Arnold quickly became the leading contender. On October 7, 2003, Californians went to the polls. It wasn't even close. Arnold Schwarzenegger won 48 percent of the vote to become the first foreign-born governor-elect in the history of the Golden State.

"Arnold seized on something, which was a profound sense of unease in California," said J. D. Heyman. "California is a state built on optimism, opportunity, the idea that you can do anything. Arnold embodies what Californians want to be: glamorous, rich, and extremely successful." On November 17, 2003, fifty-six-year-old Arnold was sworn in as the thirty-eighth governor of California. In his inauguration speech, Arnold affirmed, "We are always stronger than we know, and California is like that, too. There's a massive weight we must lift off our state. Alone, I cannot lift it, but together we can."

"Maria gave Arnold the beginnings of a social consciousness that he has expanded and taken to places even beyond where the Kennedys imagined it could go," commented Laurence Leamer. Arnold's career as a politician is very much a work in progress. Maria's distinguished career in television is on hold. In February 2004, she quit her job as correspondent for *Dateline NBC*. Whatever happens, Governor Arnold Schwarzenegger and First Lady

Maria Shriver are setting a new course for the state of California. Summed up Sandahl Bergman, "It's a wonderful story, to see a couple in Hollywood where it's famous for people splitting up and relationships never working out. This is a relationship that has survived. The magic's going to continue."

INDEX